The Best

NEW EN

Editor
Colleen Dunn Bates

Contributing Editors
Janice Brand, Becky Sue Epstein, Mary Frakes, John Mariani,
Diane Nottle, Deborah Patton, Steven Raichlen, Nancy D. Roberts,
Pat Solotaire, Al Stankus, Marilyn Stout, Jan Swafford,
Leslie Tweeten

Assistant Editors
Margery L. Schwartz, Susan Steinway

Operations
Alain Gayot

Directed by
André Gayot

PRENTICE HALL ▪ NEW YORK

Other Gault Millau Guides Available
from Prentice Hall Trade Division

The Best of Chicago
The Best of France
The Best of Italy
The Best of London
The Best of Los Angeles
The Best of New York
The Best of Paris
The Best of San Francisco
The Best of Washington, D.C.

Published by Prentice Hall Trade Division
A Division of Simon & Schuster Inc.
Gulf + Western Building
One Gulf + Western Plaza
New York, New York 10023

Please address all comments regarding The Best of New England to:
Gault Millau, Inc.
P.O. Box 361144
Los Angeles, CA 90036

Library of Congress Cataloging-in-Publication Data
The Best of New England

Includes index
1. New England—Description and travel—1981—Guide-books. I. Bates,
Colleen Dunn.
F2.3.B49 1989 917.4'0443 89-3504
ISBN 0-13-072851-9

Thanks to the staff of Prentice Hall Travel for their invaluable
aid in producing these Gault Millau guides.

CONTENTS

NEW ENGLAND

SIX STATES OF MIND IN ONE

A light at the head of the harbor. Sailboats bobbing up and down on a deep-blue ocean. Gleaming glass towers slashing through the sky. Bright-red lobsters pulled steaming from the pot. Whitecapped mountains and rolling green hills. Weathered barns and church steeples in a sea of autumn colors. Modern-day pilgrims sitting down, amid pumpkins and Indian corn, to Thanksgiving dinner.

They could be pictures on a calendar, these images that symbolize New England—and no doubt they have been, many times over. If they've become clichés, it's happened for the best of all possible reasons: They're true. Yet these pictures don't tell the whole story.

New England. The very name conjures up a place with a strong sense of past and future. So many of the values its people honor—the work ethic and the thrift, the respect for the sea and the love of the land, the striving for simplicity and the thirst for knowledge—came over on the *Mayflower* from old England, the homeland in which the Pilgrim settlers could no longer bear to live, yet could not help but love. They would always look back to England, but they would build their own world—their "New" England. For nearly 400 years now, each successive wave of immigrants has followed suit, adopting—or adapting—New England's traditions to suit its own needs while at the same time contributing new traditions. Taken as a whole, the six New England states—Massachusetts, Rhode Island, Connecticut, Vermont, New Hampshire and Maine—make up one of America's most distinctive regions, so often unified in its principles yet divided in its perceptions of life.

At the center of it all lies Boston, known abroad as "the Athens of America" and locally as "the Hub of the Universe." (Bostonians accept that status so universally that "Hub" is perfectly acceptable among the headline writers of local newspapers as a shorter synonym for Boston.) The city has a reputation for being stodgy, self-satisfied and inhospitable to change. Two much-loved anecdotes, apocryphal though they may be, nevertheless sum up Boston as personified by a nineteenth-century dowager. First, in support of the Hub theory, there's the one regarding travel. "Why should I travel?" the dowager is quoted as saying. "I'm already here." Then there's the one in which the legendary lady is asked if she has bought her new hats for the coming season. "Hats?" she sniffed. "I already *have* my hats." That's Boston—a city that does not take kindly to trends that may be here today and gone tomorrow.

Boston has survived some tough times, perhaps even more of them in this century than during the Revolution that began in its streets. As in so many other American cities, the once-vibrant downtown was for decades deserted after evening rush hour. Court-ordered busing to achieve school desegregation exacerbated the problem in the mid-1970s, prompting not only rioting in the streets but "white flight" into the suburbs. Then, suddenly, the city began to change. Young professionals with limited patience for commuting and seemingly unlimited money for renovating started moving back downtown. Some developers had the bright idea of turning decrepit old market/warehouse buildings into a restaurant/ retail complex, and Quincy Market was born. Within a few short years, downtown Boston was alive once again.

Now the phrase "world-class city" seems to be on everyone's lips, as the movers and shakers strive daily to build a bigger skyscraper, open a hotter gourmet shop, make a bigger deal—and let the world know about it in the process. These people must be out-of-towners. For true Bostonians, not just the ones who were born there but also the newcomers infused with the spirit, this has *always* been a world-class city. It's the rest of the world that's just finding out.

Yet there's another New England—or, rather, any number of others— beyond the city limits. Before long, the expressways give way to farmland and fishermen's cottages. So removed is that way of life from the city's that some people who live maybe twenty miles from Boston take pride in not having set foot there in years.

The people of New England are sturdy individualists who defy categorization. They are farmers and fishermen, stockbrokers and stonecutters, artists and accountants. What's more, you're likely to find anyone in any place—a sage on a city street, a world-class chef in a tiny mountain village. If they're not in Boston, it's not because they couldn't make it there: They simply chose not to. And the individualism extends far beyond choice of home or profession. You can never be quite sure if that dowdy-looking person next to you on the subway sleeps in a shelter for the homeless or a Beacon Hill mansion. Hence, it pays to treat everyone equally well, and that's how New Englanders like it.

Despite their reputation for being standoffish, New Englanders can be warm, welcoming people—once they get to know you a little. When that happens, anything else can. With luck, you might find yourself on an impromptu sail on a twelve-meter yacht or at a table with a family whose ancestors really did come over on the *Mayflower*. When that day comes, sit back and enjoy the ride.

New England is remarkably accessible by car, train, bus, boat—and imagination. Whether your travel plans call for walking the Freedom Trail, holing up in a secluded country inn or free-floating down a river, you've come to the right place.

ABOUT THIS BOOK

The Best of New England, as the name implies, is a collection of our personal favorites in the six New England states: Massachusetts, Rhode Island, Connecticut, Vermont, New Hampshire and Maine. The book is by no means comprehensive—one would need several volumes to do the region justice—but it is rife with romantic country inns, outstanding restaurants, intriguing things to see and do and an idiosyncratic collection of shops, primarily those specializing in antiques and New England crafts. And, of course, we devote plenty of attention to the region's hub, Boston: its restaurants, hotels, nightlife, quick-bite spots, shops and sights.

The chapter called "Basics" tells you how to get into, out of and around Boston and how to get to points beyond in the six New England states; provides information on useful services and phone numbers; details worthwhile annual events throughout New England; and suggests travel itineraries—from summer on the Cape to autumn amid the famed foliage. After "Basics" you'll find the small "Music Festivals" chapter, a guide to the best of the unique music festivals that dot the New England landscape in summer. And toward the end of the book you'll find the "Toque Tally," a roster of New England's restaurants by ranking.

If we've neglected your favorite New England inn or restaurant—and if you don't mind revealing your secret—please let us know and we'll pay it a visit for our next edition.

ABOUT THE RESTAURANTS

Restaurants are ranked in the same manner that French students are graded: on a scale of one to twenty, twenty being unattainable perfection. The rankings reflect *only* the quality of the cooking; decor, service, welcome and atmosphere are explicitly commented on within the reviews. Restaurants ranked thirteen and above are distinguished with toques (chef's hats), according to the following table:

4 toques, for 19/20, exceptional

3 toques, for 17/20 and 18/20, excellent

2 toques, for 15/20 and 16/20, very good

1 toque, for 13/20 and 14/20, good

Keep in mind that we are comparing New England's restaurants to the finest in the world. Just because the region's best restaurants don't rate four toques doesn't mean they aren't exceptionally good. Also, these ranks are *relative*. One toque for 13/20 is not a very good ranking for a highly reputed (and very expensive) temple of fine dining, but it is quite complimentary for a small place without much pretension.

Unless otherwise noted, the prices given are for a complete dinner for two, including an appetizer, main course and dessert per person, along with tax, fifteen-percent tip and a bottle of wine. It is, naturally, hard to estimate the cost of wine; for our purposes we've assumed a modest bottle at a modest restaurant and a good California wine (usually $20 to $30 a bottle) at a more serious place. Lovers of the great Burgundies, Bordeaux or Champagnes will find their tabs climbing higher than our estimations; conversely, those who like to eat lightly, sharing appetizers and desserts, will spend less. Prices, however, continue to creep up, so some restaurants may have become more expensive by the time you visit.

ABOUT THE INNS

The inns and hotels are ranked on a scale of one to four, using the following symbols:

   excellent

   very good

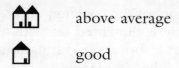

above average

good

These rankings reflect our opinions (subjective, of course) of each inn's charm, appeal, personality, warmth and comfort. Therefore, a place that is quite luxurious and expensive but has a disappointing decor and a chilly welcome may rank only a two 🏠🏠, whereas a more rustic and inexpensive inn with loads of charm and a particularly exceptional setting may rank a four 🏠.

Prices are given at the end of each review. For hotels (all but a few are in the "Boston" chapter), we give the range for singles, doubles and suites. For inns, we give the range for a room for two people. Breakfast is almost always included (as noted); when we indicate that dinner is included, we mean for *two* people, usually excluding wine.

BASICS

AT YOUR SERVICE

BOSTON ACCENTS

Contrary to popular wisdom, there is no single "Boston accent." Instead, there is a colorful, sometimes bewildering variety of accents that reflects the ethnic diversity of the city. Variations range from the Brahmin way of speaking, apparently with jaws firmly clenched, to those of recent immigrants who've introduced their native speech patterns to the local patois.

The accent most often encountered by visitors, and most confusing to them, is the one President John F. Kennedy made famous. In some words, Bostonians drop the letter r in favor of a flat *a* (as in "Aalington" for Arlington, or "Central Aahtery" for the downtown expressway). At the end of words, they'll add an *r* where it doesn't belong (as in "tuber" for tuba) and drop it where it does (hence "lobsta chowda"). Linguists have traced the accent back to seventeenth-century speech in eastern England, home of many of the Pilgrims. They brought the accent with them on the*Mayflower*, and it's been here ever since.

Boston pronunciation also has individual quirks, such as "Quinzee Maaket" for the popular Quincy Market (which is, curiously, not in the town of Quincy, as many tourists have learned the hard way).

The region has its own vocabulary, too. Here you drink a "tonic" rather than a soda or pop. You might buy it at a "spa," which is a convenience store or, in a few places, an old-fashioned soda fountain, where you may also order a "cabinet," also known as a milkshake. Dirty clothes are sent to the "cleanser's," not the cleaner's. When you ask for directions on the road, you'll be sent down "Comm Ave" or "Mass Ave"—never Commonwealth Avenue or Massachusetts Avenue. And if you're told to take the first right on the "rotary," don't look for a clubhouse; it means a traffic circle.

NEW ENGLAND WEATHER

"If you don't like the weather in New England, just wait five minutes—it'll change." A cliché, perhaps, but also a truism. New England has long capitalized on its changing seasons: snowy winters, flower-filled springs, beachy summers and, most of all, foliage-rich autumns. On a daily basis, however, the weather is more uneven. A day that begins in bright sunshine may end in a London-like fog; a morning blizzard may leave nothing but slush by noon.

Although spring officially begins in March, the best of it usually doesn't arrive until mid-May. (During one April in recent memory, only three days passed without a drenching rain.) Summers can be stifling, especially in downtown Boston's humidity, but plan on temperatures about 10 degrees cooler along the coast and on the islands. Indian summer often lasts well into the fall foliage season, but early cold snaps can bring the leaf watching to an abrupt halt. In winter, bundle up and prepare for dampness. Boston, its air warmed by coastal waters, tends to get much less snow than towns just a few miles inland. But if you're planning a ski trip even in the far north, be prepared for the possibility of no snow.

"Unpredictable" is the word for New England weather. When packing, be prepared for anything, from a January thaw to a summer hailstorm. In winter or summer, it's smart to wear clothes in layers and peel them off, weather permitting.

FOREIGN EXCHANGE

Some of the larger Boston-area banks offer currency exchange. The Bank of Boston's main office, 100 Federal Street (617-434-2200), stocks cash and traveler's checks in most major currencies. So does the Bank of New England (617-742-4000) at two of its offices—28 State Street in the Financial District and 800 Boylston Street at the Prudential Center—but there is a $200 limit on foreign-to-U.S. transactions if you don't have an account there. BayBanks (617-482-1040) stocks six major currencies (British, Canadian, French, German, Japanese and Swiss) at 75 of its branches, including most in Boston and Cambridge; other currencies may be ordered in two days. BayBanks also changes money at Logan International Airport, with booths in terminals C and E. Cambridge Trust (617-876-5500) offers immediate trading of most major currencies at its main office, 1336 Massachusetts Avenue in Harvard Square.

In downtown, Deak International at 160 Franklin Street (617-426-0016), in the South Station area, exchanges all foreign currencies and sells Thomas Cook or Barclay's traveler's checks in ten currencies. Hours are Monday to Friday 9 a.m. to 5 p.m. American Express exchanges money at 10 Tremont Street downtown (617-723-8400) and at 44

Brattle Street in Harvard Square, Cambridge (617-661-0005). Hours are Monday to Friday 9 a.m. to 5 p.m.

TELEPHONE NUMBERS

Ambulance, 911
American Automobile Association, (617) 723-9666
Amtrak, (617) 482-3660, (800) USA-RAIL
ARTS/Boston, (617) 723-5181
Bed & Breakfast Associates, (617) 449-5302
Campground Information, (617) 248-6373
Chamber of Commerce (Greater Boston), (617) 227-4500; Visitor Information, (617) 536-4100
Children's Hospital, (617) 735-6000
Coast Guard Search and Rescue, (617) 565-9200
Consulates: See Blue Pages of Boston Phone Directory
Dental Referral Service: Massachusetts Dental Society, (617) 651-7511
Directory Assistance: Local, 411; Within Area Code, 555-1212
Federal Express, (617) 391-4760
Fire and Rescue: Boston, 911; Brookline, 911; Cambridge, (617) 876-5800
Greater Boston Convention and Visitors Bureau, (800) 858-0200; Recorded Information, (617) 972-6000
Lawyer Referral Service, (617) 742-0625
Library Information (Boston Public Library), (617) 536-5400
Logan International Airport: Information on Ground Transportation, (800) 235-6426; Parking Information, (617) 561-1672; for Flight Information, call airlines directly
Mass Transit Information, (617) 722-3200; Commuter Rail, (617) 227-5070 (North and West Lines), (617) 482-4400 (South Lines)
Medical Referral Service: Massachusetts Medical Society, (617) 893-4610
Parks: National Parks, (617) 565-8888; Massachusetts State Parks, (617) 727-3180; Metro Parks, (617) 727-5215
Passport Agency (U.S.), (617) 565-3930
Poison Control Center, (617) 232-2120
Police, 911
Postal Information, (617) 654-5083; Zip Code Information, (617) 654-5767

Road Conditions, (617) 973-7500
Samaritans (Suicide Prevention), (617) 247-0220
Taxis: ITOA, (617) 426-8700; Boston Cab, (617) 536-5010; Checker
    (Cambridge), (617) 497-1500
Ticket Agencies: Teletron, (617) 720-3434; Ticketmaster, (617) 523-
    6633; Ticketron, (617) 720-3400; Concertcharge, (617) 497-1118
Time and Temperature, (617) 637-1234
Tourism Departments: Massachusetts, (617) 727-3201; Rhode Island,
    (800) 556-2484; Connecticut, (203) 566-3948; Vermont, (802) 828-
    3236; New Hampshire, (603) 271-2665; Maine, (207) 289-2423
Weather, (617) 936-1234

GETTING AROUND

AIRPORT

The hub of New England air travel, Logan International Airport accommodates nearly all domestic airlines and a number of international carriers (including British Airways, Air France, Alitalia, Sabena and Swissair) with direct flights to Europe. Commuter airlines link Logan with smaller airports throughout New England.

Logan's location in East Boston, just across the harbor from downtown, is either bane or blessing, depending on what form of ground transportation you choose. If you're driving, allow plenty of time; traffic in the Callahan and Sumner tunnels, which connect Logan with downtown, makes Route 128 look like the Autobahn. The subway system's Blue Line makes a stop at the airport, with free shuttle buses to all terminals; a one-way trip downtown costs 60 cents. The most pleasant way to make the trip is the airport water shuttle between the airport and Rowes Wharf, which runs daily except Sundays and a few major holidays; the one-way fare is $5 for adults and $2.50 for children. For more information on Logan transportation, call (800) 235-6426. A one-way taxi trip downtown costs about $10, including tolls and airport surcharge.

Smaller airports serving New England are located in Beverly, Hyannis and Worcester, Massachusetts; Providence, Rhode Island; Windsor Locks,

Connecticut (a good-size airport outside of Hartford); Burlington, Vermont; Manchester and Nashua, New Hampshire; and Portland, Maine.

CARS

If you'll be spending most of your time in downtown Boston and Cambridge, take the age-old advice, "Pahk the cah neah Hahvahd Yahd" (or anywhere it's legal), and walk or use mass transit. There are two main reasons: (1) Boston's streets tend to be congested, winding and (often) one-way, with no apparent pattern; and (2) Massachusetts drivers have a reputation for being the worst in the country, and they're proud of it. Since Boston is a compact city with a reasonably good subway system, it makes sense to leave the car in one place and proceed with your sanity intact.

Parking lots and garages are available in most parts of the city, but they fill up quickly on weekdays and tend to be expensive. Resist the temptation to park on the street for long periods. Meter maids are vigilant and generous with their tickets, and tow trucks periodically make the rounds. Read parking signs carefully: Some streets without meters are designated only for residents with permits; others, particularly those near government buildings (remember, Boston has city, state and federal offices), are designated only for official use. And if we haven't yet prompted you to turn in your driver's license for the duration of your stay, keep in mind that Boston's car-theft rate is among the highest in the country, so try to park in a well-guarded lot.

If you do need a car for trips out of Boston, the major car-rental companies have desks at Logan International Airport and many downtown hotels. Hertz (617-720-0100) and Avis (617-367-1190) also have offices at Government Center, among other locations. Budget is located on Commonwealth Avenue (617-254-0727) and in several suburbs; Dollar (617-523-5098) has an office at the Sheraton Boston Hotel in Back Bay, near the Prudential Center. You'll also find the major rental agencies in or around Harvard Square in Cambridge.

Boston-area road maps recommended by the Greater Boston Convention and Visitors Bureau are Rand McNally's ($1.95) and the Arrow folding wall map ($5). For trips farther afield, the visitors bureau recommends Rand McNally's map of Maine, New Hampshire and Vermont ($1.50) and the Champion road map of Massachusetts, Connecticut and

Rhode Island ($1.50). Maps are available from the Visitors Bureau (Prudential Plaza, P.O. Box 490, Boston, MA 02199), in the book department of the Harvard Coop stores (617-492-1000) and at the Globe Corner Bookstore, 3 School Street near Downtown Crossing (617-523-6658). The Globe Corner Bookstore, devoted entirely to travel books, has a mail-order service; call (800) 227-5199. AAA touring information can be reached in the Boston area at (617) 723-9666.

Important highways in and around Boston include the Massachusetts Turnpike (Interstate 90), which everyone calls the "Mass Pike," leading west from the city; Interstate 95, which runs north to New Hampshire and south to Providence, Rhode Island; Interstate 93 (parts of which form Boston's Central Artery and Southeast Expressway), which heads north to New Hampshire and Maine; State Route 3, leading south to Plymouth and Cape Cod; U.S. Route 6, the main road on Cape Cod; and State Route 128 (part of Interstate 95), the beltway around Boston, called "America's Technology Highway" for its heavy concentration of computer companies.

MASS TRANSIT

MASSACHUSETTS BAY TRANSPORTATION AUTHORITY (MBTA)

The MBTA, usually called "the T," is the mass transit authority serving Boston and the surrounding communities. It runs the Boston subway system, buses throughout the city and suburbs, and commuter rail lines.

Boston's subway system is the oldest in the nation (the first stretch, under Tremont Street, opened in 1898), and it sometimes shows its age. Trains are scheduled to run every eight to sixteen minutes, depending on day and time, but frequent breakdowns, rush-hour crowding and almost constant construction slow down the system. At times you may feel like the legendary Charlie (immortalized in the '60s song "Charlie and the MBTA"), who was destined to ride forever as "the man who never returned." But if you keep in hand an MBTA map and keep in mind the following general guidelines, you should have no problem either getting to or returning from your destination.

Stations are marked with circular black-on-white "T" signs. The system is divided into four color-coded major lines, all of which pass through downtown. The Red Line runs from Alewife station in north Cambridge through downtown, then splits at Andrew station into the Braintree and Dorchester lines. The Green Line runs from Lechmere in east Cambridge through downtown before branching into four lines that serve the western side of the city. The Orange Line runs from Malden to Forest Hills. The Blue Line runs from Government Center downtown to Revere Beach north of Boston.

Most trips on the T require no more than one change of trains. However, the Blue Line does not intersect with the Red—an inconvenience if you're traveling to Logan Airport from Cambridge or the South Shore. The hub of the Hub is Park Street station at Boston Common, where the Red and Green lines intersect. The Red and Orange lines meet at Downtown Crossing, where the city's two major department stores, Jordan Marsh and Filene's, are located. Blue and Orange meet at State Street in the Financial District, and Green and Blue meet at Government Center.

Most MBTA buses connect with subway stops; however, there are no free transfers unless track construction requires the use of shuttle buses. Bus hubs include Harvard Square on the Red Line, Kenmore Square on the Green Line and Ruggles station on the Orange Line.

Although fares are calculated on a zone system, the basic subway fare is 60 cents, and the bus fare 50 cents. Tokens are sold at all MBTA stations. The MBTA has a telephone-information line at (617) 722-3200. Printed schedules and maps are available at the information booth inside Park Street station; at the State Transportation Library, 10 Park Plaza in Park Square; or at the information booth in Harvard Square.

NEW ENGLAND BUS LINES

Remote parts of New England are also accessible by bus. From the Trailways terminal at 10 Atlantic Avenue, across from South Station, run three bus lines: Continental Trailways; Concord Trailways, serving New Hampshire, Vermont and Maine; and Peter Pan bus line, serving western Massachusetts and upstate New York. All three may be reached by calling (617) 426-7838. Greyhound and Bonanza, which serve Cape Cod, Rhode Island, Connecticut and parts of western Massachusetts, and Vermont Transit, which serves New Hampshire and Vermont, operate out of the Greyhound terminal at 10 Saint James Avenue in Back Bay; call (617) 423-5810 for both lines. The Plymouth & Brockton Street Railway Company (617- 773-9400) provides bus service from South Station and the Trailways Terminal (Greyhound) to Hyannis, Plymouth, Scituate and Brockton.

TAXIS

Boston's compact size makes taxi travel affordable and often preferable to driving yourself. And as in many other cities, taxis are plentiful except when you need them most. (Try finding a cab in Chinatown at 7 p.m. on a rainy Saturday night.) They may be ordered by phone or hailed on the street, or try the major hotels, especially the Ritz-Carlton in Back Bay and the Omni Parker House at Government Center. Also look for taxi stands throughout the city. But you can't rely on the light atop the car to indicate whether the taxi is free, as you can in New York; Boston cabbies are notoriously lax about turning their lights on and off.

In the Boston area, taxis are licensed by the individual town and may pick up passengers on the street only in that town. (However, they may respond to radio calls from anywhere.) Hence, a Cambridge cab will not stop for you in Boston's Financial District. Share-a-cab arrangements are prohibited except at the airport, and then only during emergencies and cab shortages.

Meter fares are based on both distance and time. If your cab is stuck in traffic, it'll cost you. In addition, a surcharge and all tolls are added to fares for rides originating at Logan International Airport, adding more than a dollar to the metered fare.

It helps to have general directions to your destination. Although the city now requires new licensees to pass a twelve-hour training course, many still don't know the city well and/or have a poor command of English.

Reliable taxi companies include Boston Cab (617-536-5810), which has extraordinarily good pickup service in the early morning; ITOA (617-426-8700); and Checker Cab of Cambridge (617-497-1500). Most suburbs have at least one cab company serving the area; check the Yellow Pages for individual towns.

Once you've made the cab connection and feel the need to register a complaint or a compliment about the service, call the Boston Police Hackney Unit's 24-hour hotline at (617) 536-8294.

TRAINS

Boston is the terminus for Amtrak's Northeast Corridor, with service to New York (about five hours away) and Washington (about eight hours). The coastal route through Providence, New Haven and Mystic passes through some particularly scenic parts of Rhode Island and Connecticut. The inland route from Boston to New Haven makes nine stops, including Worcester and Springfield, Massachusetts, and Hartford, Connecticut.

Amtrak trains terminate at South Station but also stop at the new Back Bay station, which is convenient if you're staying in that part of town or if you're running a little late. (Trains leave Back Bay about five minutes after South Station.) If you're staying in the western suburbs and have a friend with a car, the Route 128 station in Dedham is a convenient drop-off point.

Amtrak also runs commuter rail service under contract to the MBTA, providing easy access to such areas as Salem, Ipswich, Rockport, Lowell and other towns in northern and western Massachusetts from Boston's North Station (617-227-5070 or 800-392-6099). Commuter trains to the south leave from South Station and Back Bay (617-482-4400 or 800-882-1220).

South of Boston, the Cape Cod & Hyannis Railroad (617-848-7336) runs vintage railway cars from Braintree station on the MBTA's Red Line to Buzzards Bay, Sandwich and Hyannis on Cape Cod. The train leaves several times daily from Memorial Day through Columbus Day. From late May to early September, Amtrak (800-872-7245) also offers weekend service to Hyannis from New York's Penn Station; the trip takes about three hours from Boston.

Because of poor track conditions, Amtrak's popular Montrealer train from New York to Montreal through New England has been replaced by bus service. But at the time of this writing, Amtrak had begun proceedings to reestablish the route. Check with Amtrak to see if the line is running when you plan to visit.

GOINGS-ON

Special events in New England ebb and flow with the seasons. Coastal communities come alive in summer, while winter is the peak season (pun intended) for ski resorts. As for Boston proper, it's a city that never sleeps. We've put together a year-round guide to the best of the fests in the area. For up-to-date information, contact the Greater Boston Convention and Visitors Bureau at (617) 536-4100.

JANUARY

Stowe Winter Carnival (mid-Jan.), Stowe, VT; (802) 253-7321. One of the earlier Upcountry (Vermont, New Hampshire and Maine) winter carnivals, which continue in various towns through Feb.
Chinese New Year (late Jan. or early Feb.), Chinatown, Boston; (617) 536-4100.

FEBRUARY

Black History Month, Boston; (617) 536-4100. Special programs and exhibits all month throughout the city.
Beanpot Hockey Tournament (early Feb.), Boston Garden; (617) 227-3200. The Big Four of Boston's hockey-playing colleges (Boston College, Boston University, Harvard University and Northeastern University) have been competing for decades in this two-night event.
Boston Boat Show and New England Sailboat Show (early Feb.), World Trade Center, Boston; (617) 536-8152.
Valentine's Festival (mid-Feb.), downtown Boston; (617) 536-4100. A weekend of romantic entertainment, including piano bars, classic films, sightseeing tours and hotel packages.
Maple-sugaring season (late Feb.–early April), western MA, VT and NH; (413) 628-3912. Members of the Massachusetts Maple Producers Association welcome visitors to their sugarhouses. Call for details.

MARCH

Boston Globe Jazz Festival (mid-March), Boston concert halls; (617) 929-2637. New England's leading newspaper brings big-name performers to Boston for a ten-day festival.

New England Flower Show (mid-March), Bayside Exposition Center, Boston; (617) 536-9280. Sponsored by the Massachusetts Horticultural Society.

Saint Patrick's Day (March 17), Boston. A rowdy citywide celebration of Boston's Irish heritage; the annual parade through South Boston is usually scheduled for the nearest Sunday.

Great Chefs' Taste Fair (late March or early April), World Trade Center, Boston; (617) 326-7225. Samples from the best chefs, caterers and wineries in eastern Massachusetts.

APRIL

Museum-goers' Month (throughout April), Boston area; (617) 523-7170. Thirty-five museums sponsor special events organized around a different theme each year.

Newport Preservation Society mansions open for the season (April 1–Nov. 1), Newport, RI; (401) 847-1000.

Easter Parade (Easter Sun.), Boston. Bostonians in their Easter finery stroll the Commonwealth Avenue mall and Newbury Street, weather permitting.

Opening Day at Fenway Park (early April), Boston; (617) 267-8661. Batter up!

Patriots' Day (third Mon. in April), throughout MA; (617) 536-4100. Activities in commemoration of the Revolution's early days include the Hanging of the Lanterns ("One if by land, two if by sea") in the Old North Church, Salem Street, Boston; the reenactment of "the shot heard 'round the world" on Lexington Green (at 5 a.m. on April 18); and the reenactment of the Battle of Concord on April 19.

Boston Marathon (third Mon. in April), Hopkinton to Boston; (617) 536-4100. One of the world's most famous marathon runs.

Daffodil Festival (last weekend in April), Nantucket, MA; (508) 228-0925. A weekend of events to celebrate spring.

Boston Pops Orchestra, Symphony Hall, Boston; (617) 266-1492. Spring season runs from late April or early May through June.

MAY

Walk for Hunger (early May), Boston Common; (617) 227-3796. Participants walk a twenty-mile course, accepting sponsorship on a per-mile basis, to fight world hunger.

Art Newbury Street (mid-May), Boston; (617) 267-9416. A Sunday-afternoon festival with gallery shows and street performances. Repeats in mid-Sept.

Lilac Sunday (mid-May), Arnold Arboretum, Boston; (617) 524-1717.

Hidden Gardens of Beacon Hill (mid-May), Boston; (617) 227-4392. Members of the Beacon Hill Garden Club open their gates to visitors during the height of spring in the city.

Long Island Sound America Festival (mid-May–Sept.), New Haven to Norwalk, CT; (203) 579-1045. A series of events ranging from clambakes to sand-castle competitions.

Motif No. 1 Celebration (late May), Rockport, MA; (617) 546-6575. Events include a road race, and there is a craft-fair center in the red waterside shack immortalized by innumerable painters who've worked in this legendary artists' colony.

Whale-watching season begins. Cruises leave from Boston and other coastal towns. Although whales appear in Massachusetts Bay throughout the summer, the best time for viewing is late May and June. Best all-day whale watch: Bay State Cruises, (617) 723-7800.

JUNE

Brimfield Weeks, Old Boston Post Rd. (Rte. 20), Brimfield, MA; (413) 245-7479. A thrice-yearly (early June, early July and early Sept.) flea-market extravaganza that attracts antiques collectors from around the world. The tiny central Massachusetts town overflows with pieces from thousands of dealers. Plan your visit early—the inns and motels in the area (Brimfield is near Sturbridge) are often booked up to a year in advance.

Cambridge River Festival (early June), Cambridge, MA; (617) 498-9033. Live performances, crafts, environmental art and international food.

Festival of Historic Houses (early June), Providence, RI; (401) 831-7440. A weekend of tours of private homes and gardens on the city's historic east side.

Yale-Harvard Regatta (early June), New London, CT; (203) 432-1456.

Tanglewood Music Festival (early June–late Aug.), Lenox, MA; (413) 266-1492. Summer home of the Boston Symphony Orchestra. Picnicking on the lawn while listening to the music is a New England tradition. See "Music Festivals" chapter.

Bunker Hill Day Reenactment and Parade (mid-June), Charlestown, Boston; (617) 241-9511. Modern-day patriots dress in Revolutionary duds and restage the famous battle.

Jacob's Pillow (mid-June–late Aug.), Becket, MA; (413) 637-1322. Summer dance festival brings ballet, modern dance, jazz and mime to the Berkshires.

Italian street festivals (most weekends late June–Aug.), North End, Boston; (617) 536-4100. Live entertainment, processions and mountains of Italian food.

P. T. Barnum Festival (late June–early July), Bridgeport, CT; (203) 367-8495. Parade, road race, Jenny Lind concert and even the selection of a "Tom Thumb" from local elementary schools.

Williamstown Theater Festival (late June–mid-Aug.), Williamstown, MA; (413) 597-3400.

JULY

Brimfield Weeks. See "June."

Boston Harborfest (early July), Boston waterfront; (617) 227-1528.

Shawmut/U.S. Pro Tennis Championship (early July), Longwood Cricket Club, Chestnut Hill, MA; (617) 731-4500. The oldest professional men's tennis tournament in the country is held in this Boston suburb.

Fourth of July celebration, Boston; (617) 536-4100. Major events include the U.S.S. Constitution's turnaround cruise, a Boston Pops concert on the Charles River Esplanade and fireworks.

Bastille Day (mid-July), Marlborough Street, Boston; (617) 266-4351. Sponsored by the French Library, a Boston institution, the open-air party usually includes a formal dinner, a street party and dancing.

Great Woods Center for the Performing Arts (mid-July–Aug.), Mansfield, MA; (800) 233-8468. Summer home of the Pittsburgh Symphony Orchestra, as well as a site for rock 'n' roll concerts and dance performances.

Marlboro Music Festival (mid-July–mid-Aug.), Marlboro, VT; (802) 254-8163. See "Music Festivals" chapter.

Antique and Classic Boat Rendezvous (late July), Mystic, CT; (203) 572-0711. This coastal town trots out its seafaring finest.

Black Ships Festival (late July), Newport, RI; (401) 272-7790. Newport's annual Japanese festival.

AUGUST

Illumination Night (Aug. 3), Martha's Vineyard, MA; (508) 693-0085. Islanders hang paper lanterns outside their homes for an evening of color and light.

JVC Jazz Festival (mid-Aug.), Ft. Adams State Park, Newport, RI; (401) 847-3700. Bring a blanket and a picnic for a date with some of the world's best jazz musicians. Be sure to get tickets in advance for this extremely popular event.

Martha's Vineyard Agricultural Fair (mid-Aug.), Tisbury, MA; (508) 693-0085. Old-fashioned three-day country fair on the Vineyard.

Faneuil Hall Marketplace Anniversary Celebration (late Aug.), Boston; (617) 523-1300.

SEPTEMBER

Brimfield Weeks. See "June."

Gloucester Schooner Festival (early Sept.), Gloucester, MA; (508) 283-1601. A weekend of maritime activities.

Charles Street Fair (third Sun. in Sept.), Beacon Hill, Boston; (617) 227-1922.

Art Newbury Street (mid-Sept.), Boston; (617) 267-9416. See "May."

Bourne Scallop Festival (mid-Sept.), Buzzards Bay, MA; (617) 759-3814.

Eastern States Exposition (mid-Sept.), West Springfield, MA; (413) 737-2443. The East's largest annual fair, with agricultural, educational, industrial and champion-horse shows.

Essex Clam Fest (mid-Sept.), Essex, MA; (508) 283-1601. Chowder festival, shucking contest and clambake.

Providence Waterfront Festival (mid-Sept.), Providence, RI; (401) 273-9700. A weekend of arts and crafts, boat races, cruises, ethnic foods, and entertainment.

Striped Bass and Bluefish Derby (mid-Sept.–mid-Oct.), Martha's Vineyard, MA; (508) 693-0085.

New England Patriots football season opens (late Sept.), Sullivan Sta-
dium, Foxborough, MA; (508) 543-8200.

Topsfield Fair (late Sept.–early Oct.), Topsfield, MA; (508) 887-2212.
An old-fashioned fair with sheep dog trials, midway rides, ethnic
foods, and exhibits.

Fall foliage and apple festivals (late Sept.–Oct.), various towns throughout New England; (617) 727-3201.

OCTOBER

Boston Bruins hockey season opens (early Oct.), Boston Garden; (617)
227-3206.

Boston Symphony Orchestra season opens (early Oct.), Symphony Hall,
Boston; (617) 266-1492.

Harvest Weekend (mid-Oct.), Old Sturbridge Village, MA; (508) 347-
3362. Spend a weekend observing how the early Colonists harvested
crops, stored vegetables for the winter and dried fruit.

Ringling Brothers Barnum & Bailey Circus (mid-Oct.), Boston Garden;
(617) 227-3206.

Boston Celtics basketball season opens (late Oct.), Boston Garden;
(617) 523-6050.

Head of the Charles Regatta (late Oct.), Boston; (617) 864-8415. A
festive rowboat regatta on the Charles River.

New England International Auto Show, Bayside Exposition Center,
Boston; (617) 536-8152.

NOVEMBER

Boston Globe Book Festival (mid-Nov.), Boston Public Library and
citywide locations; (617) 929-2637. Ten days of speaker programs,
luncheons and workshops featuring authors of current interest.

Thanksgiving celebration (late Nov.), Plymouth, MA; (508) 746-3377.
Town celebration includes a turkey dinner for 2,000 and open houses
at historic homes. Plymouth Plantation (508-746-1622) closes for the
season with a weekend of events and authentic seventeenth-century
dinners.

Ski season opens (late Nov.), northern New England.

Edaville Railroad Christmas Lights (late Nov.–early Jan.), South Carver, MA; (508) 866-4526. Vintage narrow-gauge trains carry passengers on a five-and-a-half-mile route through a working cranberry plantation that is decorated with thousands of lights for the Christmas season.

DECEMBER

Christmas Tree Lighting Ceremony (early Dec.), Prudential Center and Boston Common, Boston; (617) 536-4100.

Nantucket Christmas Stroll (first weekend in Dec.), Nantucket, MA; (508) 228-0925. Many shops, inns and restaurants that have closed for the season reopen for this weekend of holiday cheer. But beware: Wintry weather has been known to strand merrymakers on the island.

Christmas Weekend (second weekend in Dec.), Martha's Vineyard, MA; (508) 693-0085. Holiday shopping, parade, town dinner and concerts.

Boston Tea Party Anniversary (Sun. closest to Dec. 16), Boston Tea Party Ship & Museum, Boston; (617) 338-1773. Reenactment of the historic tea-dumping, preceded by a town meeting at the Old South Meeting House and a march to the ship.

First Night (Dec. 31), throughout downtown Boston; (617) 542-1399. Boston's citywide New Year's Eve celebration begins in the late afternoon with performances, other artistic events, and fireworks on the waterfront at midnight.

The Nutcracker, Wang Center, Boston; (617) 542-1323. Performed by the Boston Ballet.

ITINERARIES

Boston may consider itself the Hub of the Universe, but there's plenty of life elsewhere. Whether you prefer the mountains or the shore, the classic or the chic, the six New England states offer unlimited opportunities for exploration. Here are some suggestions for travel beyond Boston. For details on specific towns and sights, consult the chapters on the individual states and regions.

Before beginning your excursion, you must master the basic terminology of New England geography. "The North Shore" refers to coastal communities north of Boston; "the South Shore," those south of the city. "The Cape" always means Cape Cod. (Bostonians will say they're going "down the Cape" for the weekend.) "The islands" usually means Nantucket and Martha's Vineyard. "The Berkshires" refers to the rolling hills that make up much of western Massachusetts. "Upcountry" means Vermont, New Hampshire and Maine—and northern-outpost Maine is, curiously, also referred to as "Down East."

Remember, New England's attractions are seasonal. Most of the following itineraries make pleasant trips year-round, although the peak season, especially in the coastal communities, is May through October (coastal Maine virtually shuts down from October through May). The exceptions, of course, are ski areas, which are busiest from late November through March. When you're driving in winter, especially in Upcountry, be prepared for hazardous road conditions and delays.

SALEM & CAPE ANN

Everybody knows Salem is famous for witches, but that's only part of the city's story. It's also an architectural treasure trove, boasting not only a historic district filled with restored sea captains' mansions but also the lesser-known East End with its gems of Federal-style working-class homes. From Boston, travel north by car (Route 1A) or train (the Ipswich/Rockport line from North Station) to Salem for a day of sightseeing. If you're driving, make a side trip to charming Marblehead. Continuing north (by car via Route 128), tour the Rockport artists' colony and the Gloucester fishing community before returning to 128. If time permits, continue north on 1A to the old town of Newburyport and the beaches of Plum Island before heading back to Boston. Or tour Cape Ann on your way to the Upcountry. See also "Boston Environs/ Eastern Massachusetts" chapter.

FALL APPLE ROUTE

For a pleasant autumn day-trip during the height of apple-picking season (from Labor Day to mid-October), wander the back roads west of Boston. From Boston/Cambridge, take Route 20 west through Wayland and Sudbury, stopping at Longfellow's Wayside Inn. At Marlborough, turn north on Route 85, then circle back to Boston via Stow on Route 117, passing Thoreau's Walden Pond. The roadsides will be lined with pick-your-own apple orchards and farm stands where you can lunch on hot apple dumplings and cider. To add a bit of history to your day, stray north a bit to Minute Man National Historical Park in Concord. See also "Boston Environs/Eastern Massachusetts" and "Central & Western Massachusetts" chapters.

THE BERKSHIRES

Believe it or not, there's a part of Massachusetts that has nothing to do with the sea. Less than two hours' drive from Boston, the rolling Berkshire Hills take over as nature's main attraction, and the villages that dot the landscape show another side of New England.

From Boston, take the Massachusetts Pike (Interstate 90) straight through to western Massachusetts. (En route, make a brief detour to Old Sturbridge Village.) Select one town—the best are Stockbridge and Lenox—to use as a base for several day-trips. During the summer, the chief attractions are the summer arts and music festivals, such as Tanglewood, Jacob's Pillow and the Williamstown Theater Festival. In winter, several ski areas are open in the Berkshire Hills. One trip not to be missed is a day in Williamstown, home of Williams College and the Clark Art Institute, which boasts an extensive collection of impressionist paintings. See also "Central & Western Massachusetts" chapter.

CAPE COD

If your New England dream vacation consists of a long, lazy drive toward miles of seashore, mixed with a fair bit of history and antiques hunting, you know what the song says: "You're bound to fall in love with old Cape Cod."

From Boston, travel south by car (Route 3), bus or train. If you're driving, take a day en route to visit Plymouth for a taste of early Massachusetts history. Then cross the Cape Cod Canal via the Bourne Bridge (for the Upper Cape towns of Falmouth and Woods Hole) or the Sagamore Bridge, which connects with Route 6 for Hyannis, the scenic Lower Cape and the Cape Cod National Seashore.

Hyannis is the transportation hub of the Cape, with bus service to most of the towns beyond. If your main destination is the Lower Cape and you won't need a car, consider taking the boat that runs daily in summer to Provincetown from Long Wharf in Boston (617-723-7800). See also "Cape Cod & the Islands" chapter.

THE ISLANDS

Back in the 1970s, Martha's Vineyard and Nantucket once threatened to secede from Massachusetts, and few New Englanders were surprised. Often mistakenly considered part of the Cape, the islands have a distinct air of separateness, and their people take pride in their staunch independence. Despite ever-increasing commercialization, the islands remain two of New England's best bets for a getaway weekend, week or entire summer.

For the most part, Martha's Vineyard and Nantucket are open to visitors from May to October only. From Boston, travel south to Cape Cod by automobile (Route 3), bus or train. Board ferries at Woods Hole for Martha's Vineyard or at Hyannis for Nantucket. If you intend to take a car to either island, note that ferry reservations often fill up months in advance; call the Steam Ship Authority at (617) 540-2022 for information. Ferries also run daily in summer, weather permitting, between Nantucket and Oak Bluffs on the Vineyard, offering a chance to explore both islands on a single trip. And Bay State–Provincetown Cruises (617-723-7800) now connects Boston and the Vineyard. See also "Cape Cod & the Islands" chapter.

RHODE ISLAND COAST

Once you've left Providence, the smallest of the United States turns into one of the country's biggest charmers. Whether you're looking for Newport sophistication or country quiet, it's all there, and within an hour or so of whatever base you've chosen. From Route 128 or Route 495 in Massachusetts, connect with Route 24 south to Fall River and Newport. En route, take a side trip to Tiverton (for antiques and gourmet shopping), Little Compton (home of Sakonnet Vineyards) and Sakonnet Point. Plan to spend several days in Newport, touring the millionaires' "cottages" and soaking up the atmosphere of this high-society resort. In summer, for a few relaxing days on an almost-unspoiled island, take a ferry from Newport or Point Judith to Block Island. From Point Judith, continue south along the coast toward Connecticut to charming Watch Hill, where you can ride one of the oldest and loveliest carousels in the country. See also "Rhode Island" chapter.

COASTAL CONNECTICUT

The maritime theme of New England exploration continues along the Connecticut coast. From Boston, take Interstate 95 to Providence. If time permits, take the scenic route, U.S. 1 along the coast; if not, continue on 95 to Mystic, Connecticut. The main attraction there is Mystic Seaport Museum, an entire village that celebrates America's maritime heritage, with its own restoration shipyard. Other interesting towns along the coast include Groton, New London and Waterford. Continue west, if you like, to lovely Old Lyme; to Essex, where you may board the Valley Railroad Steam Train; and finally to New Haven, home of Yale University. See also "Connecticut" chapter.

MAINE/NEW HAMPSHIRE COAST

Nobody's quite sure why you have to drive up (that is, north) to get Down East, but that's the way it is in Maine. The maritime odyssey continues as the ocean grows colder and the coastline more rugged. From Boston, drive north on Route 95, stopping at Hampton Beach or Portsmouth along New Hampshire's brief seacoast. Continue north into Maine. Wells Beach and Ogunquit are popular beaches along the route, while Kennebunkport has long been a resort for the wealthy. Continue on 95 through Portland in the Casco Bay region to Freeport, home of L. L. Bean and myriad factory outlets. Just past Freeport, you may choose to continue along the coast via Route 1 through the picturesque sea town of Camden, or to follow Interstate 95 into ski country. See also "New Hampshire" and "Maine" chapters.

NEW HAMPSHIRE LAKES & MOUNTAINS

Upcountry, the scenery grows progressively grander as the green hills of Massachusetts give way to the peaks of New Hampshire. Lake air may lack the salty bite of ocean breezes, but Winnipesaukee looks almost as big as the ocean and every bit as majestic. From Boston, take Interstate 93 north into New Hampshire, passing through Manchester and Concord, the state capital. At Franklin or Ashland, turn east toward Lake Winnipesaukee, largest of the many lakes that make up this vacationland (*On Golden Pond* was filmed in the area). Return to Interstate 93 and drive north toward Mount Washington and the Presidential Range in the White Mountains. For a longer trip, continue north through Franconia, cross the Connecticut River into Vermont and circle back to Boston via the Green Mountains. See also "New Hampshire" chapter.

VERMONT'S GREEN MOUNTAINS

The French knew what they were talking about when they called this the land of "verts mont(agne)s." The fact that Vermont's mountains do tend to turn white in winter makes the state all the more appealing as a year-round vacationland. From Boston, take Interstate 93 to just before Concord, New Hampshire, and turn onto Interstate 89. Follow 89 to the Vermont border (stopping in Hanover, New Hampshire, to look around Dartmouth College) and continue as far as Royalton. There you'll connect with Route 100 to drive north through a series of ski resorts, many of which are open (and even busier) in summer. Continue north along Route 100, crossing 89, to Stowe. If you're pressed for time, stay on Interstate 89 from Royalton to Waterbury, where you'll turn onto 100. Interstate 89 will also take you to Lake Champlain, Burlington and north into Canada. See also "Vermont" chapter.

FALL FOLIAGE

In autumn, just about any New England drive will provide a good look at the famous foliage. Of the routes suggested above, Cape Ann, the Berkshires and Upcountry trips offer the best viewing. When timing your trip, remember that the leaves start turning earliest in the far north and last the longest in the south, where ocean air keeps the trees warm until relatively late in the season.

MUSIC FESTIVALS

SYLVAN SERENADES

New England may be the only part of the world where, when vacation-ers get out into the deep boondocks and start to worry about bears, they are more likely to stumble onto a string quartet. The number of first-rate musicians among the fauna is one of the natural wonders of the region. In pursuit of them you may journey to a little brick mill town in New Hampshire to hear Bartók in a church, drive into the Green Mountains to savor Bach at Marlboro, sail out into the middle of Lake Champlain for Mozart and champagne, or park your car in a hay field and stroll into Tanglewood with picnic in hand and Beethoven in the offing. The reasons for all this sylvan serenading are many—for example, the fact that musicians like to go on vacation, too, but for financial reasons must keep at their trade for the duration. Perhaps the main reason, though, is how well the countryside and the music go together: Away from the glitz and the columned cultural mausoleums of urban concert life, the music shines in its full glory in the most beautiful of settings. Whether you are an old fan of classical music or a novice, you will rarely find a better place and time to enjoy the finest sounds there are.

THE FESTIVALS

**Bay Chamber
Concerts**
Camden, Maine
(207) 236-2823

The heart of the Bay Chamber Concerts is the estimable Vermeer Quartet, which has been in residence for more than fifteen years. The Vermeer plays the bulk of the concerts; it is joined by such high-caliber guest soloists as pianists Ruth Laredo and Jeffrey Kahane. The repertoire runs to the familiar—Haydn and Beethoven and Brahms—with a bracing seasoning of pieces by living and breathing composers. (Featured in a recent season, for example, was a string quartet by Peter Schickele, an entirely sober work by the avatar of P.D.Q. Bach.) Before each concert is a lecture and afterward a reception or dinner. Altogether, the Bay Chamber Concerts present a fine evening of treats for the ear, palate, mind and soul. There are one or two concerts a week, July and August, on Thursday and Friday evenings.

Cape and Islands Chamber Music Festival
Various locations on Cape Cod
(508) 755-7365

Founded by pianist Samuel Sanders in 1980, the Cape and Islands Chamber Music Festival is one of the newer entries in the New England summer music scene, but it's as active and popular as any. Sanders mans the keyboard in most of the programs, with added string and wind players chosen primarily from the ranks of the better American soloists. The literature is a good mixture of music familiar and otherwise; a typical program might include a Mozart flute quartet, a Telemann trio, a Villa-Lobos piece and a world premiere by a visiting composer. The festival is peripatetic, holding forth mainly at the Cape Cod Synagogue in Hyannis, the Marine Biological Laboratory in Woods Hole, the First Congregational Church in Wellfleet and the Old Whaling Church in Edgartown on Martha's Vineyard. There are also master classes, children's concerts, lectures and other sideshows. The concerts run from late July to mid-August.

Castle Hill Festival
Ipswich, Massachusetts
(508) 356-4070

We happen to be particularly fond of Castle Hill, not only because of its kaleidoscopic slate of concerts, but also because we're particularly fond of Crane's Beach, which is next door. (Castle Hill is, in fact, the Crane Estate.) An afternoon at the beach and a night of chamber music, spaced by seafood from someplace nearby, make for a pretty fine summer day. The estate's mansion is grand, the Italian Garden elegant, and the concerts and artists too wide-ranging to mention. As a sampler: The excellent Lydian String Quartet usually puts in an appearance, Boston soloists such as pianist Russell Sherman are perennial, and recent visiting soloists have included Yin Cheng-Zong of the People's Republic of China, the Mazo-Shlyam Lyfson Duo from the Soviet Union, the Boston Museum Trio and such popular groups as the Paul Winter Consort and the Dave Brubeck Quartet. July to mid-August.

Kneisel Hall
Blue Hill, Maine
(207) 374-2811

Kneisel Hall was established in 1902 by Franz Kneisel, a buddy of Brahms and leader of one of the great string quartets of the day. It developed into the first chamber-music school in the country and remains among the finest, the artists/faculty including such luminaries as violinist Roman Totenberg and pianists Artur Balsam and Seymour Lipkin. There are eight or so programs of chamber music on Friday and/or Sunday nights from early July to early August. As is often the case in summer festivals, the literature ranges more widely off the beaten path than it usually does in the winter season; you will hear Haydn and Mozart through Beethoven and Brahms to Bartók and beyond, all in an exquisite little concert hall with a sweeping view of Blue Hill Bay.

Marlboro Music Festival

Marlboro, Vermont
(802) 254-8163

Marlboro is mainly a summer chamber-music school in which experienced soloists coach and perform with younger players. The festival came to fame in the '60s, when Pablo Casals and Rudolf Serkin headed the old-world stars of a new-world musical nexus in the hills of Vermont. Today the music making is as strong as it ever was, with a yearly crop of hot young musicians showing up to polish their skills. The concerts are secondary to the learning, which is why programs are posted the day of the concert only and why there is no great effort to sell tickets (the place is usually sold out anyway). Order well ahead; the outside overflow seats are poor in sound and sight. If you do manage to find a ticket, whatever and whomever you chance to hear will likely be worth it. Twelve weekends, mid-July to mid-August.

Mohawk Trail Concerts

Federated Church,
Mohawk Trail (Rte. 2),
Charlemont, Massachusetts
(413) 774-3690

Every summer festival has its own style and traditions. In the case of Mohawk Trail, one thinks of summer twilight and folks strolling into the church for a concert; the church dinner once a season; the wry and rambling introductions to pieces by founder/director Arnold Black; and shirt-sleeved musicians getting up from the pew next to you to go play. The programs run mostly to lighter fare—lots of Vivaldi and Telemann and other masters of Baroque Muzak, with the occasional Mozart and Dvořák outing and the milder moderns. The Bolcom/Morris Duo usually makes an appearance with its show-stopping show tunes and Victoriana, and a chamber-orchestra series recently began. Mid- July to late August.

Monadnock Music

Southern New Hampshire
(603) 924-7610

Even among summer festivals in the countryside, Monadnock stands out for its closeness to audiences and its informal approach to music making. The chamber concerts, three or four a week, are held all over the southern New Hampshire landscape, most notably in the lovely brick mill town of Harrisville. These concerts are of high quality, and they're free (though contributions are countenanced). The larger (though not free) Wednesday-through-Sunday-night concerts at Crotched Mountain Foundation in Greenfield are performed primarily under the baton of founder/director James Bolle; these can range from concerto programs with top-notch Boston soloists, to recitals and chamber music, to concert versions of operas. A few years ago, a Boston critic called a Monadnock performance of Mozart's *Così fan tutte* one of the best he'd heard anywhere, and we'd say more or less ditto about a version of Stravinsky's *Rake's Progress*. The concerts run for six weeks starting in mid-July.

Music Mountain
Falls Village, Connecticut
(203) 355-0375

Music Mountain's reputation has been built on a good many years of chamber-music playing that's as solid as you'll find anywhere during the New England summer. The place was started by a string quartet back in 1929, and it remains above all a place to hear outstanding international string groups, starting with the resident Manhattan String Quartet. Otherwise, the fourteen-week schedule (starting in mid-June and held on Saturday nights and Sunday afternoons) is filled with visiting chamber ensembles and the occasional folk or jazz outfit, plus added soloists (such as pianist Ruth Laredo), puppet shows and what have you.

The New Hampshire Music Festival
Center Harbor,
New Hampshire
(603) 253-4331

We've never quite figured out how he manages to do it, but for 25 years now founder/director Thomas Nee has hauled a rather fine collection of musicians from around the country up to the foot of the White Mountains for a summer orchestral series and an accompanying chamber series. (In fact, we recollect that in the '70s, a backpacking chamber group used to play on top of the mountains.) We've heard the orchestra do Beethoven's Ninth, we've heard them do Respighi, we've heard them do world premieres, and we've usually been impressed. Orchestral concerts are held Thursday nights at Plymouth State College and Friday nights at Gilford High School.

Newport Music Festival
Newport, Rhode Island
(401) 846-1133

The thing was, Newport had all these monstrous mansions sitting around on the beach with no more Vanderbilts or Astors to party in them. Then, twenty years ago, Mark P. Malkovich III had a bright idea: Fill the places with the kind of music that was written for such hypertrophied settings— the grand Romantic style of the nineteenth century. The festival has since been drawing crowds extensive of wardrobe and expansive of pocketbook to these three-a-day orgies of Chopin, Brahms, Schumann, Rachmaninoff and the like. The festival also makes a point of introducing major soloists to the U.S.; among those first heard under the whopping grand staircase of The Breakers and similar digs are pianists Bella Davidovich, Jean-Philippe Collard and Andrei Gavrilov. Dust off that tux and recheck that bank account. Two weeks in mid-July.

The Norfolk Chamber Music Festival
Norfolk, Connecticut
(203) 542-5537

Norfolk is the summer home of the Yale School of Music and its resident Tokyo String Quartet, all housed at the Stoeckel Estate. The concert hall, a rich, wooded barn for musical thoroughbreds, was built early in this century by Carl Stoeckel so that he could present little concerts by his friends—being blessed with such friends as Sibelius, Rachmaninoff and Fritz Kreisler. These days, there are a dozen or so chamber programs from mid-June to mid-August; the

Saturday-night Tokyo concerts are the most popular and are usually sold out, so order early. One should not neglect the free weekday recitals by students, which are often quite nice. Above all, one should not neglect to arrive early and picnic on the grounds, which are of the kind that picnics were probably invented for. (Don't forget to include in the picnic basket your favorite bug stuff.)

Tanglewood
Lenox, Massachusetts
(413) 637-1600

There is a spirit at Tanglewood that has to do with more than the presence of the Boston Symphony Orchestra (BSO), the beauty of the grounds and the Berkshires, and the echoes of the masters who have played and studied there for the last 50 years. The spirit is found in the blending of the music and the place: Sitting in the Music Shed listening to Mozart and looking out across the lawn to the trees perhaps tells you something about Mozart that you hadn't realized before, something about the relationship of nature and human art. Tanglewood frames its music in such a way as to often make it unforgettable. The BSO plays three programs a weekend (plus a Saturday-afternoon open rehearsal) for nine weeks starting in late June. We offer two bits of advice. First: Yes, the lawn tickets are cheaper and the lawn is glorious, but if you want to hear the music that the orchestra is actually emitting, picnic before the concert and buy seats in the Shed; the music on the lawn is actually coming through loudspeakers, albeit cleverly disguised ones. Second: Look for the weekday programs, where you'll find the likes of Ely Ameling, the Vermeer Quartet, the Festival of Contemporary Music, student recitals and world-class chamber music from BSO players and Tanglewood faculty. Nearly any night of the week, you'll find something worth listening to.

The Vermont Mozart Festival
Burlington area, Vermont
(802) 862-7352

No, it isn't all Mozart, though Wolfie is featured prominently in these concerts, and most of the music is pre-1850, with an occasional foray into this century. The music travels around the countryside, involving a wide assortment of groups: A recent season included the Festival Orchestra, pianist Menahem Pressler and friends, the New York Chamber Soloists, the New York Trumpet Ensemble, the Vermont Gilbert and Sullivan Ensemble, and the Mitchell-Ruff Duo in a Gershwin program. Somebody up there really likes horses, too—each season kicks off with a grand dressage exhibition in Shelburne. Other programs are heard all around northeastern Vermont: Vergennes, Stowe, Colchester, Burlington and the Lake Champlain Ferry. All in all, the Vermont Mozart series is a reflection of the excitement, artistic and otherwise, that seems to hang around Burlington (a real peach of a town). Mid-July to mid-August.

BOSTON

RESTAURANTS

RESTAURANTS BY NEIGHBORHOOD

ALLSTON/BRIGHTON

Cafe Brazil   Siam Cuisine

BACK BAY

Aujourd'hui   Legal Sea Foods
Cafe Budapest   Miyako
The Colony   Morton's of Chicago
Dartmouth Street   Mr. Leung
L'Espalier   Ritz-Carlton Hotel/
Grill 23 & Bar   The Dining Room
Kebab 'N' Kurry

BEACON HILL

Another Season   Il Toscano
Hampshire House

BROOKLINE

Chef Chang's House

CAMBRIDGE

Café China   Sally Ling
Cajun Yankee   Michela's
Daily Catch   Panache
East Coast Grill   Rarities
Green Street Grill   Upstairs at the Pudding
The Harvest

CHINATOWN

Golden Palace   Ho Yuen Ting

DOWNTOWN

Anthony's Pier 4
Bay Tower Room
Blue Diner
Cornucopia
Durgin-Park
Jasper's

Julien
Locke-Ober Café
Maison Robert
Le Marquis de Lafayette
Seasons

JAMAICA PLAIN

Five Seasons

SOUTH END

Chef Chandler's
Hamersley's Bistro

Icarus
St. Cloud

THEATER DISTRICT

Bnu
Rocco's

Suntory

WALTHAM

Allegro

THE WORLD'S CUISINES

AMERICAN

Aujourd'hui
Bay Tower Room
Blue Diner
Bnu
The Colony
Cornucopia
Dartmouth Street
Durgin-Park

East Coast Grill
L'Espalier
Green Street Grill
Hamersley's Bistro
The Harvest
Icarus
Jasper's
Locke-Ober Café

Panache
Rarities
Rocco's

St. Cloud
Seasons

BRAZILIAN

Cafe Brazil

CAJUN

Cajun Yankee

CHINESE

Café China
Chef Chang's House
Golden Palace

Ho Yuen Ting
Sally Ling
Mr. Leung

CONTINENTAL

Bay Tower Room
Cafe Budapest
Hampshire House

Locke-Ober Café
Ritz-Carlton Hotel/
    The Dining Room

CREOLE

Cajun Yankee
Chef Chandler's

Green Street Grill

FRENCH

L'Espalier
Julien

Maison Robert
Le Marquis de Lafayette

HUNGARIAN

Cafe Budapest

INDIAN

Kebab 'N' Kurry

INTERNATIONAL

Another Season   St. Cloud
Rocco's

ITALIAN

Allegro   Michela's
Bnu   Il Toscano
Daily Catch   Upstairs at the Pudding
Dartmouth Street

JAPANESE

Miyako   Suntory

MACROBIOTIC

Five Seasons

SEAFOOD

Anthony's Pier 4   Durgin-Park
Daily Catch   Legal Sea Foods

STEAKHOUSE

Grill 23 & Bar
Morton's of Chicago

THAI

Siam Cuisine

RESTAURANTS

Allegro
313 Moody St., Waltham
(617) 891-5486
ITALIC
Open Tues.-Thurs. 6 p.m.-
9 p.m., Fri.-Sat. 6 p.m.-
9:30 p.m.
Cards: MC, V.

When Allegro opened in 1979, the concept seemed revolutionary: a stylish dining room specializing in Italian nuova cucina in what was formerly a working-class bar. Boutique restaurants have long since become old hat, but Allegro still delights and surprises (at least this Allegro does; the one in Boston is less successful). Owner/chef Jim Burke has an uncanny knack for making food taste just like what it is, only better. Traditional steak and potatoes takes the form of grilled aged sirloin served with roasted shallot and potato gnocchi. King salmon may be served with a grilled tomato and cilantro salsa. On one visit, lobster might be complemented by baby corn and basil; on another, it might be paired with lemon linguine and fiddlehead ferns. We'd kill for the orange-and-chocolate-truffle ice cream, and the pineapple upside-down cake with Mascarpone has been known to reduce us to tears. In the past, Allegro's chief drawbacks were the lack of a waiting area and a tendency to rush leisurely guests. Those problems have been remedied now that Allegro has a new home a few doors from its old location. The new spot has a bar and waiting area, not to mention a comfortable contemporary decor. Dinner for two will run about $100 with wine.

Another Season
97 Mount Vernon St.
(617) 367-0880
INTERNATIONAL
Open Mon. 5:45 p.m.-
10 p.m., Tues.-Fri. noon-
2 p.m. & 5:45p.m.-10 p.m.,
Sat. 5:45 p.m.-10 p.m.
Cards: AE, MC, V.

This cozy Beacon Hill restaurant is the brainchild of Odette Bery, a short, energetic English-born chef with a global grasp of cooking. Her menu, which changes monthly, might feature French pâté, Mexican-style shrimp simmered in a pumpkin-seed sauce, Mediterranean-style lamb served with pesto and couscous, and traditional Yankee shortcake. Her cooking is wholesome, attractive and mercifully understated. It is also rich in flavor, low in sodium and fat, and surprisingly reasonable in price. Bery has made the best of a Beacon Hill basement location: The murals on the walls portray Paris in the Gay Nineties, and for intimacy the dining area has been divided into several small rooms separated by French doors. The absence of music will be appreciated by people who have grown weary of raising and lowering their forks to the cadence of Vivaldi's *Four Seasons*. People with claustrophobia, however, may find the tables too closely packed for comfort. About $75 for two, with wine.

Anthony's Pier 4

140 Northern Ave.
(617) 482-6262
SEAFOOD
Open Mon.-Fri.
11:30 a.m.-11 p.m.,
Sat. noon-11 p.m., Sun.
12:30 p.m.-10 p.m.
All major cards.

11/20

Anthony's Pier 4 is probably the most famous restaurant in Boston. But whether it merits its reputation will depend on how much you appreciate dining on dreary seafood along with 600 other noisy guests. On the plus side, Anthony's boasts impressive views of Boston Harbor and the largest wine cellar in New England. On the minus side, you can't make a reservation (expect a 30- to 40- minute wait), and some of the entrées may remind you of drab cafeteria fare. (As at most fish houses, you're best off ordering the simpler items.) Waiters are dressed in buckskin and knee britches, towering popovers emerge hot from the oven, and desserts are on the gooey-rich side. Past meals have led us to suspect that some of the fish may have been frozen; only the lobster was above reproach. The sheer dimensions of Pier 4 boggle the mind: The parking lot alone is the size of several football fields, and as many as 1,600 guests dine here in a single evening. Don't forget jackets and neckties, gentlemen, or you'll be turned away. About $100 for two, with wine.

Aujourd'hui

(Four Seasons Hotel),
200 Boylston St.
(617) 338-4400
AMERICAN
Open Mon. 7 a.m.- 11 a.m.,
11:30 a.m.- 2:30 p.m. &
6 p.m.-10:30 p.m., Tues.-
Thurs. 7 a.m.-11 a.m.,
11:30 a.m.-2:30 p.m. &
5:30 p.m.-10:30 p.m., Fri.
7 a.m.-11 a.m., 11:30 a.m.-
2:30 p.m. & 5:30 p.m.-
11 p.m., Sat.-Sun. 7 a.m.-
2:30 p.m. & 5:30 p.m.-
11 p.m.
All major cards.

We like a dining room to be, well, roomy. And therefore we like Aujourd'hui. There's so much space between the tables that you'd almost need a megaphone to converse with your neighbors. Aside from its unrivaled elbow room, we also like Aujourd'hui, the formal dining room of Back Bay's Four Seasons Hotel, for its quiet elegance. Guests ascend a palatial staircase to a dining room remarkable for its mahogany paneling, antique porcelains and sweeping view of the Public Garden. The service is courteous and friendly, if not always heel-clickingly prompt. And most important, we like Aujourd'hui for its food, which is much improved now that executive chef Mark Baker has steered the kitchen away from the nouvelle cuisine of his predecessor and toward the bountiful cooking of North America. New York State foie gras is transformed into a luscious terrine; lobster is combined with corn to make a sweet, soulful chowder. A "club sandwich" served for lunch features grilled tuna, pancetta and brioche. But Baker needs to work on his pastas and lighten a few of his sauces. Weight watchers will appreciate the availability of dishes with reduced fat and calories, while devil-may-care theater-goers flock to the dessert-laden Viennese table served in the elegant Bristol lounge on weekends from 10 p.m. to midnight. Aujourd'hui is becoming a popular spot for power breakfasting. Lunch is marginally less successful than dinner. About $150 for dinner for two, with wine.

Bay Tower Room
60 State St.
(617) 723-1666
AMERICAN/CONTINENTAL
Open Mon.-Thurs.
5:30 p.m.-9:30 p.m.,
Fri.-Sat. 5:30 p.m.-
10:30 p.m.
All major cards.

We're justifiably leery of restaurants that crown skyscrapers. It's well known that people flock to such establishments less for the food than for the views. For many years, the Bay Tower Room fit the stereotype: The safest dishes to order were such simple items as oysters on the half shell, rack of lamb and chateaubriand. But recently the kitchen has been infected by the same innovative spirit that has been sweeping more earthbound restaurants in the name of the "new" American cuisine. We like the lobster strudel, the colorful vegetable terrine and especially the seafood mixed grill. The duck could use a little work—or at least a sharper knife. The food is not always inspired, but it is better than it needs to be, given the view. And after dinner, you can dance to live jazz on a tiny parquet floor under the stars. You certainly can't beat the setting: a multilevel dining room sheathed ceiling to floor in smoked glass; tables graced with snowy cloths and soft lamplight; burgundy-colored carpets and miles of burnished brass. The views of Faneuil Hall, Boston Harbor and the jets landing at Logan International Airport will take your breath away. About $135 for two, with wine.

Blue Diner
178 Kneeland St.
(617) 338-4639
AMERICAN
Open Mon.-Thurs. 7 a.m.-
11 p.m., Fri. 7 a.m.-
midnight, Sat. 8 a.m.-
midnight, Sun. 10 a.m.-
4 p.m.
All major cards.

12/20

Remember the diner—the cozy booths, the Formica tabletops? The whole country is on a remember-when diner kick, and the Blue Diner was one of the first on the bandwagon. Built in 1947, this Leather District (named in honor of the former tradesmen who worked in the area) landmark was completely refurbished and reopened in July 1986. The menu retains such vintage fare as meatloaf, macaroni and cheese, fluffy mashed potatoes and "wets" (homemade french fries slathered with gravy). We hear whisperings of nouvelle cuisine from the open kitchen: Witness the grilled fish with melon salsa. The malteds and frappés of yesteryear have been supplanted by boutique beers and vintage Chardonnays. Our only complaint with dessert (nostalgic creations like gooey custards and coconut cream pie) is the limited supply. The decor is vintage diner—down to the counter with stools and Seeburg tableside jukebox selectors—except for the unexpected (but welcome) cloth napkins and fresh-cut flowers. About $50 for two, with wine.

Bnu
123 Stuart St.
(617) 367-8405
AMERICAN/ITALIAN
Open Mon.-Wed.
11:30 a.m.-9:30 p.m.,
Thurs.-Sat. 11:30 a.m.-
11 p.m., Sun. 5p.m.-9 p.m.
Cards: AE, MC, V.

12/20

For years now, Hub theater-goers have been hungering for a restaurant that was interesting, affordable and convenient. Their prayers have been answered by a woman named Linda Criniti, who goes by the curious nickname of Bnu. Bnu has chosen to specialize in pizzas, pastas and salads—a can't-lose arrangement these days. But hers aren't your typical pizzas, not with toppings like arugula, spaghetti squash and black olives, or barbecue sauce, Cheddar cheese and grilled ham. An evening pasta special might feature manicotti with pesto ricotta, while a salad could favor grilled vegetables, polenta and balsamic vinaigrette. The lemon-flavored cannoli burst into a million buttery flakes with each bite. Do we like the decor? You bet we do: a Fellini-esque blend of faux marble, art deco, neon and lace. About $50 for two for a full meal with wine.

Cafe Brazil
421 Cambridge St.
(617) 789-5980
BRAZILIAN
Open daily 11:30 a.m.-
10:30 p.m.
Cards: MC, V.

12/20

As far as we know, the Girl from Ipanema never dined here, but we can tell you that she'd have felt right at home. This lively Brazilian café in Brighton is the next best thing to a weekend jaunt to Rio. You could start with camjiquinha, a rib-sticking stew made with hominy and pork. (The Brazilians eat it with a few drops of fiery malagata chile sauce.) "Brasil 2001" is a carnivoral orgy of beef, pork, chicken and spicy linguiça sausage, served with farofa (fried manioc flour) and garlicky collard greens. On weekends, the restaurant serves an authentic feijoada, traditional Brazilian black-bean stew. The only dishes that have failed to please us are the ones that contain seafood. For dessert, order a sugary flan and a cafèzinho (Brazilian espresso) to wash it down. The storefront dining room is attractively decorated with travel posters and hanging plants. Latin jazz and a large percentage of Portuguese-speaking customers heighten the Brazilian ambience. Unfortunately, Cafe Brazil doesn't have a liquor license. About $30 for two.

Cafe Budapest
90 Exeter St.
(617) 734-3388
HUNGARIAN/CONTINENTAL
Open Mon.-Thurs. noon-
10:30 p.m., Fri.-Sat. noon-
midnight, Sun. 1 p.m.-
10:30 p.m.
All major cards.

Many chefs pride themselves on their daily-changing menus. Not Edith Ban, the imperious owner of the venerable Cafe Budapest in Back Bay. Ban developed all the recipes herself and expects her chefs to follow them to the letter. "Chefs may change," she once quipped, "but the food at the Cafe Budapest does not." This is not a place frequented by foodies, but the cooking has soul and class. We would walk barefoot across a bed of burning coals just for a bowl of Ban's chilled tart-cherry soup. Her liver pâté has the authentic flavor of chicken fat. Other good bets are the chicken paprikas crêpes, fork-tender wienerschnitzel and a Sauerbraten à la St. Hubert that should be savored on bended knee with one's head bared. The desserts are less memorable, but you shouldn't leave without trying Ban's homemade, hand-stretched Strudel. The Cafe Budapest has been the site of innumerable marriage proposals and anniversaries, and the bar is indeed romantic, with its private alcoves, flocked wallpaper and live piano-violin duets. But the most romantic dining area is the Blue Room, with its hand-painted ceiling timbers and leaded glass. The Pink Room is not without charm; the main dining room, however, can feel as busy as Grand Central Station; dinner on Friday and Saturday nights at 8 may remind you of feeding time at the stockyards. The wine list features many outstanding Hungarian wines. Dinner will run about $100 for two, with wine.

Café China

1245 Cambridge St.,
Cambridge
(617) 868-4300
CHINESE
*Open Tues.-Thurs. noon-
2:30 p.m. & 5 p.m.-10 p.m.,
Fri. noon-2:30 p.m. &
5 p.m.- 10:30 p.m., Sat.
noon-10:30 p.m., Sun.
5 p.m.-10 p.m.
Cards: AE.*

12/20

Good things come in small packages, goes the old saying. We don't know whether Confucius coined the phrase, but we do know that he'd heartily approve of Inman Square's diminutive Café China. The 34 seats fill up quickly, and for good reason: The chef is Chinese, her husband/front man is Swiss, and the menu features good things from two continents. You could start with vegetarian Peking ravioli, honey-sweet boneless spareribs or a colorful ten-vegetable salad. For entrées, we're partial to the Chinese-style duckling à l'orange, yu hsiang scallops and roast quail, which is often served as a daily special. The place doesn't look like your typical Chinese restaurant, not with its forest-green color scheme and Babylonian garden of hanging ferns. And the service is mercifully free of the surliness one often encounters in the North End. About $45 for dinner for two, with wine.

Cajun Yankee

1193 Cambridge St.,
Cambridge
(617) 576-1971
CAJUN/CREOLE
*Open Tues.-Sat. 6 p.m.-
10 p.m.
Cards: AE, CB, DC.*

12/20

For several years now, John Silberman has been searing our palates with fiery jambalaya and pan-blackened redfish. His Cajun fare seems less revolutionary now than it did when the restaurant opened in 1984, but it still fills this funky Inman Square storefront dining room with a faithful clientele. Cajun popcorn (fried crawfish tails) and spicy shrimp rémoulade are perennial favorites; the crawfish étouffée contains enough garlic to ward off an entire legion of vampires. If we had to pick just one dessert, it would be Mary Silberman's sinful sweet- potato pecan pie. Lined with rec-room paneling and clunky tables, the Cajun Yankee isn't what we would call elegant, but that doesn't prevent it from playing to capacity crowds. About $50 for two, with wine.

Chef Chandler's

329 Columbus Ave.
No phone
CREOLE
*Open Mon.-Sat. 6 p.m.-
10 p.m.
No cards.*

11/20

This noisy hole-in-the-wall used to be one of the best-kept restaurant secrets in the South End. It's no longer a secret (yuppies clog the place nightly), but the plain dining room behind a boisterous, smoke-filled bar still serves some of the best and most reasonably priced Creole food in town. You won't find the venerable chef Chandler messing with such newfangled dishes as Cajun popcorn and pan-blackened redfish. What you will find are soulful renditions of conch pie, Creole chicken, and roast pork with old-fashioned gingersnap gravy. Did we like the sweet-potato pie? Enough to order seconds! About $45 for two, with wine or, even better, icy Samuel Adams beer.

Chef Chang's House

1006 Beacon St., Brookline
(617) 277-4226
CHINESE
Open Sun.-Thurs. noon-
9:30 p.m., Fri.-Sat. noon-
10:30 p.m.
Cards: AE, MC, V.

11/20

Chef Chang was one of the Hub's first restaurateurs to break out of the traditional Chinese orange-and-black Formica mold. His nicer-than-average decor and Szechwan-Mandarin menu still attract standing-room-only crowds. This is the place to have Peking duck: The bird is ceremoniously carved tableside, and the skin is cellophane-crisp. (For Peking duck first-timers, you use a scallion brush to paint the Peking pancake with hoisin sauce, then place a piece of skin, a piece of duck meat and the scallion on top, roll the whole thing up and pop it into your mouth.) Other good bets at Chef Chang's include General Gao's chicken and a spectacular spicy, crisp whole fried cod. If the truth be told, however, some of the stir-fries are greasy. Nonsmokers will appreciate the separate dining room attractively appointed with textured wallpaper, paintings and comfortable bentwood chairs. The waiters are somewhat more gracious than their Chinatown counterparts, but are nonetheless harried and overworked. About $50 for two, with wine.

The Colony

384 Boylston St.
(617) 536-8500
AMERICAN
Open Tues.-Thurs. 6 p.m.-
10 p.m., Fri.-Sat. 6 p.m.-
10:30 p.m.
All major cards.

Nouvelle cuisine is alive and well and hiding in—of all places—New England. If you don't believe us, just visit The Colony, located in Back Bay at the former home of Dodin Bouffant and L'Espalier. Colony owners Bruce Frankel and David Kantrowitz spent three years studying traditional New England cooking before opening their quietly elegant restaurant, and they've come up with a menu that presents an intriguing hybrid of past and present: corn oysters with spicy tartar sauce, a fiddlehead-fern turnover with smoked ham, Maine veal steak with fresh morels and potato dumplings. The cheese tray is a must, featuring handmade cheeses from farms across New England. Desserts range from whimsical upside-down rhubarb cake with "foamy sauce" to strawberry shortcake featuring a biscuit that's as light as French puff pastry—but it's the chocolate bread-and-butter pudding, made with sliced brioche, that left us weak in the knees. The wine list, unsurpassed in its selection of New England wines, includes a Chardonnay made by Crosswood Vineyards in Connecticut and a peach dessert wine made by the Nashoba Valley Winery in Massachusetts. A doorman escorts guests up a private elevator to a dining room remarkable for its brass chandeliers, elaborate moldings and Chinese Chippendale chairs. About $150 for dinner for two, with wine.

Some establishments change their closing times without warning. It is always wise to call ahead.

45

Cornucopia

15 West St.
(617) 338-4600
AMERICAN
Open Mon. noon-
2:30 p.m., Tues.-Sat. noon-
2:30 p.m. & 5:30p.m.-
9:30 p.m.; café open Tues.-
Sat. 2:30 p.m.-10 p.m.
All major cards.

The twentieth century has not been kind to a downtown thoroughfare called West Street—but in the nineteenth century, the Peabody house at number 15 was the gathering ground of the Hub's intelligentsia. It was here, in 1842, that Nathaniel Hawthorne married Sophia Peabody; it was here that Ralph Waldo Emerson and Elizabeth Peabody launched the transcendentalist journal The *Dial*. All of which is a lengthy prologue to a restaurant whose imaginative food, attractive setting and convenience to both the shopping and theater districts make it eminently worth a visit. The chef interweaves the cuisines of California and peasant Europe. A scallop ceviche garnishes a rustic black-bean soup. A braised lamb stew accompanies rack of lamb. Mesquite-grilled oysters are spiced up with jalapeño vinaigrette. Not every dish is worth crossing town during a snowstorm for, but in general the food is superior. Cornucopia is the only Boston restaurant we know of that recommends a specific wine—available by the glass—for every dish on the menu. Designed and run by architect Thomas Piatt and his wife, Christine, Cornucopia boasts a stunning decor: a yellow-and-aquamarine color scheme, ivy-clad trellises, inverted-pyramid stained-glass lamps. For formal dining, there's a sunny mezzanine with a glass cathedral ceiling. The ground-floor bar is a perfect place for a post-theater drink and dessert. Dinner with wine will set two back about $70.

Daily Catch

1 Kendall Square,
Cambridge
(617) 225-2300
SEAFOOD/ITALIAN
Open Mon.-Sat. 11:30 a.m.-
10:30 p.m., Sun. 5 p.m.-
10 p.m.
All major cards.

12/20

Squid is not a subject about which most people wax grandiloquent. But without it there would be no fried calamari, no black pasta and no linguine with squid. These are but a few of the house specialties of the Daily Catch, a tiny North End hole-in-the-wall that has grown into a popular three-restaurant chain. The Cambridge branch alone goes through 750 pounds of cleaned calamari—the equivalent of three tons of live squid—each week! The delicate flavor of calamari hints at scallop and clam, and contrary to popular belief, when properly prepared it's not the least bit rubbery. In the unhappy event that you don't care for squid, you'll find lots of other fresh seafood: broiled skate, lobster fra diavolo, and pastas made on the premises. The profligate use of garlic reflects the Sicilian heritage of Daily Catch owners Maria and Paul Freddura, as do the desserts— gelati and cannoli that are freshly made in-house. Located in a renovated warehouse at One Kendall Square, the Cambridge Daily Catch has faux marble tables, black lacquer chairs, high sunny windows and acres of quarry tiles. White-toqued chefs tend flaming sauté pans for all to watch in the open kitchen. About $50 for dinner for two, with wine.

*T*ime was when life's finer things
such as Hine Cognac were the
preserve of a privileged few.
Today, it is still the true connoisseur who
appreciates the mature, mellow flavour
of Hine.
The dictionary defines a connoisseur as "one
who is an expert judge in matters of taste".

And who are we to argue.

HINE
MAISON FONDÉE EN 1763

C O G N A C

BRASH, BOLD GUIDES
TO THE BEST OF THE VERY BEST

Also available:

Dartmouth Street

271 Dartmouth St.
(617) 536-6560
ITALIAN/AMERICAN
Open Sun.-Wed.
11:30 a.m.-3 p.m. &
5:30 p.m.-10:30 p.m.,
Thurs.-Sat. 11:30 a.m.-
3 p.m. & 5:30 p.m.-
11:30 p.m.
All major cards.

12/20

We like a restaurant that respects its customers enough to supply each table with a flask of balsamic vinegar and extra-virgin olive oil. We also like a restaurant where the pizzas are available with smoked salmon and sour cream, and where the fettuccine is blackened with squid ink. And therefore we like this subterranean bar/grill/café, the sort of place where you can come to nibble on a salad or soup (try the one with hearts of palm and buffalo mozzarella) or put away an entire meal. In a neighborhood where many of the waiters are more fixated on themselves than on their customers, it's nice to find a staff that seems to take pleasure serving the public. The owners have decorated their basement dining room with natural woods, brass rails and an abundance of quarry tiles. The bar is a popular mating ground for Back Bay trendies. Dinner for two, with wine, will run about $70.

Durgin-Park

(Faneuil Hall Marketplace),
340 N. Market St.
(617) 227-2038
AMERICAN/SEAFOOD
Open Mon.-Thurs.
11:30 a.m.-10 p.m., Fri.-
Sat. 11:30 a.m.-10:30 p.m.,
Sun. noon-9 p.m.
No cards.

10/20

The venerable Durgin-Park is probably the only restaurant in a ten-block radius of Faneuil Hall that doesn't have butcher-block tables or potted ferns. Instead it has long, crowded communal tables draped with red-checkered cloths and groaning with vast portions of hearty New England fare at prices that even a Puritanical purse can afford. The prime rib weighs in at 27 ounces; the bone is as big as a barrel stave. The chowder is mercifully free of starchy thickeners; the clams and oysters on the half shell are superbly fresh (though oysters are served in a heap, leaving those on the lower level dirty). Other good choices are the broiled seafood platter, Yankee pot roast and homemade baked beans. Durgin-Park also makes its own shortcake to serve with strawberries: It is best to order this early in the evening, for the restaurant has been known to run out. (If it does, you can always console yourself with an Indian pudding that would have done Miles Standish proud.) On the down side, there is almost always a waiting line, and the noise level makes a jackhammer seem quiet. The wait can be shortened by ordering a drink in the bar, then asking the bartender to send you up the rear staircase. Not all the waitresses are as surly as they are reputed to be. Fish buffs will be pleased to learn that Durgin-Park recently opened a street-level late-night seafood grill. Not the least remarkable thing about this most remarkable restaurant is that in its 160 years of operation, it has had only three owners and five chefs. About $40 for dinner for two, with beer or wine; considerably less for lunch.

East Coast Grill

**1271 Cambridge St.,
Cambridge
(617) 491-6568**
AMERICAN
*Open Sun.-Thurs.
5:30 p.m.-10 p.m., Fri.-Sat.
5:30 p.m. 10:30p.m.
Cards: MC, V.*

It's not what we would call elegant, and the location is far from central. Why, then, does the East Coast Grill fill its tables night after night after night? Not the least of co-owner/chef Chris Schlessinger's accomplishments is a North Carolina–style barbecue that's as authentically Southern as corn likker. But to come here simply for barbecue would be to miss out on Schlessinger's tongue-blistering jerk chicken (made with scotch bonnet chiles), triple-thick tuna steak (smokily charred on the outside and served sushi-rare in the center) and intoxicating bourbon bread pudding. The East Coast Grill is a fun restaurant where blue margaritas come with animal-shape swizzle sticks and flames leap up from an open grill. Once a vintage luncheonette, the dining room is decorated with contemporary art and playful squiggles of neon. Be sure to buy a bottle of the restaurant's Inner Beauty Hot Sauce on the way out—the stuff makes napalm seem positively refreshing. About $50 for two, with wine.

L'Espalier

**30 Gloucester St.
(617) 262-3023**
AMERICAN/FRENCH
*Open Mon.-Sat. 6 p.m.-
10 p.m.
All major cards.*

Hub foodies held their breath when Moncef Meddeb sold L'Espalier to his sous-chef, Frank McClelland. Would this fashionable Back Bay restaurant remain a temple of high gastronomy? After several months of new ownership, the answer, we're happy to report, is yes. McClelland has an artist's eye for presentation: His food would be suitable for framing in a gallery of the culinary arts. He has infused the once strictly French menu with Yankee innovation—chocolate pasta accompanies blood- rare squab; a cool corn soup harbors a grilled seafood sausage; "barbecued" lobster is served with an exotic mango "ketchup." Not all of the combinations work, but you can't fault the chef for not trying. The kitchen could use a more assertive hand with the salt. The service, thankfully, has shed its snotty airs, but the pace of dinner can tarry. Above all reproach is the setting: a Back Bay townhouse restored to Victorian splendor, filled with mammoth flower sprays and museum-quality art. Expense accounts are in for a heavy workout. About $160 for dinner for two, with a good wine.

Five Seasons

**669A Centre St.
(617) 524-9016**
MACROBIOTIC
*Open Tues.-Sat. noon-
10 p.m., Sun. 11 a.m.-
2:15 p.m. & 4 p.m.-10 p.m.
Cards: MC, V.*

12/20

Who says health food has to be Spartan or dietetic? Rob and Jon Pell, owners of this popular Jamaica Plain restaurant, have proven that macrobiotic cooking can also be gourmet. Seafood fanciers will have a field day here with the salmon teriyaki, bluefish with mustard sauce and salubrious sea vegetable salad. Vegetarians can look forward to vegetarian chili, tempura nori rolls (batter-fried vegetable sushi) and made-from-scratch french fries and onion rings served with homemade ketchup. Desserts range from the predictable granola pear crisp to a "cheesecake" made with tofu. Naturally, you can order fresh carrot juice to accompany your meal, and this is one of the few places in town that serves Anchor Steam beer. The dining room is tastefully decorated with paddle fans, wood trim, butcher-block tables and clean white walls decked with the works of local photographers and artists. To get to the bathroom, you must pass through the kitchen; you'll marvel, as did we, at the Pells' ability to produce such good food in such a small work space. About $40 for two, with wine.

Golden Palace

14-20 Tyler St.
(617) 423-4565
CHINESE
Open daily 9 a.m.-
11:30 p.m.; dim sum daily
9 a.m.-3 p.m.
Cards: AE, MC, V.

11/20

It's Saturday morning in Chinatown, 11 a.m., and already there's a waiting line. A half hour later, we take our seats in the typically decorated room (Formica and lanterns) amid a sea of exuberant Chinese eaters. The purpose of our visit? Dim sum. Dim sum translates into "bits and pieces eaten at odd moments to please the heart"—and that translates into a mind-boggling assortment of Chinese tea pastries and hors d'oeuvres. You don't need a menu; every few minutes, a cart laden with goodies emerges from the kitchen. To order, simply point your chopstick at whatever looks good: har gao (opalescent shrimp dumplings), shu mai (meatballs steamed in cabbage leaves) or, our favorite, airy steamed bao buns filled with barbecued pork. Not all the dim sum—like the bony chicken and duck feet and the intimidating tripe—will delight the average American diner, but with more than 30 different varieties to choose from, even the most timid palate will be pleased. Less than $20 for dim sum for two, with beer.

Green Street Grill

280 Green St., Cambridge
(617) 876-1655
AMERICAN/CREOLE
Open Tues.-Fri.
11:30 a.m.-2 p.m. &
6 p.m.-10 p.m., Sat.-Sun.
6 p.m.-10 p.m.
Cards: AE, MC, V.

This boisterous neighborhood-bar-turned-restaurant is not for the faint of heart or the tender of palate. St. Thomas–born chef John Levins takes almost satanic delight in igniting his food with garlic, ginger, hot sauce, peppercorns and chiles. His cracked-pepper shrimp come with a devilishly hot clam-chile relish. The merest nibble of his conch with scotch bonnet chile sauce sends us lunging for our beer. But you don't need an asbestos gullet to enjoy every dish: The loin of pork with Jamaican curry and the blackened tuna with chile hollandaise are flavorful but not too piquant. The dining room isn't much to look at—drab wooden walls, a ratty red carpet, tiny tables and uncomfortable chairs—and the service is slow, but the food speaks eloquently for itself. Most evenings there is live jazz after 10 p.m. About $50 for two, with wine.

The prices listed in this guide reflect what restaurants and hotels have informed us they plan to charge at press time. Please don't blame us if they don't coincide exactly with reality.

Grill 23 & Bar

161 Berkeley St.
(617) 542-2255
STEAKHOUSE
*Open Mon.-Thurs. noon-
2:30 p.m. & 6 p.m.-
10:30 p.m., Fri. noon-
2:30 p.m. & 6 p.m.-
11 p.m., Sat. 6 p.m.-
11 p.m.
All major cards.*

Grill 23 is Boston's answer to a traditional New York chophouse. It's masculine. Crowded. And noisier than Boston Garden during a Celtics game. But the ear-splitting decibel levels do not deter a business crowd from flocking here for Bible-thick veal chops, lengthily aged steaks and seafood grilled to smoky perfection. We adore the grilled vegetables; the steak tartare is superb. The most-unusual-dessert award goes to the grilled banana split. Located in Back Bay's historic Salada Tea building, the dining room glows with the clubby elegance of burnished brass, dark woods and massive marble pillars, around which are tables set with snowy cloths, heavy silver, and marble salt and pepper shakers. But despite the decor, this is no place for an intimate dinner à deux, unless you find shouting romantic. A recently instituted brunch features hand-cut bacon, homemade sausage and omelets filled with lobster, scallions and Camembert. About $90 for dinner for two, with wine.

Hamersley's Bistro

578 Tremont St.
(617) 267-6068
AMERICAN
*Open Mon.-Sat. 6 p.m.-
10:30 p.m.
Cards: AE, MC, V.*

Roast chicken is not generally a dish that delivers epicures into culinary nirvana. But the roast chicken at Hamersley's Bistro is so crisp, so moist, so sublimely flavored, it will make you want to nominate the chef for sainthood. This popular South End bistro is the brainchild of Gordon and Fiona Hamersley, who have staked their reputation on refined versions of such robust peasant fare as Raclette, braised short ribs and bouillabaisse. Chops and fish are grilled to order in an open kitchen manned by a team of chefs in red baseball caps (Hamersley is the one who's as tall and skinny as a bean pole). Desserts sound such homey themes as fruit compote, homemade ice cream and apple pie. The decor might be termed "no-frills bistro": stark white walls decked with gallery prints and tables topped with white paper. A well-dressed clientele of South End professionals keeps the two small dining rooms packed. Though the Hamersleys aren't exactly giving their wines away, the list harbors some well-chosen bottles. About $85 for two, with wine.

Hampshire House

84 Beacon St.
(617) 227-9600
CONTINENTAL
*Open Mon.-Fri.
11:45 a.m.-2:30 p.m. &
5:30 p.m.-10:30 p.m., Sat.-
Sun. 5 p.m.-10:30 p.m.
All major cards.*

12/20

A majestic spiral staircase lined with medieval tapestries leads to a dining room with eighteen-foot ceilings, brass chandeliers and a fire crackling away in a marble hearth. Welcome to the Hampshire House, where for one evening, at least, you can experience what it must have been like to dine in a wealthy Brahmin home in the nineteenth century. Several of the tables overlook the Public Garden; all are graced with heavy silver and burnished service plates. In keeping with the setting, the food is conservative and sturdy: baked stuffed mushroom caps, Boston scrod, steak au poivre and prettily garnished chateaubriand for two. Inspired? No, but it's competently prepared. Sunday brunch in the stately Oak Room Bar, where a pianist fields requests, is refreshingly understated: flawless eggs à la florentine, corned beef hash—fewer than a dozen items in all. The Bloody Marys are generally acknowledged to be Boston's best. Expect to see plenty of tourists milling about, because The Bull and Finch Pub in the Hampshire House's basement was the inspiration for the TV sitcom Cheers. The Hampshire House is immensely popular, so it is advisable to arrive early for drinks or brunch. About $70 for two for dinner with wine; $40 for two for brunch with drinks.

The Harvest
44 Brattle St., Cambridge
(617) 492-1115
AMERICAN
Open Mon.-Thurs.
11:30 a.m.-10 p.m., Fri.
11:30 a.m.-10:30p.m., Sat.
noon-3 p.m. & 6 p.m.-
10:30 p.m., Sun. 11 a.m.-
3 p.m. & 5 p.m.-
10:30 p.m.
All major cards.

The Harvest was, perhaps, the first Hub restaurant to serve wild game, "trash fish" (underutilized sea creatures) and dishes of the American heartland. We still find the menu as exciting and innovative as when this Harvard Square landmark opened in 1975. A shiitake flan accompanies rack of lamb; Barbary duck is sauced with pearl onions and blueberries; tournedos of buffalo replace traditional filet mignon. The bread basket harbors Irish soda bread and what is undoubtedly the finest baguette in town. There are three dining environments to choose from: a formal dining room decorated with tiny Christmas tree lights and a seasonally changing color scheme (green in spring and summer, brown in autumn and winter); an informal café festooned with bright Marimekko wall fabrics; and a shady terrace for al fresco indulging. The bar, Ben's Corner, attracts a well-heeled crowd of Cambridge professionals and is a great place to order one of the best burgers in Cambridge. Each night a half dozen interesting wines are available by the glass; beer buffs will find a bevy of interesting brews, including Geary's Pale Ale from Portland, Maine, and locally made Lightship Lager. About $100 for dinner for two, with wine, in the dining room; about $70 for two, with wine, in the café.

Ho Yuen Ting
13A Hudson St.
(617) 426-2316
CHINESE
Open Mon.-Thurs.
11:30 a.m.-9:30 p.m., Fri.-
Sat. 11:30 a.m.-10:30 p.m.,
Sun. noon-9:30 p.m.
No cards.

12/20

The first thing we look for when visiting a Chinese restaurant is the percentage of Asian clients. A sea of Chinese faces augurs well for this boisterous Chinatown hole-in-the-wall. Seafood is the house specialty: Cantonese lobster, clams with black-bean sauce, whole sea bass steamed to perfection with ginger and scallions. The pièce de résistance is the house special flounder: a whole fish whose batter-fried bones form an edible platter for the filets, which are stir-fried with vegetables. Other good bets here include the bountiful soups (we like the watercress and barbecued pork) and filling rice-in-pot dishes. Success has brought such decorative amenities as textured wallpaper and art, and the dining room on the second floor is available for large and private parties. Since the reasonable prices and excellent food have made Ho Yuen Ting one of the most popular haunts in Chinatown, arrive early or expect a wait. About $40 for dinner for two, with beer (the only form of alcohol served).

Icarus

3 Appleton St.
(617) 426-1790
AMERICAN
Open Mon.-Thurs.
5:30 p.m.-10:30 p.m.,
F ri.-Sat. 5:30 p.m. mid-
night, Sun. 11 a.m.-9 p.m.
All major cards.

We remember the Icarus of the old days: the rustic decor, the blackboard menu, the mismatched antique silverware and plates. My, how times have changed! This South End landmark recently reopened in a basement on Appleton Street, and it's as chic as a Manhattan nightspot. Extravagant flower sprays and tree branches strung with tiny white lights festoon the split-level dining room, and recessed neon casts a cool blue glow around the perimeter of the ceiling. Watching over it all is a statue of Icarus, his wings spread and ready for flight. The buttery rolls are homemade, and so are the pasta dishes and designer pizzas. (We particularly relished the pizza topped with apples, walnuts and Cheddar cheese.) The appetizers sound a grass-roots American note: grilled leeks with country ham and biscuits, and smoked cod and potato gratin. The chef stumbles on some of the entrées but recovers with the desserts. Chocoholics will swoon over a long-standing house specialty, a soufflé-light chocolate cake. Dinner for two, with wine, will run about $100.

Jasper's

240 Commercial St.
(617) 523-1126
AMERICAN
Open Mon.-Thurs. 6 p.m.-
10 p.m., Fri.-Sat. 6 p.m.-
11 p.m.
All major cards.

Any chef can work wonders with caviar, smoked salmon and foie gras. It takes a true genius to elevate such lowly ingredients as cabbage, pork and white beans to the status of culinary superstars. Such chefs are Jasper White and his second in command, Stanley Frankenthaler. Under their direction the kitchen turns out an endless profusion of delicacies: pheasant with cabbage turnovers, double-thick rib steak with shoestring potatoes, tuna medallions the size of baseballs swaddled in bacon and smokily grilled. As befits a Hub restaurant, Jasper's also serves a tasting menu devoted exclusively to seafood. A recent visit fetched us lobster sausage, fettuccine with caviar, and a breathtaking smoked-haddock chowder. There are lots of nice touches here: homemade breadsticks; the delivery of a fresh napkin every time you leave the table; jazz pianist Ed Perkins in the bar on weekends. And yet, all is not perfect in Jasper's kingdom. During a recent meal, the service, normally so attentive, wasn't just leisurely, it was slow. Sorbets have been known to be icy, and betimes, someone in the kitchen has a heavy hand with the salt. Housed downtown in a former molasses warehouse, Jasper's boasts massive ceiling timbers, handsome brick walls, black-lacquered furniture and a pleasingly eclectic assortment of flower arrangements, alabaster lamps and original art. The selection of Cognacs, dessert wines and eaux de vie is one of the most comprehensive in town. About $150 for dinner for two, with wine.

Julien

(Hotel Meridien),
2250 Franklin St.
(617) 451-1900
FRENCH
Open Mon.-Fri.
11:30 a.m.-2:30 p.m. &
6 p.m.-9:30 p.m., Sat.
6 p.m.-11 p.m., Sun.
6 p.m.-9:30 p.m.
All major cards.

Julien at the Meridien must surely be the most grandiose dining room in the city. Located downtown in the former Members Court of the old Federal Reserve Building, it boasts gilded cornices, marble walls and dizzyingly high coffered ceilings. The tables are well set and well spaced, the wing-back Queen Anne chairs are roomy and comfortable, and the place oozes an aura of opulent civility. Like most foreign hotels (this one belongs to France), the Meridien hired a consulting chef to design the menu: Olivier Roellinger of the Breton restaurant De Bricourt. Not surprisingly, Roellinger likes seafood: Twelve of the eighteen dishes on his menu are prepared with fish. We're pleased to see that he's given up trying to fly fish in from France. (Importing seafood to Boston is like carrying coals to Newcastle.) His current menu features such local specialties as roasted Maine lobster with dark rum, tartare of salmon and mahi mahi with spring vegetables, and "un mariage terre-mer"—sliced sea scallops and smoked breast of duck. Cheese buffs will be thrilled to find two "vintages" of superb aged French mountain cheese served with fruity vin jaune (yellow wine) from Chalon, and chocoholics will be transported after one bite of the bouchées au chocolat amer (bitter-chocolate "mouthfuls" with coffee sauce). Roellinger is still feeling his way with Julien, and some of his dishes sound better than they actually taste, but we are optimistic that things will only get better. We have similar expectations of the service, which has ranged from slow to satisfactory to excellent. Dinner with wine will cost two about $150.

Kebab 'N' Kurry

30 Massachusetts Ave.
(617) 536-9835
INDIAN
Open Mon.-Sat. noon-
3 p.m. & 5 p.m.-11 p.m.,
Sun. 5 p.m.-10:30 p.m.
Cards: AE, MC, V.

In the past three years, the Hub has been inundated with Indian restaurants. Despite the rash of newcomers, our favorite remains Kebab 'N' Kurry in Back Bay. Venerable by ethnic restaurant standards, KNK was opened in 1980 by New Delhi–born Vinod and Shakila Kapoor. The spices are imported from India and freshly roasted and ground each morning. The Kapoors serve six types of curry, ranging from mild korma (a delicately spiced almond and cream curry) to incendiary vindaloo (a dry curry flavored with vinegar and chili). The kebabs are marinated to Mercurochrome orange in spices, then grilled in a tandoor oven. To round out your meal, try the pakoras (vegetables fried in chickpea batter) or dahi papri (lentil crisps with spiced potatoes, yogurt and tamarind sauce). Ras malai (rosewater-scented curds) and badami kheer (Indian rice pudding) provide a dulcet touch for dessert. Decorated with peach walls, mirrors, hanging plants and batiks, Kebab 'N' Kurry makes the most of its Massachusetts Avenue basement location. Don't forget to bring your own beer: You'll need it to put out the fires. About $30 for two, without wine.

Legal Sea Foods

(Park Plaza Hotel),
35 Columbus Ave.
(617) 426-4444
SEAFOOD
*Open Sun.-Thurs. 11 a.m.-
10 p.m., Fri.-Sat. 11 a.m.-
11 p.m.*
All major cards.

At the risk of sounding older than we are, we remember
Legal Sea Foods in the old days, back when it was a fish
store with a handful of picnic tables, where guests could eat
perfectly broiled bluefish and fried haddock so crisp you
could hear each bite. Today, Legal is big business, with
restaurants across Eastern Massachusetts. Amazingly, the
fish is every bit as fresh as it used to be, and the dining
rooms are more upscale—but a certain gemütlichkeit has
been lost. The company's flagship is the Back Bay Legal, a
split-level expanse of wicker, canvas and brass rails, located
on the ground floor of the Park Plaza Hotel. The Cambridge Legal features Japanese kites and blue and white tiles,
while the Chestnut Hill branch runs more toward butcher
block and hanging ferns. Whichever Legal you visit, you can
rely on the Berkowitz family's uncompromising insistence
on freshness. Stick to the straightforward items: clams and
oysters on the half shell (each batch is laboratory tested for
contamination), broiled or fried fish, smoked bluefish pâté
and Irish smoked salmon (the latter custom-cured for Legal). Desserts include homemade ice creams and sorbets.
You no longer have to pay ahead of time, a rather quaint
custom in the old days, but the food is still served without
ceremony as soon as it is ready, and not necessarily at the
same time your companions receive theirs. The computer-
ized wine list is a treasure trove of California boutique
wines. About $50 for two, with wine.

Sally Ling

(Hyatt Regency
Cambridge),
575 Memorial Dr. ,
Cambridge
(617) 227-4545
CHINESE
*Open Mon.-Thurs. noon-
2:30 p.m. & 5:30 p.m.-
10 p.m., Fri. noon-
2:30 p.m. & 5:30 p.m.-
11 p.m., Sat. 5:30 p.m.-
11 p.m., Sun. 5:30 p.m.-
10 p.m.*
All major cards.

Before its move from downtown Boston, Sally Ling was as
good as Chinese food gets in these parts. Whether it's still as
good, now that it has relocated to plush new quarters in the
Hyatt Regency Cambridge, has yet to be seen; the just-
before-press-time move didn't give us a chance for a proper
review. And whether it's worth the price of admission will
depend on how you feel about paying as much for dinner
for two here as you'd spend to feed a family of eight in
Chinatown. But this is no Chinatown joint: The Chinese
Chippendale chairs, starched white tablecloths, scroll paintings, Oriental statuary, lavish flowers and tuxedoed maître
d' make that clear the moment you walk in. You'll find
dishes here you rarely see on Chinese menus, like peony-
blossom beef, Peking-style frogs' legs and sautéed salmon
with four vegetables, and you'll find a French-style six-
course menu dégustation. The Chinese classics—Peking
duck, Hunan imperial chicken and lobster with ginger—are,
of course, also to be found. We hope the once-high
standards are maintained. About $100 for dinner for two,
with wine.

Locke-Ober Café
3 Winter Pl.
(617) 542-1340
AMERICAN/CONTINENTAL
Open Mon.-Thurs.
11:30 a.m.-10 p.m., Fri.-
Sat. 11:30 a.m.-10:30 p.m.,
Sun. 5 p.m.-10 p.m.
All major cards.

The union of Frank Locke's Wine Room with Louis Ober's Restaurant Parisienne in 1894 resulted in a Boston landmark: the Locke-Ober Café. The waiters, many of whom have been here for 30 years, wear the black jackets and floor-length white aprons of a bygone era, but their expert service remains mercifully down to earth. The chef has little time to bother with pan-blackening or other such food fads; except for the prices, Locke-Ober's menu has remained virtually unchanged for half a century. The food is heavy by modern standards, but that does not deter a primarily male business clientele (though women crossed its sacrosanct portal in 1970) from flocking here for clams à la Gino, oyster stew (a JFK favorite), fishermen's eggs and a steak tartare so noteworthy that it was the subject of a story in Esquire. Stick with the simpler entrées: chateaubriand, rack of lamb for two (the company has a sheep farm in Rhode Island). We've never understood the fuss about the leaden lobster Savannah. No one can beat Locke-Ober's Indian pudding, but don't overlook the frothy zabaglione and booze-soaked English trifle. If this is your first visit, request to be seated in the Men's Bar and Café, decorated with gilded wallpaper, hand-carved Dominican mahogany and a gleaming silver steam table. You'll feel like you've been invited to dinner at the Vanderbilts' in the second-floor Ober room, complete with furnishings from a mansion in Newport. The private dining rooms on the third floor are popular with business folk. About $150 for dinner for two, with wine.

Maison Robert
45 School St.
(617) 227-3370
FRENCH
Open Mon.-Fri.
11:30 a.m.-2:30 p.m. &
5:30 p.m.-10 p.m., Sat.
5:30 p.m.-10 p.m.
All major cards.

This is the house that Robert built, located in Boston's grandiose Old City Hall. There are three dining environments to choose from: a sunny outdoor terrace, a formal dining room with sky-high ceilings and chandeliers, and an informal café amid the warm brick arches of what was formerly the city vault. So how's the food? It is French in inspiration, astronomical in price and popular with the expense-account lunch crowd. We have no complaints about the rich pâté, the boudin blanc (veal sausage with mustard sauce) or the fluffy but costly omelets. And the tarte tatin and frozen chestnut mousse have been known to make us weak in the knees. But we have had complaints about salty sauces, sloppily assembled salads and some overly complicated entrées; the service can be leisurely to a fault. Maison Robert was the first Hub restaurant to serve lotte, and this firm-fleshed fish, often called "the poor man's lobster," remains a house specialty, as do Dover sole and rack of lamb. The future is looking brighter for this place: Robert's daughter has brought some fresh air to the kitchen. The wine list is not for paupers, but budget-minded guests might do well to consider the Metaire Muscadet, which is specially bottled for Maison Robert. About $130 for dinner for two, with wine.

Le Marquis de Lafayette

(The Lafayette Hotel),
1 Ave. de Lafayette
(617) 451-2600
FRENCH
Open Mon.-Fri. noon-
2:30 p.m. & 6 p.m.-
10:30 p.m., Sat. 6 p.m.-
10 p.m. (closed for lunch
July-Aug.).
All major cards.

Bostonians are fond of bashing that architectural boondoggle, Lafayette Place. But you won't hear them making fun of the formal restaurant at The Lafayette Hotel, Le Marquis. Le Marquis showcases the talents of three gifted chefs. The menus are designed by Louis Outhier, the globetrotting owner of the renowned restaurant L'Oasis on the French Riviera. Not long ago Outhier designed a five-course, fixed-price menu based entirely on caviar; his toujours trois ("forever three") menu is the best antidote we know to menu indecision, featuring three different Marquis appetizers, fish dishes, meat dishes and desserts. The execution of these dishes falls to the Alsatian-born chef de cuisine, Philippe Reininger, who favors herbs, vinaigrettes and vegetable sauces over the artery-clogging butters and creams of classical French cuisine. Pastry chef Pierre Prevost has a sculptor's touch when it comes to dessert: His prune mousse, for example, is decorated with pulled-sugar rose petals. The dining room is a little chilly, but crystal chandeliers, lavish flower arrangements and costly antiques provide the appropriate aura of elegance. Romantically minded guests will appreciate the candlelight and live harp music. The cost of such joys ain't cheap: Dinner for two, with a decent wine (wines *start* at $30), will drain your wallet of $150 to $200.

Michela's

1 Athenaeum St.
(at First St.), Cambridge
(617) 225-3366
ITALIAN
Open Mon.-Wed. noon-
2:30 p.m. & 6 p.m.-
10 p.m., Thurs.-Fri. noon-
2:30 p.m. & 6 p.m.-
10:30 p.m.
All major cards.

There are precious few things in this life more pleasurable than Michela Larson's crusty Tuscan rolls. (Try them dunked in olive oil.) Among these precious few things are some of the creations of Larson's chef, Todd English: morbidelle di semolina (semolina rounds topped with Gorgonzola and grilled mushrooms), zuppa d'aglio (garlic soup) and piatto d'agnello (lamb served four ways—barbecued ribs, roast loin, grilled leg and braised shank—each more delectable than its fellow). You can share in these culinary joys at Larson's stylish restaurant in the Carter Ink Building near the burgeoning Cambridge waterfront, where chef and proprietor are collaborating to serve the most exciting nuova cucina in New England. English and Larson are not afraid to take chances: oysters might be grilled with Mascarpone and radicchio; dessert crêpes could be filled with pastry cream and grilled corn. This sort of innovation keeps the dining room packed with a young, affluent executive crowd from the computer firms in Kendall Square. To look at the dining room, you'd never guess what the fuss is about: an industrial high-tech cavern with pink walls and exposed heating ducts. The tables are strewn with homemade breadsticks; the chairs and tables are comfortable enough; the back wall is painted with pastel colors in the image of an

Italian bank note. But you'll have to pay in good old U.S. dollars: about $120 for a memorable dinner for two, with wine (less if you keep to antipasti and pastas).

Mr. Leung
545 Boylston St.
(617) 236-4040
CHINESE
Open Mon.-Fri.
11:30 a.m.-3 p.m. &
6 p.m.-11 p.m., Sat.
6 p.m.-11 p.m., Sun.
11:30 a.m.-3 p.m. &
6 p.m.-10 p.m.
All major cards.

Mr. Leung doesn't look like your average Chinese restaurant. Not with its spotlight-studded ceiling, sleek black walls and table settings of white cloths, black plates and purple Peruvian lilies. And when was the last time you dined at a Chinese restaurant (especially in New England) that had valet parking, tuxedoed captains and an affable, hovering staff? Opened by Hong Kong–born Bernard Leung, Mr. Leung reflects the latest trend in the upscaling of ethnic restaurants. The menu ranges from the familiar to the exotic. The honey-barbecued spareribs and crispy shrimp balls, for example, are variations on Cantonese classics. But we've never before seen the likes of the "grape cluster" sea bass (the fish is cut and cooked in such a way that it really does resemble a bunch of grapes). But not every dish is memorable—some of the stir-fries bear a disheartening resemblance to neighborhood Chinese takeout. As befits a haute-Chinese restaurant in Back Bay, guests have a choice of several varieties of tea, each served with a stick of rock candy for stirring. The prices are far from typically Chinese, too: about $90 for dinner for two, with wine.

Miyako
468 Commonwealth Ave.
(617) 236-0222
JAPANESE
Open Sun.-Thurs. noon-
2:30 p.m. & 5 p.m.-
10:30 p.m., Fri.-Sat. noon-
2:30 p.m. & 5 p.m.-11 p.m.
Cards: MC, V.

This Back Bay basement hideaway is the sort of place we're inclined to share only with close friends. The sushi chef has a way with fish that borders on the preternatural. We've rarely encountered a better tiger eye (octopus, salmon and avocado arranged in the form of a cat's eye). The salmon-skin temaki (hand roll) and amaebi (fresh prawn sushi) will make your taste buds sing. The kitchen does an equally fine job with cooked dishes—the broiled yellowtail, for example, melts on your tongue like butter, and the tiny shrimp dumplings called age-shumai are as succulent as the katsu (breaded pork chop) is audibly crisp. Located in the heart of the student ghetto, Miyako has an unpretentious decor of Oriental-print reproductions and Formica butcher blocks. The service is friendlier than you'd expect of a restaurant that regularly fills all its seats. About $40 for dinner for two, with wine.

Morton's of Chicago
1 Exeter Pl.
(617) 266-5858
STEAKHOUSE
Open Mon.-Fri.
11:30 a.m.-2:30 p.m. &
5:30 p.m.-11 p.m., Sat.
5:30 p.m.-11 p.m.
All major cards.

12/20

The arrival of this Chicago-based chophouse to the Hub was hyped to an excess befitting a rock star. The good news is that Morton's really does serve superlative meat: hefty steaks so generously marbled that they practically melt in your mouth. On the down side, it took three tries to get calves' liver medium rare, the way we had ordered it. Everything is done on a grand scale at Morton's (in Back Bay): Oysters are served on a mountain of ice in a salad bowl, and baked spuds are the size of footballs. As at most chophouses, you're better off sticking with the simpler items: smoked salmon, oysters on the half shell, Caesar salad. But pay no heed to the brouhaha Morton's makes over its black-bean soup, which we find lackluster. Depending on your perspective, the stucco walls, stained-glass panels, and flickering oil lamps on the tables will feel either cozily clubby or synthetically Wild West. The management needs to speed up the service at lunch if anyone's going to get any work done in the afternoon. About $80 for a steak dinner for two, with wine.

Panache
798 Main St., Cambridge
(617) 492-9500
AMERICAN
Open Tues.-Sat. 6 p.m.-
10 p.m.
All major cards.

We were alarmed to learn of the departure of Bobby Calderone, longtime chef of this ever-so-chic boutique restaurant. We rushed to Panache with our hearts full of dread, but we're pleased to report that the new chef, Anton Dodel, has taken charge without skipping a beat. Dodel has a way with seafood: Sweet Maine shrimp are served in a Cajun cream, soft-shell crabs are anointed with a tomato vinaigrette, and kingfish is married with fennel. Panache was one of the first restaurants to install a wood-burning grill; we would hate to have to choose between the grilled pizza with goat cheese and herbs or the grilled lamb chops with fiddle-head ferns. Desserts are easier: Everything else pales next to the silken chocolate marquise. The wine list is small but choice—we doubt there's a better selection of New England wines anywhere. A conspiratorial air reigns among the 36 guests who occupy the storefront dining room decorated with a black ceiling, dark-gray walls and Fiestaware service plates for splashes of color—as if they're all in on some great secret, which in fact they are. Anywhere from $80 to $100 for two, with wine.

> *DON'T FORGET: Gault Millau introduces you to the Best of New York, the Best of Washington D.C., the Best of Los Angeles, the Best of San Francisco, the Best of Chicago, the Best of France, the Best of Paris, the Best of Italy, the Best of London.*

Rarities

(The Charles Hotel,
at Harvard Square),
1 Bennett St., Cambridge
(617) 864-1200
AMERICAN
*Open Sun.-Thurs. 6 p.m.-
10 p.m., Fri.-Sat. 6 p.m.-
11 p.m.*
All major cards.

The people behind Rarities were smart enough to realize that for most diners prepared to shell out big money for dinner, courtesy counts—a lot. From the moment you call to make a reservation until the time you pay your check, courtesy is something this swank new hotel restaurant has in abundance. Alas, one does not dine on courtesy alone, and Rarities has its culinary downs as well as its ups. Our most recent dinner began auspiciously enough with deviled quail eggs, smoked-salmon-stuffed radicchio and other complimentary hors d'oeuvres. But $17.50 for a soggy foie gras napoleon will try the patience of even the most understanding guest. The menu celebrates American foods—Olympia oyster focaccia, sirloin with Navajo bread—and the flavor combinations are imaginative: turnip gnocchi with black trumpet mushrooms, braised rabbit with pears and couscous. Some combinations work better than others, but you can be assured of one thing: Your palate will never be bored. Served from a marble buffet table, desserts aren't quite up to the quality of the entrées. The contemporary dining room is done in exposed brick, expanses of glass, dark-gray carpets, black-marble trim and enormous potted plants. After dinner, you can repair to the adjacent Regattabar to take in a big-name jazz act—if you're still in the mood, which you may not be after parting with $150 to $200 for dinner for two, with wine.

Ritz-Carlton Hotel The Dining Room

15 Arlington St.
(617) 536-5700
CONTINENTAL
*Open Mon.-Thurs. noon-
2:30 p.m. & 6:30 p.m.-
10 p.m., Fri.-Sat. noon-
2:30 p.m. & 5:30 p.m.-
11 p.m., Sun. 10:45 a.m.-
2:15 p.m. & 6:30 p.m.-
10 p.m. (Ritz Café open
for breakfast daily 7 a.m.-
10:30 a.m.).*
All major cards.

It is said that more Boston business gets done at breakfast at the Ritz-Carlton Hotel (in the Ritz Café) than at any other time of day anywhere else. Hyperbole, perhaps, but it does underline the importance of this venerable Back Bay hotel as a gathering ground for Beantown movers and shakers, even at lunch and dinner. No doubt that's due in part to the setting, in which the power-suit crowd feels snugly omnipotent: a quietly grandiose dining room with a filigreed ceiling, cobalt-blue chandeliers, tinkling baby grand and magnificent view of the Public Garden. And the food? It depends on what you order, and it depends on where you eat it—we've had better luck in the formal dining room than in the bustling sidewalk café. The prices hurt: $12 for gravlax (admittedly among the best we've ever sampled), $18 for a platter of raw and poached shellfish. And that's just for the appetizers! As at most Continental restaurants, you're better off with the simpler entrées: rack of lamb, Dover sole, enormous scampi flambéed with Pernod at the tableside. The dessert soufflés are impressive—remember to order them at the beginning of the meal. The wine prices make highway robbery seem like an act of kindness; surprisingly, the best values are to be found among the older, pricier vintages. But you do get a show for your money: The sommelier actually samples each wine to make sure you don't keel over from the shock of getting a bad bottle. Sunday brunch is an orgy of steaming roasts and shimmering aspic. Above reproach is the service, which is hovering when you need it and invisible when you don't. The waiters have been known to produce coloring books and hot dogs on silver platters for kids. About $160 for dinner for two, with wine.

Rocco's
5 Charles St. South
(617) 723-6800
AMERICAN/INTERNATIONAL
Open daily 11:30 a.m.-
3 p.m. & 5:30 p.m.-
11:30 p.m.
Cards: AE, MC, V.

Nineteen eighty-eight will be remembered as the year that dining out in Boston became fun. If you need proof, just visit Rocco's, located in the Transportation Building in the heart of the Theater District. It's a visual romp through a decorative wonderland: vertiginously high ceilings covered with colorful scenes that would have done Michelangelo proud, angular bronze chandeliers, faux marble walls, iridescent green curtains, solid cherry tables furnished with hand-painted wooden animals and comfortable bow-back Queen Anne chairs. Chef Danny Wiesel, formerly of Devon at the World Trade Center, has kept his food fashionably proletarian: black-bean cakes, all-meat chili, Irish lamb stew and a wonderful dish called "old clothes in hot sauce," made with smoked haddock, fried onions and mashed potatoes. The menu is sufficiently international to include Thai soups, Cuban salads and Italian cacciatores. The bad news is that the ethnic diversity of the menu sometimes trips up the kitchen, and the service can be slow. Rocco's owner, Patrick Bowe, has made a laudable effort to stock wines and beers not normally found at restaurants. About $80 for two, with wine.

St. Cloud
557 Tremont St.
(617) 353-0202
AMERICAN/INTERNATIONAL
Open Mon.-Sat.
11:30 a.m.-3 p.m. &
5:30 p.m.-midnight, Sun.
11 a.m.-4 p.m. &
5:30 p.m.-midnight.
All major cards.

This oh-so-trendy eatery is the crowning touch of the gentrification of the South End—name another "neighborhood" restaurant where dinner for two will gobble up the better part of a C-note. The menu is as international as the U.N. General Assembly, jumping around the globe from Thai salads to Mexican guacamole to duck breasts garnished with Westphalian ham and spring rolls. The kitchen has a light touch: Fish and chops are smokily grilled and served with tangy chutneys or gossamer reduction sauces, and the rack of lamb with rosemary garlic sauce is wildly (and deservedly) popular. Desserts are presented on a flower-strewn tray and include a white chocolate–strawberry tart that made us reconsider our aversion to white chocolate. The decor is appropriately modern—black latticed ceilings, lavender tiles, spare white walls hung with abstract art—and the crowd suits the setting: yuppie, noisy and très New York. Service can be a problem: On one visit you may feel neglected, on the next, rushed. About $90 for dinner for two, with wine.

Seasons

(Bostonian Hotel, Faneuil
Hall Marketplace),
9 Blackstone St. North
(617) 523-4119
AMERICAN
Open Mon.-Thurs. 7 a.m.-
10.30 a.m., 11:30 a.m.-
2 p.m. & 6 p.m.-10 p.m.,
Fri. 11:30 a.m.-2 p.m. &
6 p.m.-10:30 p.m., Sat.
6 p.m.-10:30 p.m., Sun.
5:30 p.m.-9:30 p.m.
All major cards.

We feared that standards at this nationally acclaimed hotel dining room would, with the departure of founding chef Lydia Shire, plummet like a wrecking ball. But the former Seasons sous-chef, William Poirier, has proven himself to be as imaginative as he is skilled. His food transcends national boundaries: Quail are served with a baked enchilada; rack of lamb may be accompanied by dates and sumac rice. But he isn't too highfalutin to turn his back on such homey New England fare as cod cheeks with bean cakes and Rhode Island clam chowder. The desserts are designed to delight the child in all of us, ranging from chocolate rum pudding to pumpkin crème caramel. And to wash them down, there are lots of interesting vintages on the all-American wine list. Located on the fourth floor of the Bostonian Hotel, the Seasons dining room offers dramatic views of the Faneuil Hall market area and the Financial District skyscrapers. The decor is pleasantly contemporary: marbled fabrics, mirrored ceilings and electronically raised and lowered shades. The waiters may be snooty, but they're certainly coordinated—they raise those silver bell jars covering each dish in perfect unison. Dinner for two, with wine, will run about $150.

Siam Cuisine

961 Commonwealth Ave.
(617) 254-4335
THAI
Open Mon.-Thurs.
11:30 a.m.-3 p.m. &
5 p.m.-10 p.m., Fri.-Sat.
11:30 a.m.-3 p.m. &
5 p.m.-10:30 p.m., Sun.
5 p.m.-10 p.m.
Cards: AE, MC, V.

12/20

In the past five years, Thai restaurants have been springing up like wild mushrooms after a rainstorm; most of them are as undistinguished as yesteryear's Cantonese takeout. Siam Cuisine, however, has remained consistent and consistently good. It's more attractive than most, too, filled with hanging plants and gilded sculptures and featuring canopied booths for larger parties. Culinary pyromaniacs can blast their taste buds with "Siam madness" (shellfish stir-fried with chilis and onions) or duck choo chee (served in a fiery green curry sauce). The meek of palate will enjoy the pad Thai (sweet, nutty pan-fried noodles) and Siam chicken (sautéed with cashews and served in a hollowed-out pineapple). To wash them down, try Singha, a hopsy Thai beer. Dinner for two, with wine, will cost about $40.

Suntory

212 Stuart St.
(617) 338-2111
JAPANESE
Open Mon.-Thurs.
11:30a.m.-2 p.m. & 6 p.m.-
10 p.m., Fri. 11:30 a.m.-
2 p.m. & 6 p.m.-10:30 p.m.,
Sat. 6 p.m.-10:30 p.m.,
Sun. 5:30 p.m.-9:30 p.m.
All major cards.

We thought we'd seen it all, culinarily speaking, until we experienced Suntory's ishiyaki, a dish of thin strips of beef or seafood cooked on a super-hot stone. Suntory, in the Theater District, is the new haute-Japanese restaurant opened by the largest liquor company in Japan. (The firm has Suntorys in London, São Paulo and Singapore—the Boston branch is its first venture in the United States.) It's a veritable dining emporium, complete with a sushi bar, shabu-shabu room, teppan-style steakhouse and an elevator connecting all three floors. Shabu-shabu is a sort of Japanese fondue: a stunning selection of seafood and vegetables simmered together on a burner built right into the table. Sushi buffs will rejoice over the gyu (beef sushi), mentaiko (spicy pollack roe) and usuzukuri sashimi (a flower-petal arrangement of paper-thin slices of flounder). Other highlights include a gem-like assortment of complimentary hors d'oeuvres and fork-tender cuts of beef and fish cooked before your eyes on specially heated tables. The dining pace is leisurely, so let your waiter or waitress know if you're trying to make an 8 p.m. curtain. About $80 for dinner for two, with wine.

Il Toscano

41 Charles St.
(617) 723-4090
ITALIAN
Open Mon.-Thurs.
11:30 a.m.-2 p.m. &
5:30 p.m.-10 p.m., Fri.-
Sat. 11:30 a.m.-2 p.m. &
5:30 p.m.-11 p.m., Sun.
5:30 p.m.-10 p.m.
Cards: AE.

The neighborhood is pure Beacon Hill, but within these walls you could be in a tiny village in Tuscany. Freshly baked focaccia (a pizza-like bread), homemade pastas and hearty game dishes are but a few of the trademarks of Tuscan-born chef Vinicio Paoli. Antipasti are served from a gleaming wheeled trolley. Entrées range from vitello valdestana, a veal chop stuffed with prosciutto and cheese, pan-fried and served with mushroom sauce, to cacciuco, individually cooked catfish, lotte, swordfish and other seafood served on a thick slice of bread topped with a delicatissimo red sauce. The chef once tried to remove the tiramisu from the menu, and the patrons nearly rioted. The wine list, strong in Italian vintages, is not unreasonably priced. Like the food, the decor runs to the tasteful but understated: exposed brick walls decked with paintings of the Italian countryside. This is a favorite haunt for Beacon Hill types—the clientele is all dowagers and bow ties. About $100 for two, with wine.

Upstairs at the Pudding

10 Holyoke St., Cambridge
(617) 864-1933
ITALIAN
Open Mon.-Sat. 6 p.m.-
10 p.m.
All major cards.

As you might guess from the name, this is anything but a typical Italian restaurant. Not with dishes like tortellini with fresh ricotta and snails or fiddlehead-fern risotto. Proprietor/chef Michael Silver has an uncanny knack for juxtaposing familiar elements of Italian cuisine with exotic ingredients from all seven continents, and the results are as pleasing and unexpected as the dining room, with its high timbered ceilings and forest-green walls decked with antique show posters.

As you might also guess from the name, Upstairs at the Pudding is located on the top floor of the historic Hasty Pudding Club near Harvard Square. Pink tablecloths, brass service plates and glimmering candles create the requisite aura of elegance. The service has a Cantabrigian earthiness about it and is mercifully relaxed. Unlike at some restaurants, where the portions seem to be doled out by Lilliputians, you won't leave the Pudding hungry. Each entrée comes with a half dozen interesting vegetables, including salsify and portabello mushrooms. But regardless of how full you are, you'd have to be a fool to pass up the Queen Mother's chocolate rum cake for dessert. The fixed-price menu ($39.50) features a first course, main course and salad or dessert. About $110 for two, with wine.

Give an extra special scotch to someone who deserves it.
You.

EXTRA **12** SPECIAL

Johnnie Walker
BLACK LABEL

QUICK BITES

ASIAN

Cao Palace
137 Brighton Ave.
(617) 783-2340
Open Mon.-Sat.
11:30 a.m.-10 p.m.
No cards.

Set in a polyglot of a neighborhood in Allston, the Cao Palace is a fish market as well as a restaurant. So, naturally, this storefront Vietnamese eatery specializes in seafood. Diners can hunker down to a huge plate of soft-shell crabs done up Vietnamese style with a spicy peanut dipping sauce, noodle-stuffed squid or any of the boiling hot-pots. With the latter, diners first choose a fish from the case, which the kitchen then cuts up and a waiter finally brings to the table along with a pot of rolling broth. You cook the fish yourself, wrap it in rice paper and various sprouts and vegetables, and finish up the entire process by dipping it in a thick peanut sauce. Dinner for two, including an appetizer and main course, is about $22, without wine or beer (no liquor license).

Little Hong Kong
46 Beach St. (Chinatown Mall basement)
(617) 542-2176
Open Sun.-Thurs. 11 a.m.-midnight, Fri.-Sat.
11 a.m.-1 a.m.
No cards.

The front of the menu reads: "No M.S.G. No tipping. Just Delicious"—three good reasons to catch a quick bite or a full meal in this always-bustling Chinatown eatery. Typical of so many Chinese restaurants that cater to both indigenous and Occidental tastes, the menu here is large and peppered with such old-fashioned fare as egg foo yung and shrimp in lobster sauce. But we suggest you skip these and go a little more exotic with, perhaps, the deep-fried squid with peppered salt, the steamed sea bass, the shredded pork with pepper and onion, or the most reasonably priced Peking duck (no advance ordering necessary) in town. Dinner for two costs about $17.

The Viet Restaurant
25 Tyler St.
(617) 350-6615
Open Mon.-Thurs.
11:30 a.m.-11 p.m., Fri.
11:30 a.m.-1 a.m., Sat.
10 a.m.-1 a.m., Sun. 10
a.m.-11 p.m.
Cards: AE, MC, V.

While many second- and third-generation Chinese Americans are moving away from Boston's Chinatown into less congested neighborhoods, the Oriental flavor of the area remains strong, thanks to a large influx of newly arrived Vietnamese and Cambodians. And like their predecessors, they're finding it profitable to open restaurants. Of the many new Vietnamese restaurants in Chinatown, one of the best (and certainly the most attractive) is The Viet Restaurant. In the back, large groups of Vietnamese hang out, smoking cigarettes, eating huge bowls of soup and drinking the amazingly sweet sugarcane beverages of Southeast Asia. For the Anglo, there are fresh spring rolls filled with ground pork and noodles, frogs' legs and chicken in lemon grass, barbecued pork and beef served over noodles, and delicious Vietnamese curries made with meat and chunks of potatoes.

Dinner for two, with a shared appetizer and French beer, will be about $30.

BARBECUE

Redbones
55 Chester St.
(617) 628-2200
Open Tues.-Thurs. & Sun. 4:30 p.m.-10 p.m., Fri.-Sat. 4:30 p.m.-midnight. No cards.

An open kitchen, seemingly staffed by a U.N. roster, huge black-and-white photos of old Texas barbecue joints, a wall loaded with posters touting the finest of black Southern performers... all this leaves little doubt that Redbones of Somerville is an outpost of barbecuedom in the middle of Yankeeland. It continues to be a fairly popular place in a territory in which real barbecue is eyed skeptically. We will admit that much of the food is pretty authentic; the baby-back ribs, pulled pork sandwich, fried catfish and sausage of the day will have you whistling "Dixie." But the side dishes are uniformly boring and tasteless. Dinner for two, with beer, runs about $27.

CAFES

Caffe Paradisio
255 Hanover St.
(617) 742-1768
Open daily 7 a.m.-2 a.m. Cards: AE.

Caffe Vittoria
296 Hanover St.
(617) 227-7606
Open daily 8 a.m.-1 a.m. No cards.

If you're looking for a late-night dessert or an early-afternoon café pick-me-up, head out to Hanover Street in the North End, where within four blocks there's a bevy of cafés. But we like the Caffe Vittoria, with its combination art deco and kitschy '50s trappings, and the more conservatively decorated Caffe Paradisio best. Both open early and close late, and true to their impressive-looking machinery, each brews strong demitasses of espresso and frothy cups of cappuccino to accompany the substantial selection of Italian pastries, including a ricotta pie and filled-to-order cannolis. Both have full liquor licenses as well. A couple of cups of coffee, a shot of Sambuca and two desserts will cost about $12.

The Commonwealth Brewing Company
148 Portland St.
(617) 523-8383
Open Mon.-Thurs. 11 a.m.-4 p.m. & 5 p.m.-10 p.m., Fri.-Sat. 11 a.m.-4 p.m. & 5 p.m.-11 p.m., Sun. 11:30 a.m.-3 p.m. All major cards.

As the name implies, beer and its hop-filled cousins are brewed here. But though the room-temperature ale and bitters made in the huge copper tanks in the lower-level bar draw raves, the pub grub is actually the superior reason to stop by this cavernous room in the shadow of the historic but dilapidated Boston Garden. The potato salad, made with red potatoes, is a fine mate to the huge knockwurst, and the kitchen displays a deft touch when it comes to frying up plates of local scallops and haddock. We also come for the list of blends that combine a number of different beers, ales and ciders. Two glasses of brew and a couple of plates of fried scallops will run about $20.

Il Dolce Momento

30 Charles St.
(617) 720-0477
*Open Sun.-Thurs. 8 a.m.-
11:30 p.m., Fri.-Sat.
8 a.m.-midnight.
No cards.*

On one of the city's loveliest thoroughfares sits one of its nicest little cafés. Though you'll be inside, there are enough windows looking onto Charles Street to make sipping a cappuccino at Il Dolce Momento a good opportunity to take in the bluebloods, antiques dealers and politicians scurrying about Beacon Hill. Eggs are served at breakfast, and more substantial fare turns up after 11 a.m.; butterfat-rich bowls of gelato (hazelnut is our favorite) and all manner of delicate and gooey pastries are served whenever your system is in need of a sweet fix. Dessert and a fancy coffee concoction will cost two about $10.

The Gardner Museum Cafe

208 The Fenway
(617) 566-1088
*Open Tues.-Sun. noon-
4 p.m.
No cards.*

A trip to this 34-seat café also provides the opportunity to visit one of the city's great little treasures, the Isabella Stewart Gardner Museum (see "Sights"). The entire complex was once Mrs. Gardner's home, and the small dining area is set in the back next to one of the gardens. In season, there's romantic al fresco dining among the flowers. Naturally, the fare here is "museum food": good cream soups in winter, some nice chilled versions in summer, a variety of quiches, sandwiches (made with some of the best bread in the Hub), large salads and a surprisingly good cheesecake. In summer, the museum occasionally puts on classical-music concerts, and on those nights, the café may stay open; it's a good idea to call the museum to check on concert scheduling. A nice lunch for two, with beer or wine and dessert, will run about $30.

Harvard Book Store Cafe

190 Newbury St.
(617) 536-0095
*Open Mon.-Thurs. 8 a.m.-
11 p.m., Fri.-Sat. 8 a.m.-
midnight, Sun. noon-4 p.m.
All major cards.*

A café within a bookstore—and both the bookstore and the café are worth checking out, either individually or collectively. In summer, tables are set up on fashionable Newbury Street (in Back Bay, not in Cambridge, as the Harvard name suggests), which makes it nice for a double espresso, a slice of cheesecake and a people-watching session. The café's excellent smoked turkey appears in two sandwiches, the salad niçoise is classically rendered, and at dinner, there's always a trendy pasta dish and a good old-fashioned chicken pot pie. Lunch for two (salad, entrée, shared dessert and wine by the glass) is about $33.

Joe's American Bar and Grill

279 Dartmouth St.
(617) 536-4200
*Open Sun.-Thurs. 11 a.m.-
11 p.m., Fri.-Sat. 11:30
a.m.-midnight.
Cards: AE, MC, V.*

This superb Back Bay brownstone is loaded with mahogany and enough tinges of the past to evoke a warm feeling, yet it's populated with a lively crowd of on-the-prowl locals inhaling huge sandwiches and superb onion rings. In the upstairs section, the food and the setting are more serious, with some good pasta creations and a fine rack of lamb. But it's in the downstairs area, with its rectangular bar in the center of the room, that most of the action takes place. Individual designer pizzas (like the one with four cheeses and wild mushrooms), huge burgers, steamed mussels and stuffed potato skins are good matches for the long beer list. Lunch or a late-night snack—such as a bowl of clam chowder, burgers and beer—will cost two about $20.

Nicole's Ristorante
54 Salem St.
(617) 742-6999
*Open Tues.-Thurs.
11:30 a.m.-10 p.m.,
Fri.-Sat. 11:30 a.m.-10:30
p.m., Sun. 3 p.m.-10 p.m.
All major cards.*

Hanover and Salem, the two main east-west streets of the city's predominantly Italian North End, are dotted with modest restaurants, some deco-inspired cafés and a healthy number of excellent markets. While the cafés and markets are clearly more authentic than most of the Italian-American, red-sauce restaurants, there are plenty of spots for a tasty quick bite. One of the better homes of Boston-style Italian food is Nicole's, a pink, more-than-modest, dimly lit restaurant. There are some fine appetizers, including marinated squid, clams casino and fried eggplant stuffed with ricotta cheese. For dinner, try the wonderful chicken pescatore—stuffed chicken topped with sea scallops and jumbo shrimp, all at rest in a fish stock—or the peasant dish of thick pork chops with vinegar peppers and roast potatoes. Lunch for two, with a glass of wine and espresso, will run about $20. Dinner for two, with a glass of wine, espresso and a shared dessert, will cost about $50.

Pentimento
344 Huron Ave.,
Cambridge
(617) 661-3878
*Open Mon.-Fri. 8:30 a.m.-
9 p.m., Sat. 9 a.m.-9 p.m.,
Sun. 10 a.m.-2 p.m.
No cards.*

While it's not the counterculture haven it once was, Cambridge still marches slightly askew of center. And those Cantabs who would still rather talk about issues than escalating real estate prices can be found at Pentimento. Here, the furniture is mismatched, personal photographs and old paintings dot the walls, and a lot of folks still wearing sandals and socks start the day with what are perhaps the best muffins in creation. At lunch, there are hearty soups and thick sandwiches; the dinner crowd likes the cassoulets and stews. No liquor license. Breakfast for two runs about $8, and dinner for two, about $30.

Steve's
62 Hereford St.
(617) 267-1817
*Open Mon.-Sat. 7:30 a.m.-
9:30 p.m.
No cards.*

The most democratic establishment in high-ticket Back Bay, Steve's is a place where representatives of both the highly fashionable and the cutting-edge gather for Greek soul food. Somewhat reminiscent of the *Saturday Night Live* Greek-diner skits that had John Belushi yelling "cheesebugah, cheesebugah," Steve's has a grill man who flips eggs, bakes a tasty lamb and dishes out huge bowls of rich chicken-and-lemon soup. A good refueling stop for those whose shopping takes them to the upper end of chic Newbury Street. Lunch for two is about $16.

Taha Two
1154 Massachusetts Ave.
(Harvard Square),
Cambridge
(617) 864-4935
*Open daily 11 a.m.-11 p.m.
Cards: AE, MC, V.*

While the first Taha was a Harvard Square shoe store that is now a bank, Taha Two is a cozy restaurant/café that used to be a used-record store. And though the restaurant is relatively new, its food is rooted in Cambridge's storied collective-inspired days. Start with the ubiquitous hummus, and then proceed to the eggplant parmigiana, stuffed grape leaves or anything on a skewer; if you're still hungry, or you're just looking for a sweet treat in Harvard Square, the pistachio-laden baklava and a cup of coffee should quiet the pangs. No liquor license. Lunch for two costs about $17.

The Tam O'Shanter
1648 Beacon St.
(Washington Square),
Brookline
(617) 277-0982
Open daily 11:30 a.m.-
3 p.m. & 5:30 p.m.-
10 p.m.
No cards.

Despite the impression given by its Scottish name, The Tam O'Shanter (called "The Tam" by everyone) is an old-fashioned rock 'n' roll bar after 10 p.m. But before the likes of the Memphis Rockabilly Band hit the stage, The Tam is packed with a hodgepodge of locals who would hate to see this little place get any more discovered (sorry, folks—we mean well). The lights are dim and fresh flowers grace every table; the kitchen turns out such good starters as smoked trout and pâté. The menu changes regularly but runs to such time-warp favorites as lasagne, real double-crusted chicken pot pie and soft-shell crabs amandine; things get more modern with the grilled shark with a spicy cilantro salsa. Desserts are made both on the premises and by good local purveyors, and the wine list is well conceived and affordable. Dinner for two, with a glass of wine, will cost about $38.

DELICATESSENS

Maven's Kosher Court
95 Winthrop St. (Harvard Square), Cambridge
(617) 492-3354
Open Mon.-Thurs. 11 a.m.-
11 p.m., Fri. 11 a.m.-2
p.m., Sat. 9:30 a.m.-1 a.m.,
Sun. 10 a.m.-11 p.m.
Cards: AE, MC, V.

In a gentrified paean to their past, a trio of big-time lawyers headed by Alan Dershowitz (he defended Claus von Bulow) has opened a rabbinically approved kosher deli in WASPish Harvard Square. Step into the subterranean space and enter a treasure trove complete with huge black and white floor tiles, a tin ceiling and wonderful scenes of old Coney Island on the walls. The food, like the setting, is true to its roots. In a city where "good deli" used to be an oxymoron, there is finally a place where the mavens (Yiddish for "experts") can meet to debate life's big questions and eat brisket dinners, stuffed cabbage, and sandwiches made with superb cuts and cures of corned beef, pastrami, tongue and so on. Two sandwiches and a couple of Dr. Brown's sodas (the place has no liquor license and doesn't allow you to bring your own) will run about $15.

HAMBURGERS & SANDWICHES

Mississippi's
484 Commonwealth Ave.
(617) 247-8181
Open daily 11:30 a.m.-
11 p.m.
No cards.

The crossroads known as Kenmore Square, where baseball fans, night people, students and those on the edge congregate, is hardly a place for the food connoisseur. But at some point you're likely to find yourself in Kenmore Square and hungry for something other than pizza or fried chicken. One of the creative and well-prepared sandwiches from

Mississippi's should do you quite nicely. There are more than 50 sandwich combinations bearing such names as the Che Guevara (roast beef, Bermuda onion and Russian dressing on a bulkie) and the Mayflower (turkey with cream cheese and cranberry sauce on light rye), along with some accompaniments—a few soups and a salad bar. Soup and sandwiches for two will run about $10.

The Skewers
92 Mt. Auburn St.
(Harvard Square),
Cambridge
(617) 491-3079
*Open Mon.-Thurs.
11 a.m.-11 p.m., Fri.-Sat.
11 a.m.-midnight.
No cards.*

The Skewers is a fine place for tasty, reasonably priced Middle Eastern sandwiches and platters. Set below street level, the tiny Harvard Square eatery has a cozy dining room behind a beaded doorway; those in a hurry can place orders at the cash register and eat at the counter or in the park just across the street, which is always filled with a mix of serious readers and serious eaters. No liquor license. About $10 for a sandwich lunch or dinner for two.

INTERNATIONAL

Asmara
714 Massachusetts Ave.,
Cambridge
(617) 864-7447
*Open Mon.-Wed. noon-
10:30 p.m., Thurs.-Sat.
noon-11:30 p.m., Sun.
12:30 p.m.-11 p.m.
No cards.*

Asmara may be named for the capital of war-torn Eritrea, but most diners familiar with foreign fare will recognize the cuisine as Ethiopian. On the site of a former health-food store, the simple restaurant is filled with native crafts and some wonderful photographs; indigenous folk music plays on the stereo. There is no silverware on the tables, and when dinner arrives, so does a huge plate of fermented bread known as injera. If you're not familiar with the use of injera, the friendly waiters will show you how to pull off sections to wrap around the various main dishes. Among the best main-course offerings are the (very) spicy chicken, lamb yet-wats and thinly cut raw beef; the vegetarian selections are rather mild, but the potato salad is spiced with a "Quick, pass the beer" green chili dressing. No liquor license (there is a $2 corkage fee for BYOBers). Dinner for two will be less than $20.

Cecil's
129 South St.
(617) 542-5108
*Open Mon.-Tues. 7 a.m.-
9 p.m., Wed.-Thurs. 7
a.m.-10 p.m., Fri. 7 a.m.-
11 p.m., Sat. 6 p.m.-
11 p.m.
All major cards.*

This attractive spot located in the rapidly rediscovered area known as the Leather District (so named for the former tradesmen who toiled here) can serve any of four distinct functions, depending on the time of day you drop in. In the morning, it fuels the pinstripe set with hearty breakfasts and sends them on their way to shake up the financial world. At lunch, these executives vie with more artsy types for tables. And when the sun sets, its bar is a popular trysting place, while the dimly lit back room serves reasonably priced, rather tasty food from the Spanish-speaking tropics: tostones, double-fried plantains with a puréed black-bean sauce, ceviche, the shredded beef dish called ropa vieja, and a number of fish stews. The wine list is good, and the bar turns out properly made cocktails. Dinner for two, with a glass of wine, will cost about $33.

La Española
405 Centre St.
(617) 524-9410
Open Thurs.-Tues.
11:30 a.m.-10 p.m.
No cards.

When it opened fifteen years ago, La Espanola served the food of the Dominican Republic. After a few years, a Cuban family took over the operation, and though they changed the menu, they kept the name. Today, this friendly bilingual establishment in the Victorian-laden neighborhood of Jamaica Plain remains the most authentic spot in town for Latin American soul food. Inside you'll find lots of lights and Formica and a nice mix of Hispanic families, aging hippies and the new gentry eating huge plates of fried and roasted pork, chicken rinds (actually deep-fried and garlic-spiked pieces of boned thigh), shrimp with peppers and onions and pan-sautéed kingfish steaks. Everything comes with the perfect complements of rice and beans. If nantillas, a velvety vanilla pudding, is available, order it, along with some pick-me-up café con leche. Dinner for two, with beer, dessert and coffee, will cost about $25.

Mexican Cuisine
1682 Massachusetts Ave.,
Cambridge
(617) 661-1634
Open nightly 5 p.m.-11 p.m.
Cards: AE.

In a city where Americanized Mex is the norm, this restaurant is a different breed. Although the bartender (the restaurant shares its space with a neighborhood bar) can't seem to make a decent margarita, the chef knows how to concoct those complex sauces found in restaurants along the coast and in the interior of Mexico. Making good use of all sorts of chiles (most notably the smoky chipotle), pumpkin seeds, sour oranges, cilantro and the like, he uses his never-bland toppings to enliven all manner of seafood, including lotte and shrimp, as well as lamb and pork. Dinner for two, with Mexican beer, runs about $37.

Viceroy
569 Massachusetts Ave.,
Cambridge
(617) 354-0611
Open daily 11:30 a.m.-
2:30 p.m. & 5 p.m.-
11:30 p.m.
All major cards.

There are six fine Indian restaurants in Cambridge's Central Square, and then there is the Viceroy. The only one with atmosphere (even more so if you reserve a fabric-draped booth for four or more) and a full liquor license, the Viceroy also happens to serve food that's a full head in front of its neighboring competitors. As soon as you're seated, spicy pappadum wafers are brought to the table. Vegetarians will like the mali kofta, ground vegetables rendered into meatball shapes and then deep-fried and covered with a creamy sauce, and the saag paneer, spinach with Indian cubed cheese. From the sea, giant prawns in a hot sauce are served over puffy Indian bread, a tasty play on the pizza concept; for a dazzling appetizer, skewered lamb and chicken tikkas are finished tableside on a sizzling platter. The good spices are easily fanned by one of the beers of many nations. Service is formal. Dinner, with beer, will cost two about $30.

PIZZA

Regina's Pizzeria
11 Thatcher St.
(617) 227-0765
*Open Mon.-Thurs. 11
a.m.-11:30 p.m., Fri.-Sat.
11 a.m.-midnight, Sun.
2 p.m.-11 p.m.
No cards.*

They may have franchised the name, and Regina's may soon be popping up in malls all over America, but the flagship can never be duplicated. Even in Boston, the two new Regina's aren't even thought of as relatives of this old-time, no-frills, pizza-only joint. Those in the know swear that Regina's success is due to its ovens, which, like the pizza parlor, are more than 50 years old. Tables, some booths, a small bar, a good jukebox and a crowd of locals (including a few big shots and wise guys) combine with the thin-crusted, soft-to-the-bite southern Italian pizza with fresh traditional toppings to create an interesting harmony that could belong only to the original Regina's. A large pizza and two bottles of beer cost about $12.

HOTELS

Joshua Bennett House
78 Pinckney St.
(617) 353-1111

Built in 1829 and licensed as a lodging house since 1910, this homey six-room bed-and-breakfast is perched on Beacon Hill, just a chip shot away from famous Louisburg Square. Adhering to the less-is-more philosophy of interior design, the common areas have peach walls, lace curtains and hardwood floors. Bedrooms are a bit more plush, with thick wall-to-wall carpeting and furnishings in pale tones; all have small color TVs and two have private baths. The breakfast room is small, so the resident hosts have two flexibly scheduled breakfast seatings. Breakfasts are satisfyingly robust: fresh fruit, homemade muffins or breads and such entrées as eggs Sardou or frittatas.
Rooms: $75-$115, including breakfast.

Boston Harbor Hotel
70 Rowes Wharf
(617) 439-7000

A star from the day it opened, Boston's self-proclaimed "most expensive hotel" is indeed that. But it lives up to its price range with an understated elegance that nicely fuses the time-honored and the contemporary. The level of luxury is apparent from the moment you step into the Italian-marbled lobby. Walls are generously dotted with antique (not reproduction) maps and nautical charts and an extensive collection of maritime paintings. To take best advantage of the superb waterfront setting, the hotel occupies the eighth through sixteenth floors, allotting the lower levels to office space. Its 230 rooms are large, beautiful, perfectly equipped and blessed with marvelous unobstructed city and harbor views. Also on-site are the Harbor View Lounge, a tidy gem of a bar; the serenely lovely but culinarily disappointing Rowes Wharf Restaurant; and the less- formal Rowes Wharf Café. As part of the hotel's goal to bring back the glamour of the harborfront, a water taxi makes continuous runs (for a $6 fee) across the water to Logan International Airport—a lifesaver for those heading to or from the airport at rush hour.

Singles: $210-$220; doubles: $235-$245; suites: $350-$1,600. Weekend packages available.

Bostonian Hotel
Blackstone St. (Faneuil Hall Marketplace)
(617) 523-3600

The best of old and new Boston lies just outside your door at this gem of a hotel. A few blocks from downtown's business hub and smack in the middle of legendary Haymarket Square, which on Fridays and Saturdays hums with street vendors, the Bostonian is also right next to the shops of Quincy Market and but an underpass away from the still heavily Italian but rapidly gentrifying North End. The Bostonian is an unusual luxury hotel in that it's small and independently owned, which leads to, respectively, a sense of peace and quiet and a we-try-harder approach to service. A circa-1824 structure was skillfully blended with a new, taller wing, in which some rooms have working fireplaces, exposed beams and brick walls. All the rooms have French windows that open onto minuscule balconies (filled with geraniums in summer), hair dryers and daily fresh flowers; most have large bathrooms with two sinks. A phone call can result in a complimentary VCR or LifeCycle delivered to your room; you can also use the gym facilities at the nearby Sky Club for no charge. Our only complaints are minor ones: Some of the rooms have uninspired views of the neighboring freeway (though noise is not a problem), and the decor is perfectly pleasant but nothing special. Eating and drinking facilities include the surprisingly tropical Atrium bar, a flower-lover's paradise, and Seasons, the first of the spectacular new hotel dining rooms in Boston, which draws the pols and power brokers three meals a day.

Singles: $180-$210; doubles: $200-$230; suites: $355-$520. Weekend packages available.

A Cambridge House
2218 Massachusetts Ave. (Porter Square), Cambridge
(617) 491-6300

Dating back to Cambridge's days as farm country, this meticulously restored home and its adjacent carriage house are listed in the National Register of Historic Places. The two common areas, each with its ever-present bottle of sherry, are carefully studied blends of chintz, blue-and-white Oriental pieces and well-positioned needlepoint pillows and cushions. The eleven rooms spread about the property have their own sinks and vanities, but only one has a private bath (though the ratio of bathrooms to bedrooms is 1:2). Some of the rooms have four- poster beds, a few have fireplaces, and all have air conditioning and cable-equipped color TVs. Breakfasts are fresh and generous, parking is free, and the house is just a five-minute walk from the subway and a fifteen-minute walk from Harvard Square. A Cambridge House also serves as a referral service for other bed-and-breakfasts and short-term apartment rentals in Boston and its environs.

Singles: $49-$115; doubles: $59-$135, including breakfast. Rates vary seasonally.

Chandler Inn
26 Chandler St.
(617) 482-3450

After new owners took over in 1983, the Chandler Inn was completely refurbished. Located in the city's partly gentrified, partly polyglot neighborhood called the South End, it has now completely expunged its scandalous past, when it was the Hotel Diplomat, a favorite haunt of the city's working girls. As is so often true with older hotels, the rooms are small, but they have been tastefully redone, and the bathrooms have been modernized. The reasonable rates include a Continental breakfast at Fritz, the hotel's restaurant, which is a popular gathering spot for the area's large gay population.

Singles: $64; doubles: $74; triples: $84, including breakfast.

The Charles Hotel at Harvard Square
1 Bennett St. (Harvard Square), Cambridge
(617) 864-1200

The first luxury hotel at Harvard Square, the brick Charles Hotel blends in beautifully with surrounding Cambridge. It's set in a minicomplex called Charles Square, making it possible to shop at such chic merchants as Sisley, Matinique and Laura Ashley without facing the elements. But the elements deserve confrontation, for just outside Charles Square is Harvard Square, the shopping mecca that draws people from all over the Boston area. Everything about The Charles radiates conservative class, from the walls decorated with beautiful antique quilts and commissioned paintings of Cambridge and sculls on The Charles River to the very large rooms equipped with down quilts, plush robes and scales in the good bathrooms. Guests may swim, work out and luxuriate with a facial or a massage at the adjacent health club, Le Pli, and business travelers will appreciate the for-rent computers and modems. Rarities, the hotel's restaurant, has a loyal and deserved following; the Bennett Street Café, a vaguely tropical dining room that serves three meals a day, is more casual. And the Charles is the home of the handsome Regattabar, the only nightclub in the city devoted to mainstream jazz, where such greats as Stan Getz, Dizzy Gillespie and McCoy Tyner have played. Valet parking is $10 a day.

Singles: $186-$206; doubles: $206-$226; suites: $275-$1,200. Weekend packages available.

Copley Plaza
138 St. James Ave.
(617) 267-5300

Self-billed as "Boston's Grande Dame," the Copley Plaza is an elegant, well-preserved period piece that recently celebrated its 75th anniversary. With the exception of the suites, most rooms are on the small side, but the skillful furnishing with period pieces—right down to the TVs in the armoires—compensates for the compactness. The best, most expensive rooms overlook Copley Square and magnificent Trinity Church; the view is worth the $20 or so extra. The seemingly endless ground floor is home to the high-ceilinged marble lobby that is reminiscent of a train station; the open-air Tea Court off the lobby is home to a daily high tea; and wide halls lead to the restaurants, a florist, a newsstand and even a podiatrist, to soothe those visitors suffering from the worst of Boston's cobblestoned streets. Even if you don't stay here, make a point of visiting the Plaza Bar, where the superb pianist Dave McKenna plays in a setting right out of colonial India, with its huge palms and marble columns. Valet parking is $20 a day.

Singles: $150-$175; doubles: $170-$195; suites: $190-$750. Weekend packages available.

Four Seasons Hotel
200 Boylston St.
(617) 338-4400

A new hotel made to look old, the Four Seasons lives up to its chain's reputation by quietly pampering its guests with exceptional service. Though imposing from the outside, where it faces the Public Garden, inside it has a small, warmly lit lobby with marble floors and oil portraits on the walls, as well as a beautiful restaurant, Aujourd'hui, and the Public Garden Bristol Lounge. Naturally, the best rooms face the Public Garden, but all the rooms are large and quite comfortable, with down comforters and TVs in the armoires. A large swimming pool and whirlpool on the eighth floor are surrounded by glass, affording a wonderful view across the Public Garden to the golden dome of the State House on Beacon Hill. Valet parking is $16 a day.

Singles: $195-$260; doubles: $215-$280; suites: $350-$1,200. Weekend packages available.

Guest Quarters Suites Hotel
400 Soldiers Field Rd.
(Storrow Dr.)
(617) 783-0090

The city's first "all-suite" hotel, Guest Quarters was part of the Embassy Suites chain for its first five years. Located on a bend of the Charles River in Brighton, just across the bridge from Cambridge, the hotel comprises compact one- and two-bedroom suites stocked with lots of lacquered furniture and living room sofas that open into beds, making it an ideal place for traveling families. On the down side, the location isn't good unless you have a car; the nearest subway stop is a fifteen-minute walk away, and there's absolutely nothing else around this lonesome outpost off the Massachusetts Pike. But the hotel has a shuttle van to move guests about, and those with cars will find sights galore within a short driving distance. The wide-open common areas take advantage of the hotel's river view, and athletes will like the place for its swimming pool and its direct access to the excellent and scenic jogging trails along the river. Self-parking is free for guests.

Suites: $160-$185 (weekdays), $112-$132 (weekends), including breakfast.

Hotel Meridien
250 Franklin St.
(617) 451-1900

A little bit of France and a lot of old Yankee blueblood have gone into making the Meridien one of the city's best hotels, with plenty of the exceptionally friendly service that the chain is known for. Opened in 1981 as a hotel, the landmark Renaissance Revival building used to house the Boston branch of the Federal Reserve Bank. The transformation into hotel included a huge atrium with a glass mansard roof, which can make sitting in Café Fleuri, the casual dining area, a tad disconcerting—the view is downright downtown. But the other common areas are wonderfully grand. We especially love the Julien Bar, the very handsome former reception room for Federal Reserve officers that is stocked with dim lights, a gleaming piano, original N. C. Wyeth oils and a terrific selection of Armagnacs. Julien, the former "members' court" and now the Meridien's outstanding formal French restaurant, is a veritable vision of old-world opulence. There's little sense of the building's history in the guest rooms, which are contemporarily furnished, often with sofas and always with all the expected luxury amenities; since so many rooms were carved out of former offices, one finds a great deal of variety from room to room. The third-floor health club is well staffed, and though the pool is on the small side, the exercise equipment is first-rate.

Singles: $185-$205; doubles: $205-$225; suites: $400-$800. Weekend packages available.

Hyatt Regency Cambridge
575 Memorial Dr.,
Cambridge
(617) 492-1234

When the Hyatt, the first luxury establishment in staid Cambridge, opened in 1976, locals flocked to its bars. Since then it has quieted down and, in the process, lost some of its Cantab (the local nickname for Cambridge residents) glamour to the newer Charles Hotel. But the ziggurat-shaped, hugely atriumed hotel, designed by local wunderkind Graham Gund, still has plenty of admirers. The trademark Hyatt glass elevators whisk guests to comfortable rooms, although some of the furniture is beginning to show signs of wear. Many rooms have private balconies overlooking the Charles or the atrium; athletes will appreciate the indoor pool and health club. A thoughtful touch is the rooftop heliport, where you can catch a helicopter (and bypass snarled traffic) to the airport for $29. There's also a courtesy van that goes to both Cambridge and Boston; the hotel is located away from public transportation and is not handy for the pedestrian. Along with a couple of restaurants, the Hyatt is home to the Spinnaker, the only revolving bar in the city, which offers a sweeping view of the Charles, Boston University and the downtown skyline. Self-parking costs $9 a day.

Singles: $170-$190; doubles: $190-$210; suites: $250-$400. Weekend packages available.

The Lafayette Hotel
1 Ave. de Lafayette
(617) 451-2600

This Swissôtel is more than just the home of one of New England's finest restaurants, Le Marquis de Lafayette. It's also a good full-service, business-oriented European-style hotel in Lafayette Place, the controversial development in a rapidly gentrifying section of downtown. The stark, modern exterior (notable for its band of blue neon around the top) belies a warm, antiques-rich interior, including an elegant third-floor lobby, 500 large bedrooms, meeting and banquet facilities, the aforementioned restaurant, the less-formal Café Suisse and a lobby bar. Rooms boast comfortable king-size beds, minibars, TVs tucked into antique armoires and all the trendy amenities. Extras include an indoor swimming pool and a 24-hour concierge.

Singles: $160-$190; doubles: $180-$220; suites: $250-$450.

Lenox Hotel
710 Boylston St.
(617) 536-5300

In the heart of Back Bay and just one big city block from Copley Place, this low-rise family-run hotel dates to 1900. While its glory days were brief, today it successfully combines tradition, an excellent location, well-maintained rooms and affordability. Rooms are either Colonial reproductions or Oriental-influenced; corner rooms have fireplaces. The piano bar, Diamond Jim's, is a popular after-work gathering spot, and the restaurant, Delmonico's, is a Victorian period piece. The Lenox's van will transport guests to and from the airport for $5 a person; valet parking is $8 a day.

Singles: $85-$150; doubles: $100-$175; suites: $250. Weekend packages available.

Marriott Long Wharf
296 State St.
(617) 227-0800

Built to resemble a wharf, albeit an oversized one, this well-situated hotel has many rooms with harbor views. If you never ventured forth from the lobby, a plant-filled, five-story atrium type, you could forget where you were—you could just as easily be in Dallas, Phoenix or San Francisco. But the pastel rooms are spacious, the beds oversized, and the location (on the water and near Faneuil Hall, the North End and the Aquarium) quite good. Extras include an indoor pool, a sundeck and a well-equipped health club. Valet parking is $15 a day.

Singles: $175-$190; doubles: $195-$210; suites: $195-$900. Weekend packages and family rates available.

Quality Inn
275 Tremont St.
(617) 426-1400

If you ask a local where the Quality Inn is located, you're apt to get a vacant stare—the completely overhauled hotel superbly located near the city's small Theater District and almost-as-small Chinatown will probably always be known by its former name, The Bradford. The large art deco lobby, which dates to 1926 and just a few years ago served as the foyer to a rock 'n' roll concert hall, has been nicely restored, even if the lights are too bright. At the time of this writing, everything is new and quite cushy; if the management stays on top of things, the Quality Inn looks like a promising spot for the budget-conscious traveler. The hotel's restaurant is the first outpost of the famous Stage Deli of New York, and there's a new nightclub, The Roxy. Parking is available in nearby garages.

Singles: $83; doubles: $98; suites: $125-$137. Weekend packages available.

Ritz-Carlton Hotel
15 Arlington St.
(617) 536-5700

Despite the host of new hotels in the city, the Ritz (locals never add the "Carlton") remains the quintessential Boston hotel. Built in 1927, enlarged in 1981 and refurbished in 1985, the Ritz is as wonderful as ever—none of these changes have altered its elegance one whit. The multilingual staff is plentiful and helpful (with perhaps the highest ratio of staff to guests in the city), and the rooms, from the excellent beds to the marble sinks, are plush. Most of the suites have wood-burning fireplaces. In winter, guests are supplied with ice skates for use on Frog Pond in the Boston Common across the street; in all seasons, guests can avail themselves of the large stock of Rockport walking shoes. The first-floor Café still rates as the city's most "in" breakfast spot, the oak-paneled bar is clubby and inviting, and the health club on the seventeenth floor offers an unmatched workout panorama. Valet parking is $16 a day.

Singles: $175-$285; doubles: $210-$320; suites: $375-$1,500. Weekend packages available.

267 Commonwealth
267 Commonwealth Ave.
(617) 267-6776

Although visitors are quick to point out similarities between Boston and San Francisco, the Hub falls short of its Bay Area rival in its supply of small apartment-style hotels. That's why 267 Commonwealth in Back Bay is such a great find. It's perfect for the traveler seeking a short-term apartment in the middle of one of the city's premier residential neighborhoods. Transformed from a former rooming house by Bob Vila, the famous renovator from PBS's *This Old House*, 267 Commonwealth is a collection of five one-bedroom and four studio apartments spread over the four floors of this venerable brownstone. Ceilings are twelve feet high, furniture is an eclectic blend of old and new, there's chintz galore on the walls and windows, and every room has a working fireplace. The concierge-cum-manager will fill refrigerators, give tours of Boston and take care of your dry cleaning.

All rooms: $100; long-term rates slightly discounted.

NIGHTLIFE

BARS

Allegro on Boylston
939 Boylston St.
(617) 236-0200
*Open Mon.-Sat. 4:30 p.m.-
1 a.m., Sun. 4:30 p.m.-
midnight.*
All major cards.

Atmosphere seekers will appreciate this popular northern Italian restaurant as much as neighborhood regulars appreciate its bar and friendly staff. Trendy Boston at its very best, Allegro has a people-watching potential that's generally as high as its design: cool mint-colored walls dotted with black-and-white photographs, a black-and-white-tiled floor and a remarkable "Beamo" fixture that casts light in the shape of hearts, leaves and other seasonal tributes onto a shiny black-lacquer bar. The eclectic clientele is always well dressed and provides plenty of good theater, especially on Thursday and Friday nights.

Bay Tower Room
60 State St.
(617) 723-1666
*Open Mon.-Sat. 4:30 p.m.-
1 a.m.*
All major cards.

By day, this elegant 33rd-floor retreat is a private dining club—by night, a restaurant and lounge that ought to be on everyone's list of places to see in Boston. The rich decor is enhanced by brass railings and a lighting scheme seductive enough to make even the world's worst blind date (many first dates seem to wind up here) palatable. Still, the arresting view of downtown and the harbor has always been and likely will remain the Bay Tower's primary attraction. Entertainment is on the mellow side until about 10 p.m., when the well-dressed couples begin to sway to the sounds of a four-piece orchestra.

Dartmouth Street
271 Dartmouth St.
(617) 536-6560
*Open Sun.-Wed.
11:30 a.m.-1 a.m., Thurs.-
Sat. 11:30 a.m.-2 a.m.*
All major cards.

Friendly and attentive management has helped keep this spacious and refreshingly bright Back Bay restaurant a favorite meeting place for the city's yupscale. Thursday and Friday nights are tipped in favor of singles, most of whom are so chicly dressed that you'll think you've stumbled onto a fashion show. Co-owned and carefully supervised by the silver-haired Diego Messina, Boston's premier hairdresser, Dartmouth Street is predictably slick. The three-tiered interior of polished brass, hardwood floors and beveled glass is as beautifully manicured as the restaurant's clientele, which includes a number of local media and entertainment-industry personalities.

Fynn's
359 Newbury St.
(617) 536-1100
Open daily 11 a.m.-midnight.
All major cards.

Boston club-owner Patrick Lyons's first foray into the restaurant business is, simply put, drop-dead gorgeous. A Maltese Falcon, Bogey autographs and Mae West gowns are but a few examples of the esoterica and nostalgia that pepper the walls, which are hand-carved originals from the interior of a British priory. Add to all that a polished brass and marble bar, salmon-colored marble tiles, rich mahogany paneling and an oversized tropical fish tank, and it's no wonder such a glamorous crowd of models, TV personalities and entertainment moguls regard Back Bay's Fynn's as their home away from home.

Julien Bar
(Hotel Meridien),
250 Franklin St.
(617) 451-1900
Open Mon.-Fri. noon-1:30 a.m., Sat. 4 p.m.-1 a.m., Sun. 4 p.m.-midnight.
All major cards.

As secure in the former Federal Reserve Bank Building as certificates in a safe-deposit box, this one-time reception room for bank officers and visiting dignitaries attracts a similarly monied and influential crowd today. Anchored by a solid mahogany bar, the soothing and seductive chamber proves remarkable for its gilded coffered ceilings, N. C. Wyeth wall murals of American nobility and elegant service by waitresses draped in floor-length gowns. What with the masterful piano playing of Jeffrey Moore (whose repertoire runs from Beethoven to Bacharach) and the complimentary ramekins of goose-liver pâté, it's not a surprise that this swank hotel lounge fills up so quickly.

O'Brien's
3 Harvard Ave.
(617) 728-6245
Open daily 10 p.m.-1 a.m.
No cards.

For those in search of college-town nightlife, replete with friendly bartenders, plenty of cold drafts and better-than-average entertainers (mostly R&B and acoustic duos), O'Brien's is the answer. Boisterous (at times too much so, given the talent onstage) and unadorned, this Allston pub appeals mostly to local students, but increasingly to the growing numbers of yuppies and college grads eager to down-scale their dress and really relax. The setting is as low-key and comfortable as a campus coffeehouse.

The Plaza Bar
(Copley Plaza Hotel),
138 St. James Ave.
(617) 267-5300
Open daily 11:30 a.m.-1 a.m. All major cards.

Reminiscent of a British officers' club, this elegantly appointed sanctuary in Boston's grande dame hotel carries the irradicable odor of a long and celebrated past. Gilded ceilings, potted palms, Oriental screens, leather sofas and the world-class talents of such pianists as local favorite Dave McKenna make it easier to overlook the fact that the service in this beautiful room is too often slow and surly.

The Ritz Bar
(Ritz-Carlton Hotel),
15 Arlington St.
(617) 536-5700
Open daily 11:30 a.m.-1 a.m. All major cards.

Revered as much for its martinis as for its splendid views of the Boston Public Garden, The Ritz Bar is a formidable institution. The recent aesthetic changes may get mixed reviews, but the international fat cats, local bon vivants and blue-haired Brahmin ladies still love the place for its unrivaled sense of propriety. Though pretentious at times, the service could not be finer.

CABARET

Club Cabaret
209 Columbus Ave.
(617) 536-0972
*Open Mon.-Tues. 9 p.m.-
1 a.m., Wed.-Sun.
7:30 p.m.-2 a.m. Show
time 8 p.m. Cover varies.
All major cards.*

Just the layout and decor of this intimate South End nightclub will make you want to spend more time here. Chic without being pretentious, Club Cabaret attracts SRO crowds (including a large gay contingent) by presenting a rotating bill of dinner-theater revues and torch-song sirens, including many of the area's finest performers. The spare art deco space revives the concept of a traditional nightclub, while the quality of the performers has given the once-dilapidated South End a chic new place to play. After the evening's final notes have been sung (about 10 p.m. during the week, later on weekends), the club turns into "Moonshine," a video bar with nine monitors and a 30-foot screen.

COMEDY

Five years ago, there were only a hundred or so rooms devoted to comedy in the United States; today, there are three times that many, with more than a dozen in the Boston area alone. Seating is generally cabaret style, and the dress code tends to be informal. Despite the relaxed ambience of these places, reservations are often necessary, especially on weekends.

The newest comedy club in town is a branch of a well-known New York club—Catch a Rising Star (30 JFK Street, Cambridge, 617-661-9887), which presents a nightly double bill of comedy and live music. The atmosphere in the place (formerly Jonathan Swift's, a revered Harvard Square rock club) is basement-blah, but the talent often is on the verge of national stardom.

Still, Boston's most popular comedy club remains Stitches (969 Commonwealth Avenue, 617-254-3939). Adjacent to The Paradise, a music and dance club, this homey little laugh shop is where such current headliners as Steven Wright and Jay Leno made their first forays into the national limelight. For a candid and at times crass taste of life in the Hub, try to catch Steve Sweeney, a native of Charlestown (Massachusetts) who performs here regularly.

Two other recommended stops on the comedy circuit are the Comedy Connection (76 Warrenton Street, 617-391-0022) and Nick's Comedy Stop (100 Warrenton Street, 617-482-0930). Both are located in the Theater District and showcase the city's rising young stars.

DANCING

Axis

13 Lansdowne St.
(617) 262-2437
Open Wed.-Sat. 10 p.m.-
2 a.m. Cover varies.
All major cards.

Billed as "the industrial dance club for the '90s," Axis resembles a scene out of a Samuel Beckett play. Adjacent to Boston's largest mainstream disco (Citi), this mortar-and-steel haven of hipness is embellished with wrought-iron girders soaring from floor to rafter, eerie blue and red lights and a room-length bar lined with black-clothed punks wearing dangerous-looking jewelry. The loud music thuds and crashes as if a bombing's under way in the city's most genuine specimen of cutting-edge cool.

Boston Beach Club

(Landmark Inn,
Faneuil Hall Marketplace),
300 N. Market Building
(617) 227-9660
Open Tues.-Sun. 6 p.m.-
2 a.m. Cover $5 Thurs.-Sat.
All major cards.

Ceiling fans, bartenders in shorts, deejays in Hawaiian shirts and makeshift tables of horizontal surfboards add up to a Shasta commercial come to life. Young area professionals sip "totally tubular toxins," swoon to surf tunes and eyeball one another in Boston's newest theme bar. Has all the ambience of a USC beer blast, with live entertainment to boot.

Café Fleuri

(Hotel Meridien),
250 Franklin St.
(617) 451-1900
Open Mon.-Fri. 11 a.m.-
11 p.m., Sat. 11 a.m.-mid-
night, Sun. 11 a.m.-5 p.m.
All major cards.

Nestled in the city's Financial District, this elegant hotel brasserie serves up more than the jazz brunches and power breakfasts for which it's known. Here, visitors can soak up an atrium environment surrounded by lighted trees and lots of greenery and, on Friday and Saturday nights, some of the most danceable jazz (performed by local quartets) in town. The friendly European-style service is a plus.

Citi

15 Lansdowne St.
(617) 262-2424
Open Wed.-Sat. 9 p.m.-
2 a.m. Cover varies.
Dress code.
All major cards.

You can bet your sequins that Patrick Lyons's sprawling dance showcase—formerly called Metro—will feature state-of-the-art everything. At press time, Citi was in the throes of a top-to-bottom face-lift, expected to result in lasers and lights galore. When live bands perform here, as they occasionally do, expect top names—as in Prince, Eric Clapton and Cher, all of whom graced the stage (as well as the private upstairs VIP lounge) in 1988.

The Jukebox

(Quality Inn Hotel),
275 Tremont St.
(617) 542-1123
Open Tues.-Sat. 8 p.m.-
2 a.m. Cover $3 Thurs.,
$6 Fri.-Sat.
Cards: AE.

Richie and the Fonz visit Boston of the '80s in this subterranean salute to *Happy Days* gone high-tech. Located in the basement of the downtown Quality Inn, the club is decorated with a smattering of antique Wurlitzer jukeboxes, a drive-in mural with cars pulled up to loudspeakers, and neon signs slick enough for a Steven Spielberg movie. Music from the '50s and '60s draws long lines of casually dressed fun seekers (mostly aged 22 to 28) who can't seem to get enough of the place. Show up early on weekends if you don't want to wait in line.

The Last Hurrah
(Omni Parker House
Hotel), 60 School St.
(617) 227-8600
*Open Mon.-Thurs. 5:30
p.m.-12:30 a.m., Fri.-Sat.
5:30 p.m.-1 a.m., Sun.
4 p.m.-11:30 p.m. No cover.
All major cards.*

The Ed, Bill and Bo Winiker Swing Orchestra has transformed The Last Hurrah into a Boston institution. Though popular among the city's young professionals, the place manages to attract a steady flow of older (ages 40 to 60) folks as well. The decor is turn-of-the-century, with lots of brass, dark wood and vintage Brahmin photographs. Hotel management lost favor a couple of years ago when it transformed the space into a disco, save for Friday and Saturday, when the Winikers swing.

The Links Club
Boylston Pl.
(617) 423-3832
*Open Tues.-Sun. 9 p.m.-
2 a.m. Cover $6 Fri.-Sat.;
cover varies other nights.
Cards: AE.*

The owners of this Theater District dance club saw the Big Chill trend coming, wrapped it up in a preppy package and ran with it. Colleges like Vassar and Williams get a lot of free PR in this spacious, country club of a club where the decor includes tennis rackets, racing sculls and bathtubs filled with ice and beer. In the crowd, either sitting on bleachers or bopping on the dance floor (to occasional live music and a good selection of deejay-spun rock), are plenty of club-tied young suitors, taking long draws off of lime-topped Coronas as they try to decide which of the pretty young females would please the folks most.

Man Ray
21 Brookline St.,
Cambridge
(617) 864-0400
*Open Wed.-Sat. 8 p.m.-
1 a.m. Cover varies.
No cards.*

This combination art gallery and rock bar has brought a touch of TriBeCa to Central Square, an area once known for little else than its ethnic restaurants and discount-furniture stores. It has also provided the city's fashion crowd with a hangout. Over the years, Man Ray has become a home away from home for area artists, designers, models and musicians. The music tends toward the progressive and is sometimes obscure. Downstairs, the Astro Lounge provides a cozy conversation area with '50s furniture; an adjacent gay bar called Campus is connected by an underground tunnel.

Le Papillon
(Back Bay Hilton),
40 Dalton St.
(617) 236-1100
*Open Wed.-Sat. 9 p.m.-
2 a.m. Cover $10
($5 Wed.).
Cards: AE, MC, V.*

Once one of the most pretentious and expensive dance clubs in the city, this well-appointed mélange of neon, brass and mahogany in the basement of the Back Bay Hilton appears to have loosened up recently. Though Le Papillon is still favored by the champagne-drinking would-be jet set, management has had the good sense to slash prices and pretensions enough to maintain a loyal following of well-dressed foreigners and Boston University coeds living off of mommy and daddy's bank account. Mainstream disco makes the room hop on weekends after 11 p.m.

The Roxy

(Quality Inn Hotel),
275 Tremont St.
(617) 227-7699
Open Thurs.-Sat. 8 p.m.-
2 a.m. Cover $8.
Cards: AE.

Whether it's the novelty of the concept or the '40s-style look of the downtown room, Boston's best bet for the young professionals who want to double-date with their parents is making early waves. Though skeptics question the feasibility of filling such a vast amount of space (the capacity is 1,300), sophisticated club-goers revel at the Bogey-&-Bacall-meet-Bowie-&-the-Boss concept: A live swing orchestra plays '40s tunes for twenty minutes on the hour; the rest is deejay-spun pop-rock. On weekends, "The Roxies," an eight-member dance troupe, add to the theater.

Zanzibar

1 Boylston Pl.
(617) 451-1955
Open Wed.-Fri. 5 p.m.-
2 a.m., Sat. 8 p.m.-2 a.m.
Cover $5-$8.
Cards: AE, MC, V.

A brand-new meeting place for the city's young movers and shakers, this $1.5 million Back Bay club seems to have been inspired by too many hours watching *Gilligan's Island* reruns. Not that it really matters when you consider the immediate success of the place. Long lines of tony and properly conservative young professionals gladly wait to enter this tropical paradise, where a staff wearing Banana Republic fashions cruises along two levels amid towering Royal palms (five in all), faux marble walls and a curious collection of African and South American artifacts. The music—a smart blend of seemingly all styles—is setting new heights for the city.

JAZZ

The Regattabar

(Charles Hotel), Bennett
St. & Eliot St., Cambridge
(617) 864-1200
Open Mon.-Fri. 5 p.m.-
2 a.m., Sat. 8 p.m.-2 a.m.
Showtimes & cover vary.
All major cards.

This attractive Cambridge jazz club combines an upscale regatta environment (glass walls, parquet floors and contemporary ceiling beams that boast bright renderings of sailing flags) with the most arresting jazz performed in the area. Attracting a refreshingly diverse crowd, the Regattabar has managed to thrive despite its overpriced, thimble-size drinks by serving up top-line jazz performers, including many national acts, on a regular basis. Not designed for talkers, the club targets serious listeners and rewards them with clean lines of vision and sharp acoustics.

Ryle's

212 Hampshire St.,
Cambridge
(617) 876-9330
Open Sun.-Thurs. 5 p.m.-
1 a.m., Fri.-Sat. 5 p.m.-
2 a.m. Showtimes & cover
vary.
All major cards.

No jazz-lover's tour of Cambridge would be complete without a stop at this no-frills, no-nonsense club where fans are treated to two bands for the price of one. Home-grown favorites draw an unpretentious mix of locals stopping by for a burger and a brew on the main floor, while serious listeners head up to the second level, where bigger names in jazz, fusion and swing perform nightly. Soft and soothing, the dimly lit decor has a comfortably bohemian flavor.

1369 Club
1369 Cambridge St.,
Cambridge
(617) 354-8030
*Open Sun.-Wed. 9:30 p.m.-
1 a.m., Thurs. 9:30 p.m.-
2 a.m., Fri.-Sat. 8:30 p.m.-
2 a.m. Showtimes & cover
vary.*
Cards: MC, V.

A love of jazz literally oozes out of this smoky, 1920s-style listening room with spinning fans, tin ceilings and small, wobbly tables with red-checked cloths. Narrow and dimly lit, the 1369 is revered as a musician's club where, on some nights, there's as much talent in the audience as there is on the stage. The crowd varies with the acts, but you can always count on a strong showing of laid-back students and young professionals in need of a jazz infusion.

MUSIC

The Channel
25 Necco St.
(617) 451-1905
*Open Sun.-Tues. 7:30 p.m.-
1 a.m., Wed.-Sat. 8 p.m.-
2 a.m. Showtimes & cover
vary. No cards.*

Now in its eighth year, The Channel offers plenty of headliners and local unsigned bands to accompany its first-rate sound board. Sticky floors notwithstanding, The Channel is undeniably one of the best places to hear live bands, which explains the crowds that turn out regularly. Low cover charges ($3 to $5 most of the time), clear lines of view and a varied entertainment lineup (everything from reggae to rock 'n' roll) draw fans from all over the area. The club's steadfast commitment to local music is evidenced by the sprawling atmosphere, which is hardly conducive to social drinking. Don't show up too early; headliners don't go on until about midnight.

Nightstage
823 Main St., Cambridge
(617) 497-8200
*Open Sun.-Wed. 8 p.m.-
1 a.m., Thurs.-Sat. 8 p.m.-
2 a.m. Showtimes & cover
vary.
All major cards.*

Nocturnal Cambridge hit an all-time high when this 275-seat listening room opened a couple of years ago. Though initially a showcase for jazz and blues acts (most of them nationally known), Nightstage now puts forth a roster as eclectic as its crowds: top names in reggae, rock, Irish folk, African pop and good ol' country and western, along with such jazz and blues legends as B. B. King and Bobbie Bluebland. Better yet, the club has style to match its sound, with a sleek, seductively lighted interior and clean views of the stage from every corner of the room.

The Paradise
967 Commonwealth Ave.
(617) 254-2052
*Box office open Mon.-Fri.
noon-6 p.m., Sat. 3 p.m.-
6 p.m. Showtimes & cover
vary.*
Cards: AE, MC, V.

If you don't mind a ho-hum atmosphere, The Paradise is arguably the best live-music bar in Boston. Although it doubles as a dance club on weekends (Saturdays draw a slick crowd of 23- to 25-year-olds), it's best known for its concerts, which feature national acts and well-known local favorites—Warren Zevon, Men Without Hats, the Del Fuegos, 'Til Tuesday, Down Avenue. Dance nights tend to attract more fashion-forward types than weeknight concerts, where you'll encounter Ralph Lauren preps, cutting-edge punks and just about everything in between. The rather intimate room's three bars are well spaced, so neither lines nor stage visibility is a problem, and The Paradise is blessed with heavenly acoustics.

The Rat

528 Commonwealth Ave.
(617) 536-9438
Hours showtimes &
cover vary.
No cards.

It's dark, it's loud, and the punkish fans who file in tend to be young, restless and wearing leather—but without this venerable Kenmore Square hole in the wall, a lot of promising local bands would never be heard. Pickup bands perform for free in the upstairs balcony on Friday and Saturday nights, and these thrashers are often better than the bands you pay for downstairs. A must-see for serious music buffs.

The Tam O'Shanter

1648 Beacon St., Brookline
(617) 277-0982
Open nightly 5 p.m.-1 a.m.
Showtimes vary. Cover $5.
No cards.

If you like good, clean fun, this place could be a great discovery. In fact, we're almost afraid to mention it too loudly. For a small club, The Tam manages to provide a lot of action, not to mention some of the tastiest American regional cuisine in town. The crowd is low-key and diverse, and people flock here to enjoy frosty long-necked beers and some of the best dance music around, whether it's rockabilly imported from Louisiana or R&B from Cambridge. What makes The Tam so special is its lack of pretension. If management ever decided to take the patchwork quilts off the walls or add designer pizzas to the menu, a lot of regulars would likely rebel.

The Western Front

343 Western Ave.,
Cambridge
(617) 492-7772
Open Tues.-Sun. 6 p.m.-
1 a.m. Showtimes &
cover vary.
No cards.

This dingy but distinguished reggae club stirs it up to the beat of the islands. The decor may not be memorable, but the music (Brazilian, Caribbean, steel and reggae), the dancing and the spicy Jamaican fare have made The Western Front one of the area's most popular hangouts. On crowded nights, an upstairs room is opened to accommodate the overflow.

PERFORMING ARTS

THEATER DISTRICT

Boston's professional stage activity centers on five downtown theaters. The Shubert, 265 Tremont Street (617-426-4520), and the Colonial, 106 Boylston Street (617-426-9366), play host to pre-Broadway tryouts and national touring companies; in fact, the table in the ground-floor ladies' room at the Colonial is a show-biz legend as the spot where some of America's greatest plays were rewritten. The Wilbur, 246 Tremont Street (617-423-4008), is a smaller legitimate house recently converted for cabaret shows. Spectaculars and crowd-drawing out-of-town companies come to the Wang Center, 270 Tremont Street (617-482-9393), where the Boston Ballet also performs several programs a year, including the traditional *Nutcracker* at Christmastime. The Charles Playhouse, 76 Warrenton Street (617-426-6912), houses intimate musicals and one-man shows in its main theater, while the comedy-mystery *Shear Madness* has been playing downstairs at Stage II (617-426-5225) for most of the 1980s and shows no signs of stopping.

THEATERS

American Repertory Theater
64 Brattle St., Cambridge
(617) 495-2668

Harvard's professional theater company, which started life at Yale before moving to Cambridge in 1979, mounts about five productions a year in repertory. In its first ten years, ART produced world premieres (including Marsha Norman's *'Night, Mother,* the Broadway musical *Big River* and several works each by Sam Shepard and Robert Wilson), as well as the classics, often taking an iconoclastic approach. The company has included nationally known artists (including actor Ken Howard and playwright David Mamet) and Boston stalwarts. Performances are held at the Loeb Drama Center, 64 Brattle Street, and Harvard's famous Hasty Pudding Club, 12 Holyoke Street, Cambridge.

Berklee Performance Center
136 Massachusetts Ave.
(617) 266-7455

A facility of the Berklee College of Music, this Back Bay hall plays host to an incredible variety of concerts throughout the year. Performers come from the top ranks of rock, pop, cabaret and folk music, but Berklee's specialty is jazz.

Concerts on the Common
Boston Common,
Tremont St. side
(617) 725-3912

Every year the neighbors complain about noise, crowds and trampled grass, but Concerts on the Common have become a fixture of Boston's summer scene. Each spring wooden bleachers are erected on the Common, and by mid-June thousands of fans start trooping in to hear their favorite rock and pop headliners. One summer not too long ago, Whitney Houston was a warm-up act; the next year she came back as a full-fledged star. If you can't get a ticket (and hot acts sell out fast), there's no law against sitting on the Common outside the enclosure.

Hatch Shell
Charles River Esplanade
at Arlington St.
(617) 727-5215

Bring your blanket and picnic basket—but come early. This oversized band shell on the banks of the Charles is famous nationwide as the home of the Boston Pops' annual Fourth of July concert and fireworks finale. Thousands camp out all day at their favored spots for the evening concert. The Pops Esplanade Orchestra also performs at the shell for at least one week of free concerts each summer (see newspapers for listings), as does the Boston Ballet II, composed of the company's up-and-coming young dancers. And other events are scheduled for nearly every night during summer months.

Huntington Theater Company
264 Huntington Ave.
(617) 266-3913

As the professional theater company in residence at Boston University, the Huntington generally mounts five productions a year, fall through spring. Selections range from classics to comedy to Cole Porter musicals, with a great deal in between.

Jordan Hall
30 Gainsborough St.
(off Huntington Ave.)
(617) 536-2412

This intimate concert hall, located near Symphony Hall, is particularly well suited to chamber music and small orchestras. It hosts a full schedule of professional and student recitals throughout the year.

Opera House
539 Washington St.
(617) 426-5300

Home of Sarah Caldwell's Opera Company of Boston, the Opera House also is rented out for occasional pop concerts and other performances. OCB usually produces four or five operas a year, but its precarious finances and management make even advertised programs unpredictable. (It once canceled an entire season—after subscription tickets had been sold.) OCB seasons generally run from January through early summer but sometimes include autumn productions. One standby, Humperdinck's *Hansel and Gretel*, is performed some years during Christmas-shopping season and is worth hearing.

Orpheum Theater
Hamilton Pl.
(off Tremont St.)
(617) 482-0650

Devoted primarily to rock concerts, the Orpheum has played host to some of the biggest names in rock. (However, megaconcerts now tend to play Worcester's Centrum.)

Symphony Hall
201 Massachusetts Ave.
(617) 266-1492

The grande dame of New England's concert halls, Symphony Hall is the home of the Boston Symphony Orchestra and the Boston Pops. The BSO is in residence October through May (Friday-afternoon concerts are often the best bet for last-minute tickets), while the Pops does short seasons at Christmastime (including an annual New Year's Eve gala) and in the spring. Other groups that use the hall on a regular basis include the Wang Celebrity Series and Boston's Handel & Haydn Society.

Water Music, Inc.
Departs from
Commonwealth Pier
(617) 876-8742

A seasonal pleasure, Water Music runs concert cruises from mid-June to late summer. Jazz dominates the musical offerings (the Jazz Boat makes two trips every Friday night), but the line offers some classical concert cruises as well. A highlight of some seasons is the Royal Fireworks cruise, with a display of pyrotechnics synchronized to Handel's music.

TICKETS

Bostix
Faneuil Hall Marketplace
(617) 723-5181
Open Mon.-Sat. 11 a.m.-
6 p.m., Sun. noon-6 p.m.

This outdoor booth, a service of ARTS/Boston, provides information on arts events throughout the Boston area and sells half-price tickets (cash only) on the day of performance for many Boston theaters. The few available tickets for big hits go fast, so it pays to line up early.

SHOPS

HATS—AND THEN SOME

In his 1947 book, *The Proper Bostonians*, Cleveland Amory recounted the legendary answer to the question, where do Boston women get their hats? "Our hats? We don't buy hats—we have 'em." Lucky for us, those days of reluctant acquiring and spending are past. Today, Boston's shops offer a world (literally) of goods to demanding buyers.

The foremost shopping venue is Newbury Street in Back Bay, which is lined with both national and international boutiques. Antiques buffs frequent Charles Street at the foot of Beacon Hill. The city's two home-grown department stores, Jordan Marsh and Filene's, anchor Downtown Crossing. For European and American designer names, head to Copley Place, a glistening mall done in marble and brass. And Faneuil Hall Marketplace draws the crowds, though you'll really have to hunt out any substantive shopping experiences here.

The modern Back Bay matron (probably 35 and juggling job and family) can be found in The Limited, The Gap, Banana Republic and a Benetton or two. Her Beacon Hill cousin might shop at Laura Ashley, Bally of Switzerland and Ann Taylor, perhaps sneaking into Victoria's Secret on occasion. In other words, the big chains now inhabiting every U.S. city are just as popular in Boston.

This section of the book, though, will focus primarily on those shops and boutiques that are unique to Boston—places in which you're likely to find something you won't find at home. You might even find a new hat.

ANTIQUES

Charles Street, which skirts the western flat of Beacon Hill, is the center of Boston's antiques district. Merchandise ranges from European fine art to Americana and kitsch, and prices run from outrageous to affordable enough for an impulse purchase.

Alberts-Langdon, Inc.
126 Charles St.
(617) 523-5954
Open Mon.-Thurs. 10 a.m.-4 p.m., Fri.-Sat. hours vary; closed in summer.

This small Beacon Hill shop specializes in Oriental antiques, as well as paintings and porcelain. Prices are exquisite, but so are the pieces.

Beacon Hill Thrift Shop
15 Charles St.
(617) 742-2323
Open Mon.-Thurs. & Sat. 11 a.m.-4 p.m.; hours may vary.

When a matron on the Hill decides to clean the attic, chances are that much of the stuff will end up in the rooms of the Thrift Shop. Whether you find a good deal (an antique silver hip flask, for instance) or junk (white go-go boots from the '60s) depends on how good you are at sifting through piles and layers. Kindly little old ladies run the shop to raise scholarship money for the New England Baptist Hospital School of Nursing.

James Billings
70 Charles St.
(617) 367-9533
Labor Day-Memorial Day: open Mon.-Fri. 10 a.m.-6 p.m., Sat. 10 a.m.-4 p.m.; Memorial Day-Labor Day: open Mon.-Fri. 10 a.m.-6 p.m.

These fine English antiques and paintings speak to the excessively Anglophile Bostonian. If you aren't looking to blow your entire trust fund on antiques, poke in the store anyway. This charming shop is housed in the former Charles Street Meeting House.

Boston Antiques Co-op
119 Charles St.
(617) 227-9810
Open Mon.-Thurs. 11 a.m.-7 p.m., Fri. 10 a.m.-6 p.m., Sat. 11 a.m.-6 p.m., Sun. 1 p.m.-6 p.m.

Upstairs and downstairs in this building are the eclectic collections of fourteen dealers, whose wares ramble from the seventeenth century to the era of art deco, covering everything from jewelry to furniture. Upstairs, you may find some terrific prices on Victorian antique clothing; downstairs, check out the vintage photographs in the back corner.

Danish Country Antique Furniture
138 Charles St.
(617) 227-1804
Open Mon.-Wed. & Fri. 10 a.m.-6 p.m., Thurs. 10 a.m.-7 p.m., Sat. 10 a.m.-5 p.m., Sun. 1 p.m.-5 p.m.

If you travel with a large suitcase, perhaps you'll have room to take home one of these beautiful pine benches, chests or armoires, all over 100 years old, sanded and refinished. The straightforward, clean lines of the furniture are refreshing after all the Victoriana found elsewhere on Charles Street.

Eugene Galleries
76 Charles St.
(617) 227-3062
*Open Mon.-Sat. 10:30
a.m.-5:30 p.m.,
Sun. by chance.*

Rare prints, paintings and maps are the hallmark of this shop. You'll find old views of Boston and of many other cities as well. There are stacks of cards and bins of prints to browse through, making this a delightful place to while away an hour.

Flamingo Bay
121 Charles St.
(617) 227-5733
*Open Mon.-Fri. 11 a.m.-
7 p.m., Sat. 11 a.m.-6 p.m.,
Sun. noon-6 p.m.*

Looking for an antique dress or a funky pair of '50s pants? Then head for Flamingo Bay. It also stocks vintage costume jewelry and a quirky collection of old-fashioned accessories. For the most part the clothing attracts a punk audience, but a beautiful Edwardian dress that sold for $20 recently graced its owner at a Christmas costume ball in vintage style.

George Gravert Antiques
122 Charles St.
(617) 227-1593
*Open Mon.-Fri. 10 a.m.-
5 p.m.*

Another Beacon Hill storefront with beautiful pieces at equally beautiful prices. The fine furniture, china and tapestries are for the true connoisseur and collector.

Samuel L. Lowe Jr. Antiques, Inc.
80 Charles St.
(617) 742-0845
*Open Mon.-Fri. 10:30 a.m.-
4:45 p.m., Sat. by chance.*

Have a nautical bent? Then set sail for Lowe. It sells books, ship models, scrimshaw, fishing gear—anything and everything marine that a fish or ship fancier could fancy.

Marika's Antiques, Inc.
130 Charles St.
(617) 523-4520
*Open Mon.-Sat. 10 a.m.-
5 p.m.; closed Sat. in July
& Aug.*

Claiming to be the oldest shop on Charles Street, Marika's is an emporium of collectibles, jewelry, furniture, glassware and seemingly everything else imaginable. You might wonder if the owner really knows what his inventory is in this jumble, but it's good fun to peer and discover.

Weiner's Antique Shop
22 Beacon St.
(617) 227-2894
*Open Mon.-Fri. 9 a.m.-
4 p.m., Sat. 11 a.m.-4 p.m.*

Although not on Charles Street, Weiner's is catercorner to the State House, which is close enough. Since 1896, this shop has sold American and European antique furniture and art, and it looks as though some of the stuff has been here since the shop opened. Another jumble worth exploring.

BEAUTY

Diego at the Loft
143 Newbury St.
(617) 262-5003
*Open Mon.-Tues. & Fri.-
Sat. 9 a.m.-6 p.m., Wed.-
Thurs. 9 a.m.-7 p.m.*

Diego Messina has been a longtime fixture on the Back Bay beauty scene, and his third-floor salon caters to businesswomen and businessmen. Cuts may not shout avant-garde, but sit in one of Diego's chairs long enough and you'll see just about everyone who matters in Boston come trooping in for a color job, a cut, a perm or a blow dry.

Great Cuts

1 Eliot Square, Cambridge
(617) 576-3920
Open Mon.-Fri. 9 a.m.-
7 p.m., Sat. 9 a.m.-6 p.m.

If you think you'll go mad if you don't get your hair cut right away, this is the place to go. Don't expect to leave with a new head, though; Great Cuts takes care of you just fine if you need a trim, or your bangs shortened, or other emergency minor repairs. No appointments are taken and every cut costs a mere $8. Needless to say, this branch is popular with the Harvard kids; the Great Cuts in Boston, on Newbury Street, gets busy execs.

Lancôme

(Filene's),
426 Washington St.
(617) 357-2100
Open Mon.-Sat. 9:30 a.m.-
7 p.m., Sun. noon-6 p.m.

If traveling has left you a little frayed around the edges, you'll be glad to discover this little corner of Paris tucked away on the first floor of Filene's. The facials will refresh you (they include a foot massage), and the makeup sessions will leave you feeling like a new woman, not a painted one. It's all served up in peaceful surroundings. The operation is professional without pushing its own products.

Le Pli Beauty Salon

5 Bennett St. (at Charles
Square), Cambridge
(617) 547-4081
Open Mon.-Tues. 9 a.m.-
5 p.m., Wed. 8:30 a.m.-
5 p.m., Thurs.-Fri. 8:30
a.m.-7 p.m., Sat. 9 a.m.-
4 p.m.

Sydney Moss runs an elegant salon in Cambridge that is attached to a full-scale health spa. For those in real need of rejuvenation, there's "Day at Le Pli," a pampering package of exercise, massage and beauty treatments—including a manicure, a facial and makeup—for $225.

BOOKS & STATIONERY

Architectural Bookshop

66 Hereford St.
(617) 262-2727
Open Mon. 9 a.m.-8 p.m.,
Tues.-Thurs. 9 a.m.-6 p.m.,
Sat. 9 a.m.-5 p.m.

Across from the Boston Architectural Center, this compact store features books and magazines about—what else?— architecture and design: books about Boston, about other cities and about foreign cities, all with design in mind. There are weighty coffee table tomes and toys (like Color-forms) geared to get kids in the visual mode.

Avenue Victor Hugo Bookshop

339 Newbury St.
(617) 266-7746
Open Mon.-Fri. 9 a.m.-
9 p.m., Sat. 10 a.m.-8
p.m., Sun. noon-8 p.m.

From current titles to used books, this tiny Back Bay shop has a great selection, including back issues of such magazines as *Life* (10 cents back in the '50s, about $7.50 now). You'll also find last week's *New York* magazine and books on subjects ranging from the world wars to cooking and child rearing.

Brattle Book Shop

9 West St.
(617) 542-0210
Open Mon.-Sat. 9 a.m.-
5:30 p.m.

If you're hunting for an old book and can't find it here, you might just as well give up. This marvelous shop was established in 1825, and the current family of owners has been in residence since 1949, presiding over a legendary collection of old volumes on everything from cuisine to fly-fishing, fiction to politics. Be sure to visit the third floor of rare volumes.

Globe Corner Bookstore
1 School St.
(617) 523-6658
Open Mon.-Sat. 9 a.m.-
7 p.m., Sun. noon-5 p.m.

The present rosy-brick structure dates from about 1718, when it opened as an apothecary. For the next century, it housed a variety of businesses, becoming the Old Corner Bookstore in 1828. In the 1830s, the publishing house of Ticknor and Fields, which worked with such authors as Longfellow, Holmes, Hawthorne, Emerson and Thackeray, took up residence, and the building became a literary gathering place. Slated for demolition in the 1960s, the downtown building was saved when the *Boston Globe* decided to occupy a corner of the store, ensuring its renovation. Today, the downstairs bookstore specializes in books about Boston and New England; upstairs, the Travel Book Store covers the globe.

Goodspeed's Book Shop
7 Beacon St.
(617) 523-5970

2 Milk St.
(617) 523-5970
Open Mon.-Fri. 9 a.m.-
5 p.m.

The Beacon Street Goodspeed's specializes in prints; the Milk Street location, under the Old South Meeting House, features a veritable dustbin of the past, perfect for a rainy afternoon's crawl.

Harvard Book Store Cafe
190 Newbury St.
(617) 536-0095
Open Mon.-Thurs. 8 a.m.-
11 p.m., Fri.-Sat. 8 a.m.-
midnight, Sun. noon-8 p.m.

This bookstore, located in Boston's Back Bay despite its name, comes complete with an attractive café. Stop in for a morning coffee, croissant and newspaper, a light lunch in the back two-level dining room or an al fresco dinner on the sidewalk in the summertime. Surrounding you are books on New England, the latest in fiction and poetry, handsome art books and a world of cookbooks. The café also hosts a number of author talks.

Harvard Coop
(Harvard Square),
1400 Massachusetts Ave.,
Cambridge
(617) 492-1000
Open Mon.-Wed. & Fri.-
Sat. 9:20 a.m.-5:45 p.m.,
Thurs. 9:20 a.m.-8:30 p.m.

The official bookstore of Harvard and MIT, The Harvard Coop also carries posters, art books and general fiction. But if you want to read what the computer whizzes and business bosses of tomorrow are being assigned in class today, visit the third floor, where the class reading lists are posted.

Pad and Pen
(Copley Place),
100 Huntington Ave.
(617) 353-0250
Open Mon.-Sat. 10 a.m.-
8 p.m., Sun. noon-5 p.m.

This high-toned stationery store aims for the scribbler with a design sense, selling such things as expensive Mont Blanc pens, bizarre wall clocks, trendy marbleized writing papers and artists' supplies. If there's an architect or designer on your gift list, you'll find something here.

Papermint

(Charles Square),
5 Bennett St., Cambridge
(617) 492-0289
*Open Mon.-Fri. 10 a.m.-
9 p.m., Sat. 10 a.m.-
6 p.m., Sun. noon-6 p.m.*

Want stationery by the pound? Papermint offers a range of colors and styles, as well as cards and gifts, often with an amusing Boston bent.

Spenser and Marlowe Books

314 Newbury St.
(617) 262-0880
*Open Mon.-Sat. 11 a.m.-
7 p.m., Sun. by chance.*

This Back Bay basement spot is actually two stores in one. Spenser's Mystery Bookshop relies on the world of intrigue, in both new releases and used books, and features all the big names of the genre: Elmore Leonard, Dick Francis, Dashiell Hammett and Ngaio Marsh, not to mention Boston's own originator of Spenser, Robert B. Parker. Marlowe's is a used-book outlet, with good prices on past fiction and nonfiction.

Wordsworth

30 Brattle St., Cambridge
(617) 453-5201
*Open Mon.-Sat. 8:30 a.m.-
11:30 p.m., Sun. 10 a.m.-
10:30 p.m.*

Wordsworth claims to stock more than 50,000 titles, and we believe it; you can find practically any current title in architecture or computers or fiction. Best of all, the bookstore, just steps from the center of Harvard Square, is always a scene in itself—you may forget book shopping in favor of people watching.

CLOTHES

CHILDREN

Petit Bateau

161 Newbury St.
(617) 262-5664
*Open Mon.-Sat. 10 a.m.-
6 p.m.*

Parents with a heightened design sense or egos large enough to forgive their children for being better dressed than they are can stock up on these 100-percent cotton outfits made by France's Petit Bateau. Everything in this Back Bay shop—from Lilliputian striped dresses to minuscule madras slacks and matching cardigans—is, of course, unbearably adorable. The cotton cloth is guaranteed not to shrink, though there's no guarantee that your little angel won't outgrow her $30 play frock in no time.

MEN

Alan Bilzerian

34 Newbury St.
(617) 536-1001
*Open Mon.-Tues. & Thurs.-
Sat. 10 a.m.-5:30 p.m.,
Wed. 10 a.m.-7 p.m.*

No one would claim that Boston is the sartorial capital of the world. But when the Hub is mentioned in the pages of *GQ* and *Esquire*, it is most likely in connection with this Back Bay shop, where cutting edge is king. Here are designers from Armani to Comme des Garçons (and a host of others we've never heard of) presented in all their outrageous glory. Prices are hefty, but exquisite leather shoes and boots, jackets that would never see duty in some stuffy boardroom and a collection of slightly retro hats are worth the cost to those with avant-garde tastes. White walls, turquoise wood floors and wall sconces do a fine job of setting off the clothing-as-art displays.

Brooks Brothers
46 Newbury St.
(617) 267-2600
Open Mon.-Sat. 9 a.m.-6 p.m.

Delivering the ultimate in the proper Boston look, Brooks has been supplying the merrily conservative set with khaki pants and button-down shirts for over 50 years. The store exudes its solid charm quietly—there is no background Muzak, and austere and properly striped suits hang with nary a crease. Indeed, the nattily attired salespeople so reflect the store that it's hard to tell the help from the customers. Brooks and Bilzerian may be on the same block, but they are a million miles apart.

The Lodge at Harvard Square
109 Newbury St.
(617) 247-2802
Open Mon.-Fri. 9:30 a.m.-6 p.m., Sat. 10 a.m.-6 p.m., Sun. noon-5 p.m.

No, this store is not in Harvard Square, but its spirit is. The Back Bay shop sells sportswear for the preppy: chinos, cotton sweaters, madras shirts and deck shoes galore. But the Lodge isn't just a low-price Brooks Brothers; there is a concession to style, and the prices are certainly right for any budget. There are other locations at Faneuil Hall Marketplace and in Harvard Square.

Louis
470 Boylston St.
(617) 965-6100
Open Mon.-Tues. & Thurs.-Fri. 10 a.m.-6 p.m., Wed. 10 a.m.-8:30 p.m., Sat. 9:30 a.m.-5:30 p.m.

Louis is the last word in fashion for Boston's best-dressed—and best-heeled—men. Suits, mostly Italian in design (Lucimo Barbera, Zegna), can easily run $1,500; shirts are handmade and will cost about $145. Shoes are buttery soft, as well they should be for $350. Beware the sometimes unapologetically snooty attitude of the sales help, which can be irritating—and goad sales. We know of one young millionaire-about-town who loves to shop at Louis just to prove to the posturing salesmen that, yes, he *can* afford that $400 sweater. Louis will soon be moving across Boylston Street to the erstwhile 1863 Museum of Natural History—if you can't find the store, look for the inevitable array of Mercedes-Benzes, Porsches, BMWs and the occasional Aston Martin parked out front.

Roots
419 Boylston St.
(617) 247-0700
Open Mon.-Tues. & Fri. 10 a.m.-6:30 p.m., Wed.-Thurs. 10 a.m.-8 p.m., Sat. 9:30 a.m.-5:30 p.m.

Another mecca for the proper Boston male, Back Bay's Roots floats somewhere above Brooks's old-money look but beneath Louis's unflinching Euro-trendiness. The traditional-minded suits and jackets on the second floor are not wedded to conservative cuts or stratospheric prices. The first-floor dress shirts, sportswear and accessories bespeak a man with good taste, if somewhat restrained flair. It all feels as though you've wandered into a store at which Prince Charles might shop if he needed to pick up a pair of braces in Boston.

W.D. & Co.
165 Newbury St.
(617) 437-0888
*Open Mon.-Fri. 10 a.m.-
7 p.m., Sat. 10 a.m.-
6 p.m., Sun. noon-5 p.m.*

Tired of suits? Slip into W.D. & Co., where it's always play time. The sports jackets, cotton sweaters, shirts and slacks are bright, trendy and meant for the man with a fine sense of taste and fun. A short-sleeve summer shirt might feature galloping zebras across the collar; a handmade cotton sweater sports a giant watermelon slice; another sweater is emblazoned with a huge red lobster. Ties come in a rainbow of hues and designs that are never boring; even the paisley here packs a punch. A Back Bay relief from the workaday world for those who can afford it.

WOMEN

Alan Bilzerian
34 Newbury St.
(617) 536-1001
*Open Mon.-Tues. &
Thurs.-Sat. 10 a.m.-
5:30 p.m., Wed. 10 a.m.-
7 p.m.*

The second floor of Bilzerian features women's au courant clothing—you know, the jackets with pockets in funny places, skirts that have buttons in even funnier places, shirts with unexplainable flaps. Maud Frizon shoes, along with Bilzerian's own designs, Prada silky-soft leather handbags, outsize hats and always luxurious fabrics speak to a customer who knows her own look. If you can carry off the look, and the price tag, you'll be assured of the most in-style style.

Clothware
52 Brattle St., Cambridge
(617) 661-6441
*Open Mon.-Wed. & Fri.
10 a.m.-6:30 p.m., Thurs.
10 a.m.-8 p.m., Sat. 10
a.m.-6 p.m., Sun. 1 p.m.-
6 p.m.*

This small store has a fervent following among Cambridge and Boston businesswomen who demand natural-fiber clothing and good design. Sweaters are expensive and beautiful; accessories are trendy and fun. There's a good collection of sportswear, as well as lovely nightgowns and lingerie.

Copley Place
Copley Square
(617) 267-5300
*Most stores open Mon.-Sat.
10 a.m.-5 p.m., Sun. noon-
5 p.m.; some open later;
Neiman-Marcus closed Sun.*

Since it opened in 1984, this brass and marble mall in the heart of Boston has lured the wealthy and the window-shopper. Ralph Lauren, Saint Laurent/Rive Gauche, Gucci, Alfred Sung, Charles Jourdan—all maintain classy boutiques on the first floor. Upstairs, the prices come down a bit at The Gap, Pappagallo, Bandolino and a cute boutique called Irresistibles. There are restaurants—a branch of Durgin-Park, a fish restaurant called Arne's—and movie theaters, but most people come to Copley Place to browse and spend at such stores as Neiman-Marcus, Tiffany & Co., Williams-Sonoma and The Limited.

Fogal
115 Newbury St.
(617) 262-5338
*Open Mon.-Tues. & Thurs.-
Sat. 10 a.m.-6 p.m., Wed.
10 a.m.-7 p.m.*

Just stockings. But oh, what stockings. The imported Swiss naughtiness includes wild designs, thigh-highs, glittery nighttime hose and one-piece garter pantyhose (use your imagination). Prices are pretty wild, too, but to flatten your man of the moment, we firmly believe nothing beats a great pair of legs—even in proper old Boston.

Goods Lingerie

123 Newbury St.
(617) 536-7860
*Open Mon.-Tues. & Fri.-
Sat. 10 a.m.-6 p.m., Wed.-
Thurs. 10 a.m.-7 p.m.*

When we're feeling sexy, or when we're feeling blue, Goods has the answer. This is lingerie to inspire fantasy, not of the *Playboy* variety but of the rich-and-pampered-who-can- afford-to-drop-a-couple-of-hundred-dollars-on-things-that-never-see-the-light-of-day variety. The negligees are fluid, the tap pants are trimmed in lace, and the pajamas are of such silk they make us feel like Claudette Colbert (at $245, they should). There are thirsty cotton robes to be wrapped in, garter belts to be naughty in, Hanro undies to be loved in. Although some lingerie shops sink into the sleazy, the tasteless would never appear at Back Bay's Goods.

Jasmine Boutique

37A Brattle St., Cambridge
(617) 354-6043
*Open Mon.-Sat. 10 a.m.-
8 p.m., Sun. noon-6 p.m.*

Light pours in through Jasmine's big windows, illuminating the young and trendy collection of Esprit and other sportswear designers. Prices are reasonable, and the looks are today's. Accessories and jewelry are unremittingly fun. Jasmine is best known, though, for Sola, its shoe section, which features the latest in clunky black rubber-soled things, as well as pumps and evening shoes.

Lapis

236 Newbury St.
(617) 437-1057
*Open Mon.-Fri. 11 a.m.-
6:30 p.m., Sat. 11 a.m.-
7 p.m., Sun. noon-6 p.m.*

This tiny Back Bay store sells only clothes by Boston designers. It's rather a hit-or-miss proposition, and not much in the way of the dresses and suits is much to our taste, but the jewelry and accessories are knockouts. Very unusual stuff: The earrings are bold and bright, one jewelry line features cuff bracelets that look like crinkled paper, and another turns an assortment of buttons into statement pins and earrings. At least you know that no one back home will be wearing the same thing.

Louis

470 Boylston St.
(617) 965-6100
*Open Mon.-Tues. & Thurs.-
Fri. 10 a.m.-6 p.m., Wed.
10 a.m.-8:30 p.m., Sat.
9:30 a.m.-5:30 p.m.*

While they may not get quite the expert attention that the men get, women at Louis are not totally neglected. There are beautiful separates by Luciano Barbera, linen jackets that cost a fortune and silk skirts that are as gossamer as clouds and priced in the stratosphere. As in the men's departments, you may want to be sure you are dressed in your finest to shop here. If we had to choose just one outfit for the rest of our lives, it would be from Louis.

Roots

419 Boylston St.
(617) 247-0700
*Open Mon.-Tues. & Fri.
10 a.m.-6:30 p.m., Wed.-
Thurs. 10 a.m.-8 p.m., Sat.
9:30 a.m.-5:30 p.m.*

The men at Roots seem to get the better deal, as its suits for women are relentlessly conservative, the skirts unabashedly long and the shirts nearly all made for little bows. You almost expect to see Nikes for sale along with the Bally shoes for the '80s office look. However, Roots scores big with beautiful handmade sweaters and expertly made classic coats—you can always team them up with a more stylish skirt and shoes from Bilzerian.

Charles Sumner

16 Newbury St.
(617) 536-6225
Open Mon.-Tues. &
Thurs.-Sat. 10 a.m.-
5:45 p.m., Wed. 10 a.m.-
7 p.m.

This is *the* store for the Boston woman of means and social standing. It's not a place for the young; the French elegance of Louis Féraud dresses and the soierie silks of Ann Lawrence are too much an acquired taste for those who are not yet sartorially developed. Sumner, a classic women's store, sells dresses, lingerie, shoes, eveningwear, accessories and makeup—in short, everything for the sophisticated woman. Service is gracious; salespeople remember a regular customer's Bruno Magli size as easily as they help newcomers select the correct dress for an upcoming ball.

Talbots

25 School St.
(617) 723-0660
Open Mon.-Fri. 10 a.m.-
7 p.m., Sat. 10 a.m.-6 p.m.

For Muffy with love, Talbots is the last word in preppy dressing. Short skirts have made no inroads at this bastion of cable-stitch cardigans, Pappagallo shoes, madras shorts and cotton blouses with prim little collars. But the prices are good, and if you're looking for the classic, you'll find it here. In Talbots, you are likely to see a number of men shopping—properly preppy husbands picking up a little surprise for the wife for when she gets home from her Junior League meeting. He knows everything is bound to please. There are branches on Boylston Street and in Cambridge.

CRATS

Alianza

154 Newbury St.
(617) 262-2385
Open Mon.-Sat. 10 a.m.-
6 p.m.

In the heart of the city's art-gallery district, you can find this excellent selection of high-quality work, which is especially strong in ceramics. This is the latest of the store's incarnations; it originally carried foreign-made crafts. Though not quite at gallery level, Alianza can hold its own with neighboring stores.

The Artful Hand

(36 Copley Place), 100
Huntington Ave.
(617) 262-9601
Open Mon.-Fri. 10 a.m.-
7 p.m., Sat. 10 a.m.-
6 p.m., Sun. noon-5 p.m.

Surrounded by some of Boston's toniest stores, this eclectic shop sells wall hangings, a good selection of furniture, vases, jewelry, handmade paper, glass and ceramics both functional and sculptural—and everything is of uniformly high quality. The relentlessly contemporary work comes from artists who live all over the country, and you won't see most of these items all over the place.

Cambridge Artists' Cooperative

38A Brattle St., Cambridge
(617) 868-4434
Open Mon.-Sat. 10 a.m.-
6 p.m.

The 25 members of this cooperative create a wide variety of craftwork, but they are particularly strong in handmade paper. An added benefit: the opportunity to meet the artists, who staff the store. Though the co-op's future is threatened by a proposal to replace the building in which it does business, it's worth dropping by.

Journeyman
(The Galleria), 55 Boylston St., Cambridge
(617) 876-0170
Open Mon.-Tues. & Sat. 10 a.m.-6 p.m., Wed.-Fri. 10 a.m.-9 p.m., Sun. noon-5 p.m.

This shop is the Hyundai of the area craft stores; it puts on no gallery airs but instead concentrates on small-scale-production craft items. Most of its inventory is functional and relatively inexpensive, and the selection rests heavily on stoneware, perfume bottles, mirrors, lamps and wooden items.

Signature
Dock Square, North St.
(617) 227-4885
Open Mon.-Thurs. 10 a.m.-9 p.m., Fri.-Sat. 10 a.m.-10 p.m., Sun. noon-6 p.m.

The Quincy Market hordes often leave the riot of T-shirts and tourist trash to wander across the street to this refuge of elegance. Be sure not to miss the gallery in the back, which often displays collector-level, one-of-a-kind pieces as part of juried shows. Perhaps because they have to deal with a lot of browsers, the sales staff can be a bit abrupt if you're not there for the expensive stuff. Nevertheless, Signature is one of the city's best.

The Society of Arts and Crafts
175 Newbury St.
(617) 266-1810
Open Mon.-Fri. 10 a.m.-5:30 p.m., Sat. 10 a.m.-5 p.m.

The home of the oldest nonprofit crafts organization in the United States does more than simply sell high-quality handmade items. In addition to displaying the work of about 150 craftspeople, this small Back Bay storefront also houses an artists' slide registry and an upstairs gallery that contains changing exhibits. Good selection, good cause.

Ten Arrow
10 Arrow St., Cambridge
(617) 876-1117
Open Mon.-Wed. & Fri.-Sat. 10 a.m.-6 p.m., Thurs. 10 a.m.-9 p.m., Sun. 1 p.m.-5 p.m.

Small it may be, but this storefront on the edge of Harvard Square was the first gallery in the Boston area to devote itself exclusively to American crafts. One room often shows small-scale but sophisticated exhibits of cutting-edge work; the rest of the place offers a good selection of jewelry, glass, ceramics and wood. The owner, Betty Tinlot, is knowledgeable and more than happy to share her expertise.

Whippoorwill Crafts
(Faneuil Hall Marketplace), 126 S. Market Bldg.
(617) 523-5149
Open Mon.-Sat. 10 a.m.-9 p.m., Sun. noon-6 p.m.

This basement-level shop in the city's tourist mecca caters to the traveler shopping for his (or more likely her) grandchildren. Packed with toys, puppets and kaleidoscopes, it leans toward the wooden-cutting-board school of craft: relatively inexpensive handmade items squeezed in between more commercial wares. Whippoorwill is to craft what Quincy Market is to Rodeo Drive.

DEPARTMENT STORES

Bonwit Teller
500 Boylston St.
(617) 267-1200
Hours not available at press time.

Bonwit has moved to its new home in the New England building and added a menswear department to its slightly conservative but always correct clothing.

Filene's

426 Washington St.
(617) 357-2100
Open Mon.-Sat. 9:30 a.m.-
7 p.m., Sun. noon-6 p.m.

Long considered Boston's premier hometown department store, Filene's quality slipped when its parent company went through takeover wars. But now the fighting's over. Filene's is not where you go for high-end designer labels; it's where you go for your basic Liz Claiborne and Ellen Tracy. But there's a stylish edge here, and its second-floor juniors department has made a hit with the young crowd. Filene's upstairs, though, does not equal Filene's downstairs (see below).

Filene's Basement

426 Washington St.
(617) 357-2100
Open Mon.-Sat. 9:30 a.m.-
7 p.m., Sun. noon-6 p.m.

Old-time purists will tell you that Filene's Basement, a separate corporation from Filene's department store upstairs, isn't as good as it used to be, but we think that's just crankiness. On two floors of incredible jumble, you'll have to search and pick through bins piled with Charles Jourdan shoes, racks of Neiman-Marcus dresses and aisles of Louis linen jackets, all at eye-popping discounted prices. There are lingerie and luggage, necklaces and neckties, ball gowns and bridal dresses, towels and trinkets. There are even a back room of designer labels and a corner devoted to fur coats. Dressing rooms are the aisles (for the women), but rare is the visit that doesn't produce at least one find.

Jordan Marsh

450 Washington St.
(617) 357-3000
Open Mon.-Sat. 8:30 a.m.-
7 p.m., Sun. noon-6 p.m.

Always Filene's lesser cousin, Jordan Marsh has recently matched its neighbor across Washington Street with a better selection of designer clothes and special sizes. To blend in with the Bostonians shopping here, be sure to drop the r in the store's last name, that is, "Jordan Mahsh."

Lord & Taylor

760 Boylston St.
(617) 262-6000
Open Mon. & Wed.
10 a.m.-9 p.m., Tues. &
Thurs.-Sat. 10 a.m.-7 p.m.,
Sun. noon-6 p.m.

Next door to Saks, Lord & Taylor provides two floors of classic and sensible clothes and accessories for conservative men and women. The upstairs dress department is particularly good, and the shoe department, featuring Ferragamo, Bruno Magli, Perry Ellis Portfolio and Liz Claiborne, is one of the best in the city.

Neiman-Marcus

(Copley Place),
Copley Square
(617) 536-3660
Open Mon.-Fri. 10 a.m.-
7 p.m., Sat. 10 a.m.-6 p.m.

A jewel from the Dallas retail world is set in glittering Copley Place, Boston's most upscale mall. The three-level store is where you go for your Ferragamo handbag, your Sonia Rykiel knit dress, your Christian Dior stockings, your Victor Costa evening look, your Zhandra Rhodes statement. From men's tuxedos to home accessories, everything here carries a price tag to match its label. We wait for the sales.

Saks Fifth Avenue

(Prudential Plaza),
800 Boylston St.
(617) 262-8500
Open Mon. & Wed.
10 a.m.-9 p.m., Tues. &
Thurs.-Sat. 10 a.m.-6 p.m.,
Sun. noon-5 p.m.

The Boston Saks isn't very big, but its selection of designer dresses and sportswear can't be beat. Ralph Lauren, Anne Klein and Perry Ellis hold court here, as does a Chanel boutique and a salon of couture evening dresses. On the second floor is the best department for petites in the city.

FOOD

Bay State Lobster

379-395 Commercial St.
(617) 523-7960
Open Mon.-Wed. 8 a.m.-
5:30 p.m., Thurs.-Fri.
7 a.m.-6 p.m., Sat. 7 a.m.-
5:30 p.m., Sun. 8 a.m.-
1 p.m.

If you want to surprise the folks back home with a New England lobster dinner, Bay State Lobster will ship its crustaceans anywhere and guarantee that they'll arrive fresh for dinner. Of course, you can also arrange to have a lobster sent home to yourself.

Berenson's

(Faneuil Hall Marketplace),
Quincy Market
(617) 523-1206
Open Mon.-Sat. 9 a.m.-
9 p.m., Sun. 11 a.m.-7 p.m.

One of the last of the original tenants of the old Quincy food market, Berenson's features great, luscious cuts of red meat. This is a butcher extraordinaire among the frenzied fast-food counters in the center of the granite Quincy Market building, which is the center of Faneuil Hall Marketplace.

Coffee Connection

Seven locations
around town
(617) 254-1459
Open daily; hours vary.

Boston's caffeine mainline. In these stores you can get your fix of beans from Brazil, Guatemala, Kenya, Kona and Sumatra, including espresso and mocha java blends. Got the jitters? Try a water-process decaf. Cut coffee out of your life? Sample one of the almost 40 teas, including chamomile, gunpowder green tea, jasmine and Risheehat Darjeeling. Coffee Connection also runs an active mail-order business.

L'Espalier's Great Food Store

443A Boylston St.
(617) 262-3023,
(617) 536-6543
Open Mon.-Sat. 7 a.m.-
7:30 p.m., Sun. 9 a.m.-
5 p.m.

If you get a craving for caviar, truffles or smoked salmon—and who doesn't from time to time?—stop in here to take out some, as well as exotic meats, breads and pâtés. The Back Bay shop is tiny and a little hard to find (it's below street level), but the fresh turkey, roasted Cornish game hens, celeriac rémoulade and Linzertorte make it a must visit. The sandwiches served at lunch are perfect for al fresco picnics on a Commonwealth Avenue bench.

Polcari's

105 Salem St.
(617) 227-0786
Open Mon.-Sat. 8 a.m.-
6 p.m.

On the corner of Salem and Parmenter streets in the North End, Polcari's is a treat for the eye and the nose—the store is packed with bags of coffee beans, bins of nuts and boxes of herbs. Even if you're not in a buying mood, you owe it to your nose to go in for a whiff.

Trio's

222 Hanover St.
(617) 523-9636
Open Mon.-Sat. 9 a.m.-
6 p.m., Sun. 9 a.m.-1 p.m.

For 30 years, Tony and Genevieve Trio have had a shop in the ultra-Italian North End, specializing in—you guessed it—pastas and sauces. A trip to this gleaming little shop will reward the most Italian-minded cook with a world of macaroni shapes and flavors.

GIFTS

Communications

40 Charles St.
(617) 523-0884
Open Mon.-Sat. 10 a.m.-
10 p.m., Sun. noon-7 p.m.

When we're looking for the imaginative and artistic, we treat ourselves to a half hour at this card shop with a difference. Communications shines with its selection of jewelry, T-shirts, toys and ceramics. The back corner harbors the raunchy naked-men cards, but in the front of the shop are hand-printed and hand-painted cards. Recent finds have included a serving tray shaped like a coiled alligator, a quite useless but handsome painted wood Dalmatian and a collection of handbags fashioned from wrapping papers and wrapped in clear plastic. The music is always too loud, but if it weren't, browsers would probably never leave.

Eric's of Boston

38 Charles St.
(617) 227-6567
Open Mon.-Sat. 10 a.m.-
6 p.m., Sun. noon-6 p.m.

Eric's is next door to Communications on Charles Street, but, like Bilzerian and Brooks Brothers, couldn't be further away in taste. Nothing offensive is ever found at Eric's, where wrapping papers, stationery and pretty cards depicting Boston scenes, speak in dignified hushed tones. The kiddies will like to look at the charming doll house exquisitely furnished with miniature furniture; parents would rather not look at the prices.

Faneuil Hall Marketplace

Off Congress St.
(617) 523-3886

The granddaddy of them all, Faneuil Hall Marketplace is 160 shops stocked with things you don't really need. There are three buildings here: the central Quincy Market, a riot of food vendors, is flanked by the bilevel granite North and South Market buildings. Outside, tourists, kids and more kids crowd around performing mimes and jugglers, window-shop and sit on the benches to eat lunch. This is specialty shopping: Lefty (items for left-handed people), Hog Wild (everything in the shape of pigs), Purple Panache (everything purple) and Have a Heart (everything covered with red hearts). There are well-known chains: Crabtree & Evelyn, The Limited, Ann Taylor, The Nature Company. Marketplace Center, at the eastern end of the Marketplace, is home to Sisley, Pavo Real, Banana Republic and Sharper Image (which makes its patrons wait in line to enter the store on weekends). If you need a respite from getting and spending, duck into historic Faneuil Hall, where the history is free.

Harvard Coop
(Harvard Square),
1400 Massachusetts Ave.,
Cambridge
(617) 492-1000
*Open Mon.-Wed. & Fri.-
Sat. 9:20 a.m.-5:45 p.m.,
Thurs. 9:20 a.m.-8:30 p.m.*

Officially the Harvard Cooperative Society, the Coop (pronounced like the chicken house) is a Cambridge tradition—since 1882. Here the budding Harvard scholars get their first dorm-room appliances, their underwear, their sweaters. Here you can pick up a Harvard sweatshirt, T-shirt, mug and an assortment of other collegiate necessities emblazoned with the college's name. The record department, befitting college students, is one of the best, and the bookstore is renowned in a city of bookstores. There are also branches in Boston and other areas of Cambridge.

Kennedy Studios
31 Charles St.
(617) 523-9868
*Open Mon.-Fri. 10 a.m.-
7:30 p.m., Sat. 10 a.m.-
6 p.m., Sun. noon-4:30 p.m.*

These emporia carrying prints, posters and cards seem to pop up all over Boston like mushrooms after a rainstorm. They all feature bright and cheery watercolors of Beacon Hill streets, Back Bay, the Public Garden and other scenic sites around Boston. If you are looking for a pictorial reminder of the city that's not a snapshot, one of these views will do quite nicely. There are three branches in downtown Boston, too.

La Ruche
174 Newbury St.
(617) 536-6366
*Open Mon.-Sat. 9 a.m.-
5:30 p.m.*

If you love hand-painted ceramic ware as much as we do, you too will love La Ruche. Imports from Italy, France and Portugal include dishes, bowls, cups and hefty mugs in a rainbow of pastels. Interspersed is an eclectic collection of antiques and potpourris and assorted pricey knickknacks. The small store looks like a room of wedding presents, and the stuff is all beautiful.

Women's Educational and Industrial Union
356 Boylston St.
(617) 536-5651
*Open Mon.-Fri. 10 a.m.-
6 p.m., Sat. 10 a.m.-5 p.m.*

In 1877 a group of concerned Boston women decided to quit fretting about the city's socially disadvantaged and do something. The result was, and still is, the Women's Educational and Industrial Union. The store, which helps fund the group's philanthropic services, is the kind of place where grandmother got all that stuff: quilted knitting bags, embroidered hand towels, painted place mats, needlepoint canvases of the swan boats in the Public Garden. Here the absolutely proper Bostonian—the type who doesn't buy hats—feels utterly at home. Unless you're a grandma, you may not find anything you need, but you'll have a lot of fun browsing and people watching.

WHERE TO FIND...

A BABYSITTER

Parents in a Pinch
(617) 739-KIDS
Mon.-Fri. 8 a.m.-4 p.m.

This four-year-old agency can help out on short notice with babysitting for an afternoon or for over night.

A DRUGSTORE

Phillips Drugs
153-159 Charles St.
(617) 523-1028
Open daily 24 hours.

The only drugstore in town open 24 hours, Phillips is at the corner of Cambridge and Charles streets at the foot of Beacon Hill.

FORMALWEAR (MEN)

High Society
39 Newbury St.
(617) 266-4774
*Open Mon.-Fri. 11 a.m.-
5:30 p.m. (last fitting
5 p.m.), Sat. 11 a.m.-5 p.m.
(last fitting 4:30 p.m.).*

This store carries the latest in tux looks, but also has a selection of 1920s vintage suits to choose from.

**Read & White
Tuxedo Rentals**
54 Chauncey St.
(617) 542-7444
*Open Mon. & Thurs.
9:30 a.m.-7 p.m., Tues.-
Wed. & Fri.-Sat. 9:30
a.m.-5 p.m.*

Since 1914, the fitters at Read & White have been dressing Boston properly.

FORMALWEAR (WOMEN)

Botnes
118 Newbury St.
(617) 247-1957
*Open Mon., Wed. & Fri.
10:30 a.m.-8 p.m., Tues.,
Thurs. & Sat. 10:30 a.m.-
6:30 p.m.*

Caught with a sudden invitation to a fancy dinner and nothing to wear? Botnes, a small third-floor shop in Back Bay, rents dresses, skirts and tops to help you out of such a scrape. The store also sells its slightly used formalwear at greatly reduced prices.

A GIFT WRAPPER

Wrappers
(Prudential Plaza),
800 Boylston St.
(617) 266-9051
*Open Mon.-Fri. 7:45 a.m.-
6 p.m., Sat. 9 a.m.-6 p.m.,
Sun. noon-5 p.m.*

Do you get all nervous at the thought of having to wrap a present? This store will take the anxiety out of your hands—literally. Having at their beck and call two dozen paper designs and 100 ribbons, plus cards, balloons and all sorts of package paraphernalia, these people are experts in tying bows and making any package look great. Wrappers is also a UPS drop-off, so they can ship boxes, too.

A MESSENGER

Marathon Messenger Service
553 Boylston St.
(617) 266-8990
*Open Mon.-Fri. 7 a.m.-
5 p.m.*

This fleet of messengers comes recommended by many of the city's top hotel concierges.

A NEWSSTAND

Out of Town News
Harvard Square,
Cambridge
Open daily 6 a.m.-midnight.

No matter how out of town you are, you'll probably find word from home at this stand, which sits right in the center of the square.

A RECORD

Tower Records
360 Newbury St.
(617) 247-5900
*Open Mon.-Sat. 9 a.m.-
midnight, Sun. 10 a.m.-
midnight.*

The world's largest record store, Tower has three bright floors crammed with compact discs, records and cassettes of everything from the Motels to Mussorgsky.

A TAILOR

Pacifici of Boston
19 Hawley St.
(617) 426-7920
*Open Mon.-Fri. 8:30 a.m.-
6 p.m.*

You've just made the buy of the century at Filene's Basement—trouble is, the dress you got for $40, which was marked down from $400, is a size 12 and you wear an 8. Better see Mike Uva, owner of Pacifici, a men's and women's tailoring shop conveniently located around the corner from the Basement. Work is excellent and fast, and rates are reasonable. Uva will even talk you out of something if he thinks it's really not that alterable.

A TRANSLATOR

Academia Translation Service
11 Mount Auburn,
Cambridge
(617) 354-6110
*Open Mon.-Thurs. 9 a.m.-
9 p.m., Fri. 9 a.m.-6 p.m.*

These multilingual experts can provide an interpreter and translate technical documents.

Berlitz Translation Services
437 Boylston St.
(617) 266-6858
*Open Mon.-Fri. 9 a.m.-
7 p.m., Sat. 9 a.m.-1 p.m.*

If Berlitz can't translate it, maybe it shouldn't be read.

SIGHTS

THE SMALL-TOWN CITY

Boston is a city with a past. Far more than from the trendy shops or the skyscrapers that seem to be sprouting daily, Boston's character and charm derive from its 350 years of history. What's more, that history continues to live and breathe. You can still stumble over cobblestones (wear sensible shoes) on your way to shop at the market building Peter Faneuil gave the city in 1742. You can still have lunch at the Union Oyster House in the rooms where King Louis Philippe gave French lessons while in exile. You can ride to sea with rough-and-ready mariners or nod to socialites strolling the Commonwealth Avenue mall.

Thanks in part to that constant communion with the past, Boston remains, in spirit, a small town—or, perhaps more accurately, a conglomeration of small towns. More than any other major American city, Boston is a city of neighborhoods, each with its own temperament and texture.

The first ones that come to mind are Beacon Hill and Back Bay, the traditional dwelling places of "proper" Bostonians. Yet historically, Beacon Hill was a neighborhood divided—between the Brahmins' red-brick mansions on the slope facing the Common and the north-slope rooming houses where their servants and other working-class Bostonians lived. (Today, the division is moot, since just about everything on both sides has gone condo.) Back Bay, land reclaimed from the Charles River with landfill, made similar class distinctions more gradually, becoming progressively less fashionable as one moved west from Arlington Street. Nevertheless, Back Bay remains gracious, with its wide, straight vistas. And then there's the South End, which tried so hard to be another Back Bay but never quite made the grade of fashion and respectability. Now, after decades of decline, the neighborhood is attracting affluent, committed professionals back to the city.

Not every Bostonian is an upper-crust Yankee—in fact, few cities offer greater ethnic diversity. As a seaport, Boston has always been a gateway for immigrants, who have left their stamp on vibrant neighborhoods. Take the North End, for example. The first immigrants to settle there, the British colonists, gave way over the years to the Irish (Rose Fitzgerald Kennedy was born in the North End), Jews and, later, to the Italians, who predominate today. Now a few Asians are moving in—along with the inevitable yuppies. Meanwhile, Irish pride reigns in the working-class neighborhoods of South Boston (affectionately called "Southie") and Charlestown. Roxbury is the center of the black community, while Boston's Chinatown thrives as the third largest in the United States.

Not surprisingly, Bostonians have developed a strong sense of turf. Unfortunately, they don't always roll out the welcome mat. The most heavily publicized instance was the rioting over court-ordered busing for school desegregation in the mid-1970s. Although the city has calmed down considerably since then, racial incidents do occur on occasion.

No visit to Boston would be complete without a sashay through Cambridge across the river. Cambridge is neither a part of Boston nor a suburb, but a separate city with a strong character of its own. It's the home of Harvard University and the Massachusetts Institute of Technology, plus a number of smaller schools, and the heavily academic population gives the city an air of youth, freedom and liberal thinking. Especially in Harvard Square, there's a feeling in the air that anything can happen.

If you'd like to find out what is happening around the city, visitor-information centers are located on Boston Common (Tremont Street side, near Park Street station) and at the Prudential Center. The National Park Service also runs information centers at 15 State Street near the Old State House and at Charlestown Navy Yard near the U.S.S. *Constitution*. And Cambridge Discovery Inc. runs an information booth outside the main entrance to Harvard Square station.

EXCURSIONS

Beacon Hill & Back Bay

The two neighborhoods that say "Boston" best, where even window glass and wrought-iron fences have their own historical markers, make a pleasant unguided stroll any time of year. (But tread carefully: Sloping brick sidewalks can be slippery when wet.) Starting at the State House, walk west on Beacon Street to Joy Street; then climb the hill to Mount Vernon, the handsome street of brick row houses and free-standing mansions that once marked the boundary between the "right" and the "wrong" sides of the hill. Turn left down Mount Vernon to Louisburg Square, the private park that is one of Boston's most photographed sights. Continuing down Mount Vernon, turn left onto W. Cedar Street, pausing to look up the cobbled alley that is Acorn Street. At the end of Cedar, turn right onto Chestnut Street. Follow

Chestnut to Charles Street, the "main street" of the village that is Beacon Hill, and enjoy lunch or browse the antiques shops. Then stroll across the Public Garden to Back Bay. Take your pick of the streets, depending on whether you prefer the stately brownstones lining Commonwealth Avenue or the boutiques of Newbury Street. Better yet, leave time for both.

The Black Heritage Trail
(617) 742-1854

Not far off the Freedom Trail are many reminders of an often-neglected side of America's heritage. Throughout the nineteenth century, the north slope of Beacon Hill was home to a large black community. The center was the tiny street known as Smith Court, off Joy Street, where today typical homes of the era provide a pretty oasis in the heart of the city. Also on the trail are the African Meeting House, 8 Smith Court, the oldest black church still standing in America; the Charles Street Meeting House, built in 1807, site of many abolitionist meetings; and the Robert Gould Shaw and 54th Regiment Memorial at Boston Common, just across Beacon Street from the State House. A bas-relief by Augustus Saint-Gaudens, considered a masterpiece of public sculpture, commemorates the North's first black regiment in the Civil War. Trail maps can be picked up at the Boston Common Visitor Information Center.

The Freedom Trail

The best introduction to Boston, old and new, is this self-guided walking tour that starts out on the corner of Boston Common at Tremont and Park streets. Follow the red-brick road (or, in some spots, the red line painted on the sidewalk) to many of Boston's most historic sights. Among them are the Old Granary Burying Ground, the final resting place of famous American figures ranging from patriot Samuel Adams to Mother Goose; King's Chapel, the first Anglican church in Boston; the site of America's first public school, where Benjamin Franklin learned his letters; the Old State House, where the Declaration of Independence was first read to the people of Boston; the triangle in the middle of State Street that marks the site of the Boston Massacre; and, in the North End, Paul Revere's house and the Old North Church. The Freedom Trail continues across the Charlestown Bridge to Bunker Hill Monument and the U.S.S. *Constitution*, but that's a long walk if you've already had a full day. Freedom Trail maps are available at the Boston Common Visitor Information Center.

Harborwalk

Once the ocean practically licked the east steps of Quincy Market, but no more. Today the waterfront area—the neighborhood of the Boston Tea Party Ship, Museum Wharf and the New England Aquarium, among other attractions—alone is worth a visit, preferably by both land and sea, using

106

one of the boat lines that operate from Long Wharf or Rowes Wharf (see "Tours" in this chapter). Harborwalk is marked by a blue line on the sidewalk (similar to The Freedom Trail's red line). Visitor information centers and most hotels can supply maps for a self-guided walking tour.

Harvard Square & Brattle Street

For a taste of Cambridge at both its best and its quirkiest, spend a day in the vicinity of Harvard Square. Wander into Harvard Yard, or sign up for the walking tour that leaves from Harvard's Holyoke Center on Massachusetts Avenue in the Square. (Free tours are offered Monday to Friday at 10 a.m. and 2 p.m. and Saturday at 2 p.m. during the school year; in summer, tours are Monday to Saturday at 10 a.m., 11:15 a.m., 2 p.m. and 3:15 p.m., Sunday and holidays at 1:30 p.m. and 3 p.m.) Then head down Brattle Street, past the shops and restaurants to the red-brick buildings of Radcliffe College, the onetime home of poet Henry Wadsworth Longfellow, and Tory Row, a residential street of pre-Revolutionary homes. Wind your way back to the square via Cambridge Common, or backtrack toward the Charles River and relax in the peace and quiet of the riverfront park behind the John F. Kennedy School of Government. Whatever path you choose, be sure to leave time to browse the bookstores, the boutiques, the cafés and, most of all, the street life—they all make the square anything but square.

LANDMARKS

Boston Garden
150 Causeway St.
(617) 227-3200

Conveniently located at North Station, the big, boxy Garden (you can see it from the Central Artery) is known primarily as the home of the Celtics and Bruins teams. It's also used for ice shows, circuses, college graduations and rock concerts—any event that draws a crowd.

Boston Light
Little Brewster Island,
Boston Harbor

Built in 1716, Boston Light is the nation's oldest lighthouse, and one of the last dozen to be manned. (Automation is scheduled for 1990.) Many of the Outer Harbor cruises pass the Light, but it's a fairly well-kept secret that people are welcome to visit Little Brewster and climb the lighthouse. Most of the time you have to bring your own boat, and the Coast Guard prefers that visitors call in advance (617-925-1801) to check tide conditions. But the Friends of the Boston Harbor Islands have several cruises each year to Little Brewster; for dates, call (617) 523-8386.

Boston Public Library

666 Boylston St.
(Copley Square)
(617) 536-5400
*Open Mon.-Thurs. 9 a.m.-
9 p.m., Fri.-Sat. 9 a.m.-
5 p.m., Sun. 2 p.m.-6 p.m.
Admission free.*

From the Dartmouth Street doors sculpted by Daniel Chester French to the great hall inside, this pseudo–Italian Renaissance building, designed by Charles McKim in 1895, is a Boston classic. Avoid the new wing and bask in the nineteenth-century grandeur. The library has frequent exhibitions of books, art and photography, as well as murals painted by John Singer Sargent and Puvis de Chavannes; call or check local newspapers for current information.

Bunker Hill Monument

55 Constitution Rd.,
Charlestown
(617) 242-5641
*Open daily (except major
holidays) 9 a.m.-4:30 p.m.
Admission free.*

Climb the 294 steps to the top of the monument, if you like—but don't fire until you see the whites of their eyes. The National Park Service maintains the obelisk commemorating the Battle of Bunker Hill, as well as an exhibit area with dioramas and photographs explaining the Revolutionary War battle. Also in Charlestown, the Bunker Hill Pavilion (55 Constitution Road, near the U.S.S. *Constitution*, 617-241-7575) presents a multimedia slide show with fourteen screens and seven channels of sound reenacting the battle. The show starts every half hour daily from 9:30 a.m. to 4 p.m. (6 p.m. in summer). Admission is $3 for adults, $2 for seniors and college students with ID, $1.50 for children and $8 for families (two adults and up to six children).

Christian Science Center

Massachusetts Ave.
& Huntington Ave.
(617) 450-2000
*Open Mon.-Sat. 9 a.m.-
4:15 p.m., Sun. 11:15 a.m.-
4:15 p.m.
Admission free.*

In 1879 Mary Baker Eddy established the Church of Christ, Scientist, and she built her Mother Church in Boston in 1892. Just as Christian Science has grown into a religion observed worldwide, the Mother Church has become the centerpiece of a modern complex that houses the Christian Science Publishing Company and the church offices. The public is welcome to visit Back Bay's Mother Church, the Mapparium (see "Museums" later in this section), the publishing house, the broadcast center and "A Light Unto My Path," an audio-visual exploration of the Bible. Call for tour schedules. The public is also invited to services in the Mother Church on Sunday at 10 a.m. and 7 p.m. and on Wednesday at 7:30 p.m. Free parking is available (for services only) at the center's underground garage.

Faneuil Hall Marketplace

Off Congress St.
(617) 523-3886

A consulting firm once said it would be folly to renovate the run-down merchant and warehouse building between the waterfront and the Government Center into a retail-and-restaurant complex. Bostonians, the consultants said, would not go downtown to shop and would not spend the money to eat out. Boston and the millions of visitors who pass through each year have proved them wrong. Now in its second decade, Faneuil Hall Marketplace (often called Quincy Market, after its central building) has been a major force in Boston's downtown revitalization, and now just about every major city has followed with an imitation "Quincy Market" of its own.

Fenway Park
24 Yawkey Way
(off Brookline Ave.)
(617) 267-8661

Face the Green Monster, the famous left-field wall at the home of the Boston Red Sox, but don't be intimidated. More than 75 years old, Fenway Park remains one of the most intimate major-league ballparks in the country. The season opens in early April and runs through September—sometimes into the World Series, if the Sox have a good year.

John Hancock Tower
Copley Square
(617) 247-1976
Open Mon.-Sat. 9 a.m.-
10:15 p.m., Sun. noon-
10:15 p.m. Adults $2.75,
seniors & children $2.

Many Bostonians still don't care for I. M. Pei's 740-foot mirror-glass tower (they remember when the new building's windows used to pop out), but its 60th-floor observatory does have the best views in town. On a clear day, you can see the mountains of New Hampshire and well into the South Shore, as well as Boston's many distinct neighborhoods and landmarks. The Hancock also plays a taped commentary by late historian Walter Muir Whitehill and has special presentations on the city's history and its people. (Runner-up in the room-with-a-view category is the 50th-floor Skywalk at the Prudential Center, 617-236-3318, from which you can see the Hancock in context.)

Harvard University
Harvard Square,
Cambridge
(617) 495-1000

Founded in 1636, Harvard is America's oldest university and has the reputation as one of the best—and most elitist. Its undergraduate college and array of graduate schools, in fields ranging from law and business to education and design, have produced not only many of the Boston area's greatest minds and leaders but the nation's as well. To the casual sightseer, Harvard offers a fascinating mix of architecture covering the full range of the school's 350-plus years, as well as several world-class museums (see "Museums" in this section).

Massachusetts State House
Beacon St. & Park St.
(617) 727-3676
Tours Mon.-Fri. 10 a.m.-
4 p.m. Admission free.

Boston is not only Massachusetts's largest city but its capital as well. The gold-domed structure built by Charles Bulfinch in 1795 is actually the "new" State House (the old one is on State Street, a few blocks away). Inside, look for the impressive rotunda and the Sacred Cod, a four-foot homage in pine to the fish that has sustained the Bay State nutritionally and economically since its founding. In 1988 the State House began a ten-year renovation project that may affect some galleries, but most artworks are expected to be back in place by the time you read this.

Old North Church
193 Salem St.
(617) 523-6676
Open daily 9 a.m.-5 p.m.
Admission free.

Given the North End's domination by immigrant groups over the last century or two, it's easy to lose sight of the fact that this was the first site of the city of Boston. Paul Revere lived in the neighborhood (at 19 North Square; his 1676 wooden house, open to the public, 9:30 to 4:15 daily, except Mondays January to March, 617-523-1676, is the oldest building in Boston), and he began his famous ride by waiting on his horse in Charlestown, across the bay, for the signal from the Old North Church. The lanterns ("One if by land, two if by sea") were hung in the white steeple that still can be seen from many points in Boston, and from the harbor as well. The church, built in 1723, is Boston's oldest and is still in use.

Park Street Church

Park St. & Tremont St.
(617) 523-3383
Open in July-Aug., during services or by appt.

William Lloyd Garrison orated for abolition here. The Reverend Lyman Beecher (Harriet Stowe's father) preached here. The white-spired brick church across from Boston Common has long been a spiritual and intellectual center for right-thinking Bostonians. It's also the source of the carillon heard downtown throughout the day.

South Station

Atlantic Ave. & Summer St.

Though overshadowed by one skyscraper after another, the Beaux Arts facade of South Station remains inspirational in a sea of modernism. It's the terminus for Amtrak's northeast corridor service from New York and Washington. Since the mid-1980s the station has been undergoing major renovations that should soon leave it once again a classic of transportation design.

Trinity Church

Copley Square
(617) 536-0944
Open daily 8 a.m.-6 p.m. Admission free.

Though better known in recent years as the building reflected in the John Hancock Tower, Trinity Church has a distinguished architectural history of its own. Henry Hobson Richardson had already begun drawing up the plans when the original Trinity Church, at what is now Downtown Crossing, fell victim (along with most of the rest of downtown) to the Great Fire of 1872. The present French Romanesque–style church, built entirely on wooden pilings, is considered a masterpiece of American architecture. If you're in Boston around the Christmas or Easter holidays, check newspaper listings for special services and concerts at the church.

U.S.S. *Constitution*

Charlestown Navy Yard, Charlestown
(617) 242-0543
U.S.S. Constitution: open daily 9:30 a.m.-3:50 p.m.; admission free.
Constitution Museum: open daily 9 a.m.-5 p.m.; adults $2, seniors $1.50, children 6-16 $1, children under 6 free.

If "floating landmark" isn't a contradiction in terms, then the U.S.S. *Constitution* fits the description to a T. The U.S. Navy's oldest fully commissioned warship (1794) gained her better-known nickname, "Old Ironsides," when she withstood bombardment by British cannon fire in the War of 1812. Today the ship is docked placidly at Charlestown Navy Yard, except for July 4, when she makes her annual turnaround cruise (to ensure that the tides will wear evenly on the timbers). The ship is a masterpiece of marine craftsmanship, and guided tours are led by U.S. Navy personnel in period costume. Across the pier, the Constitution Museum contains historical documents and items relating to the *Constitution*'s history.

MUSEUMS

Boston Tea Party Ship and Museum
300 Congress St.
(Museum Wharf)
(617) 338-1773
Open daily 9 a.m.-5 p.m.

Guides costumed as Revolutionary patriots will show you around this working model of the *Beaver*, the ship on which the Colonists sent a message to George III that they found his tea too taxing. Each December, on the Sunday nearest December 16, the protest is reenacted. The ship's museum is included in the admission price, and tea is served free.

Adults $3.25, children 5-12 $2.25, children under 5 free.

Children's Museum
300 Congress St.
(Museum Wharf)
(617) 426-6500
Open Tues.-Thurs. & Sat.-Sun. 10 a.m.-6 p.m., Fri. 10 a.m.-9 p.m.; also open Mon. during Boston school vacations & holidays.

You don't need to be accompanied by a child to enjoy this museum. Exhibits favor hands-on, participatory experiences—which, in recent years, have ranged from circus performances to a re-creation of a Chinese market.

Adults $4.50, seniors & children 2-15 $3.50, children under 2 free.

Computer Museum
300 Congress St.
(Museum Wharf)
(617) 423-6758
Open Tues.-Thurs. & Sat.-Sun. 10 a.m.-6 p.m., Fri. 10 a.m.-9 p.m.

The talking computers that answer your call for information give an amusing introduction to the Computer Museum's user-friendly approach. Two floors of exhibits trace the development of the computer from room-size Univacs to today's ever-shrinking laptops. Exhibits feature films (including a videotape of the first time a computer was used to predict presidential election returns) and hands-on exhibits.

Adults $4.50, seniors & students $3.50, children under 5 free; admission half price Fri. evening.

Isabella Stewart Gardner Museum
280 The Fenway
(617) 566-1401
Open Tues. noon-6:30 p.m., Wed.-Sun. noon- 5 p.m.

Mrs. Jack (as she was known around town) may have started life as a New Yorker, but she ended up as a leading, if not entirely proper, Bostonian. (Among other outrageous acts, she used to parade her pet ocelot up and down the street.) After she built her Italian palazzo along The Fenway to house her exclusive art collection, one visitor remarked that no Bostonian need bother to travel to Rome, since Mrs. Jack had brought most of it to Boston. Her remarkably large—and rather eccentrically displayed, according to Mrs. Jack's firmly held notions regarding art and interiors—collection is particularly strong on Italian Renaissance paintings and seventeenth-century Dutch Masters; highlights include paintings by Vermeer, Titian's *Rape of Europa* (considered the greatest Titian in the New World), John Singer Sargent's *El Jaleo* and his portrait of Mrs. Jack. And paintings are just the beginning—the collection also comprises manuscripts, books, tapestries, furniture and some 2,000 sculptures and objects. Built around a flower-filled courtyard, the three-story museum also hosts frequent chamber- music concerts. Suggested donation $3, seniors & students $1.

Harvard University Museums

Art museums: Quincy St., Cambridge
(617) 495-2397
Natural history museums:
24 Oxford St. &
11 Divinity Ave.
(617) 495-1910
Art museums: open Tues.-Wed. & Fri.-Sat. 10 a.m.-5 p.m., Thurs. 10 a.m.-9 p.m., Sun. 1 p.m.-5 p.m.; Natural history museums: open Mon.-Sat. 9 a.m.-4:30 p.m., Sun. 1 p.m.-4:30 p.m.

One of the world's richest universities (it owns much of Cambridge) also has some of the world's richest museums, and they're open to the public. Art lovers will enjoy the famous Fogg, 32 Quincy Street, for its collections of American, European and impressionist works, and the newer Sackler, 485 Broadway at Quincy Street, which is known for its ancient, Asian and Islamic art. The Busch-Reisinger, 24 Kirkland Street, is noted for its Central and Northern European works of art from the Middle Ages to the present and for its collection of musical instruments. Those interested in natural history should visit Harvard's complex of four museums—the Museum of Comparative Zoology, the Botanical Museum, the Mineralogical and Geological Museum, and the Peabody Museum of Archaeology and Ethnology—fronting on either Oxford Street or Divinity Avenue. We recommend in particular the Botanical Museum, with its famous collection of glass flowers.

Art museums: Adults $3, seniors & students $1.50, children under 18 free.

Natural history museums: Adults $3, children $1.50 (good for all 4 museums); admission free Sat. morning.

Institute of Contemporary Art

955 Boylston St.
(617) 266-5151
Open Wed. & Sat.-Sun. 11 a.m.-5 p.m., Thurs.-Fri. 11 a.m.-8 p.m.

Occupying half of a Back Bay firehouse built in 1886, the ICA offers rotating exhibits of contemporary painting, sculpture, photography and drawing. Working artists sometimes give demonstrations on the premises. The ICA Cinema also runs frequent film series and video art programs.

Adults $4, students $2.50, seniors & children $1.50; admission free Fri. 5 p.m.-8 p.m.

John F. Kennedy Library and Museum

Columbia Point
(617) 929-4500
Open daily 9 a.m.-5 p.m.

John F. Kennedy may have been associated in the public mind with "Haahvaad," but when it came time to build his presidential library, his family chose to place it on the grounds of a public school—the Boston campus of the University of Massachusetts in the city's depressed Dorchester section. They made a wise choice, for I. M. Pei's breathtaking window-walled creation looks out on the ocean Kennedy loved. Inside, the library offers a 30-minute film on Kennedy's life, as well as displays of memorabilia. (For another perspective on the Kennedy legend, visit the modest house at 83 Beale Street, Brookline, 617-566-7937, where the president was born. The National Historic Landmark is open daily 10 a.m. to 4:30 p.m. Admission is $1; seniors and their guests are admitted free.)

Adults $2.50, seniors $1.50, children under 16 free.

Mapparium

Massachusetts Ave.
& Huntington Ave.
(Christian Science
Publishing Co.)
(617) 450-2000
*Open Mon.-Sat. 8:15 a.m.-
4:15 p.m., Sun. 11:15
a.m.-4:15 p.m.*

The world may have changed since 1935, but not at the Mapparium. Here's your chance to experience Earth from the inside out. Visitors walk inside a 30-foot stained-glass globe showing the nations of the world as they appeared when the Mapparium was built. There's still only one Germany, and the map of Africa looks quite different from its contemporary counterpart. A ten-minute talk provides explanations of the exhibit. The globe also makes a crackerjack whispering gallery.

Admission free.

Museum of Fine Arts

465 Huntington Ave.
(617) 267-9300
*Open Tues. & Thurs.-Sun.
10 a.m.-5 p.m., Wed.
10 a.m.-10 p.m.; West
Wing open Thurs.-Fri.
5 p.m.-10 p.m.*

You could spend a lifetime inside Boston's leading art museum and never be bored. The MFA is world famous for its large collections of important Greek, Roman, Egyptian, Asian, European and American art; of particular note are its exceptional impressionist paintings (Monet, Degas), its medieval tapestries, its Buddhist temple and its paintings by such American masters as John Singer Sargent, James McNeill Whistler (*Girl in a White Dress*) and Gilbert Stuart. As one would expect of a museum of this caliber, the MFA attracts blockbuster exhibitions, including the paintings of Renoir, the treasures of Alexander the Great, and Andrew Wyeth's Helga series. Although known as a stately old building, in recent years the MFA added a spectacular West Wing (designed by I. M. Pei) for special exhibitions, refurbished its Evans Galleries for European and American paintings and opened a full-service restaurant and an extensive museum shop.

Adults $5 during hours when entire museum is open, $4 during hours when only West Wing is open, seniors $4, children under 16 free; admission free Sat. 10 a.m.-noon.

Museum of Science

Science Park
(617) 742-6088
*Open Mon.-Wed. 9 a.m.-
6 p.m., Thurs.-Sun. 9 a.m.-
9 p.m.*

With exhibits ranging from astronomy to zoology, the Museum of Science takes a participatory approach that makes the natural sciences accessible to adults and children alike. In addition, frequent special exhibits have focused on cultures ranging from China to Kenya to ancient Egypt. Also on the Cambridge grounds are the Hayden Planetarium and the Omni Theater, with its four-story circular screen that sends you flying through space or rolling down a river. Omni tickets go fast, especially on weekends, so it pays to call for reservations.

Museum or Omni Theater tickets: adults $5, seniors & children 4-14 $3; combination tickets: adults $7.50, seniors & children $5; planetarium only: adults $4, seniors & children $2.50 (children under 4 not allowed).

New England Aquarium

Central Wharf,
off Atlantic Ave.
(617) 742-8870
*Open Mon.-Thurs. 9 a.m.-
5 p.m., Fri. 9 a.m.-9 p.m.,
Sat.-Sun. & holidays
9 a.m.-6 p.m.*

A living museum of the best kind, the New England Aquarium features more than 2,000 species of fish and sea mammals from around the world. Its massive central tank demonstrates interaction among various sea animals. Shows featuring performing dolphins and sea lions are held daily on the Discovery, the floating theater adjacent to the Aquarium. For the best free show in town, visit the seals in the outdoor tank near the aquarium's main entrance.

Adults $6, seniors, military personnel & students $5.

PARKS & GARDENS

Arnold Arboretum

The Arborway
(617) 524-1718
Open daily dawn-dusk.

This 265-acre park in Jamaica Plain is home to more than 7,000 varieties of trees. Special displays include an herbarium, greenhouses and an exhibit of bonsai trees—not to mention an excellent horticultural bookstore (open Tuesday to Sunday 10 a.m. to 4 p.m.). Although its sylvan paths make the arboretum a favorite spot for joggers, we would advise them, particularly women, to avoid running alone here.

Admission free.

Back Bay Fens

The Fenway

Back in the last century, when landscape visionary Frederick Law Olmsted designed the "Emerald Necklace," the park system that would encircle Boston, the Fens was one of its major gems. The necklace has shrunk considerably over the years, but the Fens remains a major parcel still devoted to parkland. Located just behind the Museum of Fine Arts, the park includes a 1940s-vintage "victory garden," open to all green-thumbed Boston residents, and a rose garden. One word of warning: The Fens is considered unsafe after dusk.

Boston Common

Downtown Boston
(bordered by Beacon,
Park, Tremont, Boylston
& Charles sts.)

The Common (never say "Boston Commons"—there's only one) is the oldest public park in America, and Beacon Hill residents still have the right to graze their cattle there. But these days you're more likely to see people jogging, sledding, cooling off under the sprinkler in the Frog Pond or listening to concerts. The Common is generally safe during daylight hours, but we advise against walking alone here at night. One of the city's larger parking garages is located beneath the Common; the entrance is on the Charles Street side, and there's a shuttle-bus service to other points downtown.

Boston Harbor Islands State Park
Boston Harbor
(617) 749-0051

Of the 30 or so islands in Boston Harbor, seven (so far) constitute a state park. These are accessible by boat from most cruise lines operating along Long Wharf and Rowes Wharf. The gateway is Georges Island, site of a Civil War fort, from which free water taxis carry visitors to other islands for hiking, picnicking, swimming and even overnight camping. The state and a nonprofit group, the Friends of the Harbor Islands (617-523-8386), sponsor special events on the islands from early spring through mid-November.

Boston Public Garden
Downtown Boston
(bordered by Beacon, Charles, Boylston & Arlington sts.)

Situated just across the street, the Public Garden is Boston Common's dressier sister. Its Arlington Street side marks the beginning of Back Bay. Inside the park is a large but shallow lagoon devoted to placid swan-boat cruises in warm weather and ice skating in winter. During the spring-through-fall months, the plantings change monthly. The Public Garden is decorated with some of Boston's most notable statuary, including George Washington on horseback; nineteenth-century orators; a column commemorating the first use of ether as an anesthetic, at nearby Massachusetts General Hospital; and a new addition, the Make Way for Ducklings group celebrating the classic children's book.

Charles River Esplanade
Boston side of the Charles River

Like Back Bay, this band of green was reclaimed from the Charles River in the nineteenth century. Technically, it stretches from the Museum of Science to Newton, but the widest part goes from the museum to the Boston University area. In addition to paths for walking, biking and roller-skating (in warm weather, watch the impromptu performances in front of the Hatch Shell), the Esplanade is the site of the Hatch Shell, with its live music and dance performances; Community Boating, Inc., the public club where those picture-postcard sailboats dock; several public pools run by the Metropolitan District Commission; and the outdoor Publick Theater. To reach the Esplanade, cross Storrow Drive by footbridges; the most accessible ones from Back Bay are located at Arlington and Dartmouth streets and at Massachusetts Avenue. Memorial Drive on the Cambridge side of the river completes a pleasant circuit for a run or long walk.

Christopher Columbus Park
Commercial St. near Long Wharf

Named for a hero of the adjacent, heavily Italian North End, this waterfront park isn't just a patch of green in an increasingly asphalt jungle, but one of the few remaining harbor views from street level downtown. A recent addition is a rose garden in honor of Rose Fitzgerald Kennedy.

115

TOURS

BY AIR

When you fly into Logan International Airport on a clear day, there's a fringe benefit: a fine view of Boston and the harbor, free of charge. If that whets your appetite for more, call the Boston Heliport, 31 Fargo Street, South Boston (617-482-4702). The heliport will schedule rides with one of its tenants for up to four passengers. Tours range from a basic six-to-eight-minute view of Boston (about $50) to a one-hour custom itinerary for four (about $500). The people at the heliport prefer to receive reservations as far in advance as possible but can sometimes accommodate same-day requests.

BY BUS

If you don't care to walk, you can see the city and even avoid taking on the notorious Bostonian behind the wheel. Two companies, Old Town Trolley Tours (617-269-7010) and Beantown Trolleys (617-236-2148), use San Francisco–style cable car bodies mounted on flatbed trucks. The basic tours, which stop at the majority of the major hotels, cover most downtown points of interest in about 90 minutes. You also can buy an all-day ticket and hop on and off at will.

The Gray Line (617-426-8805) runs tours year-round on more conventional motor coaches. The basic three-hour Boston tour follows the Freedom Trail as well as visiting Beacon Hill, Back Bay, the Waterfront and the university areas of Cambridge. Tours leave from the Gray Line office at 275 Tremont Street, and at the Quality Inn, with pickups at other hotels on request. The Gray Line also runs day trips to such areas as Lexington, Concord, Plymouth, Salem, Cape Cod and Martha's Vineyard.

You might think you're in London when you board a Boston Double-decker (617-661-1875). In summer these bright-red buses offer a basic Freedom Trail tour that can double as a shuttle between sights. Double-deckers run continuously from the corner of Boylston and S. Charles streets in Park Square.

If you're staying in the suburbs along Route 128, there's no need to take the car into the city. Boston Tours (617-899-1454) runs six-hour excursions into the city using passenger vans. The tour, which does not pick up passengers downtown, covers most of the city and Cambridge, with stops at the U.S.S. *Constitution*, Old North Church, Faneuil Hall Marketplace and the Mapparium.

BY FOOT

Boston is a pleasant, compact walking city, and Boston By Foot (617-367-2345) leads excellent walking tours. Four regular tours—the heart of the Freedom Trail, Beacon Hill, the North End and Copley Square—are given daily except Monday; admission is $5. In addition, a "tour of the month," which focuses on a specific neighborhood, is offered spring through fall for $6, and a children's tour, "Boston By Little Feet," will keep the kids amused for $3. Boston By Foot also books special tours for groups.

For foreign visitors, a taped tour of the Freedom Trail is available in French, German and Japanese. The tape, produced by Boston Walkabouts, sells for $10.95 at the Globe Corner Bookstore, 3 School Street (617-523-6658).

BY SEA

Boston Harbor is worth a tour in itself, but it's also a good vantage point for seeing the city. Several cruise lines run similar harbor tours from downtown docks several times a day from mid-April through mid-October. Your choice will probably be based on convenience of location and departure time. Most cruises cover either the Inner Harbor (U.S.S. *Constitution*, waterfront piers, Logan International Airport) or the Outer Harbor (harbor islands, Boston Light). Fares average $5 to $6.

From Long Wharf (near the New England Aquarium), Bay State Provincetown Cruises (617-723-7800) hosts 55-minute cruises of the Inner Harbor and 90-minute cruises of the Outer Harbor, with stops at Georges Island. Bay State also runs whale-watching expeditions, the daily boat to Provincetown and daily ferry service to Martha's Vineyard. Boston Harbor Cruises (617-227-4320) runs a similar itinerary, as well as lunchtime cruises ($1, lunch not included) twice a day in summer. At Rowes Wharf, Massachusetts Bay Lines (617-749-4500) has three sightseeing trips a day, luncheon cruises, sunset cruises Wednesday through Friday evenings and dinner boats.

The Spirit of Boston (617-542-2974), more a floating restaurant than a sight-seeing boat, cruises the Outer Harbor from Pier 7 on Northern Avenue. Afternoon cruises serve a clambake, evening trips a sit-down dinner. Prices are in the $20-to-$30 range per person, depending on the meal and the day of the week.

CUSTOM TOURS

What's your passion? Pub crawls? Chocolate? Antiques? If you'd like to see a special side of the city, Uncommon Boston (617-731-5854) will design a tour just for you. Prices start at $20 per person and range upward depending on the length of tour, form of transportation, admissions and so on. Uncommon Boston also offers a calendar of public tours, such as "A Victorian Christmas," "Graveyards and Goodies" (for Halloween), "Back Bay Beauties" (a walking tour of parks and buildings) and "Boston Architecture." Requests must be received at least one week in advance by telephone or in writing at 437 Boylston Street, Fourth Floor, Boston, MA 02116.

BOSTON ENVIRONS/ EASTERN MASSACHUSETTS

ACTON

SHOPS

Handworks
452 Great Rd. (Rte. 2A)
(508) 263-1707
Open Mon.-Wed. & Fri.-
Sat. 10 a.m.-5:30 p.m.,
Thurs. 10 a.m.-8 p.m.

If you're in the Concord/Lexington area and looking for handmade gifts, take a short side trip to this well-stocked shop, which concentrates primarily on cooking and serving ware, jewelry, children's toys and miscellaneous items of decor. The work is basically functional, traditional and of good quality, though the animal and floral motifs can get rather precious.

FALL RIVER

SIGHTS

Battleship Cove
Interstate 195
(508) 678-1100
Open daily 9 a.m.-5 p.m.
(except Thanksgiving,
Christmas & New Year's
Day).

For a close-up look at U.S. naval history in this century, check out Battleship Cove, the permanent home port for *Big Mamie*, a 35,000-ton battleship that logged more than 225,000 miles during World War II without losing a single man; the U.S.S. *Joseph P. Kennedy Jr.*, which saw action in both Korea and Vietnam; one of only two World War II PT boats on public display; and the U.S.S. *Lionfish*, an intact World War II submarine. Admission to Battleship Cove also includes the Marine Museum, which brings back, through ship models and memorabilia, the glory days of travel by sail and steam, particularly on the old Fall River Line, which ran between New York and New England for 90 years before closing down in 1937. The museum also presents *Titanic* exhibits.

Adults $6, children 6-13 $3, children under 6 free.

Fall River Heritage
State Park
100 Davol St.
(508) 675-5759
May-Oct.: open daily
9 a.m.-8 p.m.; Nov.-April:
open daily 9 a.m.-5 p.m.

Not far from Battleship Cove is Fall River Heritage State Park, which centers on a new mill building built to the plans of an old mill that once stood on this site, on the banks of the Taunton River. Relive those mill-town days by watching "The Fabric of Fall River," a 30-minute multimedia slide show on the city's history and textile industry.

Admission free.

The Fall River Historical Society
451 Rock St.
(508) 679-1071
Open Tues.-Fri. 9 a.m.-4:30 p.m., Sat.-Sun. 1 p.m.-5 p.m.

Occupying a former mill owner's mansion filled with period furnishings, china and glass, the Historical Society offers a different perspective—the opulent one—on the textile industry. Also on view is an exhibit on Fall River's most infamous native daughter, accused ax murderess Lizzie Borden.

Adults $2, children 10-16 $1, children under 10 free.

FRAMINGHAM

SIGHTS

Danforth Museum of Art
123 Union Ave.
(508) 620-0050
Open Wed.-Fri. noon-4:30 p.m., Sat.-Sun. 1 p.m.-4:30 p.m.

Not all of New England's fine-art museums are in the major cities. The Danforth Museum of Art hosts changing exhibits of traditional and contemporary art, with a special emphasis on its children's gallery. The permanent collection ranges from Old Masters to nineteenth- and twentieth-century American art.

Adults $2, seniors & children $1.

GLOUCESTER

SIGHTS

The Fishermen's Monument facing the harbor is famous the world over as a symbol of the seafaring heritage of this Cape Ann town. The Gloucester Fishermen's Museum (Rogers and Porter streets; 508-283-1940) also pays homage to the town's men who went to sea, with both hands-on exhibits on the early fishing industry and whale watching in season.

If the arts do more for you than the sea, visit Rocky Neck in East Gloucester, one of the earliest artists' colonies on the East Coast, or the imposing Hammond Castle Museum (80 Hesperus Avenue, 508-293-7673), a medieval castle transplanted to the Atlantic coast that is famous for its collection of medieval and Renaissance art and its 8,600-pipe organ. Another institution on the North Shore arts scene is the Gloucester Stage Company (267 Main Street, 508-281-4099). Led by playwright Israel Horovitz, the theater, housed in The Gorton Playhouse, a former fish-packing plant, has premiered many of Horovitz's plays.

HAMILTON

SIGHTS

Myopia Hunt Club
Rte. 1A
(508) 468-7956
*May-Oct.: polo matches
Sun. 3 p.m.*

Tally ho! What's a trip to New England without a day spent among the hunt-and-polo set? The oh-so-upper-crust Myopia Hunt Club sponsors summertime polo matches on Sunday afternoons, with the gates opening at 1 p.m. Occasionally there are special *Town & Country*–style events, such as tailgate picnics with caviar and champagne served from the hoods of Rolls-Royces (bring your own). The horsey set is blessed with another spot in Hamilton: the training center for the U.S. Olympic equestrian team (292 Bridge Street, 508-468-7377), open Monday to Saturday 8 a.m. to noon. The equestrian team's show-jumping talent derby is usually held here in early September.

Adults $5, children under 12 free.

IPSWICH

SIGHTS

The waters off the North Shore are definitely colder than those south of Boston, but that doesn't stop New Englanders from flocking on hot summer days to Crane's Beach on Argilla Road. The wealthy family of Richard Crane enjoyed the coastal breezes at Castle Hill, their elegant mansion now used primarily for private parties and special events. But Castle Hill is open for tours four days a year, once a month in April, July, October and December; admission is $5 for adults and $2 for seniors and students. In summer, chamber-music concerts are held on the grounds (see "Music Festivals" chapter). For current information, call (508) 356-4351.

DON'T FORGET: Gault Millau introduces you to the Best of New York, the Best of Washington D.C., the Best of Los Angeles, the Best of San Francisco, the Best of Chicago, the Best of France, the Best of Paris, the Best of Italy, the Best of London.

LEXINGTON & CONCORD

QUICK BITES

Willow Pond Kitchen
754 Lexington Rd., Concord
No phone
Open Mon.-Sat. 11 a.m.- 11 p.m., Sun. 1 p.m.- 11 p.m.
No cards.

There's nothing Colonial about this original New England diner on the historic road between Lexington and Concord—this kind of Americana comes from the 1930s and '40s. It was only a few years ago that the owners took out the individual jukebox selectors at each table. Fortunately, that's the only modernizing mistake they've made, simply because they haven't attempted any others: still the same pine paneling on the walls, still the same moth-eaten stuffed wildcats snarling down from their shelves, still the same pub-like local regulars (though a few high-tech and military personnel from nearby installations sneak in now and then). The prices haven't changed much, either. You can get a tasty, hearty seafood dinner—a sandwich, a bowl of steamers, an overflowing lobster roll—for well under $10, sometimes under $5. And all the rolls are homemade to boot.

SIGHTS

Among American history buffs, the names of Lexington and Concord are usually intoned together with great respect, for here (despite years of preliminaries in Boston) the concept of revolution took hold and became a full-fledged war. In Lexington, the center of activity remains the town green, where Minutemen faced the Redcoats in the early hours of April 19, 1775. The Museum of Our National Heritage ties the story together with its rotating exhibits and films on American history. The museum (Routes 2A and 4; 617-861-6560) is open Monday to Saturday 10 a.m. to 5 p.m. and Sunday noon to 5 p.m.; admission is free.

"The shot heard 'round the world" was actually fired in nearby Concord, in the midst of 750 placid acres in what is now Minuteman National Historic Park off Route 2A (508-369-6944). The Minuteman Memorial by sculptor Daniel Chester French stands guard at the little reconstructed wooden bridge, whose modesty belies the original's importance as a symbol of the American Revolution. From the bridge, move into the Battle Road Visitor Center for a film and exhibits on the Revolution. It is open April to November, daily 8:30 a.m. to 5 p.m.; admission is free.

While in Concord, drop in on the nineteenth century's transcendental-ist intellectuals and popular novelists. Two of Ralph Waldo Emerson's dwellings still stand: the Emerson House, Cambridge Turnpike at Lexington Road (508-369-2236; open mid-April to mid-October, Thursday to Saturday 10 a.m. to 4:30 p.m., Sunday 2 p.m. to 4:30 p.m.; admission is $2.50 for adults, $1 for children), where the philosopher lived from 1835 to 1882, and the Old Manse, better known for Nathaniel Hawthorne's tenure there, on Monument Road (508-369-3909; open June 1 to October 31, Monday and Thursday to Saturday 10 a.m. to 4:30 p.m., Sunday 1 p.m. to 4:30 p.m.; mid-April to May, weekends only; admission is $3 for adults, $2.50 for senior citizens, $1.50 for children 6 to 16). Louisa May Alcott and family also lived in Concord, at Orchard House, 399 Lexington Road (508-369-4118). The house is open for narrated tours April to October, Monday to Saturday 10 a.m. to 4:30 p.m., Sunday 1 p.m. to 4:30 p.m.; Sundays only in November. Admission is $3 for adults, $2.50 for senior citizens and $1.50 for children 6 to 17. Many Concord intellectuals, including the Alcotts, Emerson, Hawthorne and Henry David Thoreau, are buried at Sleepy Hollow Cemetery on Route 62.

Also just off Route 2 is Walden Pond State Reservation. The pond where Thoreau went to be alone and philosophize is now a popular summertime spot for swimming and sunning—it's a bit less peaceful than in Thoreau's day, but some still find his spirit among these trees.

LINCOLN

SIGHTS

Although generally a very private town, and one of Boston's ritziest bedroom communities (much loved among the horsey set), Lincoln has two outstanding public attractions.

**DeCordova
Museum and Park**
Sandy Pond Rd.
(617) 259-8355
*Open Tues.-Thurs.
10 a.m.-5 p.m., Fri.
10 a.m.-9 p.m., Sat.-Sun.
noon-5 p.m.*

The DeCordova Museum serves as a cultural center for the visual and performing arts. Its 30-acre park includes a dramatic modern-sculpture garden.
    Adults $2, seniors & children $1.

**Drumlin Farm
Wildlife Sanctuary**
Rte. 117
(617) 259-9807
*Open Tues.-Sun. 9 a.m.-
5 p.m. (open holiday Mon.
9 a.m.-5 p.m.).*

Headquarters of the Massachusetts Audubon Society, Drumlin Farm makes for a wonderful family outing (especially for city-slicker kids), with New England farm animals, hiking, hay rides in warm weather and sleigh rides in cold.
Adults $4, children $2, children under 3 free.

LOWELL

SIGHTS

**Lowell National
Historical Park**
246 Market St.
(508) 459-1000
*Open daily 8:30 a.m.-
5 p.m.*

Lowell's history is a tale of haves (wealthy nineteenth-century textile-mill owners) and have-nots (the poor children and young women who kept the mills' wheels spinning). Lowell National Historical Park, built around one of the restored mill buildings, presents an audio-visual introduction to the old-time Lowell, which was not only an industrial center but a hotbed of nineteenth-century feminism and the labor movement. Barge and trolley tours are also offered in summer.
Admission free.

**New England
Quilt Museum**
256 Market St.
(508) 452-4207
*Open Tues.-Sat. 10 a.m.-
4 p.m., Sun. noon-4 p.m.*

The more artistic side of New England textile work is on view at the New England Quilt Museum, whose permanent collection includes specially commissioned pieces by New England quilt artists, as well as antique quilts and donations from the New England Quilters Guild. Aficionados should stop in on Saturday mornings, when demonstrations are held.
Admission $2.

Whistler House
243 Worthen St.
(508) 452-7641
*Open Tues.-Fri. & Sun.
1 p.m.-4 p.m.*

Although he didn't like to admit it, expatriate artist James McNeill Whistler was born in Lowell in 1834. His birthplace houses historical exhibits and a collection of American impressionist paintings.
Admission $2.

MARBLEHEAD

QUICK BITES

Delphin's Gourmandise
285 Washington St.
(617) 639-2311
Spring & summer: open Tues.-Thurs. & Sat. 7 a.m.-6 p.m., Fri. 7 a.m.- 7:30 p.m., Sun. 7 a.m.- 5 p.m.
No cards.

After fourteen years of apprenticeship in his native France, Delphin Gomes was startled to find himself considered a master pâtissier at Los Angeles's L'Ermitage restaurant—being too humble and too dedicated to his art to presume such a title at home. After a few years of increasing impatience with the novelty-for-novelty's-sake view of California cuisine, Gomes moved his operation across the country to a historic red-wooden house in his wife's picturesque seacoast hometown. In this humble house he makes only classic French pastries—opera, napoleon, sucées, tartelette, brioche. At first, he had a hard time winning the locals over to such things as croissants *without* fillings, but before long the quality of his products won out. Now Delphin's is a town fixture, supplying everything from finely decorated wedding cakes to a place to meet for coffee and pastries (incidentally, it also supplies desserts for a growing number of Boston's upscale restaurants). Specials and hours change seasonally, and you'll find the best selection earlier in the morning.

SIGHTS

That's pronounced Marble-*HEAD*. One of the prettiest (and priciest) North Shore towns, Marblehead is a more chichi version of Boston's coastal suburbs. The town itself is the main attraction, with its harbor views, posh restaurants and cute boutiques, but it also offers several historic houses open to the public. The Jeremiah Lee Mansion (161 Washington Street, 617-631-1069), a Georgian mansion built in 1768, was the home of a pre-Revolutionary merchant; its three floors are furnished in period pieces, with original wallpaper and paneling. It's open mid-May to mid-October, Monday to Saturday 10 a.m. to 4 p.m.; admission is $2.25. The 1728 King Hooper Mansion (8 Hooper Street, 617-631-2608) serves as the home of the Marblehead Arts Association. The town's most famous artwork, though, is the Revolutionary icon "Spirit of '76," housed in the selectmen's room of the Victorian Abbot Hall in Washington Square (617-631-4056). It's open from late May to October, daily 9:30 a.m. to 5 p.m.; November to late May, weekdays 9:30 a.m. to 5 p.m.

NEW BEDFORD

SIGHTS

As any reader of *Moby Dick* knows, the words *New Bedford* and *whaling* were practically synonymous for much of the nineteenth century. Although the city today has a rather seedy reputation, new shops and restaurants have helped spruce it up in the last several years. The whaling era lives on, though, at the Whaling Museum (18 Johnny Cake Hill; 508-997-0046), which traces the history of the great marine hunt through ship models, scrimshaw displays, paintings and period rooms. Open Monday to Saturday 9 a.m. to 5 p.m., Sunday 1 p.m. to 5 p.m.; admission is $3 for adults, $2.50 for senior citizens and $2 for children. Other points of interest include the schooner *Ernestina* at Steamship Wharf, a gift from the Cape Verde islands (many Cape Verdean immigrants have settled in the New Bedford area); the lightship *New Bedford* at State Pier, open for boarding in summer; and the New Bedford Glass Museum (50 N. Second Street, 508-994-0115), the repository for more than 1,500 pieces of Pairpoint and Mount Washington glass. Open Monday to Saturday 10 a.m. to 4 p.m., Sunday 1 p.m. to 5 p.m. (to 4 p.m. October to April); admission is $2 for adults, $1.50 for senior citizens and students, and free for children under 6.

NEWTON CENTRE

SHOPS

Jubilation
91 Union St.
(617) 965-0488
*Open Mon.-Sat. 10 a.m.-
5:30 p.m.*

Jubilation is aptly named—the ceramics, glass and jewelry here all accent the fresh, the flip, the contemporary. No beige oven-to-table stoneware here; the functional pieces are brightly colored and as arty as they come.

QUINCY

SIGHTS

This city just south of Boston (and accessible by subway) bills itself as "the Presidents' City," and with good reason: It was the home of the second, John Adams, and the sixth, his son John Quincy Adams. They were born in the pair of modest saltbox houses at 133 and 1441 Franklin Street known in town as "the birthplace"; the surprisingly humble houses are open daily from mid-April to mid-October. Later, as the family prospered, John and Abigail bought and enlarged a home at 135 Adams Street in Quincy Center that served as the family seat for four generations. Now the Adams National Historical Site (617-773-1177), the estate has been beautifully restored, and the National Park Service leads excellent tours from mid-April to mid-November. The $2 admission price includes tours of the birthplaces.

Abigail Adams, of course, was part of the Quincy clan, and the homes of some of her relatives—the Josiah Quincy House (20 Muirhead Street, 617-227-3956) and the Quincy Homestead (34 Butler Road, 617-472-5117)—are also open to the public. Abigail herself was born in a 1685 farmhouse at Norton and North streets in nearby East Weymouth, which is open July 4 to Labor Day, Tuesday to Sunday 1 p.m. to 5 p.m. The early Adamses are buried in United First Parish Church in Quincy Center. The Quincy Historical Society, housed in the old Adams Academy building on the site where John Hancock was born, has its own museum on the city's history. It's located at 8 Adams Street in Quincy Center (617-773-1144) and is open Monday to Friday 9:30 a.m. to 3:30 p.m., Saturday 12:30 p.m. to 3:30 p.m.; admission is free. The Historical Society also runs a research library, which is open Monday, Wednesday and Saturday.

Unless otherwise noted, the prices given for restaurants are for a complete dinner for two, including an appetizer, main course and dessert. The prices also include tax, fifteen-percent tip and one of the least expensive bottles of wine on the wine list. Please don't hold it against us if you end up spending a bit more!

PLYMOUTH

SIGHTS

In Plymouth, as the song goes, everything old is new again. Ever since 1620, when the Pilgrims stepped ashore onto the famous Rock, Plymouth has considered itself "America's hometown." Although this working-class town (the largest in Massachusetts) lacks the spit and polish of such fashionable coastal communities as Marblehead, it retains its dedication to history.

Plymouth has plenty of public parking, and it's smart to leave the car and either walk or take the three-mile trolley tour that runs every fifteen to twenty minutes between major attractions. The logical starting point is Plymouth Rock, now enclosed in a Greek Revival pavilion in the Pilgrim Memorial State Park along the waterfront. A short walk away, at State Pier, you will find the *Mayflower II*, a full-scale replica of the surprisingly small trading vessel in which the Pilgrims crossed the Atlantic. The ship is open for tours by guides in costume and character: April to November, daily 9 a.m. to 5 p.m. (to 6:30 p.m. mid-June to Labor Day); admission is $3.75 for adults and $2.75 for children. The *Mayflower II* is an exhibit of Plimoth Plantation, a museum village three miles from the town center on Route 3A. The village re-creates life in 1627, when Plymouth was a tiny but prospering farming community overlooking the ocean. Open year-round 9 a.m. to 5 p.m., the Plantation (508-746-1662) costs $7.50 for adults and $4.75 for children.

Other Plymouth museums include Pilgrim Hall, 75 Court Street (508-746-1620), the nation's oldest public museum, which dates from 1824 and houses many items that belonged to the Pilgrims (open daily 9:30 a.m. to 4:30 p.m.; adults $3, children $1), and the Plymouth National Wax Museum (16 Carver Street; 508-746-6468). The town also contains a number of historic homes that are open to the public; check for details at the visitor information booth just off Court Street in the center of town.

Plymouth County remains the center of production for Massachusetts's largest agricultural crop: cranberries. Ocean Spray, Inc., the growers' cooperative, has established Cranberry World, a lively museum depicting the importance of the bouncy red berry. Cranberry World (225 Water Street, 508-747-1000) is open April 1 to November 30, daily 9:30 a.m.

to 5 p.m. (9:30 a.m. to 9 p.m. in July and August); admission is free. You can also see working cranberry bogs throughout much of Plymouth County, but perhaps nowhere more pleasantly than on the Edaville Railroad in nearby South Carver. Vintage narrow-gauge trains steam through an 1,800-acre cranberry plantation. The railroad (508-866-4526) is open daily throughout the year, with hours varying by season. And should your travels bring you to Plymouth in the winter, don't miss the railroad Christmas light display, which runs from early November to early January.

If you happen to be in the Plymouth area during Thanksgiving weekend, stick around for a patriotic dinner. On Thanksgiving Day, the Plymouth Chamber of Commerce (508-746-3377) serves a traditional turkey dinner at Memorial Hall on Court Street, with several seatings that accommodate up to 1,800 people a year. Plimoth Plantation also sponsors holiday dinners during the last weekend of its season; in 1987, it instituted a series of authentic seventeenth-century menus. For up-to-date plans, call the plantation at (508) 746-1622.

ROCKPORT

INNS

Inn on Cove Hill
37 Mount Pleasant St.
(508) 546-2701
Closed Nov.-March.
Cash & personal check only.

If for some reason you feel compelled to visit hugely commercial Rockport, with its too-cute tourist boutiques and competitive foot traffic, check into this sweet inn. After a day of crushing popcorn and taffy underfoot, dodging falling ice cream cones and tripping over toddlers, you'll need this place to recover. We are especially fond of the Inn on Cove Hill in autumn, when the hordes of tourists are home watching football. The 200-year-old home has been converted to an attractive eleven-room inn, in which new furnishings blend successfully with antiques—the soft colors, pencil-post canopy beds, lovely wallpaper, stunning spiral staircase and country wreaths combine to create a most inviting setting. Breakfast is served in bed during the winter and outdoors in the summer garden when it's warm. Seven different muffins tempt hungry guests each morning, all baked by owner John Pratt and delivered by his gracious wife, Marjorie. The gardens are pretty here, Marjorie fills the inn with sweet touches (sprigs of bittersweet, pumpkin displays, flowers), and the atmosphere is restful. The inn also makes a fine base for exploring the beautiful Cape Ann coast.

Rooms: $38-$75, including breakfast.

SIGHTS

You can't miss Motif No. 1, the fishermen's shack on Bearskin Neck that has served as the model for innumerable paintings—good, bad and indifferent. That's a fitting introduction to Rockport, the touristy Cape Ann town that, perhaps more than any other in New England, exemplifies the sea's attraction for artists in particular. Rockport has been a famous artists' colony for decades, and in summer both the galleries and the sidewalks swarm with them—and not everybody's painting Motif No. 1. The Rockport Art Association (12 Main Street; 508-546-6604) is a good rainy-day bet, with exhibitions and demonstrations by local artists and seasonal visitors.

SALEM

SIGHTS

The witches of New England are still alive, in Salem at least—practically every street corner carries some reminder of the infamous witch trials, be it a historic house that was actually standing in 1692 or a souvenir shop selling T-shirts, bumper stickers and tarot cards. But there's more to Salem than witches. After the trials, the town went on to become a major seaport in the China trade. The Salem Maritime National Historic Site (508-744-4323) near Pickering Wharf, the restaurant-and-shopping complex on the waterfront, makes a good starting point for walking the Salem Heritage Trail, which includes two museums, the Essex Institute and the Peabody Museum; the House of the Seven Gables, the same one made famous by Nathaniel Hawthorne; the Witch House, the restored home of one of the witch-trial judges; and the Salem Witch Museum, which offers an audio-visual show on that troubled time.

The House of the Seven Gables (54 Turner Street; 508-744-0991) is located in the historic East End, an area filled with gems of working-class Federal-style architecture being restored largely by affluent refugees from Boston. One that is emphatically *not* being restored is the Narbonne House, one of the last dozen seventeenth-century half houses (half one style, half another) still standing in New England. The National Park Service has decided to leave the house standing as is, in disrepair, to illustrate the progression of building techniques over the centuries. The Narbonne House is open for Sunday tours from May to September; call (508) 744-4323 for reservations. On the other side of town stands Salem's Historic District, where the gracious homes of whaling captains preside like grande dames over the city.

Incidentally, the witch hysteria actually took place not in Salem proper, but in Salem Village in what is now Danvers. There, at 149 Pine Street, still stands the home of Rebecca Nurse, one of the women executed in 1692 for practicing witchcraft. The house is open mid-June to mid-October, Tuesday to Saturday, or by appointment; call (508) 774-8799.

SEEKONK

SHOPS

Leonard's
600 Taunton Ave. (Rte. 44)
(508) 336-8385
Open Mon.-Sat. 8 a.m.-
5 p.m., Sun. 1 p.m.-5 p.m.

The Leonards are into their second generation of selling antiques, and you couldn't hope to find a nicer family to guide you through this labyrinthine store and assist you in finding the perfect antique bed. Known as "the bed kings" to insiders, the Leonards have supplied many a New England innkeeper with an innful of antique beds, stretched to fit today's king-size physiques. The reasonable prices (restoration is extra, provenances are rare) make it possible to outfit your entire home here; everything you could possibly need is available from the enormous inventory.

SUDBURY

SIGHTS

Longfellow's
Wayside Inn
Rte. 20
(508) 443-8846
Open daily 10 a.m.-9 p.m.

Henry Wadsworth Longfellow wrote down his *Tales of a Wayside Inn*, but new ones are taking place every day. Longfellow's Wayside Inn, which served as the inspiration for the book, has been restored to the way it appeared in 1700; it serves dinners by firelight and still has ten overnight guest rooms. Visitors are welcome to browse whenever the inn is open; a 50-cent donation to the historical fund is requested. The grounds also include a working gristmill, with a miller on duty every day.

Admission 50 cents.

WELLESLEY

SHOPS

The Gifted Hand
32 Church St.
(617) 235-7171
*Open Mon.-Sat. 10 a.m.-
5:30 p.m.*

The Gifted Hand specializes in Tasteful. These are the kinds of crafts one imagines genteelly complementing the decor of the immense homes around Wellesley College; many of the artists represented in the shop's broad selection are widely shown elsewhere. What is special, however, is the large, well-displayed collection of quilts, most with traditional patterns.

CAPE COD & THE ISLANDS

CAPE COD & THE ISLANDS

THE CAPE COD SPIRIT

As far north as Buzzards Bay or even Plymouth, you'll feel the Cape Cod spirit riding in on the ocean breeze. But you haven't officially arrived until you've crossed the Cape Cod Canal, itself a sight worth seeing. Cut through the "shoulder" of the Cape to save seagoing vessels the long trip around, the canal divides mainland Massachusetts from the hook-shaped peninsula that's the state's all-around favorite vacationland. Two high, graceful bridges—the Sagamore, which connects Route 3 with Route 6 to Hyannis, and the Bourne, connecting with Route 28 to the Upper Cape—make travelers think they're soaring across the canal from one state of mind to another.

Although they offer no scenic overlooks, the bridges do afford some excellent views. Of particular interest is the Cape Cod Railroad Bridge, at 534 feet the second-tallest vertical lift bridge in the world. Using counterweights in towers to raise and lower the track, the railroad bridge looks a bit like a skeletal version of London's Tower Bridge. Passengers on trains to the Cape feel as if they're just skimming the surface of the water.

To set the tone for a trip "down the Cape," cruise the canal from Onset Town Pier on the north side. Cape Cod Canal Cruises (508-295-3883) runs sight-seeing boats from early May through Columbus Day. Another good way to become acclimated to the Cape is to walk or cycle the paths along the canal's south bank.

Barnstable County, which covers the entire Cape, and Dukes and Nantucket counties (Martha's Vineyard and Nantucket Island, respectively), comprise dozens of small communities, many of which boast comfortable inns, solid New England restaurants, local museums, historic houses and public beaches—the best of which we've uncovered for you in the listings that follow.

Keep in mind that everything on the Cape and the islands is seasonal. Each summer, new restaurants, inns and shops spring up, only to die down again when the foliage withers and autumn nights grow cold. Sometimes the establishments just change hands, sometimes they change names, sometimes locations. But each summer vacation at the Cape is a time of rediscovery. Some places close completely in the off-season, and some close sporadically. In the larger towns, a few restaurants and shops are open year-round, or nearly so; there's generally some kind of agreement that if the local coffee shop closes in January, the bar down the block that serves food won't close until February, so the small community of year-rounders will have *someplace* to meet and eat.

BARNSTABLE VILLAGE

INNS

Charles Hinckley House
Old King's Hwy. (Rte. 6A)
(508) 362-9924
Closed Jan.-Feb.
Cash & personal check only.

The Charles Hinckley House is like a secret garden. Miya Patrick and her husband, Les, surround themselves and their guests with flowers: Wildflowers decorate the rooms, adorn the breakfast plates and welcome you in the front yard. But it's more than the flowers that make this inn so beautiful—for that we credit Miya's creative vision and Les's considerable prowess at restoration. The Federal-era (1809) house may seem modest (it has just four guest rooms), but it approaches sheer perfection in its authenticity, attractiveness and simplicity: Colonial colors, an understated decor, must-have quilts and a collection of wonderful antiques are skillfully combined to great effect. Our favorite room is the Summer Kitchen, with its massive brass bed, whitewashed barn-siding and country decor.

Miya runs a catering business on the side, and her interest in good food shows in the beautiful house breakfasts—fortunately, her cooking abilities rival her decorating skills. New-age music will envelop you as you devour a complete breakfast of fresh fruit, pastries, scrambled eggs with salmon, poached eggs with crabcakes, a variety of potato dishes and grits. After such fortification, take a walk down Scudder's Lane to Hinckley Pond where you can watch the locals ready their launches for a peaceful day afloat.

Rooms: $105-$135, including breakfast.

> *DON'T FORGET: Gault Millau introduces you to the Best of New York, the Best of Washington D.C., the Best of Los Angeles, the Best of San Francisco, the Best of Chicago, the Best of France, the Best of Paris, the Best of Italy, the Best of London.*

BREWSTER

RESTAURANTS

Chillingsworth
Main St. (Rte. 6A)
(508) 896-3640
FRENCH/AMERICAN
*June 21-Sept. 15: seatings
Tues.-Sun. 6 p.m., 6:30
p.m., 9 p.m. & 9:30 p.m.;
Labor Day-Thanksgiving:
open weekends & some
weekdays, hours vary.
Greenhouse Bar: June
21-Sept. 15: open Tues.-
Sun. 11:30 a.m.-2 p.m.;
Labor Day-Thanksgiving:
weekends & some weekdays
11:30 a.m.-2 p.m.
All major cards.*

Chillingsworth is located in the oldest house in Brewster. But there is nothing old-fashioned about a menu that features duck and prosciutto quesadillas, consommé with chèvre-filled won tons and sautéed skate wings with coral mushrooms and red-pepper mousse. The owners, Pat and Nitzy Rabin, are a rarity among restaurateurs: French-trained chefs who manage to merge the discipline of classical haute cuisine with the whimsy of American nouvelle. Nitzy builds his sauces from laboriously reduced stocks, while Pat turns out towering soufflés and exquisite petits fours; and together they have forged what in our minds is the most estimable restaurant on Cape Cod. Five dining rooms are scattered throughout the 300-year-old house—the largest one seats 40, the smallest, a *gemütlich* two! Throughout the place are working fireplaces, eighteenth-century French furniture, Empire paintings and a museum-quality collection of Napoleona. The service manages to be both professional and down-to-earth, skirting the dual perils of pretentiousness and familiarity. About $135 to $160 for dinner for two, with wine.

CHATHAM

INNS

**Captain's House
Inn of Chatham**
371 Old Harbor Rd.
(508) 945-0127
*Closed Dec.-Jan.
Cards: AE, MC, V.*

Chatham is a lovely coastal village filled with upscale shops and restaurants to amuse the upscale people who summer here. And for those who want to get away from the upscale, there are a wildlife sanctuary out on the point (see "Sights" below) and some lovely, calming beaches. Chatham is also home to Captain's House Inn, the best place in town to stay. The eleven rooms in this 1839 Greek Revival sea captain's home are filled with beautiful antique beds (some with lace canopies), cottage-painted and Early American furnishings, splatter-painted floors and soothing, flattering colors. Each of the rooms, including the three in the separate guest cottage built in 1930, gets its name from one of original owner Captain Harding's ships; one of the best is the large wood-paneled downstairs bedroom, which has a large fireplace. Whichever room you choose, you'll be treated to chocolates and British toiletries.

Owners Cathy and Dave Eakin staff the inn during the summer with British exchange students, who add a civilized accent to the place. These young ladies serve an extensive Continental breakfast and afternoon tea; their grace and accommodating warmth will make your stay very pleasant.

Rooms: $90-$149, including breakfast.

SIGHTS

Monomoy National Wildlife Refuge
(508) 349-2615
(Massachusetts Audubon Society)
Walking tours held April-Dec.; hours vary.

Cape Cod's constantly shifting sands mean that today's peninsula may be tomorrow's island, or may even disappear altogether beneath the waves. The two islands (once attached to the mainland) that make up Monomoy National Wildlife Refuge near Chatham are a prime example. Their stark beaches, wild dunes and sheltering thickets make them a prime habitat for wildfowl, and Monomoy boasts one of the greatest diversities of bird life along the East Coast, with 250 species in residence. The North Island's salt marsh, tidal flats and dunes attract such coastal birds as gulls, terns and plovers; the South Island, with its freshwater ponds, is home to herons, ducks and owls. The Massachusetts Audubon Society leads walking tours of the islands, from spring through early winter.

Tours $30-$45.

FALMOUTH/WOODS HOLE

SIGHTS

Spread out over much of the southwest corner, Falmouth (the largest town on the Upper Cape) is less centralized than many other Cape towns, and the resulting spaciousness is part of its charm. Its long western exposure also gives Falmouth a number of pleasant beaches, the most popular being Monument and Old Silver beaches. (Arrive early on fine summer days; parking is scarce.) Other points of interest include the Katherine Lee Bates Museum, homestead of the well-known author, at 16 Main Street in the center of town (open mid-June to mid-September) and Falmouth Playhouse in Hatchville (508-563-5922), one of the best theaters on New England's professional summer-stock circuit. Off Route 151 in North Falmouth, the Massachusetts Audubon Society's Ashumet

Holly Reservation and Wildlife Sanctuary (508-563-6390) offers self-guided nature walks on trails decked with holly.

If you follow Route 28 through Falmouth and turn right when you reach the Vineyard Sound, the winding road will take you to Woods Hole. Most vacationers know this village as simply a place to kill an hour or two while waiting for ferries to Martha's Vineyard. But Woods Hole has a strong scientific identity as home of the Woods Hole Oceanographic Institute, which studies every aspect of the oceans, from marine life to the remains of the *Titanic*. Also in town, on Albatross Street, is the National Marine Fisheries Aquarium (508-548-5123), run by the U.S. Department of Commerce. The aquarium has sixteen display tanks of exhibits on fish and invertebrates from Cape Cod and the surrounding waters, with two harbor seals in residence June through September. Open from late June to mid-September, daily 10 a.m. to 4:30 p.m.; the rest of the year, weekends 9 a.m. to 4 p.m.; admission is free.

HYANNIS

QUICK BITES

Dockside
53 South St.
(508) 775-8636
Open daily 7 a.m.-1 a.m.
All major cards.

This lively place, popular with tourists and islanders waiting for the Nantucket ferry, does an active bar business, sustaining summer people faced with a two-and-a-half-hour ferry ride surrounded by dogs and enthusiastic children. The bar is crammed with memorabilia, stuffed fish and snapshots of happy times. Dockside also boasts a wrap-around dining area overlooking the marina, with picnic tables outdoors. The food is good, though overpriced, due no doubt to the captive audience (it's the only place to eat at the ferry landing). But if you don't mind paying $5.50 for your child's cheeseburger or $2.95 for a hot dog, Dockside will be a pleasant lunchtime experience. The fare is standard New England seafood: a raw clam and oyster bar; clam, scallop and fish rolls; fried clams, scallops and fish; chowder; and shrimp cocktail with the prerequisite red chile sauce.

SIGHTS

Hyannis is not a place to get away from it all, for it's the "big city" of Cape Cod, its transportation hub and shopping center (witness the traffic jams near the Cape Cod Mall on a Saturday afternoon). Neverthe-less, it has several attractions. Nearby Hyannis Port is famous through-out America as the home of the Kennedy clan. Although you probably won't be invited into the family compound for a touch football game, some of the sight-seeing boats that leave from the Ocean Street docks do cruise past, and it's not unheard of to see young Kennedys out for a sail. In Hyannis proper, you can pay homage to the late president at the John F. Kennedy Memorial on Ocean Street.

The Ocean Street docks are also the starting point for travel to Nan-tucket. It's possible to do a day trip on the Hy-Line (508-775-7185), but start early: The trip takes at least two hours each way. The Hy-Line carries no cars but will accept bikes, (the ideal way to see Nantucket). If you'll be passing an evening in Hyannis, check current listings for the Cape Cod Melody Tent (508-775-9100). Throughout the summer this tented theater-in-the-round plays host to big-name nightclub acts and occasional musical comedies.

MARTHA'S VINEYARD

RESTAURANTS

Beach Plum Inn
North Rd., Menemsha
(508) 645-9454
CONTINENTAL
June 24-Sept. 15: open nightly 6 p.m.-10 p.m.; Memorial Day-June 24 & Sept. 15-Columbus Day: open Wed.-Sun. 6 p.m.-10 p.m.
Cards: AE, MC, V.

If you eat only one lobster a summer, eat it at the Beach Plum Inn. The delectable decapod is smokily grilled for mere minutes and is as succulent as it is sweet. And put the home-baked bread to good use, mopping up the caviar cream sauce. The inn's owners make a virtue of simplicity: There are only five items on the menu per evening, each straightforwardly and competently prepared. The fixed-price menu includes homemade soup (the chowder is excellent, the onion soup, a trifle sweet), a colorful salad of home-grown lettuces and an artery-clogging dessert. Though the selections are usually as far from nouvelle cuisine as you can get—veal dijonnaise, pepper steak, striped (the locals say "stry-ped") bass with lobster sauce—the kitchen doesn't rule out the occasional innovation, such as locally caught bluefish with pesto. The dining room is as uncomplicated as the bill of fare: an airy room with ocean views, a pleasant, college-age staff and tables set with hand-painted plates and wildflowers gathered daily. The menu may seem rather simple-minded, but during the season there's a three-week wait for a reservation, which tells you something. The inn has twelve guest rooms, which are comfortable if plain (see

"Inns" below). Menemsha is a dry town, so don't forget to bring your own wine. About $85 for dinner for two, without wine.

L'Etoile at the Charlotte Inn

S. Summer St., Edgartown
(508) 627-4751
FRENCH
*Mid-June-mid-Oct.: open nightly 6:30 p.m.-9:30 p.m.; mid-Oct.-mid-June: Fri.-Sun. 6:30 p.m.-9:30 p.m.; year-round: seatings for Sun. brunch 10:30 a.m.-12:30 p.m.
Cards: AE, MC, V.*

A velvety asparagus soup harbors butter-rich smoked salmon quenelles. A rabbit salad contains arugula, mâche, frisée lettuce and miniature yellow tomatoes. Lobster arrives in a towering soufflé, served with Pernod-flavored whipped cream. We pinch ourselves—are we really dining in Edgartown, or is this remarkable restaurant a dream? Chef Michael Brisson has brought a level of cooking to Martha's Vineyard that was simply unknown before. It might be called precious; it is definitely recherché; but the kitchen certainly gets an A for effort. Irresistibly chewy rolls are served with silver tongs from a wicker basket. Entrées arrive under silver bell jars. Why, they even gift-wrap the doggie bags! On the down side, the kitchen could do better with the basics: Our salad dressing was hopelessly bland. One thing above reproach is the setting, a greenhouse dining room lush with hanging ferns, filled with exquisite antiques and soothed with two murmuring fountains. After dinner, you can browse amid the paintings in the gallery that occupies three rooms on the ground floor, or toddle off to one of the lovely guest rooms. Two will spend about $130 for dinner with wine.

Feasts

Beetlebung Corner, Chilmark
(508) 645-3553
AMERICAN
*June 15-Labor Day: open nightly 6 p.m.-10 p.m.; Memorial Day-June 15 & Labor Day-Columbus Day: hours vary.
Cards: AE, MC, V.*

12/20

The location is Beetlebung Corner in Chilmark, but it might as well be L.A.—the menu is as ethnically diverse as Ellis Island and as trendy as a SoHo nightspot. There are clams with pesto, pan-blackened bluefish, gazpacho, fajitas and linguine with clam sauce. There are upscale duck breasts (served with locally made beach plum sauce) and down-home ribs, and the sort of rich, gooey desserts, like chocolate bread pudding, that appeal to the child in all of us. Just glorified fast food, really, but the chef starts with first-rate ingredients, such as extra-virgin olive oil and imported Parmigiano Reggiano cheese. The prices will leave you speechless, even before you look at the art in the gallery upstairs. The decor is appropriately contemporary: white walls, cathedral ceilings, high-tech lights, an open kitchen crowned with halogen lamps. Feasts is definitely not a temple of high gastronomy. It's something better: It's fun. Chilmark is a dry town, so remember to bring your own booze. (The kitchen will be happy to prepare mixed drinks as well as pour wine). About $70 or $80 for two, without wine.

Savoir Fare

Post Office Sq.,
Edgartown
(508) 627-9864
AMERICAN
May-Oct.: open Tues.-Sat.
11:30 a.m.-2:30 p.m. &
5:30 p.m.-10 p.m., Sun.
11:30 a.m.-2:30 p.m.;
Nov.-April: open Tues.-
Sat. 11:30 a.m.-2:30 p.m.
Cards: MC, V.

Edgartown has fancier restaurants, and some with better views, but none have the charm and unpretentious perfection of this little place tucked away in Post Office Square. The modest café-style space is given a touch of class (and warmth) with French doors, white linens, candlelight in the evening and an amiable staff. Once you sample the delicious, modestly priced cooking, you'll understand why Savoir Fare is one of the island's most popular caterers. Our last meal began with a perfect Caesar salad and a savory goat cheese tart with thyme and sun-dried tomatoes; progressed to a buttery brioche stuffed with sweet lobster and musky wild mushrooms in a pool of heavenly Cognac cream sauce, and a perfectly cooked pork tenderloin with crispy potato pancakes and a delicious onion marmalade; and ended with good coffee and lovely, simple desserts: a classic apple tart and a rich chocolate mousse cake. With pleasant wine by the glass, this thoroughly agreeable dinner cost two of us just $50, which earns Savoir Fare the title of best good-value restaurant on the island.

QUICK BITES

Black Dog

Vineyard Haven
(508) 693-9223
Open Sun.-Thurs. 7 a.m.-
11 a.m., 11:30 a.m.-2:30
p.m. & 5 p.m.-9 p.m.,
Fri.-Sat. 7 a.m.-11 a.m.,
11:30 a.m.-2:30 p.m. &
5 p.m.-10 p.m.
Cards: AE, MC, V.

Located right on the harbor, the Black Dog serves simple, unpretentious food in a setting to match. The emphasis is on stir-fry at lunchtime and on the freshest from the sea at both lunch and dinner. The chowder and the swordfish are justifiably the most popular dishes here. On inclement days you can sit inside in the dark paneled room, or take to the screened-in porch with its lacquered wood benches. The Black Dog is a local hangout that doesn't take reservations (so be prepared to wait) and doesn't have a liquor license (so bring your own). Lunch for two (burgers, sandwiches) will run about $12; dinner, about $45.

Humphrey's Bakery

State Rd., Vineyard Haven
(508) 693-1079
Open Mon.-Sat. 7 a.m.-
6 p.m.
No cards.

For a mid-morning pick-me-up while exploring the island, do as the locals do and stop at Humphrey's for a cup of coffee and one of the excellent homemade cookies. It's the sort of simple pleasure that you came to this island for in the first place.

Mrs. Miller's Muffins

Mayhew Ln. at the harbor,
Edgartown
(508) 627-9608
April-Oct.: open daily
7 a.m.-7 p.m.
No cards.

As Oscar Wilde said, we can resist everything except temptation. That's why we get weak in the knees when we walk past Mrs. Miller's Muffins, which sends the most devilishly tempting baking aromas into the salty air outside. These muffins live up to their olfactory advance notice—in fact, they're well-nigh the best muffins we've ever had. Such good things as apples, cinnamon, raisins, oatmeal, chocolate chips and various berries and nuts are blended with the utmost skill into warm, incredibly delicious muffins as big as softballs. Even the usually tiresome bran muffin is given new life at Mrs. Miller's. If you stop in at lunchtime, try one of the pizza muffins, which taste much better than they sound. The half dozen or so tables in the cramped shop are always filled with a happy mix of locals and tourists drinking coffee, reading the paper, gossiping and trying to decide if they should order just one more muffin.

INNS

Beach Plum Inn
North Rd., Menemsha
(508) 645-9454
Closed mid-Oct.-mid-May.
Cards: AE, MC, V.

Imagine sipping cocktails surrounded by people as attractive, suntanned and well educated as you, and being served hors d'oeuvres by attractive, suntanned, in-the-process-of-being-well-educated young people, all while watching the sun set over Menemsha Harbor. If this is your idea of island heaven, book yourself immediately into the Beach Plum Inn. You can be assured that Paul and Janie Darrow will do their best to make you feel comfortable, and at the very least, you can expect good service—the inn serves as a sort of boot camp for aspiring food servers/innkeepers, and there's always a waiting list for summer jobs among college students. Paul works hard to turn these young people into overnight pros. His philosophy is to give everyone equal treatment, so your waiter at dinner may be the chambermaid in the morning, and the gardener during the afternoon may be washing dishes at breakfast. But the talented chef, you'll be happy to know, stays put in the well-respected kitchen (see "Restaurants" above). Breakfast is served in the pretty dining room; mushroom-Brie or jelly omelets, waffles, french toast and pancakes are specialties.

The guest rooms are pretty basic—comfortable, cheerful and private. Some have wonderful views of the distant water, and all are serenaded by the gentle sounds of wind chimes. The atmosphere is akin to that of an upscale summer camp, the flowers are beautiful, and the tennis court is always in demand.

Rooms: $120-$225, including breakfast.

Captain Dexter House
100 Main St., Vineyard Haven
(508) 693-6564
Open year-round.
Cards: MC, V.

We most love this intimate inn in the off-season, when you can snuggle up in front of the fire, relax in a cozy room and luxuriate in the knowledge that you won't have to fight tourist traffic and the throngs of summertime pedestrians. Captain Dexter House is one of the most beautiful inns in New England—the eight rooms are jewels, the eighteenth-century furnishings are collectors' items, the artwork is period-perfect, and the atmosphere is luxuriously private. Lara and Beyer Parker have created an exquisite inn that rivals the best. You'll fall asleep by the light of your own fireplace, assured of sweet dreams in a canopy bed surrounded by considerable comfort: Early American art, beautiful wallpaper, cozy chairs and attractive modern bathrooms.

Breakfast leans towards such delicious baked specialties as apple bread, strawberry or lemon muffins and apple-strudel bread. The handsome dining room is so elegant that you may never want to leave the inn to tour the island.

Rooms: $55-$140, including breakfast.

Charlotte Inn
S. Summer St., Edgartown
(508) 627-4751
Open year-round.
Cards: AE, MC, V.

This lovely inn is the sort of place where grandfathers have long treated their young granddaughters to dinner. It's a tradition that continues today with the more sophisticated, upscale cuisine offered in L'Etoile, Michael Brisson and Joan Parzanese's elegantly handsome restaurant (see "Restaurants" above). You will be surrounded by other well-heeled summer people, young and older, who make Edgartown's distinctive landscape so blond and blue-eyed.

The 25 large, comfortable, one-of-a-kind guest rooms in the main house, Summer House, Coach House and Carriage House are blissfully inviting country-style retreats, with tall-post and canopy beds, overstuffed sofas and chairs and museum-quality antiques. Many of the rooms have separate entrances, some have TVs or working antique radios, and all have an abundance of quiet. A fire is always laid in the homey living room in the Summer House, where guests gather to watch TV, chat or play one of the board games on hand. Everything about the 1860 ship-captain's house radiates luxury and prosperity, but not vulgar ostentation, from the ground-floor art gallery to the excellent breakfast.

Rooms: $115-$325, including breakfast.

Daggett House
59 N. Water St.,
Edgartown
(508) 627-4600
Open year-round.
Cards: MC, V.

The Daggett House is a venerable Edgartown institution. Octogenarian owner Lucille Chirgwin keeps the traditions of another era alive at her inn, offering glimpses of life as it was when this was the island's first tavern (built in 1660). In the Secret Stairway Room, for instance, where breakfast is served each morning, time seems to have stood still—the ancient brick wall and hearth (hiding the secret stairway) date back to the Colonial era. The house may even be haunted: In a photograph of the fireplace, taken by an unsuspecting guest, two small faces appear in the flames, enough evidence for us that old souls are lingering on in this historic building.

The 24 rooms are simple and comfortable, with private baths and an unmemorable but unpretentious decor, perfectly suitable for the families who continue to make Edgartown their summer headquarters, generation after generation. Breakfast is straight-ahead Continental (homemade breads and muffins), served by those ubiquitous suntanned college students who populate the Vineyard each summer. For an additional charge you can fortify yourself with eggs Benedict, blueberry or banana pancakes, ham-and-cheese omelets or sour-cream coffee cake.

Rooms: $90-$135, including breakfast.

Lambert's Cove Country Inn

Lambert's Cove Rd.,
West Tisbury
(508) 693-2298
Open year-round.
All major cards.

If you arrive here in early summer, you'll think you've come to a secret back-road arboretum instead of a country inn—the grounds are so beautiful and the colors so vibrant that you'll want to salute the gardener. Not only does everything look gorgeous, but it also melds into a symphony of fragrance—aromatic cornflowers, irises, lilies of the valley, bridal veil, lilacs, lady slippers and wisteria. All these pretty flowers are balanced by the pine forest, apple orchards, tennis court fenced with sweet peas and trellis laden with Concord grapes. Lambert's Cove Country Inn is a true safe haven, a perfect place to recover from life's cruel blows. The 1790 farmhouse is restful, with its verdant vistas and breezy atmosphere, and the restaurant serves excellent dishes from a frequently changing menu, which offers such delights as lobster steamed in white wine, pasta with fresh island scallops, soft-shell crabs sautéed in Cajun butter, or Dijon-rosemary lamb chops. Breakfast—home-baked breads and pastries are specialties—is served in this same lovely room. The fifteen guest rooms, all with private baths, are pleasant and cheery, though not stunning. For privacy, try one of the rooms in the carriage house out back, especially the one with a private solarium-style sitting room.

Rooms: $55-$120, including breakfast.

Point Way Inn

Upper Main St., Edgartown
(508) 627-8633
Open year-round.
Cards: AE, MC, V.

If you and your family members are graduates of boarding schools, Ivy League colleges and law schools; have memories of your coming-out parties and summers in Europe with your grandparents; remember your nanny, cook and chauffeur with affection; and regularly attend the Brick Church in New York City, the Point Way Inn will make you feel right at home. Owners Ben and Linda Smith have decorated their walls with a seven-generation pictorial history of their families; sailing races, crew competitions, debuts and stately old homes give one a historical perspective on how the upper-crust lives.

Despite their lineage, the Smiths hardly give the impression of noblesse oblige: They are charming, engaging people who clearly enjoy their new lives as innkeepers. Ben abandoned his law career to spend a year aboard their 38-foot ketch, sailing the Caribbean with their children. Now, back on terra firma, he and Linda still work hard to enjoy life; you may find them relaxing in the gazebo or whacking away at croquet balls on their private court with fellow members of the Edgartown Mallet Club. But life isn't all fun and games for the Smiths, who know that their clientele expects the most out of a Vineyard inn—so you're just as likely to find them in any of the fifteen guest rooms, making sure everything is shipshape. The lovely bedrooms are well equipped with canopy beds, cheerful wallpaper, private baths and ten working fireplaces. Breakfast time finds the Smiths and guests downstairs in the sunny dining room, which is enlivened with a Jackson Pollock–inspired painted floor, indulging in carrot bread, bran muffins, sour-cream coffee cake and freshly squeezed orange juice, served on pretty china with silver flatware. The flower vases are Smith family sailing trophies, a subtle reminder of their brand of family history.

Rooms: $60-$200, including breakfast.

Thorncroft
278 Main St.,
Vineyard Haven
(508) 693-3333
Open year-round.
Cards: AE, MC, V.

Vineyard Haven is a great place to stay for those who are visiting Martha's Vineyard sans car, and for those who prefer the feeling of Up-island life over the whaling-captains' homes and society in Edgartown. It's certainly closer to Humphrey's Bakery, Menemsha and the cliffs at Gay Head. Vineyard Haven also has some wonderful restaurants, not the least of which is the venerable Black Dog tavern (see "Quick Bites" above). A stay at Thorncroft makes all this and more accessible. The inn has a Victorian look, although each of the thirteen rooms is unique. If you prefer canopy beds, Four is your room; for handsome Victorian furniture suites, choose One; and for more updated Victoriana, take the guest house out back. All have private baths and each is relaxing. Breakfast is a hearty meal: buttermilk pancakes with blueberry or strawberry honey, almond french toast, bacon-Swiss quiche, croissant breakfast sandwiches, spinach-sausage-cheese pie or old-fashioned eggs, sausage and buttermilk biscuits. After this generous start, you'll probably want to sit in the pretty antique wicker chairs in the living room to digest your meal, as well as to contemplate the day ahead. Karl and Lynn Buder, the charming, engaging owners who have made this inn so appealing, are always on hand to give suggestions and to help you find your way.

Rooms: $65-$145, including breakfast.

SIGHTS

The Vineyard, as most New Englanders call it, is nationally known as the summer playground of the rich and famous. But it isn't necessary to own a secluded estate to enjoy summertime, or anytime, on the island. Just seven miles (45 minutes by ferry) from Woods Hole on Cape Cod, the

Vineyard is not just another world—it's several. For each of its towns has its own markedly distinct personality.

Down island—that is, the southern and eastern side of this triangle of land measuring 21 miles at its hypotenuse—is dominated by Edgartown, seat of Dukes County since 1642. Edgartown is the island's business center and most sophisticated town. Once the bastion of whaling captains (many of whose stately homes still stand as museums or inns—just stroll N. Water Street), it's now the center of shopping, dining and nightlife. A few miles away, perched high above the water, is Oak Bluffs, a rather funky seaside town that takes its character from its decades as a favorite vacation spot among Wesleyan Methodists (who built the pastel-gingerbread Campground section) and well-off blacks. Up island, the rolling green fields of Tisbury and Chilmark epitomize New England farming country, while the fishing village of Menemsha falls just short of Rockport as the idealized working port for fishermen. And then, at the Vineyard's western tip, there's Gay Head, which somehow manages to pleasantly combine the high tack of souvenir shops and hot dog stands with views of spectacular clay cliffs—not to mention a popular nude beach.

The island is full of points of interest, most of which can be reached through an excellent system of bike paths. Edgartown has its museums and its Greek Revival mansions; Oak Bluffs its Flying Horses (the oldest carousel in the United States) and the State Lobster Hatchery; West Tisbury its general store and the Field Gallery, a sculpture display in, yes, an actual field. Chief among the Vineyard's attractions, though, is its coast. Although many prime beaches are open to residents only, there are several fine public ones. South Beach, just two miles from Edgartown with shuttle buses running in season, is a fine place to enjoy sun and surf. But for a truly unspoiled beach—not a condo in sight—take the tiny ferry *On Time* from Edgartown to Chappaquiddick Island and drive or bike to the Cape Poge Wildlife Refuge and Wasque Reservation, which offers miles of beach and no amusements whatsoever. Another fine spot for enjoying natural beauty is Felix Neck Wildlife Sanctuary, a 200-acre preserve for wildfowl and reptiles that is affiliated with the Massachusetts Audubon Society. Located on the Vineyard Haven–Edgartown Road, it's open daily year-round.

More and more vacationers are discovering that the Vineyard's charms don't disappear after Labor Day. (In fact, island waters often stay warm enough for swimming well into October.) As a result, more businesses and inns are remaining open past the peak season, and the weekend of Christmas events in mid-December, founded to buoy residents' spirits in the off-season, has become a drawing card for off-islanders as well. To simplify the search for lodging any time of year, the Vineyard has two reservations services: the Dukes County Reservations Service (508-693-6505) and Martha's Vineyard Reservations (508-493-4111). Both keep up to date on what's available and will help you find your place in the sun with a single phone call.

For more information about any aspect of Vineyard life or tourism, call the chamber of commerce at (508) 693-0085.

SHOPS

Eve Stone & Son
State Rd., West Tisbury
(508) 693-0396
*May 16-Sept. 14: open
daily 10 a.m.-6 p.m.*

It's hard not to miss the Stones' Vineyard shop: Just look for the admiral-clothed mannequin out front. If you miss that, the island's largest copper beech tree in the front yard ought to stop you in your tracks. This Connecticut-based family has opened its summer-home doors for the past twenty years (the Stones' main store is located in Woodbury; see "Connecticut"), supplying satisfied customers with American country pieces: yellowware, spongeware, children's toys, baskets, washed-pine kitchen tables, quilts, blanket boxes, Early American painted furniture and accessories. You may run into patriarch Charles Stone, returning from a day of bluefishing in Menemsha to share his catch with friends and customers. Don't worry if you visit the Stones à la bicyclette—they ship anywhere.

NANTUCKET

RESTAURANTS

Second Story
1 S. Beach Rd.
(508) 228-3471
INTERNATIONAL
*Seatings Tues.-Sun. 7 p.m.,
8 p.m. & 9:30 p.m.
Cards: MC, V.*

You can tell a lot about a restaurant by the way the proprietors handle unruly guests. Pat Tyler and David Toole earned our instant respect for evicting the drunken party at the table next to ours quicker than you could say "scram." And theirs is the sort of food that should be savored without distraction. The menu transcends ethnic boundaries: The kitchen is equally at home serving Portuguese littlenecks (simmered with Madeira, cumin and smoked ham), duck breast with a Thai caraway-ginger sauce, sea bass en papillote with Punjabi mint chutney, and old-fashioned American butter-crunch pie. The only less-than-felicitous dish we were served was a slightly overcooked lobster. The atmosphere is lively—this is no solemn temple of high gastronomy but a boisterous bistro where folks can have fun. Mismatched silverware and flickering hurricane lamps deck the pink-clothed tables; the walls are hung with the canvases of local artists. The wine list has been expanded to include an impressive selection of French white Burgundies, Provençal rosés and reasonably priced Portuguese vintages—175 different bottles in all. About $120 for dinner for two, with wine.

Straight Wharf Restaurant
Straight Wharf
(508) 228-4499
SEAFOOD
Seatings Tues.-Sun. 6:30 p.m., 8 p.m. & 9:15 p.m.
All major cards.

Obtaining a reservation at this Nantucket landmark can be as difficult as arranging an audience with the Pope. The reason for this can be summed up in three words: impeccably fresh fish. Whether you order an old standby, like grilled shrimp samurai (basted with teriyaki sauce) or thick swordfish steak, or a slightly more exotic daily special, like lobster and crabcakes or soft-shell crabs meunière, you can rest assured that it will be perfectly cooked and unimpeachably fresh. And to round out the meal there are comfortingly familiar desserts, such as peach cobbler and Grand Marnier chocolate mousse. We like to sit on the waterfront terrace, where a table is as hot an item as front-row seats for a Bruce Springsteen concert. Not that the main dining room, with its weathered shingles and wicker chairs, is uncomfortable or anything less than casually classy. After dinner you can take the night air, strolling around Pickering Wharf and the yacht-studded harbor. A not-too-horrifying $95 for dinner for two, with wine.

Tap Room at Jared Coffin House
29 Broad St.
(508) 228-2400
AMERICAN
Open daily 11:30 a.m.-9:30 p.m.
All major cards.

11/20

The Tap Room is an immensely popular place due, most probably, to its no-surprises cuisine, convivial atmosphere and solid, reassuring comfort. The swivel captain's chairs, active bar, dim lighting and pleasant staff make the country-club set feel right at home, as does the staid menu: stuffed shrimp, prime rib, fried clams and duckling, all well prepared but uneventful. Such dishes as the steamed salmon served over fresh pasta, the sesame chicken with ginger noodles and the pork tenderloin with sun-dried tomatoes gave us hopes of a light, modern touch in the kitchen, but our hopes were dashed by the salads drenched with dressing, uninspired pilaf, unmemorable home-baked breads and the desserts: brownie à la mode, cheesecake and cabinet custard. Nonetheless, the Tap Room is a good place to come when you're feeling insecure and need the familiar, when you want to see your friends at the next table or when you have a child in tow who much prefers running around the tables to eating. The staff is so well adjusted that they'll help babysit between courses. About $45 for two, with wine or beer. Also at the Jared Coffin House is Jared's, a more formal and expensive restaurant.

21 Federal Street
21 Federal St.
(508) 228-2121
AMERICAN
June 15-Sept. 15: open daily 11:30 a.m.-2:30 p.m. & 6 p.m.-10 p.m.; Sept. 16-June 14: open Mon.-Sat., hours vary.
Cards: AE, MC, V.

American cuisine is alive and well on the island of Nantucket. If you don't believe us, visit this popular restaurant tucked away in a Greek Revival house in the island's historic downtown. Good things come in threes at 21 Federal: witness the trio of lamb (rack, leg and thigh) and the trio of chocolate (cookies, cakes and crème anglaise). Seared tuna is accompanied by sushi rolls and smoked salmon. A wild-mushroom strudel features Smithfield ham; bread pudding is made with brioche. At times, the combinations are a trifle forced, but we commend the kitchen for trying. Meals are served in eight cozy dining rooms (seven with fireplaces) decorated in a country-elegant style, with cherry paneling, wide plank floors, brass fixtures and period prints. On sunny days, lunch is served on a flagstone courtyard, and at night, the splendid hand-sculpted bar becomes a popular island drinking spot. Like most Nantucket restaurants, this one gets unmanageably busy during the season. About $120 for dinner for two, with wine.

QUICK BITES

The Downeyflake
S. Water St.
(508) 228-4533
Open Thurs.-Tues. 7 a.m.-3 p.m.
No cards.

This family restaurant is beloved by islanders, because they know they'll get an honest meal served by fellow islanders in a sincere atmosphere—and they love to indulge in the home-baked pastries and donuts that have made the place famous. The sight of the bakery counter near the entrance will make you want to forgo a well-balanced breakfast or lunch for an extravaganza of lemon squares, brownies, cookies and donuts. But try to have a little self-restraint, only so you can try more of the menu's offerings: roast turkey dinner, veal cutlet with brown gravy, chili, crab-salad roll, quahog chowder, codfish cakes with egg sauce, baked beans, Grape-nuts custard and strawberry shortcake—food that would make any grandmother proud. Lunch for two, with a soda, will run $10 to $15.

Melos
8 Oak St.
(508) 228-0060
Open daily 7 a.m.-1 a.m.
No cards.

A stylish spot popular with islanders and the accidental tourist who finds this little diner on a side lane near the wharf. Decorated by the New York team of EON, Melos is worth a visit simply to see the wonderful painted and collaged walls. Seating may be vintage diner, but the daily-changing menu is as creative as it is good: rumaki with sesame noodles, generous burgers and all sorts of great sandwiches—Philly cheese steaks, Creole meatloaf with garlic mayonnaise, mustard chicken with tarragon mayonnaise, delicious tuna on oatmeal bread. Remember Melos for to-go sandwiches before catching the ferry for the trip back to the mainland. Less than $10 for a couple of sandwiches and sodas.

INNS

Cliff Lodge
9 Cliff Rd.
(508) 228-9480
Open year-round.
Cards: MC, V.

Cliff Lodge, without a doubt one of the prettiest inns in Nantucket and managed by the sweet, soft-spoken Mary Patton, is a delight to visit. The entire house was decorated under the aegis of Nantucket House Interior Designs, and a professional decorator's eye is clearly evident—from the splatter-painted plank floors and Laura Ashley wallpapers to a crisp room decor and accompanying aesthetic touches. Both sitting rooms are charming and lovely: the downstairs one in salmon and blue, with a monumental watermelon still life, and the other one with wicker furnishings, over-sized pillows and a subtle color scheme. As for the eleven guest rooms and one apartment (perfect for longer stays), we'd be hard-pressed to pick a favorite, but we will say that one of the nicest rooms on the entire island is One, a dazzler done in a brilliant cornflower-blue with white floors and walls. The large room upstairs, Four, is a companion piece to One, with a fireplace filled with dried flowers and a blue-and-white color scheme. The four rooms on the third floor are wonderful; some have views of the harbor, and all have air conditioning. Each room is equipped with a telephone, and TVs are concealed inside cabinets and behind secret doors.

A Continental breakfast is laid out buffet style in the breakfast room; you can eat in or take it outside to the garden during the summer. After breakfast, climb up to the widow's walk and soak in the breathtaking view while you plan your day.

Rooms: $30-$120, including breakfast.

Jared Coffin House
29 Broad St.
(508) 228-2405
Open year-round.
All major cards.

This very Victorian institution is always full with longtime regulars, tourists who prefer impersonal lodgings or new-comers who have been influenced by the inn's overrated reputation. Granted, the Coffin House is a vital part of island life—being the patron of the Christmas stroll and the Daffodil Weekend—but compared to the number of other beautiful inns in Nantucket, it pales. The 54 rooms are housed in a complex of six handsome buildings, which were built, in turn, by shipbuilder Jared Coffin, one of his relatives, second owner Eben Allen and others. The nondescript bedrooms have a sort of simulated antique look (oddly, not Victorian, which would be in keeping with the overall look of the place). But the Queen Victorial rules in the main house's chandelier-laden sitting rooms, which are full of Victorian sofas and Oriental carpets and overseen by the fair faces of Victorian mothers and their children in portraits over the fireplaces.

Jared's, the inn's well-known dining room, is a tranquil spot done in apricot and adorned with its fair share of portraits. The menu serves traditional fare: orange duck, stuffed chicken en croûte, broiled swordfish and salmon en papillote. The more informal Tap Room (see "Restaurants" above) is a gathering spot for the Topsider crowd, the women carrying Nantucket lighthouse bags with a certain style.

Rooms: $90-$150, including breakfast.

Corner House
49 Centre St.
(508) 228-1530
Closed Jan.-mid-April.
Cards: AE, MC, V.

Corner House successfully mixes Colonial authenticity and excellent twentieth-century taste. Sandy and John Knox-Johnston have done an admirable job of restoring their 1723 inn so that it looks and feels as it did during Nantucket's whaling salad days. The Colonial colors, wide-planked floorboards, handsome furnishings and odd tilts and angles give Corner House its exceptional charm. The six bedrooms are superb, each made special with such touches as sponge-painted walls, views of the gardens and harbor, working fireplaces, tall-post beds, good reading lights, Welsh coverlets, rag rugs, designer sheets, and down pillows and comforters. The third floor's farmhouse-simple rooms have rough-hewn beams, pine floors and whitewashed walls. Throughout are pieces from the owners' collection of American and English antiques.

The Knox-Johnstons recently opened two new houses, further proof of Sandy's impressive interior-decorating skill. Two guest rooms are tucked into Rose Cottage: Country Lane, with pale-yellow trim, white walls and a tall-post queen bed with a crocheted lace canopy, and Bandbox, with a white-and-navy color scheme, pinstriped detailing and a queen canopy bed. Down the street and around the corner is Swan's Nest, an example of Sandy's tenacity and ingenuity. This wonderful built-new-to-look-old house, designed and built by Sandy, has lots of wooden beams, queen canopy beds, Colonial colors and the same attention to detail that's found in the rest of the inn. True, the TVs and small iceboxes in the four rooms are concessions to the twentieth century, but they're certainly welcome, and the overall feeling is definitely from another era.

A huge Continental breakfast is produced in the kitchen (equipped with its original, gigantic hearth) and served in the sitting rooms, on the side porch or in the beautifully landscaped patio/garden. Afternoon tea in the winter and lemonade in the summer are poured to revive guests in time

for dinner at another of Nantucket's fine restaurants.
Rooms: $55-$125, including breakfast.

Fair Gardens
27 Fair St.
(508) 228-4258, 228-6609
Closed Jan.-March.
Cards: MC, V.

Fans of Shakespeare herb gardens will never be bored at
Fair Gardens, where they can spend hours trying to identify
in which of his works each herbal name appears. These
secret gardens are hidden in back of the delightful inn,
which has eight lovely rooms in the main house and two in
the garden house. Appropriately enough, they're all named
after flowers and herbs, and each has beautiful quilts and
simple furnishings. Camomile, with its wash of pink, Victorian iron bed and sleeper sofa (handy for those traveling
with older children), is one of the prettiest. It is as sweet and
light as the upstairs room, Rosemary, which boasts confetti-
print wallpaper and a star-motif quilt. Sage has an impressive
Victorian bed surrounded by wild strawberry–print walls,
and Tarragon, in the back of the house, has beautiful hand-
stenciled walls and a cannonball bed. A Continental breakfast is served in the pleasant breakfast room or outdoors
overlooking the garden in warm weather. Or, best of all,
request breakfast in bed and feel totally spoiled.

The charming and helpful innkeepers, Lee and Stuart Gaw,
live in a garden house on the grounds and also manage
Great Harbor Inn (see below), another example of their
good taste and talent in creating lovely guest houses.
Rooms: $75-$125, including breakfast.

Great Harbor Inn
31 India St.
(508) 228-6609
Open year-round.
Cards: MC, V.

This handsome eight-room inn impressively displays Lee
and Stuart Gaw's rehabilitation talents—in this case, a house
built in 1790. Rebuilt from the inside, Great Harbor Inn is
a tribute to the virtues of simplicity and restraint. Colonial
colors, unpretentious furnishings, beautiful quilts and large
beds are the rule here. Each room is named after a flower
found on Nantucket, noted on ceramic plaques made by
Lee. (A potter as well as an innkeeper, Lee sells her work at
the Museum Shop, Broad Street, 508-228-5785, next to
the Whaling Museum.)

One of the prettiest rooms at the inn is Columbine—
subtle green and cream colors, a queen canopy bed, a
window seat and a sleeper sofa make the room perfect for
traveling families. Equally attractive is Wood Lily, with pale-
rose walls and a rose-and-blue star quilt under an ivory
canopy bed. All rooms have private baths and TVs, which
look slightly out of place in such Colonial surroundings.

Continental breakfast is served in the intimate common
room or outside in the garden when the weather is warm.
After breakfast, you might want to look at some of the inn's
lovely artwork, notably the beachscape in the sitting room
and the portrait of the Nantucket steamboat upstairs. Add
to all that a quiet, peaceful neighborhood, and Great Har-

bor makes a supremely restful retreat.
Rooms: $65-$130, including breakfast.

The Wauwinet Inn
Polpis Rd.
(800) 426-8718,
(617) 228-0145
Closed Nov.-April
(closings vary).
All major cards.

The seaside Wauwinet Inn has been a Nantucket fixture for a good many years, through periods of glory and periods of ramshackle decline. We arrived in the first days of its recent metamorphosis into an ambitious and pricey place indeed. Despite the imposing tabs, there is nothing overtly sumptuous about this fine old three-story building; it's all wicker, flowers, paintings, carefully chosen antiques and an air of muted Yankee elegance. The cozy rooms are dominated by queen-size beds; out most windows are views of Nantucket Harbor. As a welcome omission, no TVs. In those first days of reopening we found various problems—gremlins in the fire alarm, confusion among the staff (for example, it was incorrectly implied that the bicycles we reserved were free)—and the restaurant didn't measure up to its prices; we also wished the sailboats had arrived. Presumably, such glitches will be resolved by the time you read this. During our visit we cycled and played tennis to our heart's content, strolled the beach and had a dandy time. On the whole, though, for all the artful elegance of the Wauwinet, we have to give most of the credit to Mother Nature: The real selling point of the place is not the decor or services but, rather, the wind, the sea and the fact that, on its splinter of land on the north end of the island, it's one of the few places in Nantucket that's really quiet and away from things.
Rooms: $295-$345, including breakfast ($177-$207 off-season).

SIGHTS

Picture yourself on a ferry rounding Brant Point, moving slowly past the lighthouse. As always, the docks and Straight Wharf are teeming with life. You sling your duffle over one shoulder, just as seamen have done for centuries, and walk toward the cobbled Main Street. You couldn't be anywhere but Nantucket.

Despite the evils of ever-increasing tourism, the island retains its old-time character. Pricey shops and restaurants may dominate Main Street, but the town has preserved a crusty charm. So have its people.

Whether you're staying a day or the entire summer, the most economical ticket to Nantucket's past is the full-season Visitor's Pass ($6.50 for adults, $2.50 for children). A self-guided walking tour of the Nantucket Historical Association's thirteen properties takes about three hours and includes the Whaling Museum, on Broad Street at Steamboat Wharf; five houses (best seen in chronological sequence) representing different stages in Nantucket's development; and the Old Mill, a still-working gristmill.

And that's just in Nantucket town. Don't neglect to explore the rest of the island, preferably by bike on the excellent system of off-street paths. Fine sandy beaches ring the island, with Surfside being the most popular and Cisco the least spoiled. Beaches on the south and west tend to get surf and sometimes a strong undertow; those on the north and east provide gentle waves—and seaweed. (Don't be alarmed if the day dawns as gray as the shingles on Nantucket's cottages; the fog generally burns off by noon.) Well worth an excursion by bike (if your legs can handle a fifteen-mile round trip) or tour bus is Siasconset, or 'Sconset, the village at the island's eastern tip that boasts several good restaurants, a general store and curving lanes lined with cottages dating back two centuries and more. It's especially pretty in May and early June, when rambling rose bushes cover the picket fences.

For more information on Nantucket, call the chamber of commerce at (508) 228-1700. For one-stop accommodations shopping, call Nantucket Accommodations (508-228-9559), Nantucket Vacation Planning Service (508-228-9010) or Nantucket Reservations (800-NANTUCK).

SHOPS

Four Winds Craft Guild
Straight Wharf
(617) 228-9623
Summer-fall: open daily 9 a.m.-6 p.m.; off-season hours vary.

Reputed to be the oldest shop on the island, Four Winds sells such traditional Nantucket crafts as woven lightship baskets and scrimshaw. The wares are pricey (what on Nantucket isn't?), but they're among the best of their kind, and the selection can't be matched.

Nantucket House Antiques
1 S. Beach St.
(508) 228-4604
Open Mon.-Sat. 10 a.m.- 5 p.m., Sun. by appt. only.

You can expect to find lots of overpriced everything at this crowded shop. Apparently the owners expect visitors to be in a carefree, slaphappy vacation mood, succumbing to unconscious whim and forking over high-limit credit cards in exchange for majolica, painted tables, carved wooden swans and geese, dioramas, barnyard art of one sort or another, splint baskets, glazed jugs and other antiques that sell for a small fortune. This is a great place to browse, but it's no place for the serious collector who values a fair price for quality.

PROVINCETOWN

"We offer a ten-percent lesbian discount," the cashier in the feminist craft shop said matter-of-factly. "Do you qualify?" In most resort communities, that question would constitute an invasion of privacy, but in Provincetown few people do a double take. Yes, P'town is a heavily gay community, both in season and out, but that shouldn't scare heterosexuals away.

Otherwise, Provincetown is known for its triple heritage: history, art and the sea. The Pilgrims made their first landfall here in 1620 before they decided the tip of the Cape was too rugged for them and moved on to Plymouth. But other settlers followed, and cottages dating back to the eighteenth and nineteenth centuries line the two main streets, Commercial and Bradford. (Following the shape of the spit, the town is long and narrow; it takes about five minutes to walk "across" town and an hour to walk its length.) P'town has forgiven the Pilgrims, commemorating their short stay with a bas-relief behind the Town Hall and with the town's one and only "skyscraper," the 252-foot Pilgrim Monument, which offers breathtaking views from the top of the tower.

Less than 40 miles from Boston by sea (see "Getting Around" in the "Basics" chapter) but more than 100 by land, P'town has an otherworldly atmosphere, a peace and solitude that are attracting more and more vacationers year-round. And consider this: P'town is the only place in America where you can watch the sun set over the Atlantic Ocean.

RESTAURANTS

Ciro & Sal's
4 Kiley Ct. (behind 430 Commercial St.)
(508) 487-0049
ITALIAN/AMERICAN
June-Oct.: open nightly 6 p.m.-10 p.m.; Nov.-May: open Fri.-Sat. 6 p.m.-10 p.m.
Cards: MC, V.

10/20

Ciro & Sal's is a Provincetown classic that's been around since a few starving artists and art lovers decided to cook spaghetti for one another back in the '50s. The menu has remained provincially Italian, successfully resisting the lure of nouvelle or California Italian. This is sturdy, hearty fare at moderate prices, with respectable desserts and recommendable daily specials. Still consistently crowded, year after year, with local artists, as well as tourists. Dinner for two, with wine, will run about $55.

Ciro's Flagship Restaurant
463 Commercial St.
(508) 487-1200
AMERICAN
July-Aug.: open daily noon-1 a.m.; Sept.-June: hours vary.
Cards: MC, V.

10/20

Ciro opened his Flagship Restaurant on the water side of Commercial Street a few years ago; it was slow to take off, though we don't understand why, since we prefer the food and less-hectic atmosphere here over those of his other place. We're especially fond of the Dory Bar (made of an actual Nova Scotia rowing boat), a spacious, well-populated room with a comfortable lounge area affording a view of the moonlit bay. Dining tables are set in a large, barn-like room protruding out over the sand, also with a bay view. Ciro's Flagship is a must-visit not only for the view but also for the clam chowder, just about the best we've ever had—the broth is rich yet light, the clams cooked to tenderness and not beyond into chewiness, as they are almost everywhere else.

In the summer of 1988, Ciro brought up a New Orleans chef, and the menu took on a curious Italian/Louisiana cast—something for everyone, we suppose—while retaining the Cape Cod emphasis on fish and seafood. The success of this new menu is evident in the considerable presence of year-rounders, summer locals and artists, who actually out-number tourists. About $75 for dinner for two, with wine.

QUICK BITES

Pepe's Wharf
371 Commercial St.
(508) 487-0670
June-Sept.: deck open daily noon-4 p.m.
Cards: AE, MC, V.

Pepe's is a traditional seashore joint that dishes up high-priced, not-so-wonderful food for large parties or intimate dates. If you eat in the restaurant, try the baked stuffed lobster for a typical (if unenlightened) regional dish, or maybe the rich New England boiled-lobster dinner. But we prefer to skip the restaurant altogether and, after a few hours on the beach or as a relief from the narrow, tourist-clogged Provincetown streets, head for the rooftop deck. While gazing out over Cape Cod Bay and doing some serious people watching, you can order from the raw bar or have a grilled hamburger, fish and chips or other fried or grilled seafood offering—the kind of substantial protein that doesn't particularly stand out, gustatorily, but goes well with a Bloody Mary, a beer or a frosty diet cola. About $15 for a burger and beer for two.

SIGHTS

Cape Cod National Seashore

The Cape Cod National Seashore, which stretches all the way from Chatham Light, includes 30 miles of windswept beaches in Provincetown alone. Parking for the seashore is available in Provincetown at Herring Cove and Race Point. Meanwhile, the fishing and lobstering boats that use MacMillan Wharf as their home port serve as a reminder that the sea isn't all play and no work.

Provincetown Art Association Museum

460 Commercial St.
(508) 487-1750
Open daily noon-4 p.m.; also open 7 p.m.-11 p.m. in summer.

Early in this century, the town became a summer colony for writers, actors and visual artists; Eugene O'Neill was among the many who tested their wings professionally at the Provincetown Playhouse. Today, the visual-arts community continues to thrive with a number of galleries, while the Provincetown Art Association, established in 1914, has through the years attracted such members as Robert Motherwell and Helen Frankenthaler. It now boasts more than 400 working artists in various media, many of whom live or summer in P'town. The association's museum shows its permanent collection—which spans American art from early impressionism to contemporary pieces—and periodically holds special exhibitions, including those devoted to its members' works.

Adults $2, seniors, students & children $1.

Provincetown Heritage Museum

Commercial St.
& Center St.
(508) 487-0666
Mid-June-Columbus Day: open daily 10 a.m.-6 p.m. Admission $2.

The Provincetown Heritage Museum houses an ever-growing collection of Cape Cod memorabilia, including whaling artifacts, exhibits on the fishing industry and scenes from Victorian Provincetown.

SHOPS

Ellen Harris Gallery

355 Commercial St.
(508) 487-1414
Hours vary.

On a street clad in T-shirts and stuffed with pizza-by-the-slice, this gallery stands as a refuge from the hordes in suntan oil. Surprisingly, it is strong in Southwestern crafts, such as Indian pottery and kachina dolls, though it also carries a lot of well-done ceramics, art glass, jewelry and sculpture.

SANDWICH

SIGHTS

Sandwich makes an ideal day-trip from Boston, especially since it's a prime stop on the vintage Cape Cod & Hyannis Railway (see "Getting Around" in the "Basics" chapter). Few towns exude more old-fashioned

New England atmosphere than Sandwich Center, founded in 1637 by ten settlers from Saugus, north of Boston. (In Sandwich, when you see "1639" above a cottage door, it's not the street address.) The Greek Revival Town Hall dominates the center of town, which was built around a small triangular green.

Just across the green from the Town Hall, you'll find the Sandwich Glass Museum, the repository for Sandwich glass, made at several local factories for 63 years in the nineteenth century. (Ironically, because of impurities, the glassworks couldn't use Cape Cod sand; it imported its raw material from, of all places, New Jersey.) The museum (508-888-0251) is open April to October, daily 9:30 a.m. to 4:30 p.m.; November, December, February and March, Wednesday to Sunday 9:30 a.m. to 4 p.m.; closed in January. Admission is $2.50 for adults, 50 cents for children aged 6 to 12, free for those under age 6.

Sandwich Center also has two other museums within easy walking distance. The Yesteryears Doll Museum at Main and River streets has collected just about every kind of doll imaginable, from French bisque to Javanese puppets to Raggedy Anns. The museum (508-888-1711) is open May to October, Monday to Saturday 10 a.m. to 4 p.m. and Sunday 1 p.m. to 4 p.m.; admission is $2.50 for adults and $1.50 for children. The Thornton W. Burgess Museum, 4 Water Street (508-888-6870), celebrates the work of the naturalist and children's-book writer, a Sandwich native, best known for his Peter Rabbit stories. Open Monday to Saturday 10 a.m. to 4 p.m., Sunday 1 p.m. to 4 p.m.; admission is free.

A bit farther afield, less than two miles from Sandwich Center, lies Heritage Plantation of Sandwich, a 76-acre estate that serves as a museum of Americana, with relics ranging from a working carousel to a Shaker round barn to an extensive Currier & Ives collection. The Plantation, at Grove and Pine streets (508-888-3300), is open May to October, daily 10 a.m. to 5 p.m.; admission is $6 for adults, $5 for senior citizens, $2.50 for children aged 5 to 12, free for those under age 5.

DON'T FORGET: *Gault Millau introduces you to the Best of New York, the Best of Washington D.C., the Best of Los Angeles, the Best of San Francisco, the Best of Chicago, the Best of France, the Best of Paris, the Best of Italy, the Best of London.*

TRURO

SHOPS

The "Downtown Truro" Shops
Truro Center
(next to post office)
(508) 349-2929
Summer: open daily 9 a.m.-7 p.m. (hours may vary).

We've always found it odd that so many culinarily sophisticated people from New York and New England have seemed content to leave their takeout-gourmet cravings at home when they summer on the Cape. And there's certainly been little or no evidence of neoregional American, California nouvelle Italian, Cajun or any other upscale ready-to-go foods in these parts—until the summer of 1987, that is, when Mark Rosenthal opened Jams, a truly citified gourmet takeout/deli/wine/convenience store in the middle of "downtown" Truro (the joke being that this is the only retail establishment on the road that runs past the Truro post office).

At first, everyone in Truro resented Jams, fearing that it would bring tourists flocking to this hitherto unknown (and unpronounceable) little town. Now they resent Jams because they didn't think of it first; it's doing so much business that locals have forgotten how they ever got food and wine for the daily cocktail parties that define the summer set's social life. Then, in the summer of 1988, Rosenthal vastly expanded his domain with a seafood shop called Splash, which offers fresh fish, chowder and lobster dinners; Rosie's Fruit and Produce; and a souvenir, fishing, surf and beachwear store called (what else?) the Truro Beach Club.

WELLFLEET

SHOPS

Blake Gallery
Wellfleet Center, Main St.
(508) 349-6631
Late May-mid-Oct.: open Mon.-Sat. 10 a.m.-6 p.m., Sun 10 a.m.- 4 p.m.; mid-Oct.-late May: open weekends & holidays; hours vary.

Unlike most "arty" shops on the Cape, the Blake Gallery in Wellfleet Center could translate directly to New York or Los Angeles, so select are its handcrafted jewelry, ceramics, art glass and kaleidoscopes, woven clothing and painted silk scarves. There are pieces by local artists on the walls, but don't worry—you won't run across yet another framed study of Nauset Light or any clever seashell concoctions. Susan Blake has assembled an elegant collection of truly fine baubles, objets d'art and gifts.

CENTRAL & WESTERN MASSACHUSETTS

AGAWAM

SIGHTS

Riverside Park
1623 Main St.
(413) 786-9300
Memorial Day-Labor Day:
open daily 11 a.m.-11 p.m.;
April-May & Sept.: open
weekends; hours vary.

Massachusetts doesn't have many amusement parks left, now that Revere Beach has gone condo and Nantasket's Paragon Park has been demolished. But Riverside Park in Agawam, near Springfield, still moves into high gear for summertime fun. Its 50 rides include three roller coasters whose names—the Cyclone, the Thunderbolt and the Black Widow Loop—should tell you something about what to expect. Riverside also has water rides and a 1909 hand-carved carousel, one of the oldest in the United States.

Adults $12.99, children 3-9 $9.99, children under 3 free.

AMHERST

SIGHTS

The midst of the Connecticut River Valley's rolling farm country is home to no fewer than five colleges: Amherst, Hampshire, Smith, Mount Holyoke and the main campus of the University of Massachusetts. The Belle of Amherst, Emily Dickinson, lived and wrote here in The Mansion, 280 Main Street, which is open Wednesday to Saturday 1:30 p.m. to 3:45 p.m. Reservations are essential; call (413) 543-8161.

SHOPS

River Valley Crafts
236 N. Pleasant St.
(413) 253-7919
Open Mon.-Sat. 10 a.m.-
5:30 p.m.

Sprawling through the rabbit-warren rooms of this home-turned-shop is a large and varied selection of well-made items, most of them designed for daily use. Though much of the work is off the production line, every nook and cranny holds something interesting—a browser's paradise.

BECKET

SIGHTS

Jacob's Pillow
George Carter Rd.
(off Rte. 20)
(413) 243-0745

Each summer, the acclaimed Jacob's Pillow dance festival brings to the Berkshires an international array of performers in ballet, modern dance, jazz dance and mime. The festival runs through July and August in its own theater; call for up-to-date schedules and ticket information.

BRIMFIELD

SIGHTS

Brimfield Weeks
Brimfield streets
(413) 235-7479

If you can't resist a bargain and don't mind having to hunt for one, time your New England travels to see Brimfield at its busiest. Most of the time this community near Sturbridge is something of a one-horse town, but three weeks a year—in early June, early July and early to mid-September—the town fills with dealers and shoppers for the biggest flea market and antiques fair on the East Coast. Up to 50,000 visitors browse through 3,000 or so dealers' booths in search of anything from fine English bone china to knick-knacks made in occupied Japan. It may take some time (and a sharp eye) to tell the treasures from the trash, but that's half the fun—and haggling with the dealers for a better price is the other half. One warning: The tremendous crowds indicate that the few inns and motels nearby are booked up to a year in advance, so plan your visit early, or be prepared to drive a distance to a bed for the night.

Unless otherwise noted, the prices given for restaurants are for a complete dinner for two, including an appetizer, main course and dessert. The prices also include tax, fifteen-percent tip and one of the least expensive bottles of wine on the wine list. Please don't hold it against us if you end up spending a bit more!

DEERFIELD

SIGHTS

Historic Deerfield, Inc.
Rte. 5 & Rte. 10
(413) 774-5581
*Open daily 9:30 a.m.-
4:30 p.m.*

Who would believe that this quiet town in the Connecticut River Valley was once considered a Western frontier? Yet it's true, and Historic Deerfield has preserved some of that atmosphere with twelve house-museums containing lovely collections of American furniture, silver, textiles, ceramics and other household objects, with a particular emphasis on the arts in early American life.

Adults $7.50, children 17 & under $4; admission good for 2 days.

HADLEY

RESTAURANTS

**Carmelina's
at the Commons**
96 Russell St. (Rte. 9)
(413) 584-8000
ITALIAN
*Open Sun. & Tues.-Thurs.
5 p.m.-9:30 p.m., Fri.-Sat.
5 p.m.-10 p.m.
All major cards.*

11/20

With the demise of its main competitor a while back, Carmelina's assumed the crown of premier Italian restaurant in the area. Would that it had a touch more artistry under the crown. The place is stripped down for eating: a few room dividers, philodendrons, servers bustling in every direction and patrons gabbing noisily and tearing into enormous platters of great-looking stuff. As every Italian place ought at the very least to do, Carmelina's makes you famished as soon as you walk in the door. The menu features the expected pastas, veal and seafood tagged with such cutesy-poo titles as "Crazy Alfredo" and "Convict's Macaroni." On our last visit, our server was the standard jolly and helpful sort; she admitted that the bread was not made in-house and pushed the mussels Roberto appetizer, which proved to be quite pleasant and nearly the high point of the meal. We tried both choices of salad dressing: watery blue cheese and over-the-hill olive oil and vinegar. The ensuing main courses confirmed our opinion that Carmelina's is a fickle operation. Our zuppa di pesce was properly teeming with fish and satisfying (we took two-thirds of it home), as was a pasta a l'oglia; chicken piccata was good enough, if nearly French in approach; but a dish of seafood on a bed of stuffed red peppers was reminiscent of American diner chow. In short, the kitchen is capable but has no particular point of view, and few dishes here have the elegant simplicity found in authentic Italian food. So Italy this isn't. On the other hand, it's not too pricey, and until something better comes along, it's close enough for Hadley, Massachusetts. About $50 for two, with wine.

HANCOCK

SIGHTS

Shaker Village
Rte. 20
(413) 443-0188
Late May-Oct.: open daily;
guided tours hourly
10 a.m.-3 p.m.

"'Tis the gift to be simple, 'tis the gift to be free, 'tis the gift to come down where you ought to be." To the Shakers, the nineteenth-century religious sect known for its gyrating dances and sexual abstinence, western Massachusetts was the right place to "come down" after their founder, Mother Ann Lee, brought her followers to America from England. Although their sexual abstinence, not surprisingly, led to the Shakers' extinction, this museum village re-creates their life in America with restored buildings and reproductions of their craftwork, including the simple, classic furniture seen frequently of late in chic interior-design magazines.
Adults $5.50, seniors $4.85, children $1.50.

HARTSVILLE

RESTAURANTS

Hillside
Rte. 57
(413) 528-3123
CONTINENTAL
Open Tues.-Sat. 5 p.m.-
10 p.m., Sun. 4 p.m.-
9 p.m. (hours vary in
winter).
All major cards.

10/20

The Hillside is in its sixteenth year, during which time it has become a staple among Berkshire-boonies eateries. In the summer, one can sit on the deck and enjoy soaring hills and valleys; otherwise there is the pleasant paneled dining room with Swiss hearts and flowers all over the place. The menu runs to Continental meat dishes—six kinds of veal plus the familiar chops and chicken. The menu also has a startling propensity to misspell such items as prosciutto, veal piccata, avocado and so on—an ominous indicator, as is the skimpy wine list that starts with Blue Nun. Further bad signs: The cottage-cheesy mom-and-pop glop that arrives with crackers; pâté maison that could pass for liverwurst; and excessively crumbly stuffed clams. On this particular visit, the house wine, Pere Patriarche, came in an overflowing carafe, which compensated somewhat for its lack of character. After good bread and serviceable salads, we were revived by two typically solid, if unsurprising, main dishes—a delicate and tender veal piccata and a fine, firm and moist flambéed duck with skin precisely medium-crisp as ordered. But the overall carelessness continued in an oversweet orange sauce for the duck (fortunately to the side) and a plate of good peeled asparagus compromised by a hollandaise that may not have been from a mix but gave a good impression of it. Our dessert of strawberries Romanoff was so rich and riveting that it gave us a start. As is sometimes the case with the Hillside, this visit was quite the hit-and-miss evening. The reputation of the place is based on high-quality ingredients expertly made into familiar dishes—an admirable goal, but not attainable unless the kitchen is wide awake. About $75 for two, with wine.

HILLSDALE, NEW YORK

RESTAURANTS

L'Hostellerie Bressane
Rte. 22 & Rte. 23
(518) 325-3412
FRENCH
Summer: open Tues.-Sat. 5:30 p.m.-9:30 p.m., Sun. 4 p.m.-8:30 p.m. No cards.

In 1985, Jean Morel, proprietor and chef of L'Hostellerie Bressane, received the Chef of the Year award from the exclusive L'Association des Maîtres Cuisiniers de France. Having had some of the meals of our lives here, we weren't a bit surprised. For some years, this fine eighteenth-century brick Colonial in little Hillsdale, New York, just a truffle's throw from the Massachusetts border, has housed one of the Berkshires' greatest bastions of la grande cuisine. The meals are the kind you remember through the years: poached salmon dotted with red peppercorns and basking in a lake of green sorrel sauce, framed by an exquisite plate from the chef's collection. It was here that we had our first and still best floating island, and here that we learned how soufflés, a house specialty, can transform a familiar taste into something ethereal. Morel, in other words, is an authentic master (and, by the way, he holds cooking classes on the premises).

Well, even Nijinsky fell on his duff once in a while. We have to report that our latest meal at L'Hostellerie was beset with goofs. A chicken-liver soufflé was exquisite on the top but runny on the bottom, and the fish pâté from the fixed-price menu was bland. Roast duck with black-currant sauce was perfectly done, the skin nicely crisp, but neither sauce nor duck was particularly tasty, and the same held true for chicken in a balsamic vinegar sauce. Moreover, the duck dish we ordered did not turn out to be the one we were served. And the wild rice flanking the duck had the consistency and interest of Styrofoam packing material. Our dessert soufflés, big and light and imposing as always, were no more than pretty good.

Do we still admire the place? In remembrance of things past, we remain believers, and thus our two toques. When the food is good here, it is spectacular; it would take more than one disappointing visit to shake our faith. About $95 for dinner for two, with wine.

LENOX

RESTAURANTS

Church Street Cafe
69 Church St.
(413) 637-2745
AMERICAN
Open Sun.-Thurs. 11:30 a.m.-2:30 p.m. & 5:30 p.m.-9 p.m., Fri.-Sat. 11:30 a.m.-2:30 p.m. & 5:30 p.m.-9:30 p.m.; closed Sun. Nov.-May.
Cards: MC, V.

When weather allows, the Church Street Cafe has the dandiest deck on downtown Lenox's restaurant row. Inside are cozy, low-ceilinged rooms whose plainness sets off the art on the walls. Its menu presents a survey of American regional cooking, ranging from Creole dishes to "pasta Santa Fe" to Chesapeake Bay crabcakes. The wine list, a well-chosen French and California selection, is gentle on the pocket. On our last visit a gumbo was particularly fine—thick and smoky, with a bracing slate of spices to tickle the epiglottis. We've had better gumbo, maybe, but not in this neck of the woods. As an experiment, we tried a beef stew to see if the kitchen could dress up this plain sister of a dish; the result, while satisfying, did not transcend its beefstewishness. From the Church Street's usual devastating selection of desserts, we passed up such siren calls as a bittersweet-chocolate and raspberry cake for a crème brûlée that proved to be a joy with each bite. All in all, the thing about the Church Street is that the chefs will not allow it to be a mere pleasant grazing field in downtown Lenox, which in itself would bring in the customers. The loyalty so many patrons (including us) have for this bistro stems from its striving for excellence and from the fact that, for the price, it succeeds so consistently. Our only real complaint centers around Church Street's popularity; despite three expansions, the owners often can't keep pace with the tourist hordes at lunch. But we consider the wait worthwhile. About $65 for dinner for two, with wine.

Wheatleigh

W. Hawthorne St.
(off Rte. 183)
(413) 637-0610
CONTINENTAL
Open Sun. & Tues.-Thurs.
6 p.m.-9 p.m., Fri.-Sat.
6 p.m.-9:30 p.m. (open at
5 p.m. during Tanglewood
season).
All major cards.

Wheatleigh resides around the corner from Tanglewood in an Italianate palazzo built in the last century by some countess or other. These days it is known for serving extravagantly pricey food in a haute-robber-baron atmosphere. A black-tied maître d' shepherded us from the grand foyer into one of the dining rooms (white damask, flowers, candles) and graciously offered us glasses of Champagne; it would have been gauche to refuse (first mistake). After contemplating the two-page menu that included a $55 prix-fixe meal composed of appetizer, entrée and dessert, we picked two first-course prospects from among several delicious titles: fresh Monterey prawns on lobster concassé with a flan of wild mushrooms, and duck confit and foie gras in a savoy cabbage pocket with two truffle sauces. After a complimentary and excellent serving of melon and prosciutto, we found that you can indeed tell these appetizers by their titles. The confit and foie gras were layered inside a veiny cabbage leaf and handsomely complemented the truffle-dotted white and brown sauces; the prawns and concassé made a pretty picture ringing the flan, and we never knew prawns could be so tender and so sweet. These dishes received the highest compliment: We shut up and ate, savoring every bite. One of our party, who came with a stiff neck, announced he was miraculously cured.

Now we were in a pretty sublime mood, but it was not to be unsullied. Since the wine list was being overhauled and we had to travel, we agreed to our maître d's suggestion to have glasses of house California Chardonnay with our entrées (second mistake). Passing up veal and venison, we settled on two seafood entrées. A filet of halibut proved perfectly done, but its blandness wasn't overcome by the crayfish sauce, which was too subtle for its own good—a distant whiff of ginger and nearly tasteless morels. Our fricassée of scallops and lotte, in a mild and agreeable genevoise sauce, verged on the memorable. However, the julienne vegetables and hearty saffron rice were stronger than the seafood, and the Chardonnay made too robust an accompaniment to such delicate sauces. Dessert restored unambiguous good cheer with the gamey sweetness of chèvre and raspberries unforgettable in delicate pastry, and a dandy fresh-fruit tart flanked by strapping New Zealand blackberries. It was the bill that left a bad taste in our mouths. Our four glasses of middling Champagne and ill-advised Chardonnay totaled $38, enough to have covered a bottle of good wine. Did the food earn a tab that implied virtual perfection? If we'd had the venison entrée and gotten better advice on wine, the answer might have been yes (and our rating would have climbed to three toques). As it was, the answer has to be a qualified no: The beginning and end were extraordinary and the kitchen is clearly very fine; but the main courses were good food at the great-food price of about $190 for two, with wine and the two regrettable glasses of Champagne.

INNS

Blantyre

Rte. 20
(413) 637-3556
Closed Nov.-May.
All major cards.

Built in 1902, Blantyre is one of the Berkshires' grand old "cottages," and true to its castle-like appearance, it coddles and comforts its well-heeled clientele. And like a first-rate restaurant that warrants its high prices, Blantyre delivers. Inside, it is a Gothic fantasy: leaded-glass windows, a sweeping oak staircase, an immense fireplace and intimate parlors with antique sofas, chairs and knickknacks. Upstairs, the eight guest rooms are the rarely seen ideal of what sophisticated country-inn rooms should be.

Blantyre's 85 acres include trim, rolling lawns that we'd swear are not mown but clipped with scissors. From the glassed-in breakfast conservatory, you can look out over the championship croquet lawn. Down a winding drive are the tennis courts, swimming pool, hot tub and sauna. The service is impeccable. The setting is outstanding. *This* is how the other half lives—and we do, too, at least for one night.

Rooms: $175-$400, including breakfast; two-night minimum on weekends.

Walker House

74 Walker St.
(413) 637-1271
Open year-round.
Cash & personal check only.

Music lovers who hope for symphonic inspiration while lost in a deep sleep have a hideaway in the Walker House. Each of the eight enormous rooms is named after a composer, with a decor that evokes the composer's works. Handel has a Hallelujah Chorus brass bed; Debussy, impressionistic wallpaper; Verdi, a garden of wicker and summer colors; Mozart, an antique harmonium; and so on. As you will have gathered by now, owners Peggy and Dick Houdek are in love with music and the arts. Classical music greets guests, instruments serve as decorative objects, and the doorbell chimes out Big Ben's tune.

Breakfast is served in the large dining room, where guests are warmed by a winter fire and comforted by childhood memories of their own menageries—a family of oversized stuffed animals waits patiently at its own table for breakfast and afternoon tea. In addition to their love of music, the Houdeks are cat crazy, and none-too-subtle cat motif runs rampant, competing with the virtuosos. Walker House certainly ranks as one of the more memorable inns in New England, and it's great fun in its eccentric way.

Rooms: $45-$130, including breakfast.

Wheatleigh

W. Hawthorne St.
(off Rte. 183)
(413) 637-0610
Open year-round.
All major cards.

If you're in the inn business and believe that your architecture is your destiny, you are well advised to live up to that destiny. The nice people who own this neopalazzo should take such advice. One can only assume that the $385 it costs to sleep in the deluxe room is a contribution to the inn's restoration fund, or perhaps it goes toward the cost of printing Wheatleigh's slick brochure. It is certainly not for luxurious accommodations and superb bathrooms; nor is it for a historical decor. One feels slightly unbalanced walking into a sixteenth-century foyer and being greeted by faded contemporary furnishings that would look more appropriate in an art gallery. (Linfield and Susan Simon are indeed former Chicago gallery owners, and their personal collection is on display throughout the inn.) Putti and ornate carvings intermix with contemporary ceramics; it is an ambitious plan at best.

Nonetheless, Wheatleigh is filled to fifteen-room capacity each summer; demand for upscale accommodations near neighboring Tanglewood brings a steady stream of guests for whom price is never an issue. Granted, the mansionette built by the wealthy H. H. Cook as a wedding gift for his daughter affianced to a Spanish count is architecturally stunning, the surrounding 22 acres designed by Central Park architect Frederick Law Olmsted are lovely, the tennis court and pool are welcome, and the extraordinary abandoned clock tower is worth speculating about. But Wheatleigh bends toward the pretentious, from the guest rooms to the common areas to the costly but not-quite-right restaurant (see "Restaurants" above). Wheatleigh is quite an experience, but we only wish that the promise of such luxurious living were better delivered.

Rooms: $110-$425.

Whistler's Inn

5 Greenwood St.
(off Rte. 7A)
(413) 637-0975
Closed March-April.
Cards: AE, MC, V.

Whistler's Inn offers a taste of the good life that will whet most appetites. The 1870 inn, the former home of James McNeill Whistler's nephew George, is filled with architectural nostalgia that evokes a carefree, affluent turn-of-the-century life. The music room, its oversized mirror reflecting the gilt chairs and grand piano, is as handsome as the Falstaffian dining room, with its large hearth and putti-infested candelabra. The library, designed on a more human scale, proves the perfect place to chat with owners Richard and Joan Mears, an absolutely charming literary couple with whom there is never a dearth of good, intelligent conversation. If you prefer more privacy, the library doors open onto the grassy terrace, popular with sunbathing guests. The eleven bedrooms are decorated in Joan's personal style. Each is different, some retain the flavor of the history of the house, and all have private baths and cooling ceiling fans; even the smallest room is as sweet as the master suite.

Breakfast—home-baked breads and muffins, cheeses, pastries and fresh fruit—is served on the side porch during the summer and in the formal, baronial dining room during the winter.

Rooms: $70-$170, including breakfast.

SIGHTS

The Mount
Rte. 7 & Rte. 7A
(413) 637-1899
June-Aug.: tours Tues.-Sun.; Sept.-Oct.: tours Fri.-Sun.

Outdoor performances of a different nature than those at acclaimed Tanglewood (see below) take place at The Mount, the Georgian Revival home that author Edith Wharton designed for herself. At The Mount's outdoor amphitheater, director Tina Packer's Shakespeare & Co. (413-637-3353) performs plays by the Bard and others during the summer. The Mount and its gardens are also open for tours in the summer and early fall.

Tanglewood
Rte. 183
(413) 637-1600
Open July-Aug.

If the urge strikes to hear fine music under the stars, do as many New Englanders do: Hit the road (Route 183, to be exact) for Tanglewood, summer home of the Boston Symphony Orchestra. From early July through August, the BSO moves itself lock, stock and kettledrums to the Berkshires for a summer of music making, as a full orchestra and in small ensembles, with guest artists ranging from world-class performers (Leonard Bernstein, who cut his conducting teeth here, still appears several times each season) to promising students and its own Tanglewood Festival Chorus. Preconcert picnicking on the lawn is a favorite pastime—Champagne bottles and candelabra often emerge from those special baskets—but be sure to bring a sweater, especially late in the season. (See also "Music Festivals" chapter.)

SHOPS

Hand of Man
Main St. & Walker St.
(The Curtis Shops)
(413) 637-0632
Summer: open daily 9 a.m.-6 p.m.; off-season hours vary.

The diverse stock here includes a great deal of standard craft-shop items plus a few twists: leather masks with flame-like shapes, an iron hobbyhorse that looks like a piece of sculpture, even a water fountain. It's not worth a special trip, but drop by if you've got time to kill before a Tanglewood concert. As with most Berkshire stores, hours vary with the season.

Hoadley Gallery

17 Church St.
(413) 637-2814
Open Mon.-Tues. &
Thurs.-Sat. 10:30 a.m.-5
p.m., Sun. noon-4 p.m.;
hours may vary.

As befits an enterprise owned by potters, this shop is heavy on ceramics, many intended for daily use; the owners know quality in their colleagues' work, and you'll get a good overview of styles and techniques. The store also has a smattering of baskets, scarves, jewelry and the like.

Towne Gallery

28 Walker St.
(413) 637-0053
June-Aug.: open daily 10
a.m.-5 p.m.; Sept.-May: open
Tues.-Sat. 10 a.m.-5 p.m.;
hours may vary.

This is craft as fine art. The gallery has a sophisticated collection of large sculptural ceramics, such as Linda Levine-Madori's softly folded raku pots highlighted by iridescent metallic oxides. The work here is expensive but elegant.

NORTHAMPTON

RESTAURANTS

Beardsley's

140 Main St.
(413) 586-2699
FRENCH
Open Mon.-Thurs. 11:30
a.m.-2:30 p.m. & 5:30
p.m.- 10 p.m., Fri.-Sat.
11:30 a.m.-3 p.m. & 5:30
p.m.-10:30 p.m., Sun.
10:30 a.m.-4 p.m. & 5:30
p.m.-10 p.m.
Cards: AE, MC, V.

Since it is the only fancy French restaurant in Northampton, Beardsley's has a dependable clientele, heavy on businessmen and visiting parents of Smith College students. Thus there is a danger of complacency in the kitchen; and those locals who occasionally dine here, but can't really afford it, tend to resent the big-city prices. We've celebrated special occasions in its dark-wooded booths for years, and often enjoy the fine Sunday brunch and excellent lunch pastas. The French and California wine list ranges from a $12 Entre-Deux-Mers to a $1,200 magnum of Château Latour. At our last Beardsley's dinner, we started with the always-serviceable pâté accompanied by some crisp asparagus that was topped with a hollandaise as good as any we can recall. The main courses of sautéed trout with almonds and a grilled salmon were flanked on the plate by a phalanx of a half dozen vegetables plus buttery rice. The fish, done to perfection in both dishes, was wonderfully flavorful. When it came to dessert, our generally diffident waitress advised against adding ice cream to a fresh-fruit tartelette with Bavarian cream. She was right: The tartelette was ravishing and unimprovable, with fat strawberries and a lingering aftertaste of almonds. In the afterglow we reminisced about how we've usually gone into Beardsley's kvetching about the prices and have come out singing its praises. Dinner for two is about $80 with wine.

QUICK BITES

Curtis & Schwartz
116 Main St.
(413) 586-3278
Open Tues.-Sat. 7:30 a.m.-
4 p.m., Sun. 8 a.m.-3 p.m.
Cards: MC, V.

Like most of our acquaintances, we can never remember the name of Curtis & Schwartz, but simply refer to it as The Yuppie Place. This moniker is not intended to disparage what happens to be our favorite breakfast spot in Northampton and nearly the best place for lunch as well. We show up in this airy brick bistro most often for its breakfast and brunch specials, which run to arty and expert pancakes, waffles and omelets. There's always good soup for lunch, and the smoked-turkey sandwich on focaccia is reliably excellent. Young urban vegetarians can feast on falafel, gado-gado and the like. For many in the area, The Yup, that is, Curtis & Schwartz, is an at-least-once-a-week sort of place. Breakfast for two will run about $14, lunch about the same.

SHOPS

The Artisan Gallery
150 Main St.
(Thorne's Market)
(413) 586-1942
Open Mon.-Wed. & Sat.
9:30 a.m.-5:30 p.m.,
Thurs.-Fri. 9:30 a.m.-
9 p.m., Sun. noon-5 p.m.

Most of the work here is the fairly standard, midlevel jewelry, woodenware and pottery you see displayed at a good craft fair—until you get to the kaleidoscope counter. The store represents 65 different kaleidoscope makers, and prices range from $10 to a $1,200 beauty. These are no kids' toys, and people tend to stand there spinning the ends of the beautifully decorated tubes and uttering out loud, "Wow, look at this one!"

Don Muller Gallery
16 Main St.
(413) 586-1119
Open Mon.-Wed. & Fri.-
Sat. 10 a.m.-5:30 p.m.,
Thurs. 10 a.m.-9 p.m.

Long one of the premier craft stores in an area rife with craftspeople, this gallery offers a high-quality selection of art glass, sculptural ceramics, jewelry, stained glass, wood and soft sculpture in a handsomely designed space that features free-form sculpted shelves and display cases. Always fun to browse.

Peacework
263 Main St.
(413) 586-7033
Open Mon.-Wed. & Sat.
9:30 a.m.-5:30 p.m.,
Thurs.-Fri. 9:30 a.m.-9
p.m., Sun. noon-5 p.m.

If you're vacationing in New England only because all the flights to Santa Fe were booked, fear not. You can get authentic American Indian craftwork here, and because Peacework is a member of the American Indian Arts Association, the quality exceeds that of many of the tourist traps in the Southwest. In addition to dramatic shields, pottery, fine art and weavings, the store also carries some brightly colored clothes, purses and belts woven in Guatemala.

Pinch Pottery
179 Main St.
(413) 586-4509
*Open Mon.-Wed. & Sat.
10 a.m.-6 p.m., Thurs.-Fri.
10 a.m.-9 p.m., Sun. noon-
5 p.m.*

As the name implies, the specialty here is sculptural and functional ceramics, many from local potters. The excellent selection leans toward the postmodern but covers the bases—from raku to salt-glazed to brightly colored porcelain. Jewelry, both ceramic and glass, is also prominent. If you're here between October and December, drop by the annual invitational exhibit of teapots and tea sets; you'll feel as though you've been seated between Alice and the Mad Hatter.

Skera
221 Main St.
(413) 586-4563
*Open Mon.-Wed. & Fri.-
Sat. 10 a.m.-5:30 p.m.,
Thurs. 10 a.m.-9 p.m., Sun.
noon-5 p.m.*

Classy. Elegant. Pricey. Any upscale adjective you care to select can be applied to this sophisticated store, which does nothing to destroy Northampton's reputation as the trendiest small town in the Northeast. Exquisite work, including excellent furniture, precious and costume jewelry and gorgeous hand-painted silk garments, is exquisitely displayed. Fabulous.

NORTHFIELD

INNS

Northfield Country House
School St.
(413) 498-2692
Open year-round.
Cards: MC, V.

When you finally find this beautiful inn on a back road, secreted behind lush foliage, you may want to settle in for a long stay. Owner Andrea Dale has a beautiful piece of property; sixteen acres of lawns, gardens and stunning views, complete with barn and swimming pool. Guests rock away the afternoons admiring the surroundings; during the winter, they gather in front of the oversized hearth or in any of the seven feminine bedrooms. Iron beds, stone fireplaces, wicker, and bright floral-print walls are Andrea's design signature. The handsome dining room's hand-carved wood paneling and exquisite corner cupboards make it the centerpiece of the inn. Traditional hearty breakfasts are the norm, preceded by fresh fruit and freshly squeezed orange juice.
Rooms: $50-$80, including breakfast.

We are always happy to hear about your discoveries and to receive your comments about ours. We want to give your letters the attention they deserve, so when you write to us, remember to state clearly exactly what you liked or disliked. Be concise, but convincing. Do take the time to argue your point.

SHEFFIELD

SHOPS

**Hutchinson
& Good**
Rte. 7
(413) 229-8832
*Summer: open Mon.-Sat.
10 a.m.-5 p.m., Sun.
1 p.m.-5 p.m.; winter: open
some weekends (varies).*

When you enter this little overstuffed store, David Good may greet you with the good news that he is in the mood to sell some antiques that day. That is indeed good news, because you can be sure he'll charge you a fair price for the treasures he and partner Robert Hutchinson have collected from local estates and private owners. In all the dense clutter, you may come across such joys as a mint-condition Massachusetts Chippendale chest, a Hepplewhite bow-front bureau, a heartbreaking Japanese carp plate or a striking pair of Chinese ginger jar lamps, surrounded by mediocre oils and forgettable knickknacks.

Susan Silver
Rte. 7
(413) 229-8169
*Open Wed.-Mon. 10 a.m.-
5 p.m.*

It is most considerate of Susan Silver to include a line of furniture cream and polish in her shop so that her customers can buff up the $7,500 Scottish Sheraton tall clock, massive $22,000 Georgian mahogany wardrobe, $6,500 English sideboard or $8,500 George II walnut chest they'll be carting off. Cards on each piece offer mini furniture-history lessons, price tags are rather high, and the passports on almost all of her merchandise carry the Queen's crown. We've come across some wonderful surprises here: a handsome pair of watercolors of the last Dowager Empress and her Consort; a stunning crystal chandelier; an affordable Regency writing desk; and a tempting creamware basket. The personable Silver is helpful and informative.

SHELBURNE FALLS

RESTAURANTS

**Marty's Riverside
Restaurant & Bakery**
4 State St.
(413) 625-2570
INTERNATIONAL
*Open Tues.-Thurs. 8 a.m.-
9 p.m., Fri.-Sat. 8 a.m.-
10 p.m., Sun. 9 a.m.-9 p.m.
Cards: MC, V.*

12/20

The cozy ten-table bistro that calls itself the Riverside Restaurant sits alongside the Deerfield River, its back room overlooking the Bridge of Flowers, so famous among retirees. We've been fond of the Riverside for years, not only because its down-home atmosphere and calico curtains go nicely with a time-warp town like Shelburne Falls, but also because the food is consistently better than it has any particular reason to be—the local competition is primarily pizza joints and diners. After checking the tattered wine list of reliable cheapies, we recently chose a Bully Hill white and then fell to contemplating the perennial menu (filet mignon, chicken teriyaki, pastas, some vegetarian items); as usual, we settled on the daily seafood specials. Our pleasantly flaky waitress needed help opening the wine and kept asking us to remind her what we ordered—all par for the course. Over our homemade bread and crisp salads with exceptional vinaigrette, we wondered if the sautéed catfish could hope to equal the trout. Well, it turned out to be the catfish of our lives—fresh, actually melting in the mouth, showing how respectable a formerly low-class fish can become. The trout, tricked out in a rich herb sauce, was nearly as good. About the time the folk singer warmed up, we were enjoying some of the locally notorious desserts: pecan pie that is traditional (as in cloyingly sweet) and chocolate mousse of the type usually described as sinful. We'll be back soon. Dinner for two, with a modest wine, runs about $45.

SHOPS

Salmon Falls Artisans Showcase
Ashfield St.
(413) 625-9833
Open Mon.-Sat. 10 a.m.-6 p.m., Sun. noon-5 p.m.

Perched above the river that runs through the center of town, this old grain and feed warehouse has been transformed into one of the biggest and most charming craft centers in the area. The timber rafters and broad-beamed wooden floors have been left intact in the store on the top floor, which sells the work of many regional artisans. On the lower floor, visit Bald Mountain Pottery, which houses potters at the wheel; Briar and the Rose, where a couple sells handmade furniture and silk lingerie; and a basket maker.

SOUTH EGREMONT

QUICK BITES

Gaslight Store
Main St. (Rte. 23)
(413) 528-0870
Open Wed.-Mon. 7 a.m.-4 p.m.
No cards.

This delightful café will get your day off to an optimistic start, especially if you order one of the pancake specials: blueberry, strawberry and, in the winter, apple. Lunches are equally delicious—daily homemade soups, grilled and cold sandwiches, and such specials as open-faced Reubens and turkey-broccoli melts. The Gaslight is also known for its soda-fountain specialties, and the ice cream sodas, malts and sundaes are perfect for the soda-parlor setting, a throwback to gentler times, with wire-back chairs and tables, a small selection of groceries and a candy counter for the kids.

SHOPS

Bird Cage Antiques
Main St. (Rte. 23)
(413) 528-3556
Open daily 9 a.m.-5 p.m.

The peppy lyrics of Broadway show tunes frequently cheer up this slightly eccentric, on-the-dark-side store, which is filled with an odd assortment of whatever Marilyn and Arnold Baseman have recently found: children's twig chairs, oversized baskets, silver spoons, comic-character toys of the '30s, turn-of-the-century dolls and toys, and country-painted furniture.

Geffner & Schatzky
Main St. (Rte. 23)
(413) 528-0057
Summer: open daily 10 a.m.-5:30 p.m.; winter: open Fri.-Mon. 10 a.m.- 6 p.m., Tues.-Thurs. by chance.

This charming shop showcases the latest finds of owners Sheldon Geffner and Sidney Schatzky. Yellowware bowls, primitives, hobo art, antique costume jewelry, children's toys, decorative objects—you can find just about any small thing here. It's worth stopping in from time to time for that chance find of an antique bench, Swedish crayfish plates or a honey pot. The shop is easy to find, just across the street from the Gaslight Store.

SPRINGFIELD

RESTAURANTS

The Student Prince
8 Fort St.
(413) 734-7475
GERMAN
Open daily 11 a.m.- 11 p.m. (sandwiches until midnight).
All major cards.

German cuisine is generally better known for sticking to the ribs than for subtlety, and the common run of ersatz rathskellers only tend to confirm that reputation. That's why we've long admired The Student Prince, which for 50 years has maintained its status as one of the best restaurants of any nationality in Springfield (admittedly, competition is not fierce). The place divides into two dining rooms—The Student Prince proper, with its rows of steins and its antlers on the walls, and The Fort, hung with lots of fancy crockery and, on our last visit, decked out with a Maypole and streamers. As is proper, all this ethnic texture is kept in motion by waitresses ferrying huge steins of brew from some inexhaustible source. Here we've had the best Rippchen we've encountered outside Germany, here we've come to appreciate marinated herring, and here we've often been well marinated ourselves. (One of the fine things about German restaurants is that when you're tucking into the main course you're also well into the first stein, which is perhaps why the food does not require much subtlety.) Dishes we've tried include excellent, firm-fleshed smoked salmon with dill and horseradish sauces, a subtle and savory (if a bit dry) house pâté and a surprisingly lighthearted special of Geschnitzel (strips of veal in a white sauce). The regular-menu Jaeger Schnitzel is only fair, but in both entrées we appreciate the temperate portions (not that anything approaching nouvelle cuisine has contaminated the place). Don't make the mistake we've made by ordering the mousse, which tastes as if it had been made by some French-hating German, rather than the usual Strudel or whatnot. No matter; after dinner and a couple of drafts of Dortmunder and a glass or so of sweet dessert wine, we emerge in a fair state of bliss, our accustomed response to this deservedly long-lived eatery. About $45 for dinner for two, with beer.

STOCKBRIDGE

INNS

Inn at Stockbridge
Rte. 7
(413) 298-3337
May-Oct.: open daily;
Nov.-April: open weekends.
Cards: AE, MC, V.

To bypass the Berkshires' summer traffic and tourist crowds, come to this lovely inn, perched on a hillside far from the madding crowd. The handsome 1906 inn, with an impressive colonnaded front and symmetrical side porches, is a first-class overnight ticket. Owners Lee and Don Weitz believe that guests should be pampered, and you'll share their belief after spending a night in any of the seven beautiful rooms. Outside your room, you can relax in the formal living room or watch TV in the more casual sitting room, anticipating the morning's fabulous breakfast: breakfast soufflés, french toast with Grand Marnier butter, herbed scrambled eggs, blueberry pancakes and the Sunday-traditional eggs Benedict, all served on pretty china with matching silver flatware in the impressive dining room, adorned by an elongated table and Queen Anne seating. Outside are twelve acres to explore, the side porches to escape to with a book, and a refreshing pool with which to beat the summer heat.

Rooms: $80-$190, including breakfast; winter weekend packages, $200-$400, including breakfast and dinner.

Red Lion Inn
Main St.
(413) 298-5545
Open year-round.
Cards: AE, MC, V.

New Yorkers who visit the Red Lion Inn are likely to run into their neighbors—the place is so big that in the summer it looks like a Berkshires branch of the Upper East Side. Earnest waiters serve drinks to guests relaxing on rocking chairs on the front porch, watching the tourists stroll through this lovely town, which boasts a sleeper of a drawing card, the Norman Rockwell Museum at the Old Corner House.

The 105 rooms are modestly Victorian, some even more modest with old-fashioned washbasins in the room. It's all a bit frumpy and dated, but the masses who come here seem to enjoy themselves. Locals also like the Red Lion for its dining room, where they dine on traditional fare. A lunch of Welsh rarebit, creamed chicken, broiled scrod, prime rib hash or corn fritters with sausage always seems comforting in this confusing day of Burmese-Caribbean, Tunisian-Italian and Polynesian-Greek cuisine.

Rooms: Oct. 31-May 19, $45-$155; May 20-Oct. 30, $50-$212.

SIGHTS

Chesterwood
Rte. 183, 3 miles west
of Stockbridge
(413) 298-3579
*May 1-Oct. 1: open daily
10 a.m.-5 p.m.*

Houses of historical or cultural interest abound in New England, but Chesterwood is in a class by itself. The summer home of sculptor Daniel Chester French, famous for works ranging from the Minuteman Memorial at Concord Bridge to the mammoth seated Lincoln inside Washington's Lincoln Memorial, includes the painstakingly preserved artist's studio. Many of his working models in plaster are still on display, as is the innovative railroad-track system he used to take his massive sculptures outside for daylight viewing. The main building, a two-story Georgian Revival house, is also open, and as in French's time, the 120-acre estate still makes a pleasant spot for walking in the woods or gazing up at Monument Mountain.

Adults $4, children $1.

Norman Rockwell Museum
Main St.
(Old Corner House)
(413) 298-3822
Open daily 10 a.m.-4 p.m.

Stockbridge is a town straight out of a Norman Rockwell painting, with tree-lined streets, quaint little stores, white picket fences and the veranda of its famous Red Lion Inn. Little wonder, then, that Rockwell chose it as his home for the last 25 years of his life. And Rockwell was instrumental in setting up the town's memorial to him in the Old Corner House, where summertime visitors line up outside the door and way down the street to wait for outstanding docent-led tours that include 40 to 60 original paintings from the museum's collection of 600.

Adults $4, children 5-18 $1, children under 5 free.

SHOPS

Holsten Gallery
Elm St.
(413) 298-3044
*June-Aug.: open daily
10 a.m.-6 p.m.; Sept.-May:
open Fri.-Sun. 10:30 a.m.-
5 p.m.; hours may vary.*

Even if you're not planning to drop multiple thousands of dollars, you should stop in to see work by the top names in art glass today, such as Dale Chihuly and Harvey Littleton. There's also a small exhibit room in the rear for frequent one-man shows. If you're looking for fake Tiffany lampshades or a little glass birdie for the window, forget it.

STURBRIDGE

SIGHTS

Old Sturbridge Village
Rte. 20 off I-84
(508) 347-3362
Open daily except Mon. in winter, Christmas & New Year's Day; hours vary by season.

Even in Massachusetts, a lot of people don't realize there's a Sturbridge outside Old Sturbridge Village, the 200-acre museum that re-creates life and work in 1830s rural New England. Opened in 1946, it is among the oldest and most respected museum villages in the Northeast. More than 40 restored buildings, brought to the site from throughout New England, are populated by costumed guides who demonstrate trades ranging from blacksmithing to mechanized wool-carding to running a sawmill. If you're visiting in fall or winter, make reservations early for the weekend package at the Publick House, which includes admission to the village, accommodations at the period inn, game dinners and old-fashioned conviviality around the fireside. Adults $9.50, children $4, children under 6 free.

SUNDERLAND

QUICK BITES

Bub's Bar-B-Q
Amherst Rd. (Rte. 116)
(413) 259-1254
Open daily 5:30 p.m.-9 p.m.
No cards.

You don't see Bub and his magnificent belly around the place so much anymore; he's usually off fishing or collecting ribbons at cookoffs down South. But whether Bub's personally slinging those great gobbets of flesh onto the grill or not, over the years his ribs and pork and beef and catfish have maintained and even improved their fine quality, the Rolling Rock is still sweet from the tap, and the jukebox still belts out Hank Williams for free. Things don't change a whole lot here—there's still the same brothy soup, jambalaya, potato salad and barbecued beans in the all-you-can-eat bar. We figure it'll be a cold day in hell when Bub doesn't make some of the best damn barbecue in the East and the best cheap meal in Asparagus Valley. When you need to eat stuff that's bad for you, in quantity as well as quality, there's no better place. About $16 for two, with beer or good cheap wine.

WEST STOCKBRIDGE

SHOPS

G/M Galleries
Main St.
(413) 232-8519
Hours vary.

If you feel like you'll scream if you see one more quaint New England artifact, head for this grab bag of exotica. Behind its unassuming exterior hides a cache of tribal crafts imported from Africa and South America, as well as an eclectic selection of jewelry, much of it made by co-owner Marie Bonamici-Woodcock. Her creations respect no boundaries of geography or time; a necklace may feature an antique bead excavated from a Tibetan dig next to a contemporary African glass tube next to a Czech bauble.

WILLIAMSTOWN

RESTAURANTS

The Orchards
Main St. (Rte. 2 near North Adams)
(413) 458-9611
AMERICAN/CONTINENTAL
Open Mon.-Thurs. 7:30 a.m.-10 a.m., noon-2 p.m. & 6 p.m.-8:30 p.m., Fri.- Sat. 7:30 a.m.-10 a.m., noon- 2 p.m. & 6 p.m.- 9 p.m., Sun. 8 a.m.- 11 a.m., noon-2 p.m. & 6 p.m.- 8:30 p.m. (lunch in lounge daily noon- 5 p.m.).
All major cards.

12/20

There are no orchards in sight around The Orchards, and the exterior of this inn/restaurant is glumly fortress-like; but once inside, we found the dining room to be a treat— muted-pink damask tablecloths garnished with fresh flowers, green plush velvet on the walls, a garden with a summer dining deck, and an acoustic design that keeps the sound pleasantly muted. The dinner menu changes daily, the specials running to colorfully named and ambitious dishes like "Poached Filet of Salmon, Massachusetts Bay Colony" and "Roast Duck The Orchards." There is a changing and much-recommended two-menu table d'hôte for $25. A largely middle-priced wine list also includes a few luxurious French varieties. We found the house New England clam chowder silky smooth and satisfying, if a bit complacent; ditto the veal pâté, which was savory with herbs and flanked by cornichons of eye-opening piquancy. We also tasted a gentle, buttery filet of scrod handsomely laid out on the plate, with a lemon slice discreetly bound in cheesecloth. The pastry tray (there is a regular pastry chef) can only be called bewitching; as an example, the chocolate-raspberry gâteau does just what it's supposed to– dazzle with heady, fruity chocolate. All in all, the elegance of the dining room is reflected in the food, and together they are a welcome touch of class in the area of Williams College and the Clark Art Institute. About $75 for two, with wine.

SIGHTS

You'd be hard-pressed to find a more picture-perfect college town than this one. Home of Williams College, the town has vast green lawns, churches with white steeples, and romantic inns. Despite its small size, Williamstown is also a cultural center, thanks in large part to the college. The chief year-round attraction is the Sterling and Francine Clark Art Institute (South Street on campus; 413-458-9545), with its dazzling collection of impressionist paintings, some of which have been lent to museums in lands as far away as New Zealand. In summer, the Williamstown Theater Festival (413-597-3400) draws well-known actors (Christopher Reeve and Blythe Danner are among the regulars) for a season of classic and experimental works.

WORCESTER

SIGHTS

Mechanics Hall
321 Main St.
(508) 752-5608

Worcester's leading center for the performing arts is Mechanics Hall, an 1857 jewel of a concert hall that was due for demolition before its restoration in 1977. With acoustics considered second only to those of Boston's Symphony Hall, it's especially suited to solo recitals and chamber groups. In addition, it boasts the oldest four-manual organ in the Western Hemisphere (1864). International Artists Series, a chief tenant of the hall, has been bringing world-class musical performers (including Yehudi Menuhin, Itzhak Perlman, Jessye Norman and major orchestras) to the city for more than a decade. The nearby Worcester Centrum (Foster and Commercial streets; 508-755-6800) ranks as central Massachusetts's major convention center and arena; it's a favorite among big-name acts, especially rock musicians.

New England Science Center
222 Harrington Way
(508) 791-9211
Open mid-April-Labor Day: Mon.-Sat. 10 a.m.-5 p.m., Sun. noon-5 p.m.; Sept.-mid-April: open Wed.-Sat. 10 a.m.-5 p.m., Sun. noon-5 p.m.

As the home of Worcester Polytechnic Institute, as well as a number of smaller colleges, Worcester has its scientific side. Visitors and residents benefit from this scientific bent via the admirable New England Science Center, which offers exhibits on natural science, a planetarium and a 59-acre park and zoo that's home to a polar bear family.

Adults $3.50, children $2.75, children under 3 free.

Worcester
Art Museum
55 Salisbury St.
(508) 799-4406
Open Tues.-Fri. 10 a.m.-
4 p.m., Sat. 10 a.m.-
5 p.m., Sun. 1 p.m.-5 p.m.

Worcester has an unfortunate reputation as a dull, depressed industrial city, but it has experienced something of a renaissance in recent years, especially on the cultural front. The Worcester Art Museum has long been known for its superb collection spanning the centuries and the world, including the Western Hemisphere's largest collection of medieval armor. It also has an Asian gallery and one of the first collections of pre-Columbian art in the United States.

Adults $3.50, seniors & students $2, children free; admission free Saturday.

SHOPS

The Prints
and the Potter
142 Highland St.
(508) 752-2170
Open Mon.-Tues. &
Thurs.-Fri. 9 a.m.-5:30
p.m., Wed. 9 a.m.-9 p.m.,
Sat. 9 a.m.-4 p.m.

A surprisingly savvy selection of contemporary craftwork, including jewelry, handmade paper items, ceramics, glass and wood. The store's staff is accustomed to working with interior designers and is happy to offer advice.

Worcester Craft
Center
25 Sagamore Rd.
(508) 753-8183
Open Mon.-Sat. 9 a.m.-
5 p.m.

The gift shop at this large educational institution is nothing remarkable—the work of local and national artists jumbled with gift items and Caswell-Massey soaps. But the other end of the building has a good exhibit space, and as you walk down the hall, you can peep through the windows of the various studios and see the craftspeople at work. There's also a supply store that's stocked with tools and books for such crafts as woodworking, basketry and weaving.

RHODE ISLAND

BLOCK ISLAND

RESTAURANTS

Block Island Broiler
Water St.
(401) 466-5811
SEAFOOD
*Memorial Day-Labor Day:
open nightly 5:30 p.m.-
10:30 p.m.; late April-
Memorial Day & Labor
Day-Oct. 31: open Fri.-Sat.
5:30 p.m.-10:30 p.m.
Cards: AE, MC, V.*

12/20

The Block Island Broiler is a rarity among dining establishments: a resort-area restaurant with a chef who's actually a native. Perhaps this explains the affinity Donald Hauser seems to have for the local snapper, tuna and swordfish. The snapper might be cooked au poivre, the swordfish served with a Grand Marnier butter sauce. All the dishes feature Block Island–grown vegetables and herbs. The decor is as simple and tasteful as the bill of fare: white walls with green trim and antique photographs of Block Island, polished cotton tablecloths with matching seat covers, and plants and flickering candlelight on each table. The servers—dressed in white shirts and khaki trousers—are personable and efficient. The recently renovated bar has become the island's hottest watering hole. And speaking of water, bottled spring water is used for both filling the water glasses and cooking. About $60 for two, with wine.

INNS

**1661 Inn
and Guest House**
Hotel Manisses, Spring St.
(401) 466-2421
*Closed Nov. 16-April 3.
Cards: AE, MC, V.*

1661 was a good year for Block Island: That's when the first English settlers made this lovely island their home. And 1970 was another good year for Block Island: That's when the Abrams family opened the 1611 Inn, a rambling place with sensational ocean views. The rooms (named for those early settlers) range from serviceable to spectacular, and all are decorated with Colonial antiques; some have private baths, kitchenettes, and private decks overlooking the harbor. If we can't have the spacious Samuel Deering Room, which has a large oceanfront deck, we'll settle for the John Akurs Room, which also has a deck. And if we can't have the Akurs Room, we prefer to seek lodging elsewhere—usually at the Hotel Manisses, which is, conveniently, also owned and run by the Abrams family. Built in 1870, the Victorian hotel has eighteen individually decorated guest rooms, all named for ships wrecked in Block Island waters in past centuries. All rooms have private baths, and some have Jacuzzis and king-size beds. Other amenities include a garden terrace with Victorian lawn furniture, high tea in the lobby, and staff in period dress. Breakfast only is served at the 1661 Inn in an ocean-view dining room; lunch and dinner are served daily (from May 21 to October 21) in the Hotel Manisses's dining rooms.
Rooms: $48-$190, including breakfast.

SIGHTS

Just twenty miles off Newport, Block Island still has the rustic maritime charm that characterized such places as Nantucket and Martha's Vineyard before tourism ran rampant. Oh, it has a few condos and time-shares now, but essentially Block Island remains unspoiled, a place for enjoying sunshine, fresh air, peace and quiet. Beloved of pleasure-boaters and a frequent stop for windjammers out of Newport, Block Island can be reached by ferry from Point Judith or Providence (Interstate Navigation Co.; 401-789-3502), New London, Connecticut (Nelseco Navigation Co.; 203-442-9553), and Montauk, Long Island (Viking Fishing Fleet; 516-668-5700; no cars). Although the ferries do carry cars (book as early as possible, especially for summer weekends and holidays), a bike is a more-than-satisfactory means of getting around. On-island, you can enjoy the ocean vistas from the island's many beaches or from Southeast Lighthouse, perched 200 feet above the sea on Mohegan Bluffs. And for perspectives on the island's far-reaching (by American standards) history, visit the Block Island Historical Society's museum on Old Town Road (401- 466-2481), which is open from late June to mid-September, Wednesday to Monday 10 a.m. to 4 p.m. The island can also be reached by plane on New England Airlines (800-243-2460).

CRANSTON

RESTAURANTS

Twin Oaks
100 Sabra St.
(401) 781-9693
AMERICAN
Open Tues.-Sun. 11:30 a.m.-1 a.m.
All major cards.

12/20

Twin Oaks defines New England hospitality to a T. It's one of those enormous family restaurants: You enter a foyer, give your name to the hostess, then retire to the bar for an hour or so to drink whisky-and-water and watch the lake out back. Then you hear your name called and are ushered to a roomy booth, where a smiling waiter takes your order and begins bringing trays laden with shrimp cocktail, rolls and butter, salad and dressings, soup, a slab of good roast beef or steak, potato, and desserts big enough to satisfy a hungry New England Patriot after a big win. When the bill comes, you see that you've spent no more for your family of four than you would usually pay for you and your spouse at even a moderate restaurant in downtown Providence. You go out full, you go out happy, and you go home feeling lucky that such places as Twin Oaks still exist. Two people, with drinks, probably won't spend more than $45.

LITTLE COMPTON

SIGHTS

The many bays and inlets along Rhode Island's coast tend to cut off some areas, and the Tiverton/Little Compton/Sakonnet area is actually more accessible from Massachusetts (approaching through Fall River) than from the rest of its own state. This comparative isolation works in its favor, for this section has more rural New England charm (albeit of the upscale, gentleman-farmer variety) than any other part of the state. From Route 24, turn onto Route 77 south. The first stop should be Tiverton, a village known for its few but select shops, especially Provender (see "Tiverton").

From there, continue south to Little Compton, a community of rolling estates and gracious homes that fall just short of mansion status. But the town's claim to fame is pure salt of the earth: Little Compton was the birthplace (in 1854) of the Rhode Island Red. A fitting monument to the breed stands at the junction of routes 81 and 179 in Adamsville. Another kind of Rhode Island red—the kind made from grapes—is produced at Sakonnet Vineyards, 162 W. Main Road (401-635-4356). The winery is open year-round for tours and tastings (the fall harvest is an especially good time to visit) and offers special programs, such as cooking classes at the main house with some of New England's top chefs. Continue by car or bike down winding Route 77 to its end at quiet Sakonnet Point to watch the gulls and the boats go by.

NEWPORT

RESTAURANTS

Clarke Cooke House
Bannister's Wharf
(401) 849-2900
FRENCH/AMERICAN
Open Mon.-Sat. 6 p.m.-
10 p.m. & Sun. 11:30 a.m.-
3 p.m. & 6 p.m.-10 p.m.
All major cards.

Of all the restaurants in Newport, Clarke Cooke House is by far the most enchanting. The Colonial (1790) house seems completely at home with its surroundings, the history of the city and the sophistication of its clientele, who come here for special evenings when they don't feel like beer and oysters at the Raw Bar across the wharf. Jackets are required, but feel free to wear your most outlandish pink, green or madras sports jacket if you wish to dress like the visiting yachtsmen.

Clarke Cooke House is set above the commendable Candy Store Cafe, which serves a simple American menu with some eclectic touches and functions as one of the most dynamic bars in the harbor area. You enter from the wharf, go upstairs past another bar and find yourself in a third-floor dining room with hardwood floors, flickering candles in hurricane lamps and a wonderful view of the harbor's yachts. The tuxedo-clad staff is respectful though not particularly swift-footed. The wine list is exceptionally deep, especially in overpriced old Bordeaux; when we asked for a $35 Bordeaux, the captain apologized that they were out of it and offered instead a choice of two wines, without telling us the prices (one turned out to be $35 and the other, $53).

Chef Brian Halloran, who is also chef at Boston's Locke-Ober Café, is talented but perhaps overworked. He tries to keep up with his contemporaries but sometimes goes overboard with such dishes as a quail salad with sesame, radicchio and melon balls or fried zucchini-flower beignets in a too-rich beurre blanc. But his steak au poivre in the style of Roger Vergé is near perfect, and his tuna with a tapenade stuffing and coulis of Provençal tomatoes shows he knows how to cook in the modern style. His desserts include a very American "snowball in hell"—chocolate terrine with ice cream and coconut in a wine glass—and a very French raspberry charlotte with an apricot coulis. You may get Locke-Ober's famous macaroons here, too. Two people should expect a tab of at least $120, including a bottle of wine.

The Mooring

Sayer's Wharf
(401) 846-2260
AMERICAN
Open Sun.-Thurs.
11:30 a.m.-10 p.m. &
Fri.-Sat. noon-11 p.m.
Cards: AE, MC, V.

11/20

When that sea air sets your appetite racing, race on over to The Mooring, which is set right on the water at the Newport harbor, where the sunsets can take your breath away. As delightful as it is to sit on the veranda and sip Bloody Marys or piña coladas, it's also worthwhile to eat inside in the high-ceilinged, spacious dining room decorated simply with yachting prints and populated with a clientele whose entire wardrobe seems to consist of Lacoste shirts, khaki slacks and Top-siders. You won't feel out of place in a blue blazer, but leave your necktie in your hotel room.

The service is of the "How we all doin' here?" variety, and the food is fresh and good, though it won't win any prizes for creativity. You'll be happy with a lunch of pita-bread sandwiches or lobster salad, or you might want to dig into a massive slab of prime rib or a boiled lobster served with nothing more than drawn butter and a baked potato. The place is always jammed, but The Mooring gets a somewhat tonier breed of customer than the cheaper tourist spots lining Newport's main drag. Two people can dine heartily, with wine, for about $75 or $80.

QUICK BITES

Island Omelette Shoppe
1 Farewell St.
(401) 847-9389
Open daily 6 a.m.-2 p.m.
No cards.

While we cannot say that the Island Omelette Shoppe is among Newport's more stylish eateries, we can say that we've loved every morsel of the hearty breakfasts we've had here. The Shoppe has been here for decades and, sad to say, looks as if it hasn't been scrubbed down in a good long while; its yellowed walls bear witness to a laissez-faire attitude. But you won't mind once you've tasted the fluffy, buttery omelets of every description and the freshly baked blueberry, corn, oatmeal and other muffins that are buttered and quickly grilled to achieve a moistness that goes well with the good coffee. Breakfast for two will cost you no more than $10.

INNS

Admiral Benbow Inn
93 Pelham St.
(401) 846-4256
Closed Jan.
Cards: AE, MC, V.

Glorious Palladian windows greet you at this 1855 home, which was built by Admiral Augustus Littlefield as a guesthouse for his sailor cronies (his own, more spectacular house is located down the block) and which today serves as a pleasant, if somewhat impersonal, fifteen-room inn. All bedrooms have private baths, some have brass beds, others have canopy beds, and one has a private deck (that room is usually booked well in advance for the summer season). Breakfast, served in the cool basement breakfast room, comprises such light fare as muffins and fruit breads, which will well prepare you for shopping, sight-seeing and the de rigueur visit to the nearby summer palaces on Ocean Drive.
Rooms: $45-$100, including breakfast.

Cliffside Inn
2 Seaview Ave.
(401) 847-1811
Closed Nov.-April.
Cards: MC, V.

Cliffside has an eccentric history and, appropriately enough, a slightly eccentric owner: the always-endearing Kay Russell. She has an offbeat approach to just about everything, from the peculiar naming of her French cat, Oiseau (you may hear Jacques Brel singing to Oiseau on the stereo, which helps keep the cat bilingual), to hanging a corner cabinet upside down for a better fit. Cliffside is alive with festive colors, a unique decor, lots of energy and a haunting past. Original owner Beatrice Turner, a Philadelphia Main Line runaway, devoted herself to a career as a painter, to the chagrin of her upper-crust family. To their horror, her main pictorial subject was her own naked body. When her father finally died, she painted his portrait in death (legend has it she propped him up for two weeks in her dining room) as some sort of tribute, then painted the entire exterior of the house black in mourning.

Things are considerably cheerier here today. Russell has decorated the ten rooms in her own interpretative style, using pastels and unusual paint schemes; each is unique and upbeat, and each has its own bath. A former home-economics teacher, she prepares classic breakfasts: chocolate donuts, apricot coffee bread, strawberries-and-cream cake and so on. During the season, the inn is filled with attractive young people with the prerequisite windsurfer-laden BMWs in the driveway; they keep the atmosphere festive on the lovely front porch as they prepare for a day filled with upwardly mobile activities.

As the name suggests, Cliffside is perfectly located at the beginning of Cliff Walk, the scenic pathway that dates back to Colonial times and is the best way to get an up-close-and-personal look at the summer castles dotting Newport's shoreline. This voyeur's walk allows you to eavesdrop on gardeners helping their employers keep up appearances, to get a glimpse of Marble House's brilliant red teahouse and to look out for famous faces framed by their large awning-shaded windows. This walk is one of the most pleasant ways to get a private look at turn-of-the-century mansion life.

Rooms: $65-$90, including breakfast.

**The Inn
at Castle Hill**
Ocean Dr.
(401) 849-3800
Closed Dec. 24-25.
Cards: AE, MC, V.

If you fancy yourself a latter-day Jay Gatsby, The Inn at Castle Hill will make you feel right at home. You'd better be compulsively organized, too, because you'll need to book a room far in advance. Although not quite on the scale of The Elms or The Breakers, this minimansion is still quite impressive. Original owner Alexander Agassiz left many of his precious world-travel souvenirs in place—a considerate move that allows you to tour his collection of Orientalia and imagine owning his mansionette and the staff that came with it.

The inn has the atmosphere that makes the very rich feel comfortable: an understated decor, fabulous views, a true sense of privacy, and oversized bathrooms (we sometimes wonder just what went on in these ballroom-size bathrooms back then). All ten bedrooms are charming, with upper-class wallpapers, occasional sitting rooms, serene color schemes, antique furnishings and rampant luxury; owner Paul McEnroe keeps things in good shape indeed. In summer, the inn is a fairytale-come-true for tourists who have only read about life of the privileged classes. The graceful awnings shade a bevy of well-tanned, well-heeled guests who sip dry martinis while they admire one another and the perfect summer sunset, awaiting their fashionably late dinner reservations. The men wear the required jackets, and *no one* wears jeans. The formal dining rooms are always crowded with those who like their country-inn food to have a sophisticated French accent: lobster mousse with morel sauce, escargots in puff pastry with brandy cream, chicken breast stuffed with a truffle-perfumed mousse, breast of duck in raspberry sauce and a salmon filet with beurre blanc. Lunch is another tuxedoed-waiter event, and breakfast features a full buffet loaded with pastries, bagels, cheeses, breakfast meats and fresh berries with cream.

Local Newporters also come here in the off-season, when all the sherbet-color-clad tourists have gone home. They congregate at the manly bar to gossip, and they relax around the handsome, palatial inn as though they own the place.

Rooms: $55-$230, including breakfast.

Inntowne
6 Mary St.
(401) 846-9200
Closed Dec. 24-25.
Cards: AE, MC, V.

There is a profusion of flowers at Inntowne. In the seventeen bedrooms, flowers (in the form of fabrics) climb the walls, are spread across the bedspreads and curtains, hang above you on the canopies, cover the chairs, show up in the modern bathrooms and even decorate the wastebaskets. It is a fresh approach to conventional inn decor that saves itself from being oppressive by being tasteful. The feminine touch so evident in the hothouse florals and choice of furnishings belongs to owner Betty McEnroe (wife of Paul McEnroe, king of Castle Hill). She is also dedicated to service, so her guests find the staff eager to help them plan a day exploring Newport's public and private sides. Her marriage helps guests score an otherwise-impossible-to-obtain table at The Inn at Castle Hill for a coveted Thanksgiving dinner or a romantic table for two at the height of the season.

Betty serves a light breakfast in a charming dining room in which the furnishings are for sale—you can purchase the chair in which you sit, the table at which you eat and the English bone china teacups and saucers in which your coffee is served. You'll find yourself surrounded by parents visiting their children at local boarding schools, couples weekending with boat-owning friends, and well-manicured yuppies getting away from their claw to the top.

Rooms: $80-$140, including breakfast.

SIGHTS

Ah, Newport in season! When High Society left old New York for the summer, they headed for Newport. No other New England resort had quite the same cachet. Today many of the old families have died out or found new spots for summering, but they've left their mark on the town in a way that any visitor, rich or not so rich, can enjoy.

Newport is brimming with attractions, but the best known are the summer "cottages" built by various Vanderbilts, Astors and their cohorts. The greatest concentration lines Bellevue Avenue, among them

Château-Sur-Mer, built in 1852 in high Victorian style for a merchant made rich by the China trade; Marble House, designed by Richard Morris Hunt; The Elms, built in 1901 as the home of a Pennsylvania coal-mining mogul; and Rosecliff, designed by Stanford White on the order of the Grand Trianon at Versailles. Each mansion seems more opulent than the last, but the hands-down winner is surely The Breakers, a northern Italian palace on Ochre Point Avenue designed by Hunt for Cornelius Vanderbilt. The Newport Preservation Society (401-847-1000) maintains seven historic houses, which are open from April to November on varying schedules. Admission to individual houses ranges from $2 to $4.50, but a better bargain is the combination ticket, ranging from $7 for any two mansions to $25 for all seven plus Green Animals, a topiary garden in nearby Portsmouth. Other cottages worth seeing include Beechwood, John Jacob Astor's mansion (580 Bellevue Avenue, 401-846-3774; open June to December); Belcourt Castle, containing Newport's largest antiques collection (Bellevue Avenue, 401-846-0669); Hammersmith Farm (Ocean Drive, 401-846-7346), summer home of the Auchincloss clan and the site of Jack and Jackie Kennedy's wedding reception; and Salve Regina College, an early cottage by Richard Morris Hunt that teenyboppers of the 1960s will remember as the exterior of Collinwood in the TV soap opera *Dark Shadows*. While you're touring the mansions (which are spread out over several miles; plan to travel by car or bike if you hope to see them all), be sure to stroll Cliff Walk, a National Recreation Trail high above the Atlantic that looks into the backyards of many of the mansions.

The high-society emphasis of the last century or so tempts one to forget that Newport began life long before the age of summering millionaires. Its early history revolved around the sea, and Newport has served New England as a strategic defense point since its earliest days. Fort Adams State Park on Ocean Drive (401-847-2400), the second-largest fort in the United States, was the key to the U.S. defense of Narragansett Bay from 1799 to 1945, housing 2,400 troops on its 21 acres. The fort has turned to more peaceful uses, with such facilities as public beaches, boat-launching ramps and sports fields. Although the fort itself is not open to the public, the park is open daily year-round from 6 a.m. to 11 p.m.; an admission of $1 for Rhode Island cars and $2 for out-of-state cars is charged in summer only. Newport's maritime heritage remains very much in evidence along the waterfront, although many of the wharf buildings that once stored cargo have been turned into boutiques catering to tourists. Among them are the Brick Market, which stretches for blocks along Thames Street, and Bowen's Wharf, off Thames near Pelham Street.

Newport also has a long religious heritage (remember that Rhode Island was founded by religious refugees from Massachusetts), including just about every faith that has ever made its way to America. Among the historic houses of worship are the 1725 Trinity Church in Queen Anne Square, where George Washington occupied pew 81; Touro Synagogue, 85 Touro Street, the oldest Jewish house of worship in America (1763); Channing Memorial Church, 135 Pelham Street, dedicated to Unitarian leader William Ellery Channing; and St. Mary's Church, Spring Street at Memorial Boulevard, center of Rhode Island's oldest Roman Catholic parish, where John F. Kennedy married Jacqueline Bouvier in 1953.

As might be expected in a city of such wealth, Newport abounds in museums and galleries that boast fine collections. A good orientation point is the Newport Historical Society's museum and research library, 82 Touro Street (401-846-0813), which is open year-round Tuesday to Friday 9:30 a.m. to 4:30 p.m. and, from mid-June to Labor Day, on Saturday 9:30 a.m. to noon; admission is free. The Newport Art Museum, 76 Bellevue Avenue (401-847-0179), another Richard Morris Hunt design, houses changing exhibitions of art from Newport and throughout New England. It's open Tuesday to Saturday 10 a.m. to 5 p.m., Sunday 1 p.m. to 5 p.m. Nearby, the Redwood Library and Athenaeum at 50 Bellevue Avenue (401-847-0292), a subscription library housed in the oldest continuously used library building in America (since 1748), also contains an outstanding collection of American paintings, including some Gilbert Stuarts. It's open Monday to Saturday 9:30 a.m. to 5:30 p.m. (to 5 p.m. in July and August); admission is free.

The same people who brought society to Newport also gave it a penchant for upscale sports. Tennis's first National Singles Championship was held in 1881 at the Newport Casino, the building that today houses the International Tennis Hall of Fame, the world's largest museum devoted to tennis. The museum (194 Bellevue Avenue, 401-849-3990) features displays covering a century of the sport's history, and a Grand Prix tournament is still played on its grass courts every summer. It's open May to October, daily 10 a.m. to 5 p.m.; November to April, daily 11 a.m. to 4 p.m.; admission is $4 for adults and $2 for children, with a $10 family rate.

PROVIDENCE

RESTAURANTS

Adesso
161 Cushing St.
(401) 521-0770
AMERICAN/ITALIAN
*Open Mon.-Thurs. 11:45
a.m.-2:30 p.m. & 5 p.m.-
10:30 p.m., Fri. 11:45
a.m.-2:30 p.m. & 5 p.m.-
midnight, Sat. 5 p.m.-mid-
night, Sun. 11:30 a.m.-
3 p.m. & 5 p.m.-10 p.m.
Cards: AE, MC, V.*

12/20

Adesso, which means "now" in Italian, is a restaurant with a subtitle that says it all: "California Cafe." Indeed, the name would be a mere contrivance were it not for the fact that you can get some delicious food here if you pick and choose among all the frightfully trendy items on the overly large menu.

Entry to Adesso is through a parking lot perfumed with the aroma of a garbage dumpster. A valet takes your car and tells you there's a ten-minute wait for tables (no reservations are taken). You enter through glass doors and are met by a stout maître d' who tells you the wait will be 35 minutes. When you voice your dismay, he shrugs and tells you to wait in a stifling hallway outside the glass doors, where you sit on lawn furniture and pray that time will fly. Finally, you are ushered into a handsome dining room of gray walls, black ceiling, track lights, open kitchen, large windows—oh, you know the look from L.A. The tablecloths look like silver industrial fabric. The waiters are in blue jeans and black shirts.

True, we ordered the more exotic items out of a sense of duty, but we found the less-eccentric dishes to be the better ones. Pizza topped with barbecued chicken, cilantro, red onion, smoked gouda and mozzarella tasted bizarre, but one with eggplant, garlic, red onion, oregano, Parmesan and mozzarella was delicious. Half-moon ravioli stuffed with Mascarpone cheese and sauced with sage and butter was comforting, but angel-hair pasta in a broth of chicken, sun-dried tomatoes and leeks was quite dull. Tomato ravioli with a jambalaya sauce was, shall we say, odd. Entrées are a bit more inviting—tuna with a tomato-mint salsa and delicious sea scallops with mandarin-orange cream stand out. But the fine thick veal chop smothered in a poorly rendered mushroom demi-glace and cream was a shame. The desserts are all right, though a bit gloppy. The wine list, however, is commendable, especially in Italian bottlings. Plan for a couple, with wine, to spend about $75.

The prices listed in this guide reflect what restaurants and hotels have informed us they plan to charge at press time. Please don't blame us if they don't coincide exactly with reality.

Al Forno

7 Steeple St.
(401) 273-9760
ITALIAN/INTERNATIONAL
Open Tues.-Sat. 5:30 p.m.-
10 p.m.
Cards: AE, MC, V.

One of the things that marks so many of the best new chefs in American restaurants is that so many come not out of a cooking school or restaurant training but out of another career entirely. Such a trajectory may bring an interesting slant on a restaurant's operation and cooking style. In the case of George Germon, the switch was from architectural designer and teacher at the Rhode Island School of Design; for his partner, Johanne Killeen, the road curved from photography into baking. From this union came Al Forno (which translates as "from the oven"), a minuscule restaurant strikingly done in black, with a blue-tiled bar area the size of a darkroom. From an equally small kitchen emerge a variety of dishes with an emphasis on Italian tradition but with occasional nods to the Orient or to wherever the owners have recently traveled.

At both Al Forno and Lucky's (see review below), their other restaurant, Germon and Killeen have been innovators, drawing on their New England larder to fashion robust, Italian-inspired dishes—pasta with grilled chicken, pancetta, cream and five cheeses, for instance, or a Tuscan bean and vegetable soup—along with their celebrated "grilled pizzas" (see Lucky's) topped with such items as Gorgonzola, tomato, garlic and Bel Paese. They do wonderful sausages, as well as a veal tenderloin with rapini and Gorgonzola butter, and their brief dessert menu features Killeen's toothsome New England specialties, like the strawberry and rhubarb tart or an almond-stuffed baked apple gratin. The breads come from one of the best bakeries in the region, Original Palmieri's Bakery (at 147 Ridge Street in Providence), and you can be sure that Germon and Killeen are using the finest olive oil, peppers and regional produce they can find.

The only bad news is that Al Forno is cramped; its few tables make it a difficult spot to get into most nights of the week. Dinner for two, with wine, should be about $95 to $100.

The Bluepoint Oyster Bar and Restaurant

99 N. Main St.
(401) 272-6145
AMERICAN/SEAFOOD
Open Sun.-Thurs. 5 p.m.-
11 p.m., Fri.-Sat. 5 p.m.-
11:30 p.m.; oyster bar: open
daily 5 p.m.-midnight.
All major cards.

Given the region's historic link to the seafaring trade, it has always surprised us that not every New England city has a good little seafood house like The Bluepoint. And in such an unassuming, unpretentious spot (blue-neon logo, tavern-like booths and casually dressed waitresses, most of whom are recruited from Brown University up the hill), it is even more surprising to find one of the most amazing wine lists in the Northeast. There are bottlings from all over the globe, including some of the finest Bordeaux, Burgundies and California Chardonnays to be found anywhere, and the catalog of beers is almost as impressive.

But you come here primarily for the seafood, simply cooked and pristinely fresh. You try hard to read the blackboard menu in the dim lights, you go along with the waitress when she suggests for the specials that evening, and you settle down with a good white wine to nibble on the oyster crackers and enjoy a classic New England chowder or a peppery Manhattan clam chowder full of tender tomato morsels. The more "inventive" the kitchen becomes, the less successful the dish, as with the angelfish with apples and cream sauce or the overseasoned sole Dugléré. But you'll feast on the scallops in a sauce of garlic, wine and pine nuts, the Block Island swordfish with tarragon butter or the grilled prawns—and you need not save room for the run-of-the-mill desserts. Dinner for two, with wine, should cost about $80.

Leo's
99 Chestnut St.
(401) 274-3541
AMERICAN
Open Mon.-Thurs. 11:30 a.m.-1 a.m., Fri. 11:30 a.m.-2 a.m., Sat. 5 p.m.-2 a.m., Sun. 5 p.m.-1 a.m. No cards.

11/20

The story goes that Leo's is rumored to be named after a fellow who was stabbed by a woman a long time ago, which lends the place a certain grisly, antic charm. Set in the bottom of what was once a jewelry vault, this has been for some time the meeting place for Brown and Rhode Island School of Design professors and students, as well as the unofficial watering hole for Trinity Square Repertory actors and directors. So Leo's draws a crowd that dresses and acts a bit more bohemian than the crowd at the blue-collar taverns around town. The fabric-mâché figures by Kay Ritter and the murals of favorite customers by Dan Gosch are part of the artsy atmosphere, and the food is several notches above pub fare: excellent soups, hearty chili with beans, and quite luscious desserts, especially the pecan pie. On most nights of the week, expect a good wait for a table, but you won't mind terribly—the clientele and the action are easy on the eyes. Two will spend about $60 for dinner with wine.

Lucky's
577 S. Main St.
(401) 272-7980
ITALIAN/FRENCH
*Open Tues.-Sat. 5:30 p.m.-10 p.m.
Cards: AE, MC, V.*

Almost single-handedly George Germon and Johanne Killeen have boosted Providence's gastronomic reputation, first with the opening of Al Forno (see review above) and in 1987 with Lucky's. This appealing brick-walled converted nineteenth-century stable, with its fireplace in the bar, its hanging dried herbs and its wood-fired oven, is set along the river, although the landscape at this particular bend is nothing much to delight in.

Lucky's serves some remarkably faithful renditions of provincial French and Italian classics, from a first-rate pissaladière to a garlic potato cake of real flavor. There are several interesting lasagnes, good cassoulet and perfectly grilled chicken, pork chops and skirt steak over wilted watercress. But you cannot visit Lucky's without trying one of its justly famous "grilled pizzas," a brilliant, if accidental, idea that came about when the owners were trying to reproduce the crisp, toasty crust of true Italian pizza. The result is a very thin, ill-shapen crust that is simultaneously chewy and crisp, lavished with aromatic seasonings, tapenade, cheeses and other toppings. At $9.95, it's a sumptuous meal in and of itself (remarkably, given the quality of food, none of the prices at Lucky's rise above the moderate). Do not miss desserts, either: The crème brûlée, apple tart and lemon-soufflé tart are the perfect way to finish off such a savory meal. The wine list is small but well chosen, including several Provençal selections; and just to complete the illusion that you are dining on the Riviera instead of the Providence River, Germon and Killeen offer pots of teas imported from Fauchon. Plan to spend about $100 for dinner with wine for two.

Toscano's Restaurant
265 Atwells Ave.
(401) 274-8820
ITALIAN
Open Mon.-Sat. 11:30 a.m.-2:30 p.m. & 5:30 p.m.-10:30 p.m.
Cards: AE.

Federal Hill is Providence's Little Italy section, and as in other cities, most of the restaurants are garishly decorated food halls serving red sauce–white sauce Italian-American clichés that would instantly disorient a visiting Italian. Toscano's, the exception to this rule, is a singular Italian restaurant that originally found its niche in Boston.

After several disappointing meals in other Federal Hill restaurants, we were supremely happy to settle in among Toscano's pleasant, sedately furnished surroundings: red-brick walls, outdoor patio with Cinzano umbrellas and widely separated tables. The wine list has been chosen with some care but with no bargains in mind. The menu is short—a good indication that the kitchen doesn't try to pander to every taste. You are offered good Italian bread and focaccia (a bit stale on our visit); next, you indulge yourself in one of the good, zesty pastas, perhaps spaghetti all'arrabbiata or a soothing tortellini with cream, Parmesan and prosciutto. Also excellent is the orecchiette in a veal and cream ragoût. We have no complaints about the flavor of the roast pork with rosemary and garlic (though it came only tepid to our table), the pheasant rubbed with rosemary and pieces of pancetta, the excellent veal medallions with porcini mushrooms and cream, or the stracotto alla fiorentino, a hefty platter of stewed beef with a vegetable purée. After all this, dessert is unnecessary, but we've been known to thoroughly enjoy the rich crema di caramella and near-perfect espresso. Toscano's is a place we'll happily return to any time we pass through Providence. Dinner for two, with wine, should be about $85 to $90.

DON'T FORGET: Gault Millau introduces you to the Best of New York, the Best of Washington D.C., the Best of Los Angeles, the Best of San Francisco, the Best of Chicago, the Best of France, the Best of Paris, the Best of Italy, the Best of London.

QUICK BITES

Big Alice's
100 Hope St.
(401) 273-5812
*Open Mon.-Sat. noon-
11 p.m., Sun. 2 p.m.-
10 p.m.
No cards.*

You'll find Ben 'n' Jerry's of Vermont and Emack & Bolio's of Massachusetts all over New England, as well as in Providence itself, but you won't (yet) find another Big Alice's anywhere but in the city of its birth, set near Brown University. Big Alice was the nickname of owner Robert Petteruti's big brother (for reasons we shall not begin to imagine), and the name was thereafter applied to this very good ice cream parlor, where you get several high-butterfat ice creams offered in that ingenious style known as the "Mix-In," a blending together of ice cream with all manner of candies and crunchy toppings that we must admit add remarkable texture to the basic commodity. On any given night, Big Alice's is jammed with students and locals, and it is even rumored that this is where John F. Kennedy Jr. took Brooke Shields on a date one evening.

HOTELS

Omni Biltmore Hotel
Kennedy Plaza
(401) 421-0700
*Open year-round.
All major cards.*

Providence's Kennedy Plaza, the heart of the city, has benefited greatly from extensive, much-needed renovation during the last several years; the showpiece of the plaza, the grand Biltmore Hotel, has also received a top-to-bottom make-over. The result is a modern hotel in a stately old brick package. Although it lacks the intimate charm and personality of the inns in such smaller towns as Newport and Block Island, the Biltmore is a quite comfortable, well-equipped full-service hotel that makes a fine base for exploring Rhode Island, especially for those who prefer city living to country quiet. Most of the 289 rooms are large, and despite the chain-hotel affiliation, the mood is relatively old-world and gracious.

Singles: $110-$125; doubles: $125-$140; suites: $280; weekend packages available.

SIGHTS

Too many New Englanders turn up their noses at the mere mention of Providence, capital and largest city of the nation's smallest state. They think of it as a second-class city, a center of underworld activity and sleazy politics, and in many cases, unfortunately, they're right. But thanks to a mixture of historic preservation and urban renewal, Providence has some eminently worthwhile attractions.

Chief among them is its old-time architecture. Benefit Street on the city's east side was a crossroads of Revolutionary America, where people like George Washington, John Adams and General Lafayette passed through en route to making history. Luckily, the area was an early beneficiary of the historic-preservation movement. Later sections of the city, such as the Elmwood neighborhood, retain an air of the nineteenth century's Colonial Revival and Victorian periods. Visitors are welcome at a number of historic buildings, including the 1785 Betsey Williams Cottage on Elmwood Avenue at the entrance to Roger Williams Park (open Sunday afternoons from March to September); the Brick School House, 24 Meeting Street, which dates back to pre-Revolutionary times (open Monday to Friday 9 a.m. to 4:30 p.m.); the 1707 Gov. Stephen Hopkins House, 10 Hopkins Street, home of Rhode Island's signer of the Declaration of Independence (open April to December, Wednesday and Saturday 1 p.m. to 4 p.m.); and the John Brown House, 52 Power Street, a Georgian mansion that John Quincy Adams described as "the most magnificent and elegant mansion that I have ever seen on this continent" (open Tuesday to Saturday 11 a.m. to 4 p.m., Sunday 1 p.m. to 4 p.m.). The Providence Preservation Society (401-831-7440) offers escorted tours of the Benefit Street area. Each June the Society celebrates the city's architectural past with its Festival of Historic Houses, a full weekend of house and garden tours, with accommodations packages available.

Also worth inspecting is the exceptionally lovely 1895 State Capitol on Smith Street (401-277-2311), which houses an impressive portrait of George Washington and the original charter granted to Rhode Island by King Charles II in 1663. Call for information on the free guided tours given Monday to Friday.

In education and the arts, Providence tends to fall in the shadow of nearby Boston. Yet Providence's cultural institutions are well worth a special trip. The 1917 movie house at 201 Washington Street has been converted into the home of the Tony Award–winning Trinity Square Repertory Company, one of the nation's leading regional stages, which mounts productions year-round; for current schedules and ticket information, call (401) 351-4242. The Benefit Street area is also the home of the Ivy League's Brown University, the nation's seventh-oldest college and, in the 1980s, one of the most sought-after among prospective students. Brown's historic campus in the vicinity of Prospect and College streets includes several museums and galleries open to the public: the

Bell Gallery, 64 College Street, in the imposing List Art Center, designed by architect Philip Johnson; the John Carter Brown Library, with one of the world's largest collections of books printed in America during the Colonial era; and the John Hay Library, with collections of sheet music, Lincolniana and American poetry and plays. For more information on any Brown facility, call (401) 863-1000.

The Rhode Island School of Design, one of the nation's best in the fine arts, has its own small museum (224 Benefit Street, 401-521-5010), which houses an impressive collection of art ranging from ancient to modern, including important holdings in graphics and textiles. Open Wednesday to Saturday, noon to 5 p.m. (hours may vary seasonally). The $1 admission fee is voluntary on Saturday. For a taste of a different kind of academic achievement, visit Johnson and Wales College, which specializes in the hospitality and culinary industries. The professional school at Abbott Park Place offers a wide variety of one-session classes, cooking weekends and summer weeks on campus; for information and reservations, call (800) 225-2454. J & W also operates its own inn (a training facility) in Seekonk, Massachusetts, just over the border from Providence; for information, call (508) 336-8700.

Although its coastline lacks the cachet of Newport's, Providence has at least one excellent place to enjoy the outdoors. Roger Williams Park, 950 Elmwood Avenue on the waterfront (401-785-9450), is a 430-acre Victorian park with a variety of gardens, a Museum of Natural History and its own zoo. The park is open daily 7 a.m. to 9 p.m.; zoo hours vary by season. And if your route takes you through East Providence, take a break to ride the Crescent Park Carousel on Bullocks Point Avenue (401-433-2828). Built in 1895, it features 66 unique carved figures and a neobaroque organ carved with figures that move.

SHOPS

Copacetic Rudely Elegant Jewelry
65 Weybosset St.
(The Arcade)
(401) 273-0470
Open Mon.-Wed. & Fri.-Sat. 10 a.m.-6 p.m., Thurs. 10 a.m.-8 p.m.

As you may have guessed from its name, this is no ordinary jewelry store. It specializes in handmade pieces from 30 or 40 different artists who work with every medium from precious metals and glass to leather and watch gears. There is some striking, expensive work, but the most unusual pieces include holograms and the electronic jewelry that features moving patterns. This is the place to buy for that teenage girl who wears the wild clothes.

Po
346 Wickenden St.
(401) 521-6260
Open daily noon-5 p.m.

This small shop features the work of about 50 local artists, most of them educated at the nearby Rhode Island School of Design. The brightly colored weavings are exceptional—many are by one of the owners—and the ceramics, art glass and jewelry are novel. The name, by the way, is pronounced just as it looks; ask the owners about its meaning.

The Spectrum
65 Weybosset St.
(The Arcade)
(401) 273-1590
Open Mon.-Wed. & Fri.-Sat. 10 a.m.-6 p.m., Thurs. 10 a.m.-8 p.m.

This is part of a group of six stores (the others are in Newport and in Massachusetts at Brewster, Wellfleet, Hyannis and Nantucket), and the chain-store touch shows—both for the good and the bad. The selection isn't particularly adventurous, but the quality is good and the assortment of both New England and national artists covers, yes, the spectrum of craft.

TIVERTON

QUICK BITES

Provender
3883 Main Rd.
(401) 624-9991
Open Mon.-Thurs. 9 a.m.-6 p.m., Fri.-Sun. 9 a.m.-7 p.m.
Cards: MC, V.

You are driving along a country road through some of the most beautiful New England countryside you have ever seen, and you come to a crossroads that seems to have come straight out of a Currier & Ives print. To your left is Gray's Ice Cream stand (and very good American ice cream it is), to your right an antiques store, and on the corner is Provender, a fine food shop that sells everything from boxed lunches to gorgeous little chocolate- truffle cakes and some of the best packaged pastas, relishes, cheeses, smoked fish, mustards and other items from around the world. Breads are baked on the premises—pumpernickel, sourdough and a French-style loaf called "South of Commons." The staff will happily pack a picnic basket for you from the array of cold salads and sandwiches. We tried several of the overstuffed sandwiches—with silly names like Old Smokey, Brideshead Revisited, Lady Macbeth and Geronimo—whose first-rate meats and cheeses were sometimes compromised by a cloyingly sweet pepper jelly you should tell them to hold. The staff here is cheery, and you may eat out on the front porch and watch the cars go down the country lane. Prices are modest for the amounts of food you get. About $12 for a sandwich lunch for two.

WAKEFIELD

SHOPS

Saywell's
557 Main St.
(401) 783-0630
Open Mon.-Fri. 9 a.m.-
6 p.m., Sat. 9 a.m.-5 p.m.

This "contemporary country store" carries quaint rather than creative crafts: raku pottery eggs in sizes ranging from quail to dinosaur, wood-and-stained-glass ship models, large wooden model cars, duck decoys, woven scarves and blankets. Half the store is geared toward the kitchen, and there's a lot of commercial stuff, but the place has a distinctly New England feel to it.

WARWICK

QUICK BITES

Little John's Pizzeria
625 Warwick Ave.
(401) 785-2241
Open Mon.-Sat. 11 a.m.-
11 p.m.
No cards.

Little John's may not be the only pizzeria in New England to bake its product in one-inch pie tins, but it may well be the best. Little John is five-foot-tall John Poulos, a Greek by birth but a fellow with quite a knack for crafting a good crisp crust with good fresh tomato sauce and plenty of pepperoni. The place itself, on the edge of Providence, looks like every other pizzeria within 50 miles, but its fame is far more widespread and every bit deserved. Two people probably won't spend more than $10 between them.

WATCH HILL

SIGHTS

This quaint little seaside town was a Newport-style summertime resort for the second-string (or perhaps just less ostentatious) wealthy set of yore. With its handsome old shingle-style "cottages," romantic brass-ringed carousel (on Bay Street; said to be the oldest operating carousel in the country), yachts bobbing in the harbor, appealing little shops and the lighthouse, Watch Hill makes for a fine half-day trip from your country-inn base in Westerly or Newport. Also nearby are some fine sandy beaches, including Weekapaug and Misquamicut.

WESTERLY

INNS

Shelter Harbor Inn
Rte. 1
(401) 322-8883
Open year-round.
All major cards.

The inn at Shelter Harbor is a simple sort of a place where you can get a good meal and a good night's sleep in an unmemorable room; it makes a fine stopping-off place en route to more scenic parts of New England. It's also a convenient place to stay if you get a sudden urge to play paddle tennis, since a court is provided.

Owners Jim and Debbye Dey oversee the historic 1800s inn, also a popular restaurant and watering hole for locals and travelers. It has fourteen light, cheery bedrooms, some with balconies and fireplaces and all with private baths. These rooms are a welcome sight after a full meal—and a good one at that—of Rhode Island johnnycakes, hearty soups, manly meat entrées and frothy desserts. Breakfast is equally fine: gingerbread pancakes, Brie-and-ham omelets, french-toasted croissants, eggs Benedict or a healthful granola–fresh fruit combination.

The winters on the coast here are on the brutal side, which makes the inn all the more inviting. Summer visitors are kept active with excursions to the shore, bicycling along the lowlands, visiting nearby Watch Hill's ancient carousel or catching a performance at Theater-by-the-Sea, which stages popular Broadway musicals and children's events.

Rooms: $82-$92, including breakfast.

WICKFORD

SHOPS

Different Drummer
7 W. Main St.
(401) 294-4867
Open Mon.-Sat. 10 a.m.-
6 p.m., Sun. 11 a.m.-5 p.m.

A sister store to J. W. Graham (see below), this small, quaint storefront features smaller, functional craft pieces that are more New England–traditional in design than most of the work down the street. Though there is some tourist-oriented commercial stuff, it's nice to poke around here on a lazy Saturday afternoon.

J. W. Graham
26 Brown St.
(401) 295-0757
Open Mon.-Sat. 10 a.m.-
6 p.m., Sun. noon-5 p.m.

This bright space in a charming small village offers contemporary rustic blue-and-white stoneware, elaborately quilted soft-sculpture flowers, baskets and a varied assortment of other crafts. Middle-of-the-road.

SIGHTS

The tiny village of Wickford, tucked into a picturesque cove in the middle of the larger town of North Kingstown, is well worth a visit and a stroll for its eighteenth-century architecture and charming postcard views of the sailboat- and fishing boat–studded harbor. In July, the town goes all out for the annual Wickford Art Festival.

CONNECTICUT

AVON

SHOPS

The Fisher Gallery
Avon Park North (Farm-
ington Valley Arts Center)
(203) 678-1867
*Jan.-Oct.: open Wed.-Sat.
11 a.m.-4 p.m.; Nov.-Dec.:
open Wed.-Sat. 11 a.m.-
8 p.m.*

This adventurous display space for crafts from across the
country is part of a complex that also includes twenty studios of working artists. Visitors can meet the artists, whose
hours vary, and in some cases buy work directly from them.
The shop inventory is small but carefully selected, and works
in the exhibits, which are more challenging than one might
expect from suburban Hartford, are also for sale.

BRANFORD

SHOPS

**Bittersweet
Handcraft Village**
779 E. Main St.
(203) 488-4689
*Open Tues.-Sat. 11 a.m.-
5 p.m., Sun. noon-5 p.m.*

This revamped collection of farm buildings offers an excellent opportunity to browse through a series of studios that
house, among others, a paper cutter, a pottery cooperative,
a weaver and an art glassblower.

BROOKLYN

RESTAURANTS

**Golden Lamb
Buttery**
Bush Hill Rd.
(203) 774-4423
AMERICAN
*May 25-Jan.: open Tues.-
Thurs. noon-2:30 p.m.,
Fri.-Sat. noon-2:30 p.m.
& seatings 7 p.m.-8:30
p.m.
No cards.*

Knowing about the Golden Lamb Buttery has been, for a
quarter of a century, like being a member of a private club.
Tucked away off a side road in Connecticut's remote northeast corner, it's not easy to find; and since it offers nothing
more than farmhouse cooking, it's not on the jet set's short
list. But this is farmhouse cooking at its zenith, and—as
initiates know—the Golden Lamb more than justifies a few
hours spent trekking the back roads of the northeast corner.
The restaurant, part of Bob and Virginia (Jimmie) Booth's
Hillandale Farm, is appropriately rustic: rough-wood walls,
hurricane lamps, lots of fresh flowers and a warm "welcome
to our farm" attitude. With the help of one assistant, Jimmie
does all the cooking for the 60 dinner guests, eschewing salt
in favor of fresh herbs, plenty of lemon and an abundance of

fresh eggs, butter and cream. There's no menu; while you are served cocktails in a 200-year-old barn, the waitress gives you a choice of three soups and four entrées. At the risk of being unadventurous, we've always chosen the duck soup (a thick, meaty potage that draws upon the universal memory of every farmhouse cook in history) and the roast duck (simply because no one cooks a crisp-skinned, tender roast duck better than Jimmie Booth). Be assured there are also vegetable soups, fruit soups and such entrées as chateaubriand, roast lamb and baked shrimp. Any entrée, however, serves merely as a centerpiece for the piles of farm vegetables, scooped out of large bowls by lithe, strong-armed waitresses. Though the vegetables change according to availability, the ones we had on our last visit were typical—mushrooms vinaigrette, summer squash baked with cheese, caraway-flecked cabbage poached in beer, diced parsnips in orange sauce, broccoli and onions roasted inside the duck (oh, those thrifty farmhouse cooks). For dessert, hope that Jimmie has baked the butter cake with a warm lemon-custard sauce; it's just like grandmother used to bake (grandmother, however, probably never thought to decorate her desserts with fresh geranium blossoms). To complete the mood, the Booths offer a predinner hayride and have hired a young folksinger with a golden voice and guitar to serenade the already enchanted diners. Because the Golden Lamb hosts these dinners only on weekends, reservations are essential. The restaurant also serves light lunches during the week—an appetizer, as it were. Dinner is a prix-fixe $40 per person, not including drinks and tip.

CENTERBROOK

RESTAURANTS

Fine Bouche
Main St.
(203) 767-1277
FRENCH
*Open Tues.-Sun. 6 p.m.-
9 p.m.*
Cards: MC, V.

From the outside it looks just like a small, pleasant Main Street home—gray shingles, wraparound latticework and a front lawn. Serious diners, however, have known for nearly a decade that the house belongs to Steve Wilkinson, one of the finest young chefs in the Northeast. And it's what comes from the kitchen that counts here. (Currently preoccupied with building a small inn out back, Wilkinson has turned over line duties to some of his assistants, with no discernible slip in quality. But he's still the main force here—he just can't stay out of the kitchen.) The menu changes monthly, but we've eaten at Fine Bouche often enough to proffer some advice. If the menu lists anything that sounds like quenelles or mousse, order it; Wilkinson has the light touch of an angel with such creations. We recently sampled a sole mousse dropped in an oyster shell, topped with the shell's original inhabitant and baked briefly with a cream and Riesling sauce, and we nearly died of delight. The memorable sautéed duck breast with a Cognac–green peppercorn sauce that we encountered on one visit reappeared a week later with a new outfit: port and figs. Obviously there are recurring themes; other dishes you're likely to encounter include grilled salmon (with various partners) and rack of lamb roasted with Provençal herbs. Vegetables, cooked just long enough to intensify their natural flavors, elevate supporting players to stars. But decadent desserts are the Wilkinson trademark. Watch for marjolaine—layers of almond and hazelnut meringue and layers of crème fraîche, all encased in layers of chocolate. That's decadence. The wine list (an unpretentious computer printout) is especially fine. Reservations for two of the 45 seats are essential. If this place has a flaw, it's that the diners are almost too reverential—everyone should have as much fun as Steve Wilkinson is having. Dinner for two, with wine, will come to about $115. The $36 prix-fixe dinner is one of the Western world's last great bargains.

CHESTER

RESTAURANTS

John B. Parmelee House
(The Inn at Chester)
318 W. Main St.
(203) 526-4961
FRENCH/AMERICAN
Open Mon.-Thurs. 6:30 a.m.-9:30 a.m., noon-2:30 p.m. & 5 p.m.-9 p.m., Fri. 6:30 a.m.-9:30 a.m., noon-2:30 p.m. & 5 p.m.-9:30 p.m., Sat. 7 a.m.-10 a.m., noon-2:30 p.m. & 5 p.m.-9:30 p.m., Sun. noon-2:30 p.m. & 5 p.m.-9 p.m. All major cards.

12/20

This handsome barn dating back to the Bicentennial promises a peaceful country dinner, what with the authentically aged barn-siding, the solarium garden bursting with flowers, the view of the green lawns and pond and the quaintly romantic atmosphere. Couples toast themselves with Champagne, friends catch up, the few business dinners look to be most successful, and the private parties in the back rooms sound festive. You notice these things because you have plenty of time to look around... and wait. When the dining room is barely filled, it may take you an hour to be served your meal. Is the chef not feeling well? Are the waitresses trying to antagonize you? Did they run out of food? You wonder and you wait.

On Mondays, a special tasting menu offers four courses for the bargain-basement price of $18—and gives the chef a chance to be more experimental. Clams on the half shell with ginger-and-caper sauce, mushrooms stuffed with pecans and herbs, and sautéed shrimp with garlic, leeks and tomato are all well prepared. But a cream of pheasant soup can be more reminiscent of canned cream of chicken soup than the subtler pheasant flavor you expect. Entrées are more successful: sautéed salmon with grapes, pink peppercorns and white Zinfandel; a decent grilled steak with black pepper and cream; excellent sautéed scallops with lime beurre blanc; and an ever-popular roast breast of duck served with pears and mint.

The standard menu offers more mannered dishes, such as filet mignon with a lobster cream sauce (not a success) and a demi-glace (better); sautéed lobster with basil, chives, tomato, Cognac and cream (a bit laborious); sautéed veal with wild mushrooms, apples and leeks (quite nice); roast duck stuffed with dates, figs and wild rice in orange sauce with Madeira and port (too sweet); and rack of lamb delicately flavored with rosemary (just right). The dessert cart carries such home-baked pastries as Linzertorte, chocolate mousse cake stuffed with more of those dates and figs and lemon mousse cake. The pianist in the lobby keeps things lively, ensuring that you stay awake for the (lengthy) duration of your meal. The service is friendly and apologetic, and you are so grateful that you have finally received dessert that you leave with fond memories of this pretty place. About $90 for two, with wine or beer.

Restaurant du Village
59 Main St.
(203) 526-5301
FRENCH
Open Wed.-Sun. 5:30 p.m.-10 p.m.; hours vary seasonally.
Cards: MC, V.

With tongue in cheek, Charlie van Over calls Restaurant du Village a "high-class bistro." Charlie van Over can call it anything he likes, because he's co-owner and the man responsible for those high-class bistro dishes that emerge from the kitchen. Partner Priscilla Martel is responsible for the restaurant's near-legendary French bread and for desserts that have been many a dieter's downfall. The small, storefront restaurant in Chester also shows influences of Michel Rostang, Jean Paul Lacombe and Jacques Pepin—all close friends of the owners. Bistro, indeed.

On our last visit, we started off with classic, straight-from-the-shoulder escargots swimming in garlic-Pernod butter (this is where the near-legendary French bread came in mighty handy), and with sinfully rich baked goat cheese rescued from cholesterol depravity by a surrounding chorus of fresh salad greens. Moist, perfectly roasted poussin with a morel sauce was a simple dish at its finest. (Van Over's simple secret: He roasts the chicken, quarters it and puts the dark meat back for touch-up roasting.) Lotte served with roasted garlic, bacon lardons and cream-sherry sauce, and deglazed with sherry vinegar, was the best thing that ever happened to lotte; it comes through the process tender rather than rubbery. It was only by sheer willpower (and critical integrity) that we refrained from ordering our usual entrée: roast duck under a skin crisped with care and passion. Vegetables included paillasson ("straw mat") potatoes, which were so good we begged for—and received—seconds. We finished with lemon curd tart (a Martel special, not always on the menu but always worth asking for) and chocolate cake filled with chocolate mousse, a pool of coffee crème anglaise on the side—a caloric time bomb if ever there was one. The simply decorated restaurant is quite popular, especially on summer and fall weekends. But it's worth the effort and the trip to Chester, if only to see what a "high-class bistro" is all about. Dinner for two, with wine, will run about $95.

INNS

The Inn at Chester
318 W. Main St.
(203) 526-4961
Open year-round.
All major cards.

The Inn at Chester is a well-organized operation particularly attractive to business clients. The meeting rooms, conference centers, good restaurant and pastoral setting promote a relaxed managerial pace. The 48 rooms range from the most functional and childproof to the slightly more romantic, with tall-post beds, working fireplaces and the random antique. Tabard curtains, muted Colonial-print wallpapers, telephones and TVs hidden inside chests and cabinets complete the look. The private baths are modern, and the overall feeling is impersonally pleasant.

The sitting area downstairs is impressive, with its massive stone fireplace. More sitting areas upstairs are stocked with game boards to keep you busy. And a chatty computer gives you the latest information about the Connecticut River Valley restaurants and accommodations, including, of course, The Inn at Chester and its restaurant, the John B. Parmelee House. It is an entertaining advertising device.

Rooms: $80.

COLCHESTER

SHOPS

Nathan Liverant & Son
Main St. (Rte. 85)
(203) 537-2409
Open Mon.-Sat. 10 a.m.-5 p.m.

Housed in an airy, spacious former early-nineteenth-century church, the Liverants' varied collection of antiques includes many with local Connecticut River Valley origins. Amid the scrimshaw, teapots, wooden bowls, splint boxes, exportware (antique Chinese blue-and-white porcelain), baskets, inlaid boxes and brass candlesticks, you may find a superb pair of Delft bowls, a rare set of Federal Massachusetts shield-back chairs, Queen Anne and Chippendale high-boys, a tiger-maple bow-front bureau with its original label intact or a signed tall-case clock. You are free to browse, and the owners are helpful, especially if it looks like you are truly interested in adding to your collection. The prices are as varied as the merchandise.

DEEP RIVER

INNS

Riverwind Inn
209 Main St. (Rte. 154)
(203) 526-2014
Open year-round.
Cards: MC, V.

Riverwind has a distinct Southern accent; the cheerful Barbara Barlow is apt to exclaim, "My daddy's a hog farmer back home!" This piece of information will no doubt emerge in the morning, when you are treated to a delicious Southern breakfast of piglet-shape biscuits and down-home gravy, her daddy's Smithfield ham and hot fruit curry in the winter or fresh-fruit compote in the summer. And Riverwind has a distinct country look, too. Barbara is an inveterate collector who has filled her eight-room inn with quilts, antique kitchen gadgets, handmade baskets, antique weather vanes, her family's furniture and a whole barnyard of pig-motif extras. It's clear that though Barbara has left the farm, the farm will never leave Barbara. Her guest rooms are just as country-charming as the downstairs living room and side porch and the upstairs sitting room. The Barn Rose Room is romantic, with a crocheted lace canopy over the double bed; the Smithfield Room (commemorating those hogs) is dominated by an oversized maple bed and decorated in flag colors; the Havlow Room features wall stencils Barbara created to match the painted headboard; and the four new rooms in the annex are just as appealing as the rest of the house. One has a private balcony and Japanese steeping tub, another has its own private porch, and still another has two oversized four-poster beds.

Barbara did all the restoration and renovation of her 1850s house herself—even down to the heart-shape patches on the window screens—proving to her traditional Southern family that she is more comfortable with a hammer than a sewing machine. Her second restoration project is just down the street: Riverwind Antique and Country Shop (46 Main Street), which is filled with Barbara's brand of country furnishings and decorative objects.

Rooms: $75-$135, including breakfast.

EAST HADDAM

SIGHTS

**Goodspeed
Opera House**
Rte. 82
(203) 873-8668

New England's undisputed champion of the American musical theater is perched above the Connecticut River here in East Haddam, a few miles from Essex. For more than 25 years, the Goodspeed Opera House has been presenting revivals of classic shows and new productions, many of which have gone on to Broadway (among them *Man of La Mancha* and *Annie*). Built in 1876 by shipping magnate William Goodspeed, the theater—decorated in high Victorian gingerbread—nearly fell to the wrecker's ball before its restoration in 1963. The theater has its own scene shop, rehearsal studios, company housing and library, with extensive collections of playbills, libretti and other theatrical memorabilia. The Goodspeed's season, which runs from April to October, is heavily supported by subscriptions, which account for 70 percent of ticket sales, so call ahead if you hope to get a seat. The Goodspeed also operates the 200-seat Norma Terris Theater in a converted yarn factory in Chester, five miles away.

ESSEX

RESTAURANTS

Griswold Inn
48 Main St.
(203) 767-1812
AMERICAN
*Open Mon.-Thurs. noon-
2:30 p.m. & 5:30 p.m.-
9 p.m., Fri.-Sat. noon-
2:30 p.m. & 5:30 p.m.-
10 p.m., Sun. 11 a.m.-
2:30 p.m. & 4 p.m.-9 p.m.;
light menu served weekdays
2:30 p.m.-4 p.m.
All major cards.*

Since 1776 a landmark in the picture-perfect yachting town of Essex, the Griswold Inn is the quintessential New England inn near the sea. That is to say, it's hospitable, clubby and as masculine as a musket. Walls of the various dining rooms are lined with Currier & Ives steamboat prints, gun collections, old posters, mooseheads, fireplaces—all sorts of manly things. There's always some kind of live music, and plenty of popcorn in the Tap Room. With all that going for it, it's almost a lagniappe that the Gris serves dependably fine food—and that it keeps its prices at such an old-fashioned (if not quite 1776) level.

This is pure New England food: a relish tray with crackers, clam chowder, broiled scrod, roast beef, Yankee pot roast, apple pie. And there's lots of it. The chicken pot pie for one could handily serve eight, and the inn's homemade sausages (three kinds, served with Sauerkraut and potato salad) are downright daunting. On a recent Sunday evening we dined "lightly" on the smallest steamed lobster in the kitchen (just under two pounds) and meaty barbecued ribs (just over two and a half pounds) slathered with a tangy sauce. To caulk the chinks, we also consumed hot rolls, giant baked potatoes and New England tossed salad (that is, no radicchio and no mâche)—all included, in the hospitable New England manner. Because everyone likes both a bargain and a genuine Yankee inn, the Gris can get very crowded, especially during the summer sailing season and in fall, when out-of-state leaf-watchers swarm over the landscape. Sunday's buffet Hunt Breakfast (scrambled eggs, chicken livers, fish, creamed chipped beef, cheese grits, fried chicken, bacon, biscuits...) is always packed. Dinner for two, with wine, will come to about $65.

INNS

Griswold Inn
48 Main St.
(203) 767-1812
Closed Dec. 24-25.
Cards: AE, MC, V.

For an authentic taste of the real thing, visit the Griswold Inn, the circa-1776 living testament to Yankee longevity that has been feeding and sheltering guests for more than 200 years. The 22 small guest rooms are wallpapered in Colonial prints, are furnished with durable antiques and have exposed-beam ceilings and tiny private bathrooms. But the sleeping rooms are not the main attraction. The Griswold is basically a lively two-century-old roadhouse; Banjo Night sometimes has guests in the main building springing out of bed late at night when happy customers downstairs break into another enthusiastic round of "Yankee Doodle Dandy."

The Griswold is known for its dining rooms (see review above), in which Colonial-inspired cuisine is dished up to a host of tourists and town regulars, who virtually own their own tables. And during the month of December, the Griswold's staff snaps to attention in Colonial dress to serve Christmas dinner every day (except Christmas Eve and Day). It is immensely popular, so you'd best reserve well in advance.

Rooms: $75-$170, including breakfast.

SIGHTS

Connecticut River
Foundation Museum
Main St.
(203) 767-8269
April-Dec.: open Tues.-Sun.
10 a.m.-5 p.m.

Long before America became the United States—back as far as 1656, in fact—early settlers ran a thriving wharf at the site of this museum, now housed in a restored 1878 dockhouse. The adjacent waterfront park includes a replica of America's first submarine, the *Turtle*, circa 1776, which is open to the public. And the museum will gladly provide you with a walking-tour map of historic Essex.

Adults $1.50, seniors $1, children under 16 50 cents.

Valley Railroad

Railroad Ave.
(203) 767-0103
*Late April-Nov. & Dec.
weekends: hours vary.*

For a classic trip up the Connecticut River Valley, board the Valley Railroad's steam train at Essex Station. The vintage train, with its big black steam engine and brass trim, carries passengers through the Connecticut countryside to Deep River Landing for connections with two riverboats, the *Becky Thatcher* and the *Silver Star*, for a one-hour cruise. The river trip affords views of such historic houses as Gillette Castle in Hadlyme and East Haddam's Goodspeed Opera House. The combined train/riverboat trips run from late April through mid-November; the train alone makes Christmas-season trips, with Santa and the elves on board, through December 23.

Adults $9.95, children $4.95.

SHOPS

Francis Bealey American Arts

3 S. Main St.
(203) 767-0220
*Open Mon.-Sat. 11 a.m.-
4 p.m.; closed Sat. July-
Aug.*

You have just bought your 30-room dream house overlooking the ocean a discreet distance from the shore on Greens Farms Road in Southport—and every room is empty. Fear not. Gentle Francis Bealey, with whom you have established a working relationship and whom you trust implicitly, is standing ready to outfit your home in the style to which you think you're accustomed. Your bedroom will look impressive with one of his tall-post beds, Hepplewhite tiger-maple and mahogany bow-front bureaus and delicate maple side tables; your dining room will be ready for *Town & Country* company with his Maryland serpentine-front Hepplewhite sideboard, Salem Queen Anne table and Duncan Phyfe chairs; your living room will sparkle with a pair of double-lemon andirons and Federal bumper, reflected in a sensational gilt-eagle mirror hanging over your newly acquired Hepplewhite camelback sofa covered in golden yellow brocade; and your yard will wow the gardeners with its 1840 wrought-iron twig-pattern lawn furniture. Everything is exceptional; the serious prices are worthy of serious collectors. The truly spoiled should note Bealey's $15,000 miniature Chippendale tabletop chest—its secret compartment is the perfect place to store those Schlumberger diamond clips.

Limited Editions

59 Main St.
(203) 767-1071
*Open Mon.-Sat. 10:30
a.m.-5:30 p.m., Sun. 12:30
p.m.-5:30 p.m.*

Occasional interesting touches of originality in art glass and ceramics keep the inventory here from being too "ye olde gifte shoppe." The store has a split personality—one side is crafts, the other clothing, though some of the clothing is hand-painted.

Portfolio
73 Main St.
(203) 767-2243
*Memorial Day-Labor Day:
open Mon. & Wed.-Sat.
10:30 a.m.-5:30 p.m., Sun.
noon-5 p.m.; Labor Day-
Jan. 1: open Thurs.-Sun.
11 a.m.-5 p.m.; closed
Jan.-mid-Feb.*

This small but exquisite gallery tucked away in the back of the Griswold Square complex of shops displays the art of craft. Ceramics are the focus, and they lean toward sculptural items, but even the more functional pieces are clearly design oriented. The town's pace is conducive to restful contemplation here.

GRANITE SPRINGS, NEW YORK

RESTAURANTS

Maxime's
Tomahawk Rd.
(914) 248-7200
FRENCH
*Open Wed.-Sun. noon-3
p.m. & 6 p.m.-10 p.m.
All major cards.*

No, this is not another of Pierre Cardin's franchise operations named after the Paris landmark. Maxime's proudly takes its name from owner Maxime Ribera, who, in opening Auberge Argenteuil in Hartsdale, New York, in 1972, literally led the way for all the fine French chefs who have since settled in the suburbs north of Manhattan. He went on to open Auberge Maxime in North Salem, New York, in 1977 and Buffet de la Gare in Hastings-on-Hudson in 1980, sold those, and then opened Maxime's in the almost nonexistent town of Granite Springs (about twenty minutes from the Connecticut border on Route 35). Breton-born Ribera had been owner/chef at New York's Café Argenteuil in its heyday, and he is now working at his peak, combining a flawless classic technique with a taste that draws the essential flavors from everything he creates, which is why he continues to deserve the rating we awarded him in the first edition of our New York guide.

You drive through the sylvan countryside (sadly in the throes of development) and find Maxime's set against a wooded hillside. From the outside it looks like a suburban home, while the interior, with its warm, golden lighting, fine antique paintings, working fireplace and exquisite table settings, has all the charm of a well-run provincial dining room. A lovely patio is opened in good weather.

Begin your meal with delectable little amuse-gueules, perhaps rillettes of sweetbreads or a tiny pizzette. Then enjoy the sautéed duck foie gras with sherry vinegar and wild greens or the zephir aux morilles. Ribera's roast lobster on a galette of buttery potatoes has grown to legendary status among his peers, and no one does venison better. But that would mean bypassing the extraordinary soupe de pêcheurs or the simply done halibut and salmon in a light beurre blanc. The cheeses are in good condition, as is the exceptionally strong wine list. And Maxime's desserts are of a high order (though we expect more variety in a restaurant of this caliber)—the chocolate terrine is a candy bar for the gods, but the pears in puff pastry can be too sweet; petits fours are irresistible.

Changes in staff over the years have not much affected the general bonhomie and professionalism here, for Madame Ribera oversees things most nights; in fact, a good many restaurateurs have learned their best lessons in genteel management from Maxime's. The best chefs now cooking in the suburbs have taken not only inspiration from Maxime but also a good deal of courage in opening up their ideal country dining rooms against all odds. The five-course, fixed-price dinner menu is $45, excluding wine.

GREENWICH

RESTAURANTS

Bertrand
253 Greenwich Ave.
(203) 661-4459,
661-4618
FRENCH
Open Mon.-Fri. noon-
2 p.m. & 6 p.m.-10 p.m.,
Sat. 6 p.m.-10 p.m.
Cards: AE, MC, V.

When word got out that Christian Bertrand, sous-chef for more than a decade to André Soltner at Manhattan's esteemed Lutèce, was going to open his own place, everyone assumed his menu would reflect his long New York tenure and not stray too far from the master's inspiration. Wisely, Bertrand has maintained his respect for Soltner's refined sense of classicism—but at the same time he is expressing his own style, which is best demonstrated when you put yourself in his hands. We began our last meal here (the evening's fixed-price dinner) with a hearty starter of fresh foie gras served with veal sausage and apple purée. This was followed by a light lobster ravioli with green beans, a lovely rendering of a classic bass à la nage, succulent sweetbreads and veal filet on a bed of spinach and fried celery, a salad of warm asparagus and radicchio, a selection of rich ice creams and sorbets and an apple tart that would have made Soltner blush with pride for his protégé.

On other visits, when we ordered from the printed menu, not everything was quite so satisfying. We remember a chicken consommé with truffles that tasted as if it had been thinned with tap water, calves' liver that was overcooked until gray, and marinated artichokes with coriander and saffron that might just as well have been bought at a good local delicatessen. Bertrand is a bit hesitant with his seasonings, but you won't go wrong ordering his luscious rillettes of duck with warm brioche, his fricassée of squab with rosemary or his filet of lamb with couscous and pistachios.

Desserts are a bit old-fashioned, but the vanilla-and-cassis succès is quite good.

The three-level setting is impressive, with tiled archways and successive landings; the third level over the windows is the most pleasant dining spot. Service, which begins with the greeting by Madame Bertrand at the door, is extremely knowledgeable, and the wine list isn't too terribly over-priced, especially for some Burgundies that are much more expensive in comparable restaurants. Dinner for two, with wine, will come to about $140.

La Grange at The Homestead

420 Field Point Rd.
(203) 869-7500
FRENCH
Open Mon.-Thurs. noon-
2:30 p.m. & 6:30 p.m.-
9:30 p.m., Fri. noon-
2:30 p.m. & 6:30 p.m.-
10:30 p.m., Sat. seatings
6:15 p.m. & 9:15 p.m.,
Sun. 6:30 p.m.-9:30 p.m.
All major cards.

Picture the ideal New England country inn set on rolling farmland and filled with exquisite American antiques and you have The Homestead, a 1799 mansion restored and decorated by one of New York's top interior designers to look exactly as you hoped it would. Owners Lessie Davison and Nancy Smith have seen to every detail in every corner of the inn, including the evocative dining room called La Grange, with its stone fireplace, Colonial furniture, chande-liers, patterned wallpaper and wraparound windows over-looking the greenery outside. We can think of few places where we'd rather spend a weekend; and to chef Jacques Thiebeult's credit, we wouldn't mind eating all our meals here, either.

You drive up a winding path, the valet takes your car, and if you're staying, you check into one of the beautiful rooms. If you're a man, you dress for dinner in a blazer and striped tie to blend in with the regulars, who have just come from a game of tennis at the club or stepped off the train from Manhattan. You visit the little Chocolate Bar for a cocktail before settling into a captain's chair to read over the menu, warmly contented.

Thiebeult has a solid grounding in French classicism, which means his sweetbreads with wild mushrooms, his veal with chestnuts and his cream soups are all wonderful. But though he has lightened his menu a bit in the last year or two, he still has a heavy hand when it comes to sauces and seems to lack the kind of subtlety that defines modern French cook-ing. None of this apparently matters to the faithful and affluent clientele, who can be sure of ample portions of first-rate ingredients, good beef and old-fashioned desserts. The wine list is one of the finest in New England, but the prices *start* at the expensive and soar to the stratospheric, with few bargains to be found. Two people will spend $130 to $150, with wine, on dinner.

Restaurant Jean-Louis

61 Lewis St.
(203) 622-8450
FRENCH
Open Mon.-Fri. noon-2
p.m. & 6:30 p.m.-9 p.m.,
seatings Sat. 6:30 p.m. &
9 p.m.
All major cards.

Not too long ago, Greenwich's gastronomic reputation was based on the brunch-and-buffet fare served at the exclusive country clubs that dot the region, places where the natives dined when they weren't heading into Manhattan for lunch at La Côte Basque or a pretheater dinner at "21." But all that has changed in the last few years, and Restaurant Jean-Louis has had much to do with elevating the taste and service in this bedroom community 40 minutes from Grand Central Station.

Owner/chef Jean-Louis Guerin had been executive chef to one of our favorite Paris restaurateurs, Guy Savoy, who originally opened this Connecticut dining room as his American outpost. The food was excellent, but the monthly commute from Paris to Greenwich proved too exhausting for Savoy, so a few years ago he sold it to Guerin, who transformed it into one of the finest French restaurants in the country. The tiny dining room, with its coral-pink wallpaper and shining mirrors, is a perfect setting for the kind of personal cuisine Guerin serves. He is obviously much in love with the local provender, for he does wonderfully original things with dishes like free-range chicken with braised endive, a ragoût of shrimp with pink lentils, and lotte in a red-wine sauce. He can update a classic but rarely seen dish like poulet Souvaroff by serving it with basmati rice, and his dark rum baba with fresh berries is as exciting as it is comforting. There is always a good selection of cheeses, excellent petits fours and chocolates, as well as a well-culled wine list that is primarily French, with several good California bottlings. Service, overseen by Jean-Louis's wife, Linda, is formal but friendly; the complete experience here reminds us of those well-run relais in Provence in which the wife invests the dining room with her own personality and the husband works his will in the kitchen, all in perfect equilibrium.

We highly recommend the superb four-course menu dégustation at $45 per person (without wine); otherwise, two people will spend about $140 to $150 for dinner with a bottle of wine.

INNS

The Homestead

420 Field Point Rd.
(203) 869-7500
Open year-round.
All major cards.

Nancy Smith and Lessie Davison, owners of the venerable Homestead, firmly believe that a weekend in the country should be anything but a struggle. That's why this beautifully restored 1799 farmhouse mansion has modern bathrooms, luscious Hammacher Schlemmer spa towels and terrycloth robes, telephones, TVs and an impeccable country-inn decor. Whether you prefer the snug Robin Suite in the main house, which has the oldest wall stencils in Fairfield County, or the General's Suite in Independent House, which is country-elegant and spacious, all 24 rooms are attractive and geared toward the sophisticated traveler.

The Homestead has beautiful dining rooms (see "Restaurants" above), and breakfast is served on the sunny side porch by tuxedo-clad waiters at 7:30 in the morning, a bit of a visual jolt to the uninitiated; dinner is equally formal. But catering to the affluent is nothing new at The Homestead—New York City's wealthy turn-of-the-century matrons and their children stayed here en route to their summer homes while the servants went on ahead to open the beachfront mansions for the season.

Rooms: $80-$165, including breakfast.

SHOPS

The Elements Gallery
14 Liberty Way
(203) 661-0014
Open Tues.-Sat. 10 a.m.- 5 p.m.

Inside this converted livery stable is one of the most exciting craft galleries in the state. The work of nationally known artists is given spacious display (though the space itself is less than elegant), and the inventory contains a large percentage of nonfunctional, cutting-edge work. Though this is a commercial store, the frequent themed exhibits are educational as well as opportunities to buy.

GRISWOLD

QUICK BITES

Stott Brothers
Rte. 164 & Rte. 395
(203) 376-5051
Open Mon.-Wed. 5 a.m.- 2 p.m., Thurs.-Sat. 5 a.m.- 7:30 p.m., Sun. 7 a.m.- 7:30 p.m.

Popular with farmhands, elderly locals, women with children in tow and the occasional accidental tourist, this country diner is the real thing. A piece of one of Janet's nine home-baked pies (coconut cream, French apple crumb and strawberry rhubarb are among our favorites, though we love them all) will top off an honest sandwich or delicious franks-and-beans blue-plate special. About $10 for sandwiches and pie for two.

SHOPS

John Walton
Call for directions
(203) 376-0862
Open Mon.-Sat. by appt. only.

Personable Joel Lionetti has been in the antiques business with and without John Walton for 30 years. He now runs the late Walton's enterprise and can answer any question imaginable about the stunning pieces housed in this large red barn out in the country. These are investment-grade pieces for serious collectors only—the $125,000 Queen Anne highboy or $65,000 dining table will send novices spinning into antiques shock. These mirrors, side chairs, card tables, beds, tea tables, marble-topped kitchen work-tables, sewing tables and stunning desks make the Walton a sort of à la campagne version of New York City's Israel Sack.

GROTON

SIGHTS

Several New England port towns relive the days of whalers and clipper ships, but only one is known for its submarines: Groton, the site of the U.S. Naval Submarine base. The U.S.S. *Nautilus* Memorial on Route 12 allows you aboard the world's first nuclear-powered submarine; displays in the on-site library and museum trace the history of submarines from the Revolutionary era to the present. Hours vary widely by season; call (203) 449-3174 for information. And if the very idea of underwater life brings on an attack of claustrophobia, you can tour the subs from water level. A company called See Submarines By Boat, at 185 Thames Street off Interstate 95 (203-445-8111), runs one-hour cruises of Groton harbor and the Thames River that pass by the *Nautilus*, the U.S. Coast Guard Academy at New London, the U.S. Naval Submarine Base and the General Dynamics shipyard, where new submarines are built. The cruise costs $5.50 for adults and $3.50 for children.

For a closer look at ocean life, sign on for a working cruise with Project Oceanology (203-445-9007). In operation daily from late June through late August, the project sends its two 50-foot vessels out for two-and-a-half-hour cruises to perform such tasks as chemical analysis of seawater and sediment. Passengers receive lectures on marine life while putting out nets and gathering samples; no previous training is needed. The boats leave from Avery Point on the University of Connecticut's Groton campus; reservations are suggested. The cruises cost $10 for adults and $8 for kids under 12.

GUILFORD

SHOPS

**Guilford
Handcrafts**
411 Church St.
(203) 453-6237
*Open Mon.-Sat. 10 a.m.-
4 p.m., Sun. noon-4 p.m.*

Hop off I-95 and browse this well-lit center for craft exhibits, classes and sales of work from all over the country. In the back of the store, which features high-quality items in a variety of media, a gallery often displays exhibits of surprisingly sophisticated work, and the skylit second floor contains larger pieces. Not to be missed is the Guilford Handcrafts Exposition, held in mid-July on the village green.

HADLYME

SIGHTS

Gillette Castle
67 River Rd.
(203) 526-2336
*Late May-mid-Oct.: open
daily 10 a.m.-5 p.m.; mid-
Oct.-mid-Dec.: open Sat.-
Sun. 10 a.m.-4 p.m.*

Onstage, actor William Gillette was famous as America's first great Sherlock Holmes, but in private life he was the master of Gillette Castle, now the centerpiece of a state park. Built in 1919 to resemble a medieval castle, the fieldstone mansion is filled with memorabilia of Gillette's career, including playbills and photographs, as well as hand-carved furnishings that the actor designed in his spare time.
Adults $1, children 50 cents.

SHOPS

**Black Whale
Antiques**
Rte. 82
(203) 526-5073
Open daily 10 a.m.-5 p.m.

This shop makes a charming headquarters for owner Tom Rose's hand-painted cabinets and bureaus. Barnyard animals show up on just about everything, making Black Whale a good stop for collectors who appreciate the naïf approach to country furnishings. City meets country here in the collection of English and American antiques, which will suit most tastes and more modest pocketbooks.

> *Remember to phone ahead to reserve your table or your room and please, if you cannot honor your reservation, be courteous and let the restaurant or the hotel know.*

HARTFORD

RESTAURANTS

L'Américain
2 Hartford Square West
(203) 522-6500
FRENCH/AMERICAN
Open Mon.-Fri. 11 a.m.-
2 p.m. & 6 p.m.-9 p.m.,
Sat. 6 p.m.-9 p.m.
All major cards.

For some years now, L'Américain has been considered one of the best restaurants in New England, praised for its commitment to French cuisine with a regional American twist. Or is it really American cuisine based on French principles? Well, whatever it is, dish by dish, L'Américain is aptly named, and it continues to be the most significant restaurant in the Hartford region. Set in a red-brick building on the edge of town, the premises are broken into one modern and one traditional dining room; at the entrance is an enchanting little lounge where you may take a cocktail or a Cognac after dinner. The extremely friendly staff seems genuinely delighted to see you, and chef Chris Pardue does his best to come up with some novel ideas based on the New England seasons.

Sometimes Pardue's creativity gallops ahead of his good taste—for instance, when he combines fruits with herbs in a way that overpowers the prime ingredients of a dish, as in a smoked shrimp salad with apples, an herbed crêpe with horseradish applesauce. You might also consider (as we did) his squash soup to be much too sweet and heavy for an appetizer. But if you choose carefully, you'll be quite happy with such dishes as ravioli stuffed with oyster mushrooms, squab salad with summer fruits, roast loin of lamb with chutney and woodruff, peach-and-pepper duck breast with a brandied peach sauce, salmon with an avocado mousseline, and coffee cheesecake. The wine list is creditable, but why must the management babble on so in print about its holdings? And Pardue need not give us his philosophy of seasonal cooking on the menu, which reads like a Taoist tract translated by a Yankee evangelist. Two may dine here for about $150, with wine.

HOTELS

Hartford's bland chain hotels hardly reflect Connecticut's history and charm, but they'll do the trick if you need a comfortable bed for the night. And since they're oriented toward midweek business travelers, most offer bargain-basement weekend packages. The best of the bunch are The Summit (5 Constitution Plaza, 203-278-2000), which charges $105 for a midweek double; the Sheraton-Hartford (315 Trumbull Street, Civic Center Plaza, 203-728-5151), which charges $99 to $138 for a midweek double; and the Parkview Hotel (1 Hilton Plaza, 203-249-5611), which sells midweek doubles for $104 to $152.

SIGHTS

Connecticut's capital is as full of history as any in New England—or, for that matter, in the nation. The present Capitol, 210 Capitol Avenue, is a good starting point; in addition to the state executive offices and legislative chambers, it houses historic displays, including the Marquis de Lafayette's camp bed from the American Revolution. Free tours are offered on weekdays; call (203) 240-0222 for current schedules. The original State House, 800 Main Street (203-522-6766), was designed by Charles Bulfinch in 1796. In addition to housing a Gilbert Stuart portrait of George Washington, this National Historic Landmark serves as a site for chamber-music concerts and outdoor programs in summer. It's open Monday to Saturday 10 a.m. to 5 p.m., Sunday noon to 5 p.m. Among the city's many historic houses are two on the grounds of Nook Farm, on Farmington Avenue at Forest Street (203-525-9317). Harriet Beecher Stowe lived at Nook Farm in a modest 1871 cottage that stands in stark contrast to the Gilded Age mansion, built just three years later, that was Mark Twain's home during his later years. Nook Farm is open year-round Tuesday to Saturday 10 a.m. to 4 p.m., Sunday 1 p.m. to 4 p.m. Admission to both homes is $6.50 for adults, $2.75 for children and free for kids under 6; admission to just one is $3.50 for adults and $1.50 for children.

As any viewer of TV commercials knows, one of Connecticut's leading modern-day businesses is insurance, and one of the industry's leading companies offers insights into this ever-thrilling world. At the Travelers Tower, 700 Main Street (203-277-0270), a museum (free admission) traces the history of the Travelers Insurance Co. from the 1860s onward. The tower's observation deck also affords panoramic views of the Hartford area. Open during company business hours: Monday to Friday 8:15 a.m. to 3:45 p.m.

IVORYTON

RESTAURANTS

Copper Beech Inn
46 Main St. (old Rte. 80)
(203) 767-0330
CONTINENTAL
Open Tues.-Sat. 6 p.m.-
9 p.m., Sun. 1 p.m.-9 p.m.
All major cards.

We are seated on Chippendale-style chairs at a table graced with heavy silver, a glimmering hurricane lamp and napkins rising like tapers from the wine glasses. A huge picture window frames one of the largest and oldest beech trees in Connecticut. Welcome to the Copper Beech Inn. There's nothing rustic about this restaurant/inn, which specializes in the sort of classical Continental cuisine we thought was all but extinct. Beef Wellington, rack of lamb and chateaubriand are but a few of the dishes that keep the conservative, monied crowd returning time and again. Some newer dishes have been added to the traditional menu, including wild mushrooms in puff pastry and roast duck with apple rhubarb sauce. But it's clear the chef has been instructed to follow orders, not showcase his own innovations. Nonetheless, we have never been disappointed (just a tad bored) with the skillfully made food. About $120 for dinner for two, with wine.

INNS

Copper Beech Inn
46 Main St. (old Rte. 80)
(203) 767-0330
Open year-round.
All major cards.

After completing a serious, solid dinner here, you'll be happy to know that you can waddle to a room, insulated from the harsh reality of finding your way home on the back roads of Ivoryton. The current owners have fourteen rooms that are furnished with period antiques and feature mixed prints and soft colors; a number also have their own Jacuzzis. The large Master Suite in the main house is quite grand, with two sitting areas, a fireplace, a large canopy bed and oversized windows. Its truncated Victorian bath comes as a surprise, but it's authentically in keeping with the house's nineteenth-century architecture (Copper Beech was built in 1886 by a wealthy ivory merchant named Comstock; Ivoryton was formerly famed for its ivory combs and corset stays). The new rooms in the Carriage House will satisfy more contemporary tastes, with Jacuzzi baths, muted-pastel colors and antique reproductions that were designed to withstand the tests of time, future tense. A simple breakfast is served in the Ivoryton Room, which has a relaxed view of the tree-shaded side lawn. The inn is located within easy striking distance of the Ivoryton Playhouse and the Florence Griswold Museum (famed for its collection of American impressionists).
Rooms: $75-$135, including breakfast.

LAKEVILLE

SHOPS

Suzanne Feldman's Americana
Main St.
(203) 435-2494
Open daily 10 a.m.-5 p.m.

This little shop is worth a visit for its fabulous collection of quilts. They're often discounted ten to twenty percent, and there is a selection for less than $450; otherwise, be prepared to spend nearly $950 for one of these exquisite Early American heirlooms. The collection of Victorian linens (square pillowcases, runners, tablecloths, place mats, pillow shams) is also worthy of note. Reproduction Victorian bed linens, Crabtree & Evelyn products, a smattering of majolica, vintage costume jewelry, country prints and artwork and some uninspired flea market–grade items fill out the inventory.

LITCHFIELD

INNS

Tollgate Hill Inn
Tollgate Rd. (Rte. 202)
(203) 567-4545
Closed last 2 weeks of March.
All major cards.

If Disney were to create a new amusement park called Colonial Land, Litchfield could serve as its role model. This beautiful town is almost a cliché, what with its large white Federal-style homes, enormous lawns and old money. Tourists can drive through town listening to audio-cassette tours, an innovative (if Disneylandesque) way to capture a slice of New England life.

Located at the far eastern end of town, Tollgate Hill Inn is nestled in a grove of pine trees. The barn-red building houses six guest rooms, two dining rooms, a ballroom/ dining room and a cozy bar; the adjacent schoolhouse has four more sleeping rooms. The larger rooms (One and Two) in the main house are spacious and spare, with tall-post beds, beamed ceilings and fireplaces. The three rooms on the third floor have a more contemporary decor and are quite snug, with equally snug bathrooms. Of the four rooms next door, two are suites, and all are decorated with the same simple finesse as the main house. These annex rooms also have cable TV and direct-dial telephones, for those who can't handle *really* getting away from it all. Breakfast is served in bed: a tray laden with muffins, freshly squeezed orange juice and coffee or tea.

The wood-paneled Tavern Room and the lighter, more elegant Formal Room are always filled with secure-looking people who return regularly for Tollgate's good brand of country cooking. The inn is especially popular with New Yorkers, who can practically commute home after dinner, relaxed after a break from the city's fast-forward pace.

Rooms: $85-$125, including breakfast.

SIGHTS

This storybook town in Connecticut's northwest corner is a fine place for enjoying the outdoors. The White Memorial Foundation, on Route 202 (203-567-0857), is the site of the state's largest nature center, a 4,000-acre preserve with trails for hiking, riding and cross-country skiing, which serve as a reminder that nature appreciation doesn't have to be a spectator sport. Open daily year-round; admission is free. The Conservation Center on the Foundation grounds maintains a self-guided nature trail, as well as exhibits and a library. It's open year-round; admission is $1 for adults and 50 cents for children. The White Flower Farm, on Route 63 three miles south of Litchfield (203-567-0801), has 10 acres of gardens and 30 acres of growing fields. Open mid-April through late October; admission is free.

MOODUS

SHOPS

Down on the Farm
Banner Rd.
(203) 873-9905
June-mid-Jan.: open Tues.-Sun. 11 a.m.-5 p.m.; April-May: open Thurs.-Sun. 11a.m.-5 p.m.

Once you've found your way here (from Route 9, take Exit 7 to Route 82, then bear left onto Route 149, take a left at the flashing light in Moodus Center and follow the signs), you're entitled to cackle right along with the chickens that stay in part of the huge renovated coops that now house a craft shop and studios. In addition to the jewelry, functional ceramics and glass that display a high degree of artistry, the shop has an outstanding collection of quilts in contemporary designs and a line of handcrafted cabinetry and furniture.

A Touch of Glass
N. Moodus Rd.
(203) 873-9709
Open Tues.-Sun. 1 p.m.-5 p.m.

What better way to see stained glass displayed than in a former Methodist church–turned Jewish community center–turned stained-glass shop? The unique setting contains the work of about two dozen artists; especially strong in lamps, the selection includes Tiffany reproductions, bent-glass lampshades and large window pieces. The directions for getting there are the same as for Down on the Farm (see above).

MYSTIC

SIGHTS

Mystic Seaport Museum
Rte. 27
(203) 572-0711
May-Oct.: open daily 9 a.m.-5 p.m.; Nov.-April: open daily 9 a.m.-4 p.m.

Among scholars and casual tourists alike, the words "Mystic" and "seaport" almost always go together. Founded in 1929, Mystic Seaport Museum Inc. is dedicated to keeping alive the days when men went down to the sea in ships. The complex consists of seventeen acres of historic homes, a working preservation shipyard, a planetarium and a children's museum, plus more than 300 floating vessels, ranging from America's sole surviving wooden whaleship, the 113-foot *Charles W. Morgan* (1841), to the smallest of craft. The seaport is also a center for special activities year-round, including gallery talks, the annual lobster festival in late May and various regattas.

If you bring your own boat (docking privileges may be arranged by calling the Seaport dockmaster), you can get a good view of the village by sea. But if your yacht is in dry dock, the museum also operates the *Sabino*, a 57-foot coal-fired steamboat built in 1908, which cruises the Mystic River. The cruises run daily from late May to mid-October, leaving hourly from 10 a.m. to 4 p.m. ($2.50). There's also a 90-minute cruise at 5 p.m. ($6) and another at 7 p.m. in the summer.

Other attractions in Mystic include the Mystic Marinelife Aquarium on Coogan Boulevard (203-536-3323), with more than 6,000 specimens, a Marine Theater and an outdoor seal island.

Adults $11, children $5.50, children under 5 free.

Unless otherwise noted, the prices given for restaurants are for a complete dinner for two, including an appetizer, main course and dessert. The prices also include tax, fifteen-percent tip and one of the least expensive bottles of wine on the wine list. Please don't hold it against us if you end up spending a bit more!

SHOPS

**The Company
of Craftsmen**
43 W. Main St.
(203) 536-4189
*Labor Day-Memorial Day:
open Mon.-Sat. 9:30 a.m.-
9 p.m., Sun. 9:30 a.m.-
6 p.m.; Memorial Day-
Labor Day: open Mon.-
Sat. 9:30 a.m.-6 p.m.,
Sun. noon-4 p.m.*

Functional, kitchen-oriented stoneware and wooden items predominate here, along with woven items, such as rag rugs, and pieces in the customary variety of craft media.

Whyevernot
17 W. Main St.
(203) 536-6209
*Labor Day-Memorial Day:
open Mon.-Wed. 10 a.m.-
5:30 p.m., Thurs.-Sat.
10 a.m.-9 p.m., Sun.
11 a.m.-5 p.m.; Memorial
Day-Labor Day: open
Mon.-Sat. 10 a.m.-5:30
p.m., Sun. 11 a.m.-5 p.m.*

Why open a shop that is part New Mexico, part Vermont and part the Hamptons? Whyevernot? This fresh, eclectic store starts with painted, patterned furniture in the trendiest of pastels and finishes with reasonably priced Mexican woven rugs, lace brooches and ceramics that work with the rest. *Metropolitan Home* readers will have fun here.

NEW CANAAN

SHOPS

**English Heritage
Antiques**
13 South Ave.
(203) 966-2979
*Open Mon.-Sat. 10 a.m.-
5 p.m.*

We thought we'd walked into an elite, private dining club by mistake—tables were set with Minton china, English Coalport porcelain and Sheffield flatware, and a Georgian silver coffee service and Spode tea service waited on an impressive inlaid Hepplewhite sideboard. Everything in this shop dazzles with that English brand of notice-me detailing. The price tags read like fashion copy; they'll give beginners an introductory lesson in British antiques. But you may be perfectly happy to leave with a set of six Royal Crown Derby demitasse cups and saucers in an Imari pattern for a mere $175. Collins has thoughtfully put together a pamphlet on ten easy steps to buying antiques, no doubt to assure cautious shoppers that the set of six Adams-style side chairs is *really* worth $9,500.

Sallea Antiques
110 Main St.
(203) 972-1050
Open Mon.-Sat. 10 a.m.-
5 p.m., Sun. by chance.

This intimate, distinctly feminine shop, awash in pastel blue and pink, is the perfect place to find storage pieces—Sallea advertises that "boxes are our business." If you need a tortoiseshell box for your tuxedo studs, a mother-of-pearl box for your ten-millimeter strands, a captain's box to protect your gold futures certificates, a Japanese lacquer box for spare change or an exquisite little watch box for safety pins, you'll find it at Sallea—along with a collection of tea tables, an occasional table created from a Chinese shawl box mounted on legs, brass weights (perfect for upscale weight-watchers who must measure their portions) and small-scale antique furniture. And if you can't find it, owner Sally Kaltman will find it for you.

Silvermine Guild Center for the Arts
1037 Silvermine Rd.
(203) 966-5617
Open Tues.-Sat. 11 a.m.-
5 p.m., Sun noon-5 p.m.

Hidden in the rolling suburbia of Connecticut is this cooperative, whose galleries sponsor year-round high-level shows of members' contemporary craft and art. The shop is tiny but has items of the same quality as the galleries in a variety of media.

NEW HAVEN

RESTAURANTS

Azteca's
14 Mechanic St.
(203) 624-2454
MEXICAN/SOUTHWESTERN
Open Mon.-Thurs. 5 p.m.-
9 p.m., Fri.-Sat. 5 p.m.-
10 p.m.
Cards: MC, V.

Good Mexican restaurants in Connecticut are as rare as the proverbial hen's teeth. Finding one of the Northeast's best Southwestern restaurants in Connecticut is well-nigh miraculous. Behold the miracle. Located in an unprepossessing side street in one of New Haven's historic districts, Azteca's fits nineteen tables into a small space decorated in a minimalist Southwestern fashion. Black vases, green cacti and a few palm fronds accent peachy pastel walls the color of the desert at sunset.

Connecticut owners Lynne De Leo and Deborah Allen haven't got a Western ancestor between them, but they're such brilliant interpreters of what folks eat within a 1,000-mile radius of Santa Fe that you'd think they were burrito born. Ordering from the buff-colored Mexican menu, we stumbled on the best pollo mole poblano ever—sautéed chicken breasts blanketed by that complex, slow-simmered sauce that makes stoic Yankees weep for joy. From the pink "Southwestern" menu (which changes every two weeks) came opalescent scallops, arranged like Tiffany pearls on a black plate, accented by a grainy pumpkin seed–chili sauce, and artistically separated from blue-corn cakes by a red ribbon of salsa. "Sizzling" fajitas in an incendiary chipotle sauce (same menu) were surrounded by plenty of guaca-mole, sour cream, shredded lettuce and chopped fresh tomatoes to cool things down. Grilled rib eye with corn cakes and a bracing black bean–chorizo–tomato sauce satis-fied one of our group, the most voracious trencherman in New England, who snared a couple of the tortillas served with fajitas with which to mop up his plate. Only the quesadilla disappointed—bland and boring, with all the chiles sliding off to one side. For dessert, try the whimsical combination of buttermilk, sour cream and star anise called Texas Ice Cream; it is, believe it or not, quite refreshing. Azteca's service is fast—too fast if the waiter decides he needs your table. Ignore him, savor slowly and weep those stoic Yankee tears of joy. Dinner for two, with margaritas, will be about $65.

Bruxelles Brasserie and Bar
220 College St.
(203) 777-7752
AMERICAN
Open Sun.-Thurs. 11 a.m.-midnight, Fri.-Sat. 11 a.m.-1 a.m.
Cards: AE, MC, V.

The Palace and Shubert theaters are the headliners on New Haven's newly gentrified "Theater Row," but the rising star is two-year-old Bruxelles. An uptown ingenue, a bright-lights brasserie roaming around two floors, Bruxelles devotes itself to giving gentrified customers a good meal and a good time. It's all quite jolly—Crayolas provided for scribbling on paper tablecloths, Bloody Marys served in brandy snifters, and breadsticks supplied for nibbling... or for playful dueling. With its mesquite grills, pizza ovens, rotisserie grills and penchant for pasta, Bruxelles is as "now" as tomorrow's newspaper, as suited for grazing as a spring meadow. Accordingly, we skipped gaily among such now dishes as hot potato crisps fresh from the fryer; thin-crust pizza with sun-dried tomatoes, black olives, basil and smoked mozzarella; steamed mussels in a light-garlic/bold-basil broth; tortellini with slivered duck, watercress, mushrooms, tomatoes and cream sauce; and a couple of items from the rotisserie. A bit of advice on the last: Skip any specials—such as the lamb—and any rotisserie dish with an overly con-trived sauce. Stick to the crisp-skinned, unadorned chicken. A momentary attack of health consciousness inspired us to order the Grand Salon salad, which proved a heavy path to health: roasted peppers, roasted chicken, roasted beef, sun-dried tomatoes, Fontina cheese and a dressing that tasted like Durkee's. Desserts were as unabashedly decadent as the Chocolate Truffle Decadence and the Midnight Mousse Cake (doused with three different liqueurs). Because nearly everyone loves a jolly time, Bruxelles can get terribly crowded and terribly noisy (the acoustics are awful) on weekend evenings and opening nights. Nevertheless, the enthusiastic, accommodating staff keeps things moving along briskly. Dinner for two, with wine, will come to about $60.

Delmonaco's
232 Wooster St.
(203) 865-1109
ITALIAN
Open Mon.-Fri. 11:30
a.m.-2:30 p.m. & 5 p.m.-
10:30 p.m., Sat.-Sun.
5 p.m.-11 p.m.
All major cards.

12/20

An academic once told us that we should never take seriously the restaurant recommendations of professors because they generally have neither the time nor the income to allow for eating at the best places. Alas, this may be true, for New Haven is a city with little gastronomic interest except for Robert Henry's and a few ethnic eateries where the food is cheap and filling. Delmonaco's is in this class, but its generosity and its consistency make it a consistently good choice for dinner in this university-dominated city. The place is enormous, the waiters rush around like Keystone Kops, and the atmosphere rings with the guffaws of traveling businesspeople and the restrained laughter of Yalies out to dine with their philosophy professors. The menu breaks no new ground in cucina italiana, but the portions are enormous and the food quite good—from the rich, creamy spaghetti alla carbonara to the fist-thick veal chop. Seafood is dependably fresh and nicely prepared. Desserts shouldn't be necessary after all this food, and, of course, you'll be asked if you want anisette with your coffee. You don't. For all this, with wine, two people will pay about $80.

The Elm City Diner
1228 Chapel St.
(203) 776-5050
ITALIAN/AMERICAN
Open Mon.-Thurs.
11:30 a.m.-4:30 p.m. &
5 p.m.-12:30 a.m., Fri.
11:30 a.m.-4:30 p.m. &
5 p.m.-1:30 a.m.,
Sat. 5 p.m.-1:30 a.m.,
Sun. 11 a.m.-3:30 p.m.
All major cards.

11/20

The Elm City Diner is an upscale version of an eatery that's been in place since 1955, a classic old stainless-steel diner—your basic clean, well-lighted place. The idea is to serve familiar dishes done with care and class, and that's generally accomplished; another major virtue is Elm City's late hours in a town that tends to close up early. Snacks and appetizers run to nachos, potato skins, baked Brie and huge, sculptural beer-batter onion rings. Entrées are primarily Italian, plus fancy burgers and a smattering of Cajun blackened things. The only beer on tap, alas, is Miller Lite. Our last meal included a big crackling salad with gutsy Gorgonzola dressing and a shrimp and scallop scampi that proved quite good and surprisingly delicate, with lots of sauce for the rice to soak up. Servings are substantial, the kinds that make you take the extra home when you're being good, and clean your plate when you're being bad. The German chocolate cake is a respectable rendition of the familiar transgression. As usual, we left satisfied with everything but the prices, which are much too high, and the music, which is rather trite rock 'n' roll oldies: Hearing Elvis wail about his blue suede shoes three times in one meal lacks subtlety. About $65 for two, with beer.

Some establishments change their closing times
without warning. It is always wise to call ahead.

Robert Henry's
1032 Chapel St.
(203) 789-1010
FRENCH
Open Mon.-Thurs. noon-
2 p.m. & 6 p.m.-9:30 p.m.,
Fri. noon-2 p.m. & 6 p.m.-
10 p.m., Sat. 6 p.m.-10 p.m.
Cards: AE, MC, V.

It's as perfect as a stage set—gleaming crystal on the tables, pink-marble columns flanking a formal fireplace, turn-of-the-century stained-glass fan windows, enough fresh flowers to fill a cathedral altar... or two. Originally built to house the Union League Club, the place reopened not long ago as Robert Henry's, which immediately put New Haven on Connecticut's dining map. Come to think of it, Robert Henry's put Connecticut on anyone's dining map. Service is skilled, pleasant, unobtrusive; and the food—produced by chef Jean-Michel Gammariello—astonishes. On a recent astonishing evening, not one dish faltered. An ethereally light asparagus timbale sat on a glaze of morel sauce, with a few sautéed morels off to the side. It was an inspired combination. Under a sprinkling of chopped herbs, seven different salad greens glistened with a haunting truffle vinaigrette. Crêpe-like lasagne layered with scallops, Swiss chard and pine nuts elevated itself to immortality by the addition of a light, saffron-scented sauce. Lobster and steamed spinach under a crown of crisp, thinly sliced potatoes was every bit as good. (Gammariello does serve more than seafood: Spit-roasted lamb with goat-cheese ravioli, a lusty duck confit, veal piccata flanked by a curry-sauced vegetable strudel have been among his creations.) Ripe raspberries and sabayon made a refreshing dessert, but it was the nougatine that won our hearts. Tucked in a crisp shell shaped like a hinged scallop, three sorbets had been drizzled with an intense cherry sauce. It was beguiling enough to soften the hardest of hearts. The menu changes frequently, so these may have been once-in-a-lifetime pleasures, but we look forward to sampling their successors. The coffee is particularly good, blended especially for the restaurant—but of course. Because good news travels fast, don't count on dropping in without a reservation. Dinner for two, with wine, will empty your wallet of $115 or so, more if you splurge on a major-league bottle from the extensive wine cellar.

Hot Tomato's
1195 Chapel St.
(203) 789-8468
ITALIAN
Open Mon.-Thurs. 5 p.m.-
9:30 p.m., Fri.-Sat. 5 p.m.-
10:30 p.m., Sun. 5 p.m.-
9 p.m.
All major cards.

12/20

We were fans of the late, lamented Northampton branch of Hot Tomato's, which introduced that area to the news that Italian cooking is more than generic red sauce and meatball subs. We were curious to see how the New Haven place compared, and were happy to find it even better. At the end of a scorching day, we settled into the breezy outside balcony and surveyed the daily specials, which cycle among chicken, rabbit, veal and seafood dishes. The last, on this visit, was Cajun catfish, which seemed fishy indeed for an Italian place, so we chose the regular-menu shrimp fra diavolo. But first we sampled a wild-mushroom sauté, whose chanterelles, shiitakes, tree ears and regular old mushrooms, all redolent of olive oil and balsamic vinegar, were light, tart and fine, the character of each mushroom coming through clearly. Since the house wine is a Soave, we ordered a what-the-hell Zinfandel; its tab of $3.75 a glass was the only thing we'd call unearned. The fra diavolo came out bracingly spicy but not too heavily so, the shrimp, sausage and sauce all making their points both individually and collectively, as is right and proper. The service, too, was strong and reliable, each course marching in at just the right time. Lightness and reliability are the keynotes at Hot Tomato's: You'll get a good to very good meal and leave happy and not over-filled. About $80 for two, with wine.

QUICK BITES

Louis' Lunch
261 Crown St.
(203) 562-5507
Open Mon.-Fri. 9 a.m.-4:30 p.m.
No cards.

McDonald's may have sold billions, but Louis' sold it first—the first hamburger, that is. Supposedly, original owner Louis Lassen came up with the meat-and-bun combo back in 1900, in an effort to please a hungry customer in a hurry. The rest is history. The humble but highly revered brick lunch joint is still run by the same family, and the burger is made exactly the way it was on that fateful turn-of-the-century day: Tasty, juicy meat is cooked on a vertical grill (less fat that way), topped with tomato and onion and stuck between pieces of toast.

Frank Pepe Pizzeria Napoletana
157 Wooster St.
(203) 865-5762
Open Mon. & Wed.-Thurs. 4 p.m.-10:30 p.m., Fri.-Sat. 11:30 a.m.- 11:30 p.m., Sun. 2:30 p.m.-10:30 p.m.
No cards.

This review comes under the heading of Quick Bites, but don't expect anything quick at Pepe during the dinner hours: On an average evening, the wait in line is about 45 minutes, plus another 30 or so waiting for the pizza to arrive. Is the best pizza in the world worth that wait? As it happens, Pepe's once was declared the best pizza in the world, in an inane book called *The Best of Everything*. We'll just note that after a few slugs of Genesee, the only beer on tap, any pizza would taste pretty good. And herewith we'll stop kvetching and confess that what comes out of that gigantic brick oven is one hell of a pizza pie: a thin crust with a sauce that tastes more of fresh tomato than of sauce. You put together your own combinations; we chose mozza-rella, mushrooms, pepper and sausage, the latter fragrant with fennel and utterly greaseless. The whole effect was surprisingly light (two people can comfortably eat the middle size) and entirely satisfying. We'll be back—but only in the off hours. Pizza and beer for two will run about $15.

HOTELS

Although a dynamic, interesting town, New Haven is curiously bereft of noteworthy inns and particularly wonderful hotels. But there are a couple of places to try, should you wish your visit to extend overnight. The nicest place in town is the Colony Inn (1157 Chapel Street, 203-776-1234), which is a bit '80s-hotel-generic but certainly comfortable and well appointed; doubles are $94. New Haven's hippest hotel is the Duncan Hotel (1151 Chapel Street, 203-787-1273), which may not be elegant but is certainly well located and possessed of a certain faded charm, as well as great prices: $50 for a double and $60 for a suite.

SIGHTS

New Haven Theater
Long Wharf Theater: 222 Sargent Dr.
(203) 787-4282
Yale Repertory Theater: Chapel St. & York St.
(203) 432-1234

Among theater aficionados, New Haven is famous as the place where many an ambitious show has bombed—but many have gone on to make theatrical history. Although the pre-Broadway tryout circuit has dwindled in recent decades, New Haven still boasts two fine professional companies: the historic Long Wharf Theater and the Yale Repertory Theater, the training ground for the university's illustrious drama school.

Yale University
(203) 432-2300
(university),
(203) 432-4771
(museums)

The hometown of Yale University, New Haven is one of America's intellectual capitals, as well as a cultural center. The Old Ivy campus is a pleasant place for strolling and sight-seeing, and the university offers free one-hour tours Monday to Friday at 10:30 a.m. and 2 p.m. and Saturday and Sunday at 1:30 p.m. Tours leave from the Phelps Gateway, across College Street from New Haven Green.

As is appropriate for one of the country's most prestigious centers of learning, Yale has a wealth of superb libraries and museums. Among them are the Yale Center for British Art, 1080 Chapel Street; the Yale Collection of Musical Instruments, 15 Hillhouse Avenue, which documents the history of music in Europe and America from the sixteenth century to the present; and the Yale Art Gallery, 1111 Chapel Street, a showcase for American painting from 1700 to the present, along with collections of pre-Columbian, Asian and African art. The Beinecke Rare Book Library, 121 Wall Street, counts a Gutenberg Bible and original Audubon bird prints among its collection. And last but certainly not least, the Peabody Museum of National History, 170 Whitney Avenue, is New England's largest natural history museum, with exhibits on everything from dinosaurs to the birds of modern-day Connecticut. The Peabody is open Monday to Saturday 9 a.m. to 4:45 p.m., Sunday and holidays 1 p.m. to 4:45 p.m. Admission is $2 for adults, $1.50 for seniors, $1 for children and free for kids under 5.

SHOPS

Edwin C. Ahlberg
441 Middletown Ave.
(203) 624-9076
*Open Mon.-Fri. 8 a.m.-
noon & 1 p.m.-5 p.m.,
Sat. 8 a.m.-noon, Sun.
1 p.m.-5 p.m. (closed Sun.
June-Aug.).*

If you need to have your beloved antiques repaired, re-stored or reupholstered, the Ahlberg brothers will do a nice job. These sincere gentlemen charge an honest price and do fabulous work. Proof positive is on display in their simple shop filled with lovely American pieces for sale. We found a gorgeous serpentine-front sideboard for $8,500, a maple Chippendale five-drawer chest for $6,750 and an Abraham Edwards tall clock for $4,750. Suffice it to say, the Ahlbergs' prices are slightly more reasonable than their peers' strato-spheric counterparts. Whether you have fallen in love with a Queen Anne drop-leaf table, a Sheraton inlaid secretary or tall-post twin beds, you can expect the Ahlbergs to give you a fair deal. The wooden Indian at the door stands for as much.

NEW LONDON

SIGHTS

**Monte Cristo
Cottage**
325 Pequot Ave.
(203) 443-0051
*Open Mon.-Fri. 1 p.m.-
4 p.m.*

Partly because of its proximity to New York City, Con-necticut has many and varied connections with the world of the theater. New England's most famous theatrical resident was America's greatest playwright, Eugene O'Neill. In New London, Monte Cristo Cottage—named for the role that made and, ironically, destroyed father James O'Neill's ca-reer as an actor—was the O'Neill family's summer home, which the playwright immortalized as the setting for both his only comedy, *Ah, Wilderness!*, and the darker *Long Day's Journey into Night*. Today it's a National Historic Landmark and is open for tours.

Adults $2, children 50 cents.

**Eugene O'Neill
Theater Center**
305 Great Neck Rd.,
Waterford
(203) 443-5378

In nearby Waterford, the Eugene O'Neill Theater Center is a living memorial to the Nobel Prize winner. At the Playwrights' Conference each July, selected playwrights test out their scripts on professional actors, and the public is invited to performances in the rough.

U.S. Coast Guard Academy
Mohegan Ave.
(203) 444-8270
Visitors' Pavilion—May-Oct.: open daily 9 a.m.-5 p.m.; museum—Nov.-April: open daily 9 a.m.-5 p.m.

Like so many coastal New England towns, New London has strong ties to the sea, and as the site of the U.S. Coast Guard Academy, it helps keep those ties alive. The Visitors' Pavilion traces the history of this vital but often overlooked branch of America's military service with a multimedia show on cadet life; the museum on the Coast Guard grounds delves deeper into Coast Guard history.

Admission free.

NEW MILFORD

SHOPS

Voltaire's
337 Kent Rd.
(203) 354-4200
Open Mon.-Sat. 10 a.m.-5 p.m.

The owners here are committed to displaying functional craft within the context of its use, as it would be in your home. As a result, you'll find stoneware lamps next to Seiko clocks, a handmade brass colander next to Orrefors crystal. The craft items hold up well to their mass-produced counterparts, and though this is clearly a commercial gift shop, the design quality is above average for such functional items.

NEW PRESTON

RESTAURANTS

Hopkins Inn
Hopkins Rd.
(203) 868-7295
CONTINENTAL
Open Tues.-Thurs. noon-2 p.m. & 6 p.m.-9 p.m., Fri. noon-2 p.m. & 6 p.m.-10 p.m., Sat. noon-2 p.m. & 5:30 p.m.-10 p.m., Sun. 12:30 p.m.-8:30 p.m. No cards.

Over the outside dining terrace, a fantastical chandelier made of wrought iron, copper and lights seems to hang from the stars. Inside are small rooms, big stone fireplaces, inviting corners and the headstone of a long-departed former owner embedded in the floor. It's all very New England. But the blackboard menu has a bit of an Austrian accent, as do the dirndls costuming the young waitresses. Explanation: The Hopkins Inn's owner/chef, Franz Schober, is Austrian, and his Connecticut-born wife, Beth, is a New Englander through and through.

The food is appropriately multinational, the classic dishes of many countries expertly and creatively prepared. Under a sprinkling of finely chopped bacon, garlic and peppers, plump, barely cooked clams casino sizzle in herb butter. A surprisingly sophisticated barley soup dotted with shreds of beef and prosciutto belies its peasant origins. Not surprisingly, Wiener Schnitzel is a real star. Served with lemon and anchovies curled around capers, it is golden-crisp and as tender as a first kiss. Ah, those Austrians. Broiled filet mignon is all that filet mignon should be—and we like the notion of serving béarnaise sauce on the side, in a pudding glass. Trout (served meunière) as fresh as a Rocky Mountain morning is snatched just minutes before cooking from the inn's trout tank. Rösti potatoes are every bit as good as you'd expect with an Austrian in the kitchen, and the salad dressing raises a mere tossed salad to a sensual experience. Though often importuned, the Schobers refuse to part with the recipe. All we can say is that it tastes like it's got curry in it—but it doesn't. Dessert runs to such things as a quite respectable rum-spiked white-chocolate mousse and a butterscotch sundae. And these days there just aren't many places left where you can get a really good, old-time butterscotch sundae. Reservations are necessary at this country-inn restaurant, especially on weekends, when just about everyone goes to the country. Dinner for two, with wine, will come to about $75.

INNS

Boulders Inn
Rte. 45
(203) 868-7918
Open year-round.
Cards: AE, MC, V.

This 1895 country manor overlooking Lake Waramaug is an inn for all seasons. Winter finds guests cross-country skiing, ice fishing and snowshoe hiking; in summer, they take advantage of the many lake sports. Aptly named for its unique boulder architecture, the inn has a rustic look and feel. Five modestly decorated guest rooms are in the main house, and eight private cottages, with a slightly more contemporary decor, sit on the hill; all thirteen rooms have private baths. The common rooms are considerably more interesting than the bedrooms, especially the Lake Room, which has a wonderful oversized fireplace and an enormous window with a view of the lake. The summer terrace is a perfect place to watch another day fade below the horizon, and the dining room—a converted porte-cochère, with walls made of the house's original boulder siding—is striking. Its large windows bring in nonstop views of the lake, and its ceiling is dripping with ferns. A variety of omelets (fresh dill and tomato, ham and sweet pepper), eggs, and pancakes spiked with blueberries, pecans or apples and floating in Vermont maple syrup are served for breakfast. Dinner is a pleasant, eclectic blend of country-Continental cuisine, and lunch runs from the light (salads and pastas) to the hearty (international sandwiches).
Rooms: $125-$160, including breakfast and dinner.

NOANK

QUICK BITES

Abbott's Lobster in the Rough
117 Pearl St.
(203) 536-7719
April-Labor Day: open daily noon-9 p.m.; Sept.: open Mon.-Tues. & Thurs.-Sun. noon-7 p.m.
Cards: MC, V.

Abbott's is the quintessential Maine lobster house—except that it's nowhere near Maine, located as it is in the coastal town of Noank near touristy Mystic. Come here for lobster served the way God intended it: steamed simply and eaten on a picnic table overlooking the ocean, with butter dripping down your elbows. To complete the picture, all the other Maine lobster-house staples are served as well—steamers, crab rolls, lobster rolls and good coleslaw—and, true to form, you'll have to bring your own beer or wine. From $10 to $20 for a lobster lunch for two.

NORFOLK

INNS

Greenwoods Gate
105 Greenwoods Rd. East (Rte. 44)
(203) 542-5439
Open year-round.
Cards: AE.

If you want a weekend of seductive romance, more often than not the last place you'd want to go is a country inn. Most of these otherwise-charming places have Colonial-era wall insulation, which is to say, none; your every cry and whisper is public domain. But that's not the case at Greenwoods Gate. With a perfectionist's drive and a rare attention to detail, owner Deanne Raymond has created one of the best and most romantic country inns in New England. Her 1797 house is superb. The decor is lovely—from the pale-yellow living room filled with handsome antiques to the flattering rose dining room with a fire blazing in the winter to the inviting barn-sided kitchen. But it is the bedrooms that are truly magical. The Levi Thompson Suite is perfect: Separated from the rest of the house, it offers privacy in a storybook garret hideaway, brought into the '80s by an ultra-modern bathroom and Jacuzzi. And in all the rooms, your bed will be turned down at night and couture fragrances provided; pretty cotton bed linens, British toiletries and oversized bath towels are charming trademarks of Raymond's luxurious style of hospitality. The Darius Phelps Room has a subtle peach shimmer to its walls, two three-quarter beds and a generous Victorian bathtub forged for extra-long bodies. The cheerful E. J. Trescott Suite, with blue-and-white floral-print wallpaper and a brass-and-iron double bed, is a showpiece for Ralph Lauren's home furnishings. The adjoining single room makes the suite perfect for traveling threesomes.

Raymond's energetic nature results in magnificent breakfasts. You may be fortunate enough to dine on a fresh-fruit compote with yogurt, followed by old-fashioned Irish oatmeal and topped off with Grand Marnier french croissant-toast filled with crème fraîche. Or you may be treated to frothed juice, an apple-pear compote and eggs Benedict Florentine. And those under ten years old may be served paper-doll or heart-shape pancakes.

Rooms: $125-$155, including breakfast.

NORWICH

INNS

**Norwich Inn
and Spa**
607 W. Thames St.
(Rte. 32)
(800) 892-5692,
(203) 886-2401
Open year-round.
All major cards.

Exhausted people come to Norwich to revitalize themselves with the country-elegant atmosphere and all the pamperings of a spa. The blissed-out doves in the lobby give you a preview of what to expect: a peaceful atmosphere, an attentive, helpful staff and affluent, overstressed guests.

The inn's interior designer clearly has a love affair with seafoam green and English chintz, with a pleasing result. The look is calculated country, up to the strategically placed twig furniture that dots the rolling lawns. The spa has a restful California-pastel look, complete with new-age music that will put you to sleep the minute you walk through the door. Plates of fresh fruit and bottles of Evian are plentiful, and a miniboutique sells workout and casual-chic clothes. The fairly expensive spa services range from paraffin hand treatments and manicures to body scrubs and thalassotherapy. The cosmically inclined can indulge in polarity therapy, guided imagery and aromatherapy. Whatever fix you require, you'd best reserve at least two weeks in advance to make sure you get the massage you've been working up to.

Norwich's new villas can be leased or bought; the developers have considerably furnished these blue condos, for those with no imagination. The pretty dining room, with intense rose moiré walls and cabbage-rose print on wicker, is a pleasant place to refuel for the next activity. We can only assume that the hot pastrami and sirloin-strip sandwiches and the medallion of pork with avocado and Monterey Jack that we spied on the daily-changing lunch menu are for guests who have neither cholesterol problems nor any interest in healthful cuisine.

Rooms: $95-$150 (winter and spring), $115-$185 (summer and fall); spa packages available.

OLD GREENWICH

RESTAURANTS

Café du Bec Fin
199 Sound Beach Ave.
(203) 637-4447
FRENCH/AMERICAN
Open Tues.-Thurs. noon-
2 p.m. & 6 p.m.-9 p.m.,
Fri. noon-2 p.m. & 6
p.m.-10 p.m., Sat. 6 p.m.-
10 p.m.
All major cards.

The bucolic charms of Old Greenwich are well complemented by the rustic ambience of Café du Bec Fin, with its faux-Colonial facade, oak accents and fin-de-siècle-inspired murals. This small, convivial bistro, which opened in 1979, is a good neighborhood spot, though it lacks the elegance and polish that would make you want to go out of your way. The china and silverware look cheap, the wine glasses are as thick as beer steins, and a tiled wall cuts the small dining room in two for reasons we cannot begin to imagine. The cooking is of a commendable, if amateurish, order, though it can be compromised by a staff that sometimes chooses to spend more time at the cash register than at your beck and call. Want your soiled butter plate replaced? Perhaps on your second request. Want wine with your meal? Perhaps three urgent pleas will bring some. Need a menu? Some silverware? Your order taken? Wine poured? Well, only if you insist, our waitress indicated with a roll of her eyes.

Chef Joseph Cizynski uses good ingredients and has a light touch—too light with seasonings, as if one more garlic clove or another basil leaf might upset his clientele's conservative palates. How much better his vegetable lasagne or smoked chicken with saffron pasta would be if prepared with just a pinch more salt and pepper! Gravlax is in perfect condition, and his crab crêpes with corn and basil is a toothsome dish, mildly sweet, with a good texture to the thin crêpes. At our last meal, a salad came with Bleu d'Auvergne cheese that had seen fresher days and whose rind had not been cut away. Entrées are quite good, however: soft-shell crabs in season come with a delicious hazelnut-butter sauce, free-range chicken is accompanied by a roasted potato sauce, a veal chop with wild mushrooms is pink and succulent, and even wild boar has real flavor to it. Desserts may include a surprisingly good lavender ice cream or a nicely browned coconut tart. If you're nearby for lunch or want a quiet, though not particularly cheap, dinner, Café du Bec Fin is worth a visit. Two people should spend about $90 to $100 for dinner, including a bottle of wine.

Condé's

(Hyatt Regency Hotel)
1800 E. Puttnam Ave.
(203) 637-7620
CONTINENTAL
*Open Mon.-Fri. 6 p.m.-
10 p.m., Sat. 6 p.m.-
10:30 p.m.
All major cards.*

Long ago, this suburban Connecticut site was the head-quarters of the Condé-Nast publishing company. Now it is a posh hotel that opened a couple of years ago to great fanfare. Much of the hype was devoted to Condé's, the hotel's elegant restaurant. Rather like an English club in decor and atmosphere, the overly ambitious Condé's had a rocky beginning. The too-familiar headwaiter would have been better suited to coaching a softball team, and the food was just plain strange. One of the early disasters featured baked oysters nestled on a bed of ill-chosen seaweed that reeked of low tide. Fortunately, the restaurant pulled up its socks, hired a new chef and has improved immeasurably. Simple dishes are the best. A country salad of wilted arugula, pancetta and a soft-boiled egg is well executed, as is a perfectly grilled filet of beef topped with a thin slice of tomato and melted Gorgonzola. A brace of quail stuffed with a budget-stretching mixture of wild and white rice isn't half bad, either, though marred by a "Pinot Noir" sauce that tastes suspiciously like bottled barbecue sauce. Shrimp with pasta, sun-dried tomatoes and chives is perfectly adequate, though a little flat. The flaky raspberry napoleon is by far the best of the desserts. Though the dining room attracts a few locals, your dining companions are likely to be hotel guests who see no need to go any farther than this for a good meal. Dinner for two, with wine, will run $100 or so.

OLD LYME

RESTAURANTS

Bee and Thistle Inn

100 Lyme St.
(203) 434-1667
AMERICAN/CONTINENTAL
*Open Mon. & Wed.-Sat.
8 a.m.-10 a.m., 11:30
a.m.-2 p.m. & 6 p.m.-
9 p.m., Sun. 8 a.m.-9:30
a.m., 11 a.m.-2 p.m. &
6 p.m.-9 p.m.
Cards: AE, MC, V.*

Take an Early American home, set it on five acres next to a sleepy river immortalized on canvas by turn-of-the-century American impressionist painters, and you've got a classic New England inn. Light fires in all the fireplaces, add lots of flowers and candlelight, put a smart young English chef in the kitchen, and you've got an inn restaurant several notches above expectations. All in all, this is a very romantic place to dine. Not hedonistic, glitzy romantic, mind you, but well-bred, leisurely romantic, where innuendos ripple beneath polite conversation and subtle sauces. Chef Francis Brooke-Smith changes the menu seasonally, combining Early American dishes with modern international offerings. Our last meal started off with classic, robust New England clam chowder (Early American) with plenty of clams, and surprisingly light spinach tortellini stuffed with Gorgonzola and braised with cream, garlic and prosciutto (modern international). In a haze of candlelight and wine, we moved on to slices of tender venison under a Burgundy-based sauce, and to shrimp that snapped our attention back to the food. These shrimp were wrapped in parchment paper along with roasted garlic, pine nuts, sun-dried tomatoes, white wine, oil and fresh herbs, then baked until all the flavors alchemized into something different and quite wonderful. And we discovered that having both apéritifs and coffee in the old-fashioned parlor, right in front of the fireplace, was so romantic that we checked into the possibility of a room for the night. Alas, there was no room left at the inn. Plan ahead (see "Inns" below). Dinner for two, with wine, will come to about $95.

Old Lyme Inn

85 Lyme St. (Rte. 1)
(203) 434-2600
FRENCH/AMERICAN
Open Tues.-Sat. noon-
2 p.m. & 6 p.m.-9 p.m.,
Sun. noon-9 p.m.; light
supper served in the bar
Tues.-Fri. & Sun. 6 p.m.-
9 p.m.
All major cards.

Don't look for hand-hooked rugs or Aunt Fanny's plum preserves at the Old Lyme Inn. No rough-hewn New England hostelry, this is a beautifully restored nineteenth-century home—elegant, formal, even a little reserved. There are hand-painted murals on the walls, royal-blue carpeting on the floors, formal drapes on windows that soar to the ceiling, and a single, always-perfect rose on every table. The chilled butter for the hot rolls is shaped like a regal swan. In his two-plus years here, chef Chris Hansver has made his mark on the menu (which changes three or four times a year), while leaving many of the traditional dishes in place—like the Irish smoked salmon served with slices of sweet Bermuda onion, which is always perfect. Left to his own devices, Hansver turns positively lyrical. Consider the sautéed sweetbreads surrounded by manzanilla olives and wild mushrooms and accented by bold kale, all bound together with reduced cream. At least *we* certainly thought it was lyrical. Then he took a plain trout, stuffed it with tiny scallops, hazelnuts and almonds, baked it and served it with a light cream sauce. We thought that was pretty lyrical, too. The currently inescapable sliced duck breast (whatever do they do with the rest of the bird?) is more tender and flavorful here than in most places. On our last visit, it was partnered with a brandied raspberry sauce, which managed deftly to avoid cloying sweetness. Everything is up to date at the Old Lyme. Vegetables are of the tiny type, bred like bonsai trees for small perfection. Desserts (which change daily) are as perfect as you might expect: chocolate mousse in a champagne flute, flaky-crusted fruit tarts and other sweet successes. While dinner in the main dining rooms is always a regal experience, we sometimes opt for a "light meal" in the bar. It's not really "light," and the blackboard menu is rather extensive, but it's a little less formal and a little less expensive. Of course, you still get a single, always-perfect rose on the table, and you can always get the Irish smoked salmon. Dinner for two, with wine, will set you back about $110.

INNS

Bee and Thistle Inn

100 Lyme St.
(203) 434-1667
Closed 2 weeks in mid-Jan.
Cards: AE, MC, V.

The Bee and Thistle is the quintessential New England country inn. The architecture and grounds give you hope of something exceptionally charming, but inside, unfortunately, it's slightly fatigué. The decor is a bit aged, the rooms are small and simple, the bathrooms are basic, and the pace is sleepy indeed. It's the sort of place that is forever popular for a countryside weekend luncheon, where guests and local residents gather in the sun-drenched side-porch dining alcoves to take a break from domestic chores and the exhausting strain of antiquing and gallery-hopping around the Connecticut River Valley. If you stay here, request Room One, a spacious room with a large canopy bed and a view of the bucolic front yard. The other rooms are pleasantly modest and unmemorable. The best thing about the Bee and Thistle is its fine restaurant (see above), one of the most romantic around.

Rooms: $80-$110, including breakfast.

Old Lyme Inn

85 Lyme St. (Rte. 1)
(203) 434-2600
Closed first 2 weeks in Jan.
All major cards.

Like its excellent restaurant (see above), the Old Lyme Inn is more elegant than homespun, albeit in a New England sort of way—refined, restrained and anything but showy. Owner Diana Atwood added some new bedrooms and a new parlor (Sassafras's Library, named for her beloved, now-dead cat) a few years back, bringing the room count up to thirteen. The best are the two corner rooms at the end of the corridor; one overlooks the yellow barn, which has been on the property since the 1850s, and the other has a view of some lovely trees. The original rooms in the old house are typical of that era and that part of the country—up a step here, down a step there—and are tastefully and comfortably furnished, if not exceptionally spacious. All the rooms have private bathrooms, most with tubs and showers, and all are blissfully quiet, despite the proximity to Interstate 90. The refinement of the restaurant and the comfort of the inn make the Old Lyme an ideal refuge.

Rooms: $85-$115, including breakfast.

SIGHTS

One of America's oldest artists' colonies, this coastal town still has a keen eye for the visual arts, and several fine galleries are located on Lyme Street. The Lyme Academy of Fine Arts, 84 Lyme Street (203-434-5232), is housed in an 1817 building listed on the National Register of Historic Places; it offers year-round classes for professionals and students, as well as changing exhibitions of painting and sculpture. Open Monday to Friday 9 a.m. to 4 p.m.; admission is free. Another 1817 building, the late-Georgian Florence Griswold Museum, 96 Lyme Street (203-434-5542), hosts changing exhibits on such subjects as American impressionism and the decorative arts in New England. Open June to October, Tuesday to Saturday 10 a.m. to 5 p.m. and Sunday 1 p.m. to 5 p.m.; November to May, Wednesday to Sunday 1 p.m. to 5 p.m.; admission is $1 for adults, 50 cents for seniors and free for children. And the Lyme Art Association puts on five or so shows each summer in its gallery at 70 Lyme Street; for information, call (203) 434-7802.

SHOPS

The Cooley Gallery
25 Lyme St.
(203) 434-8807
*Open Tues.-Sat. 10 a.m.-
5 p.m.*

Jeff Cooley moved out of his home in Salisbury into this fresh, spacious gallery, in which he displays his lovely collection of eighteenth- and nineteenth-century American landscapes. If gentle views of an impressionistic nature or Hudson River scenes are what you're looking for, you'll be sure to find something to take home, assuming a $14,000 or $35,000 price tag doesn't faze you. There is also a less impressive collection of twentieth-century works downstairs.

POMFRET

INNS

Cobbscroft
Rte. 169
(203) 928-5560
*Open year-round.
Cards: MC, V.*

If you were one of the privileged few who inherited Queen Anne chairs, antique clocks and Federal-period furnishings, perhaps you'd decide that you had little choice but to show them off in a beautiful country inn. At least that's what Tom and Janet McCobb decided, to help cure the postretirement doldrums. You couldn't hope to find a lovelier place to spend the night, and your stay will be made even more memorable by your sensitive, attractive hosts. Tom McCobb is a busy man: In addition to running the inn, he paints, teaches and lectures. Guests have been known to leave Cobbscroft with one of his charming watercolors under one arm—the sitting room doubles as a gallery, where Tom sells his own works along with those of local artists.
   The elegant five-room inn is a civilized alternative to the tourist-trap lodgings in and around nearby Sturbridge, Massachusetts. The affectionately named Bridal Suite up-

stairs has Empire-style furnishings, a working fireplace and a bathroom that would make Napoleon's Josephine happy; its dazzling gold fixtures and elongated Empire bath are the talk of the Pomfret plumbing world. Downstairs, a cheery blue-and-white wicker room adjoins a handsome double done in red. The rest of the bedrooms are just as attractive, each with its own beautiful private bath. Janet serves breakfast in the country-formal dining room—perhaps hot apple crisp, almond puff pastry, homemade coffee cake and fresh fruit.

Rooms: $60-$70, including breakfast.

RIDGEFIELD

RESTAURANTS

Le Coq Hardi
Big Shop Ln.
(203) 431-3060
FRENCH
Open Mon.-Fri. noon-2 p.m. & 6 p.m.-9 p.m., Sat. 6 p.m.-10 p.m.
All major cards.

In exclusive, exurban Ridgefield, people turn old barns into guest cottages and smithies into restaurants. In the case of this former smithy, the owners soft-lit the 150-year-old stone walls, shored up the beamed ceilings with new two-by-fours and hired a chef who knows how to forge some mighty wonderful dishes. Then they decorated it with a lot of roosters (painted, etched, porcelainized, printed on butter pats) and called it Le Coq Hardi. The small, romantic restaurant accommodates only about 60 people and has plenty of alcoves for relatively private dining. We suggest that you at least try to avoid the main dining area, with its elbow-to-elbow seating along one wall. Though the place can be crowded on weekends—when New Yorkers decamp to Ridgefield—we've found that on quiet, midweek nights we've been able to get an alcove, as well as the pleasant, intelligent staff and chef's best efforts, practically to ourselves.

The food ranges from the hearty to the ethereally light. Delicate salmon mousse, sprinkled with black caviar and resting in a puddle of beurre blanc spiked with green and pink peppercorns, is truly memorable—no wonder that it's Le Coq Hardi's signature dish. Hearty, coarse-textured sausage made of veal, pork and duck, grilled until its casing has just burst, is served with a gingery mustard sauce and crisp slices of Granny Smith apple. Sautéed calves' liver (this is one of the few restaurants you can trust to do a tricky dish like calves' liver just right) comes with a sage-flecked Madeira sauce and a generous portion of wild rice tossed with pine nuts. Sometimes the dishes overreach (squid with pasta, artichoke hearts, grapefruit and white wine), so stick to the reliable specialties—rack of lamb with roasted garlic cloves and Burgundy sauce, veal chop with Stilton and caramelized apples. During the week, dessert offerings may be on the skimpy side, but they burst into full flower on weekends. Le Coq Hardi knows it's special: Jackets are required for gentlemen at dinner. (Note: Le Coq Hardi has opened a second restaurant in Stamford's Westin Hotel, which is every bit as good, though there's nothing like dining in a smithy.) Dinner for two, with wine, will come to about $110.

INNS

Stonehenge
Stonehenge Rd. (off Rte. 7)
(203) 438-6511
Open year-round.
All major cards.

If you consider yourself to have the same good taste as Barbara Walters, Barbra Streisand and the invincible Elizabeth Taylor, Stonehenge is for you. The inn can be trusted for its privacy and discretion, not to mention its seductive charm, which is why it is a country home for stars on the road—and for ordinary people who consider Stonehenge their own secret hideaway for special-event celebrations and the stuff that good dreams are made of. Each of the thirteen updated-country-style rooms is different. The four suites in the guest house are particularly spacious, with Chippendale-period furnishings and ultra-modern bathrooms. The three bedrooms in the 1724 farmhouse are just as attractive as the suites, and the guest cottages are also furnished with authentic antiques, without sacrificing the modern-day conveniences that make Stonehenge a business-traveler's paradise.

There's no need to leave the well-equipped inn once you get there. The dining room serves quality cuisine, the romantic pond brims over with swans and wild geese, and autumn's drop-dead foliage, combined with the inn's Colonial architecture, makes Stonehenge picture-perfect.

Rooms: $95-$135, including breakfast.

> *We are always happy to hear about your discoveries and to receive your comments about ours. We want to give your letters the attention they deserve, so when you write to us, remember to state clearly exactly what you liked or disliked. Be concise, but convincing. Do take the time to argue your point.*

RIVERTON

SIGHTS

Hitchcock Museum
Rte. 20
(203) 379-1003
*April-May: open Sat. 1 p.m.
-4 p.m.; June-Oct.: open
Wed.-Sat. 11 a.m.-4 p.m.,
Sun. 1 p.m.-4 p.m.*

To antiques-crazy New Englanders, authentic Hitchcock chairs are among the most prized of all heirlooms. If you love their simplicity but aren't lucky enough to own one, make a detour to this museum housed in an old church, which displays a collection of nineteenth-century Hitchcock furniture. In fact, not all Hitchcocks are antiques—the nearby factory is still making a number of the lines by hand. Admission free.

RYE, NEW YORK

RESTAURANTS

La Panetière
530 Milton Rd.
(914) 967-8140
FRENCH
*Open Mon.-Fri. noon-2:30
p.m. & 6 p.m.-9:30 p.m.,
Sat. 6 p.m.-10 p.m., Sun.
noon-8:30 p.m.
All major cards.*

Many are the well-meaning American restaurateurs who have sought to replicate the character and quality of their favorite French auberges. But despite the resources and the will, most have fallen back on the clichés that continue to mark French suburban restaurants in the United States. Of the very few who have succeeded, Jacques Loupiac of La Panetière has done so splendidly. Indeed, we might readily compare La Panetière to some of our favorite restaurants in France, like Le Vieux Moulin in Bouilland, La Flamiche in Roye and La Crémaillère in Orléans. Curiously enough, Loupiac had been maître d' at a venerable (though long past its prime) restaurant in Banksville, New York, called La Crémaillère, but the comparison stops there. Here Loupiac has fashioned a dining room with a rustic decor and lots of fresh flowers, not five minutes from the Connecticut border. His wine cellar is one of the finest in the United States, and he has trained his impeccable staff to know a great deal about what's on the list, so you can trust them to choose a good bottle for your meal.

The sad death in an accident of chef Yves Gonnachon not long ago threatened to detract from the reputation La Panetière had so carefully built over two years, but Gonnachon's sous-chef, Gérard Bertholon, has bridged the gap with respect and imagination. The resulting cuisine is a delight: little foie gras and truffle sandwiches, sweetbreads on a bed of wild greens, tian of lamb on a tart of spring vegetables. We were enchanted with his swordfish done in a reduction of beurre rouge, and happy to see such a fine selection of cheeses. Desserts have improved, especially the warm fruit gratins, and the petits fours are perfect nibbles at the end of a splendid meal. Plan to be $150 poorer after dinner for two, with wine.

SOUTH NORWALK

RESTAURANTS

Pasta Nostra
116 Washington St.
(203) 854-9700
ITALIAN
Open Tues.-Wed. 11:45 a.m.-2:45 p.m., Thurs.-Sat. 6 p.m.-9:30 p.m.
No cards.

Just what possessed Joe Bruno to open the best Italian restaurant in Connecticut in drab South Norwalk (albeit on a pretty street full of antiques stores and other eateries) is a mystery. Just why he gave his little trattoria the frivolous name Pasta Nostra ("Our Pasta") is another indication that perhaps he aimed too low at the start and doesn't know just how good he is. But the locals know, which is why this Italian deli/restaurant is packed at lunch and dinner with customers who appreciate the fresh, crusty loaves of bread, the lightly cooked, sweet tomato sauces, the admirable spicing of his dishes and the fair prices (with the exception of some desserts).

You enter the unpretentious storefront and breathe in the perfume of garlic, tomato and pork. You pass a counter stacked with breads and takeout foods, and sit down in a barely decorated dining room, which at full capacity seems as loud as the din at an Italian soccer match. A casually dressed waitress suggests a glass of the good Italian house wine, and as you spread a pungently delicious black olive paste and Robiola cheese on a piece of crisp toast and sip the wine, you think you could make a lunch of this several days a week. But there's much more: sweet, ripe figs with thinly cut prosciutto; an assortment of pastas that includes freshly made cannelloni, as light as it is flavorful; and a luscious pork and Provolone cheese sausage over linguine with a spicy marinara sauce. Other pastas of the day may be agnolotti with three cheeses, red-pepper linguine with asparagus sauce, or soft-shell crab over linguine alla marinara.

Desserts are decent enough, but paying $3.50 for three pignoli macaroons is disturbing, since a lunchtime pasta may cost only $9. Incidentally, the menu notes that you will be automatically charged a fifteen-percent gratuity along with the seven-and-a-half-percent Connecticut sales tax, which should make it easy for visiting Europeans but perhaps a bit off-putting for Americans.

Pasta Nostra started out as a drop-in sort of place, but now it's tough to get in at all (reservations aren't taken). We hope Bruno never loses his ingenuousness, and we do hope more New England entrepreneurs will follow his example. Two people may dine here, with wine, for $70 to $75.

SOUTHPORT

SHOPS

Pat Guthman
281 Pequot
(203) 259-5743
Open Tues.-Sat. 10 a.m.-5 p.m.

Pat Guthman has had her hands in the kitchen for years—and she's been writing about antiques for a long time, too, as a columnist for the *Newtown Bee* and *Arts & Antiques Weekly*. So it was only natural for her to start collecting marvelous antique kitchenware. Her bright, cheerful store is filled with vintage rolling pins, choppers, wooden bowls, country cupboards, clothespins, cookie cutters, hearth cooking tools, stoneware ceramics and painted boxes. A second room is devoted to contemporary folk art (quilts, wreaths, children's toys), and a third serves as a gallery featuring the work of local contemporary craftsmen. Guthman is enthusiastic and helpful, and she will search for that must-have hearth or keeping-room utensil, ceramic jug or creamware basket to complete your own country kitchen.

STAMFORD

RESTAURANTS

See Le Coq Hardi in Ridgefield.

SHOPS

United House Wrecking Co.
535 Hope St.
(203) 348-5371
Open Mon.-Wed. & Fri.-Sat. 9:30 a.m.-5:30 p.m., Thurs. 9:30 a.m.-8 p.m.

Home restorers, home builders, antiques buffs, browsers—United House is a dream come true for all of them. Allow plenty of time to wander its five acres of relics, architectural elements, nostalgia, furniture and the like. Of particular note are the 300 to 400 pieces of stained glass, the incredible selection of new and used beveled glass (windows, mirrors, etc.), the array of new and used doors (French doors, arched doors, carved oak doors...) and all sorts of odd stuff you won't find anywhere else.

STONINGTON

SHOPS

Quester Maritime Gallery
77 Main St. (on the green)
(203) 535-3860
*Open Mon.-Sat. 11 a.m.-
6 p.m., Sun. 1:30 p.m.-
5 p.m.*

Man of the sea Jim Marenakos masterminds this extraordinary revolving collection of maritime art, which is coupled
with a collection of "non-jib" impressionistic works that are
overseen by his daughter Ann. Jim moved his fabulous
works out of his home into his new gallery, the former site
of a 105-year-old pharmacy in the stunning town of Ston-
ington. He travels throughout the world to uncover first-
rate ship models (including coveted French prisoner-of-war
pieces), John Stobart oils, China trade paintings, campaign
furnishings, refined Frederick Myrick scrimshaw (Myrick
invented this art form), navigational instruments and James
E. Buttersworth's to-die-for ship paintings. The gallery also
houses a sampling of Frank Bensen and Sir Edwin Landseer
sporting oils, along with works by the impressionists. Marenakos is a happy person who loves his avocation, and his
enthusiasm quickly makes maritime converts of the uninitiated, even if they have to save up for decades to afford some
of these treasures.

Marguerite Riordan
8 Pearl St.
(203) 535-2511
Open by appt. only.

The gracious Marguerite Riordan believes that if you don't
love it from the inside and underneath, it's not worth
investing in. At any given time, her collection of eighteenth-
and nineteenth-century antiques may include a Townsend
and Goddard card table, a Connecticut River Valley corner
cabinet deaccessioned from the Metropolitan Museum of
Art in New York, a 1790 Chippendale dining table and
some exquisite folk-art portraits. These one-of-a-kind finds
are displayed in a handsome gallery on the ground floor of
the amazing building she and her good-natured husband
call home. The prices are staggering to the novice, but fair
when you're accustomed to dealing in five figures for extraordinary pieces.

*We are always happy to hear about your discoveries
and to receive your comments about ours. We want
to give your letters the attention they deserve, so
when you write to us, remember to state clearly
exactly what you liked or disliked. Be concise, but
convincing. Do take the time to argue your point.*

WESTPORT

INNS

Cotswold Inn
76 Myrtle Ave.
(203) 226-3766
Open year-round.
Cards: AE, MC, V.

This little cottage looks like something out of the Brothers Grimm. Tucked away on a back street in Westport, it is a home-away-from-home for those accustomed to living in the lap of luxury. Owners Richard and Judy Montanaro have created a country inn that pampers guests and provides privacy. The four rooms are Laura Ashley showpieces, combining handsome reproduction furniture with every '80s convenience: discreetly hidden TVs, phones and fabulous modern bathrooms. It's no wonder that this stunning little inn is the darling of the expense-account crowd, who choose charm and good taste over a more impersonal ambience.

But maybe they come here just because they're hungry, for the Cotswold serves a superb breakfast: eggs Benedict, fresh mushroom-and-Cotswold-cheese omelets, eggs with dill, tomatoes and country sausage, heart-shape waffles with strawberry butter and Vermont syrup, fresh fruit and yogurt, and authentic Irish oatmeal are some of the choices that await you in the inn's cheerful eat-in kitchen, which is manned by the pleasant resident innkeepers. This place is a first-class ticket that's worth the price, whether you're a harried business traveler looking for something off the beaten path or someone simply interested in spoiling yourself for a weekend.

Rooms: $175-$225, including breakfast.

WILTON

SHOPS

George Subkoff
643 Danbury Rd.
(203) 834-0703
Open Tues.-Sat. 10 a.m.-
5:30 p.m., Sun. noon-5 p.m.

George Subkoff has the perfect store for those a bit intimidated by serious antiques. There's plenty of space to browse, jazz music keeps the pace alive, and Subkoff may likely be involved in a game of backgammon with a friend when you arrive, so there's no feeling of high sales pressure. You are free to wander throughout his spacious store, where you'll discover the fabulous clipper-ship painting by Antonio Jacobsen (a pricey $22,000); a reverse serpentine Connecticut oxbow chest (a mere $38,000); a Duncan Phyfe drop-leaf breakfast table (a more reasonable $7,500); a pair of nonmatching Federal mahogany card tables ($16,000); a George

II mirror (a bargain at $8,500); and a Queen Anne burl-elm and walnut chest (an investment at $15,000). There is a lot of everything, so the merchandise suits a variety of tastes and pocketbooks: bronze Chinese dogs, Chippendale highboys, country-painted fancy chairs, hunt paintings and Chinese barrel side tables, just for starters. Index cards carry the prices and a minimal amount of information about each piece.

WOODBURY

SHOPS

David Dunton
Call for directions
(203) 263-5355
Open by appt. only.

David Dunton loves to surround himself with beauty. His private collection of eighteenth-century American antiques is housed in a lovely New England home and barn that are surrounded by beautiful grounds, gardens and a peaceful stream. The garden bench is an appropriate place to sit and meditate on the abrupt reality that you are about to invest in a $10,000 inlaid card table, a $17,000 Connecticut River Valley lolling chair, an $18,000 mirror attributed to Nathan Ruggles, or one of the other exquisite pieces Dunton has to offer. There are some charming oil landscapes, dazzling tea tables, handsome Queen Anne armchairs and the occasional inlaid box or neoclassic architectural mirror priced for those who aren't yet in the big leagues. Dunton helps young collectors invest in his museum-grade pieces over time, nurturing those poor souls stricken with the lifelong obsession to acquire hard-to-pay-for treasures.

Kenneth Hammett Antiques
Main St. South
(203) 263-5676
Open Mon.-Sat. 10 a.m.-5:30 p.m.

If you don't have time to drive to historic Deerfield, Massachusetts, or Shelburne, Vermont, to admire sensational eighteenth-century American antiques *in situ*, come to this impressive store in Woodbury. Kenneth Hammett's passion is revealed in the architecture of the building that houses his business: a 1753 Federal house listed in the National Register of Historic Places. The rooms, done in appropriate Colonial colors, are filled with an extensive collection of chests, tables, chairs, card tables, fire fenders, clocks, writing tables, occasional chairs, mirrors, Oriental rugs and maybe even a Sheraton bed. Upstairs is a large collection of English ceramics. The prices are not for the faint of heart, and you need to know what you're looking for, as printed information on each piece is minimal. But Hammett himself is generally on hand, and he'll be happy to fill you in on any missing data and seduce you into leaving with a $4,750 Salem side chair.

Eve Stone & Son
319 Main St.
(203) 266-4802
Open Wed.-Sun. 10 a.m.-
5:30 p.m.

It would be perfectly reasonable to assume that the owners of this unprepossessing clapboard house sell gingerbread cake rather than $14,500 Chippendale highboys, $22,000 Hepplewhite sideboards and $7,500 Sheraton card tables. The effervescent Eve Stone and her family have an ongoing love affair with rarefied American antiques. A visit to their overflowing shop is always a surprise, and there's always something for everyone: lots of shiny antique brass, bed linens, Chinese lamps, ceramics, mirrors and clocks. Everything is exquisite and most everything is expensive. But the Stones make it easy for you—they'll help you succumb to the inevitable by giving you their best price and allowing you to buy these stunning pieces over time. The basement isn't exactly of the bargain variety, but it does have some affordable country items (fish lures, baskets, exportware). Every summer Eve takes up residence in West Tisbury on the Vineyard, where she has a branch shop that features country antiques and brass (see "Martha's Vineyard" in "Cape Cod & the Islands" chapter). And the Stones' savvy, personable son, Michael, rules the roost at their new location in New York City's Place des Antiquaires (212-935-3780), where his young connoisseur's vision and good taste are amply evident.

VERMONT

ARLINGTON

INNS

The Arlington Inn
Rte. 7
(802) 375-6532
Open year-round.
Cards: MC, V.

The Arlington Inn is one of the few places in New England where you can still find planked salmon (the fish is baked on an oak plank, which keeps it moist and smoky). But to come here solely for the food would be to overlook one of the finest examples of Greek Revival architecture in Vermont. Built in 1848 by railroad magnate Martin Deming, The Arlington Inn boasts a majestic staircase, unusual parquet ceilings and the original Victorian moldings and wainscoting. You won't find the uniformity of a Sheraton here: There are thirteen rooms, each named for a member of the Deming family and furnished with one-of-a-kind antiques. Located as it is near Stratton and Mount Snow ski areas, the inn gives its guests ample opportunity to work off calories. Fly-fishermen will appreciate the proximity to the Batten Kill River. During the fall foliage season, the chestnut and maple trees on the inn's well-maintained grounds have been known to stop shutterbugs dead in their tracks.
Rooms: $48-$125, including breakfast.

BARNARD

RESTAURANTS

Barnard Inn
Rte. 12
(802) 234-9961
FRENCH/CONTINENTAL
June-Sept.: open Tues.-
Sun. 6 p.m.-9:30 p.m.;
Oct.-May: open Wed.-Sun.
6 p.m.-9:30 p.m. (closed
parts of April, May &
Nov.).
Cards: AE, MC, V.

This is one of those country restaurants you hope to find and seldom do. Located ten miles north of Woodstock, the inn (somewhat misnamed, as there are no overnight accommodations) is home to owner/chef Sepp Schenker, Swiss born and trained, who has created a gracious little world within a red-brick house from the 1700s. Nothing stuffy, you understand—just a setting worthy of the food: five beamed-ceiling dining rooms, with candle and firelight gleaming on old wood; knowledgeable service by women in long black skirts working from movable warming tables; and a fairly well-dressed clientele. The chef follows the seasons, using wild morels in spring and chanterelles in fall; crisp, moist roast duck is served year-round, with seasonal sauces like fresh elderberry or frost grape. The cream of leek soup is delicately veined with cheese, and thinly sliced veal is sautéed in a buttery sauce of lobster, tomato, brandy and herbs. Fresh vegetables are always treated with care. Dessert is selected from seductive contenders arrayed on a tableside trolley; the light, lovely Viennese Bienenstich cake is one of the winners. Dinner for two, with wine, can go to $100.

BARRE

SIGHTS

Rock of Ages
Rte. 89 (Exit 6)
(802) 476-3119
May-Oct.: open Mon.-Fri.
8:30 a.m.-5 p.m., Sat.
10 a.m.-2 p.m.

Among Vermont's most prized products is its granite, the raw material of public and private buildings throughout America. Rock of Ages, the world's largest monumental granite quarry, gives visitors the opportunity to take a peak behind the scenes in a working quarry. The narrated tour-and-train-ride shows a working quarry, then takes you through the finishing plant, where you can watch the engraving and polishing processes.
Adults $1.95, children 50 cents.

BENNINGTON

QUICK BITES

Blue Benn
Rte. 7
(802) 442-8944
Open Mon.-Tues. 5 a.m.-
5 p.m., Wed.-Fri. 5 a.m.-
8 p.m., Sat. 5 a.m.-4 p.m.,
Sun. 7 a.m.-4 p.m.
No cards.

It's rare to find the real thing when it comes to diners—most have been retrofitted with iridescent flagstone facades and Aegean menus. But Blue Benn is an inspiration of stainless steel, food-themed stained glass and a vintage '40s decor. Whether you sit in a booth or at the counter, you'll overhear Bennington College students chat while you enjoy a reasonably priced Vermont cheeseburger, hot roast-pork sandwich, Havarti cheese melt, corned beef hash, pot roast dinner or spaghetti-and-meatballs platter.

SIGHTS

Situated in Vermont's southwest corner within a few miles of both Massachusetts and New York State, Bennington is best known as the home of Bennington College, the exclusive, highly progressive (some would say eccentric) college with a special emphasis on the arts. The Bennington Museum on W. Main Street (802-447-1571) is well known for its collection of Americana, including glass, sculpture, furniture and paintings, particularly those of Grandma Moses. It's open daily (except on major holidays), 9 a.m. to 5 p.m.; admission is $4 for adults and $3 for senior citizens and children 12 to 17, with children under 12 admitted free. Also worth a look is the Bennington Battle Monument, a 306-foot tower with an observation deck that offers views of the surrounding mountains. (Bennington is in the midst of a number of ski areas, including Prospect Mountain, Mount Snow and Dutch Hill.) The monument (802-828-3226) is open April 1 to October 31, daily 9 a.m. to 5 p.m. And Bennington's acclaimed brown-glazed pottery, as beautiful as it is practical, is on display at Bennington Potters, Inc. Located at 324 County Street, it is open year-round and offers free guided tours through the factory, as well as a showroom and a factory-outlet shop (802-447-7531).

SHOPS

Hawkins House
262 North St. (Rte. 7)
(802) 447-0488
Jan.-June: open Mon.-Sat. 10 a.m.-5:30 p.m.; July-Dec.: open Mon.-Sat. 9:30 a.m.-6 p.m., Sun. noon-5:30 p.m.

Although crafts must coexist with commercial "gift shop" items here, they manage to survive. The collection is eclectic—hand-painted egg ornaments, wrought-iron chandeliers, Woody Jackson cow stools—and there's new-age music in the background. This is, after all, Vermont.

BRANDON

INNS

Beauchamp Place
31 Franklin St. (Rte. 7)
(802) 247-3905
Open year-round.
Cards: AE, MC, V.

While cruising Route 7, admiring yet another perfect little New England village, you'll feel compelled to stop at the crossroads in Brandon to stay at this well-edited piece of Victoriana. It's easy to see that owners Georgia and Roy Beauchamp are Anglophiles—their English furnishings and sense of decor make this inn a set piece of which Queen Elizabeth herself would be proud. The beautifully decorated house is on the formal side; the dining room alone, with its heritage wallpaper, silver tea service, chandelier and impressive table, gives new meaning to the Continental breakfast served here. The serene living room is equally attractive, with flattering colors, intimate seating and an overall feeling of the lush life. And the eight bedrooms upstairs are perfect. Every detail has been attended to, from replacing the tin ceiling with era-authentic reproductions to the selection of Victorian furniture and vintage decorative linens. Die-hard romantics should choose Room One, a tribute to the Queen Mum with feminine pink colors and a sheered canopy over the expansive bed. Naturalists should try Room Three, an English garden filled with poppies—on the walls, canopy, cushions and spread. The third floor hardly qualifies as servants' quarters; its three rooms are even more enticing than those downstairs. The entire house is carpeted, which adds to the muffled tranquility.

Rooms: $75-$85, including breakfast.

BRATTLEBORO

RESTAURANTS

The Common Ground Community Restaurant
25 Elliot St.
(802) 257-0855
INTERNATIONAL/VEGETARIAN
Open Mon. & Wed.-Sat. 11:30 a.m.-5 p.m. & 5:30 p.m.-9 p.m., Sun. 10:30 a.m.-1:30 p.m. & 5:30 p.m.-9 p.m.
No cards.

10/20

Climb past notices of meditation classes and peace walks and feel the hustle and bustle of hectic life fall away. By the time you step into the second-floor Common Ground, with its mismatched chairs and cooks in T-shirts rolling whole-wheat rolls in an open kitchen, the mood of the '60s is upon you. A group of owner/workers runs the place cooperatively, following in the footsteps of the commune-based founders. Everything, from the Sauerkraut to the ginger ale, is made on the premises. That it is the oldest natural-food restaurant in New England would be no reason to come if the food weren't so good. The burrito, for example, is a heaping plateful of whole-wheat chapati loosely wrapping spicy refried beans, jack cheese, curly lettuce and herbed tomatoes and topped with a mound of sour cream and excellent house sauce. Fish and chicken are served, but the ethnic vegetarian fare is the most interesting. International Night, on Wednesdays, features a full meal from Africa, India or the Middle East. Ten Speed Press published The Common Ground's dessert cookbook, but let the restaurant make the poppy-seed torte for you. And don't light a cigarette. Dinner for two, with wine or beer, is about $25.

INNS

See Marlboro, Newfane, West Dover, Wilmington; in New Hampshire, Chesterfield, Marlborough, Westmoreland.

SHOPS

Vermont Artisan Designs
115 Main St.
(802) 257-7044
Open Mon.-Thurs. & Sat. 10 a.m.-5:30 p.m., Fri. 10 a.m.-8 p.m.

This large, cleanly designed store mixes a good variety of small-scale production work with touches of whimsy, such as stuffed-fabric animal heads. You'll find a little of everything here, though the place is particularly strong in woolens; there's a wool shop in the rear.

BRISTOL

RESTAURANTS

Mary's
11 Main St.
(802) 453-2432
AMERICAN/INTERNATIONAL
Open Tues.-Sat. 11:30 a.m.-3:30 p.m. & 5 p.m.-9:30 p.m., Sun. 10:30 a.m.-3 p.m. & 4 p.m.- 9:30 p.m. All major cards.

12/20

We've all had the fantasy of driving down the main street of an unprepossessing little town far from the big city and happening upon a memorable restaurant. It's happened to us at Mary's. About fifteen years ago, there really was a Mary; her converted lunch counter gradually expanded into the next storefront. From the start, the menu blended the vegetarian, the ethnic and the homespun culinary classics of the '70s, and the standard was fresh ingredients carefully and imaginatively prepared and moderately priced. Several owner/chefs may have come and gone since those days, but Mary's spirit remains. The decor is still comforting and simple, with mismatched chairs and plates, local art, and massive plants by the small-pane window. True, the food is fancier now, and the prices are higher, but freshness and careful attention to detail are still the watchwords. In fall, try the pumpkin soup (bring a red leaf and get a discount on your meal). Tradition is found in the satisfying pear chutney alongside the country pâté; modern touches include apples and cranberries in the pasta Alfredo. On a cold night, there's nothing better than Mary's braised rabbit in a creamy wine sauce, followed by pecan pie sweetened with maple syrup. With a bottle from the pricey wine list, two will spend about $70 for dinner.

BURLINGTON

RESTAURANTS

The Daily Planet
15 Center St.
(802) 862-9647
AMERICAN/CONTINENTAL
Open Mon.-Thurs.
11:30 a.m.-3 p.m. &
5 p.m.-10:30 p.m., Fri.-
Sat. 11:30 a.m.-3 p.m. &
5 p.m.-11 p.m., Sun.
5 p.m.-10:30 p.m.
All major cards.

12/20

As Rick's was to Casablanca, so The Daily Planet is to Burlington. Everyone passes through. Some only get as far as the bar, but you shouldn't stop there. It has been called the city's hippest restaurant and bar, but that's only part of the story; at lunch, there are enough suits and ties to prove that its appeal crosses demarcation lines. What we have here is an above-ground cellar that serves excellent, mostly ethnic food made from the freshest ingredients. The only nod toward decorating is the annual spring painting of the brick walls and exposed pipes; the room is small and so are the tables, which are dressed with tablecloths but also with paper napkins. But we don't come here for the decor—we come for the food and the fun. Why, just the other day we were lusting after a blue-corn tostada topped with sour cream and salsa, and we found one here. We also have had Moroccan mahi mahi in a spicy Berber-style sauce served with a delicious red-onion and orange relish, and "Wild Earth" pasta in a creamy red-pepper pesto with wild and cultivated mushrooms and leeks. You get the idea. The menu changes frequently but always makes a number of stops around Southeast Asia. With a bottle from the moderately priced wine list, two will spend about $40 for dinner.

Déjà Vu Café
185 Pearl St.
(802) 864-7917
FRENCH/INTERNATIONAL
Open Mon.-Thurs.
11:30 a.m.-2:30 p.m. &
5:30 p.m.-9:30 p.m., Fri.-
Sat. 11:30 a.m.-2:30 p.m.
& 5:30 p.m.-10 p.m., Sun.
11 a.m.-3 p.m. & 5:30
p.m.-9:30 p.m.
All major cards.

12/20

The story behind Déjà Vu's mellow, woody sanctum is that its original owner put a modest bar into a Rip van Winkle trance for four years, before it finally emerged in the late '70s as the restaurant with the most pleasant ambience in town. There are quirky little booths, etched glass, brass and lamps that look like bending frosted petals and morning-glory horns. Bare floors and tables keep it humble, but the food soars—attention to detail is paid here. Nouvelle touches grace the generally French menu, but there is an equally good café-style menu, with such tasty dishes as cassoulet américain, a lively mix of black beans, venison sausage, lamb and duckling. Fish is well prepared; we like the smoked trout with tarragon mayonnaise as much as the seafood stew in a wine and tomato sauce. Desserts are an event— go light with a mimosa sorbet or heavy with the Black Russian Pie. Afternoon tea is served with unlimited little cakes. The long bar stocks the largest foreign-beer selection in town. Dinner for two, with wine, will be about $40 for a café-style entrée or about $65 for selections from the regular menu.

The Ice House
171 Battery St.
(802) 864-1800
SEAFOOD/AMERICAN
Open Mon.-Sat.
11:30 a.m.-2:30 p.m. &
5 p.m.-10 p.m., Sun.
10:30 a.m.-2:30 p.m. &
5 p.m.-10 p.m.
Cards: AE, DC, V.

12/20

The Ice House is a stone's throw (with a good arm) from Lake Champlain and Burlington's waterfront, which is edging toward the south but still has a working-waterfront feel to it. The restaurant comfortably inhabits a reconditioned ice house from the last century; from a table on its wide deck during the brief but glorious summer, the view of the lake is only slightly obscured by a lumberyard. At entry level, there is a pleasant bar, but the main action is below in the dining room, which has wide windows, stone walls and exposed beams. The menu has settled down to a small but dependable variety of fish and meat, plus several nightly specials. You select the method of cooking and the sauce from a choice of several options. We have had a nicely prepared grilled rainbow trout with a red-pepper purée, as well as grilled Vermont lamb loin with roasted garlic in a demi-glace tinged with balsamic vinegar. Vegetables are always fresh and crisp, even in the long nongrowing season. Linger over the white-and dark-chocolate mousse. Wine is served only by the glass. About $55 for two, with wine.

Pauline's
1834 Shelburne Rd.,
South Burlington
(802) 862-1081
FRENCH/AMERICAN
Open Mon.-Sat. 11 a.m.-
2 p.m. & 5:30 p.m.-
9:30 p.m., Sun. 10:30
a.m.-2 p.m. & 5:30 p.m.-
9:30 p.m.
All major cards.

Pauline's is like a pearl in an oyster—the oyster in this case being a strip of car dealers. Its food is, in fact, a jewel among local restaurants. The attractive chalet has a café on the ground floor and a more formal dining room upstairs, where lace curtains make you feel like you're in a side-street place in Montparnasse. The cuisine both upstairs and down is a fine confluence of French and new American, with an emphasis on fresh local ingredients. Our last meal here started with smoked chicken breast from the nearby Shelburne Farms estate and delicately sautéed fiddlehead ferns with morels. (Fiddleheads, which taste a bit like asparagus that has spent time in the woods, are a spring treat seldom found in restaurants.) Then came thin, tender slices of Vermont lamb with chèvre, the meat appropriately rosy. The signature dessert, a crêpe stuffed with vanilla ice cream and capped with hot praline sauce and pecans, put us in caramel heaven. We have also enjoyed the crabcakes and cioppino (fisherman's stew) in the café. Plan on parting with at least $65 for two, with wine, in the dining room and about $20 less in the café.

> *DON'T FORGET: Gault Millau introduces you to the Best of New York, the Best of Washington D.C., the Best of Los Angeles, the Best of San Francisco, the Best of Chicago, the Best of France, the Best of Paris, the Best of Italy, the Best of London.*

Sakura

2 Church St.
(802) 863-1988
JAPANESE
Open Tues.-Thurs. 11 a.m.-
2 p.m. & 5 p.m.-9:30 p.m.,
Fri. 11 a.m.-2 p.m. &
5 p.m.-10:30 p.m., Sat.
11 a.m.-2:30 p.m. &
5 p.m.-10:30 p.m., Sun.
5 p.m.-9 p.m.
Cards: AE, MC, V.

12/20

It seems only right that a state that buys a lot of four-wheel-drive Subarus finally gets to eat sushi. Upscale Chinese restaurants have proliferated in the Burlington area, but Sakura is the state's only Japanese restaurant. The serene atmosphere and peach-and-beige decor perfectly complement the authentic Japanese culinary treasures. A little wooden platter of glistening sushi is a comforting sight on a snowy northern evening. The tekka-maki (fresh tuna and rice wrapped in seaweed) is first-rate; a satisfying light lunch can be made from a variety of sushi combinations. We like the crisp tempura (shrimp and vegetables), which can also be served on a bed of soba noodles in clear broth. The menu includes pork and beef dishes in interesting sauces. At the sushi bar on one side, the carving and rice rolling are on view; the rest of the place is made up of enclaves of blond tables and a tatami room. With a warm saké or a Kirin draft beer, two will dine for about $35.

HOTELS

See also Waterbury.

Radisson Hotel Burlington

60 Battery St.
(802) 658-6500
Open year-round.
All major cards.

This is Vermont's only real big-city hotel. A link in the far-flung Radisson chain, it sets a comfortable standard, offers all the expected upscale amenities and is the favorite for Burlington's business visitors. While not actually on the Lake Champlain waterfront, it is close enough to offer a prime view of the lake and the Adirondacks from the bar and the upper-floor front rooms ($10 extra, and worth it). The tastefully subdued lobby has islands of sea-green chairs, an indoor garden of big-leaf plants and an adjacent coffee shop and gift shop full of Vermont products, from cow T-shirts to blueberry preserves and maple candy. The mezzanine level has an indoor pool. Rooms are bright, thanks to large windows, and are decorated in deep, soothing colors. Among the 257 rooms are 14 poolside cabanas, 16 one-bedroom suites and 12 rooms for the disabled; the top floor (the seventh) is devoted to the Plaza Club, one of those extra-service executive floors so common in today's better hotels.

Singles: $79-$89; doubles: $94-$104; Plaza Club rooms: $125-$135; suites: $150-$165.

SIGHTS

On the shores of Lake Champlain, Burlington is a gateway to the lake area, so naturally some of its most popular activities center on the water. It's a great place to go exploring by boat, and there are several options. From late May through early October, the *Spirit of Ethan Allen*—a 64-foot, 150-passenger diesel-powered replica of a Mississippi paddle-wheeler—takes passengers on sight-seeing trips, dinner cruises, sunset cruises and, on Fridays and Saturdays during summer, moonlight cruises with live dance music. For schedules, call (802) 862-8300.

Marine Explorers (802-985-8825) offers scenic cruises, lake tours and snorkeling and scuba diving trips on a 25-foot cabin cruiser for up to six people. The territory covers the lake islands as well as the Vermont State Underwater Historic Preserve, where a number of sunken lake boats await exploration. Visits to restaurants on both shores of Lake Champlain may also be arranged. Cruises leave from Perkins Pier in Burlington, with pickups at other points also available.

For more information on private boat rentals, water sports and Lake Champlain–area sights, contact the chamber of commerce at (802) 863-3489.

SHOPS

Apple Mountain
30 Church St.
(802) 658-6452
Open Mon.-Fri. 9:30 a.m.-9 p.m., Sat. 9:30 a.m.-6 p.m., Sun. noon-5 p.m.

You don't have to trek off to distant farms to find Vermont's sophisticated new food products—they're right here in downtown Burlington. Among such frivolities as cow T-shirts, Apple Mountain has a tidy food section stocked with Blanchard & Blanchard toppings and dressings and Rathdowney's culinary herb packets, including interesting mixtures for salsa, spreads and cheese. The handmade chocolate cow by Champlain Chocolates is hard to resist.

Designer's Circle
21 Church St.
(802) 864-4238
Open Mon.-Thurs. 10 a.m.-6 p.m., Fri. 10 a.m.-8 p.m., Sat. 10 a.m.-5:30 p.m.

Located at the end of the city's colorful pedestrian mall, this basement-level shop mixes one-of-a-kind pieces with smaller production-line items. It specializes in New England contemporary crafts, and because its owners also have organized a number of professional craft fairs around the state, they have stocked it with goods of uniform high quality.

CHITTENDEN

INNS

Mountaintop Inn
Mountain Top Rd.
(800) 445-2100,
(802) 483-2311
Open year-round.
Cards: AE, MC, V.

It's hard to imagine a better mountaintop view. The lake glistening beyond the golf course, with trees and hills in the distance, sets up a Grandma Moses picture. In the winter it is fairyland, in the fall, an explosion of color, in the summer, a study in green, and in the spring, a little bleak. Seasons aside, Mountaintop is a great place for active people. There are horses to ride, a pool to swim in, a lake for water sports, trails for hiking and cross-country skiing (along with a ski shop and maps of routes through the inn's 1,000 acres), sleigh rides, hayrides, tennis and croquet, along with a sauna and whirlpool in which you can recover from all that activity.

The 33 rooms are monastically simple, with a Scandinavian-style decor: pastel colors, simple furnishings and the occasional quilt-motif wall art. All have private baths and most have fabulous views, and there are cottages and so-called chalets for those who want to camp out comfortably. The attractive sitting rooms in the main house boast beamed ceilings and large hearths, as well as simple print fabrics; also downstairs is the dining room, which serves filling country meals. Such starters as baked Brie, smoked trout, escargots and scallops sautéed with chutney and mustard are followed by anything from baked ziti and stir-fried beef topped with hollandaise (a culture clash of the highest magnitude) to New England seafood stew served over fresh biscuits and chicken breast sautéed with rosemary and artichoke hearts (a welcome return to simplicity). The children's menu offers such things as "giggle" noodle soup.

Rooms: $144-$246; cottages and chalets: $163-$301. Prices include breakfast and dinner.

We are always happy to hear about your discoveries and to receive your comments about ours. We want to give your letters the attention they deserve, so when you write to us, remember to state clearly exactly what you liked or disliked. Be concise, but convincing. Do take the time to argue your point.

CRAFTSBURY COMMON

INNS

Inn on the Common
Off Rte. 14
(802) 586-9619
Open year-round.
Cards: MC, V.

Even if you could care less about tennis, you must wander out to the court here, where you may just have a sporting religious experience: The setting is so extraordinary that you may feel compelled to grab a racket and start bashing away at the ball as though struck with divine inspiration. It's no accident that this part of the world is called the Northeast Kingdom—watching the sunset from this dramatic vantage point will make you a true believer. And while you amble back to the inn by way of the manicured croquet court, rose gardens and well-kept lawns, you may instantly decide to make an offer to owners Penny and Michael Schmitt to buy the inn—before you even see the rooms. The location is so stunning that you could sleep in a hovel and be happy. It's your good fortune, however, that the inn lives up to its promise, with eighteen charming rooms in the main house and the annex across the street.

The Schmitts believe in pampering their guests, so there are plenty of videos, a refreshing pool, fluffy robes and down quilts. The inn also serves some pretty fancy food for its location in this rural Colonial town. Vegetable roulade, wild mushroom soup, onion tart, chilled cucumber soup, Provençal tomato tart or artichokes with hollandaise may be the starters of the evening; the equally ambitious entrées run to such things as sweetbreads in white wine, veal Marsala, lamb chops with sorrel sauce, chicken portugaise, shrimp with herbed sour cream and scallops in white wine. Desserts lean toward the chocolate, with truffles headlining. Your dinner mates are apt to be other sophisticated travelers, some with their offspring, since this is one of the rare inns that welcome children.

A country breakfast will greet you in the morning, preparing you for the many small-town activities ahead: the local banjo contest, the Old Home Day parade and the summer schedule of the Craftsbury Chamber Players.

Rooms: $180-$220, including breakfast and dinner.

> *Remember to phone ahead to reserve your table or your room and please, if you cannot honor your reservation, be courteous and let the restaurant or the hotel know.*

DANBY

SHOPS

**Danby
Antiques Center**
Main St.
(802) 293-9984
Open daily 10 a.m.-5 p.m.

Aficionados of country furniture and accessories and those who love searching for one of those rare bargains in life should hie themselves to the Danby Antiques Center to see what the 25 dealers have to offer in this crowded, honeycombed, two-story Federal house. Ersatz Shaker boxes, authentically old quilts, pricey baskets, unchipped yellowware bowls, the occasional cannonball child's bed, single-drawer bedside tables and a laundry list of other charming treasures can generally be found here. The prices are usually fair, and you can call any of the exhibitors to ask for a volume discount if you find you've bought out the store.

DORSET

INNS

The Barrows House
Rte. 30
(802) 867-4455
Open year-round.
Cash or personal check only.

At The Barrows House, you can stay in your own house, while spending your days playing tennis and swimming and your nights enjoying fabulous dinners and meeting other good-looking couples. The five outbuildings remind us of childhood sleepovers at friends' houses; the decor is functional, the furnishings durable and the environment comfortable. The ten rooms in the main house are more charming, with a welcoming sitting room and pleasant dining rooms. The food here is quite good: The wintertime fare includes such warming dishes as curried onion soup, fettuccine carbonara, venison and duck pâté, steak with four peppercorns, liver with Madeira, rack of lamb with honey and thyme, and Alsatian cabbage or fabulous carrots with maple syrup. Desserts are just as filling: apple, pecan or maple-walnut pies and pumpkin cheesecake. The overall mood is cheerful; some guests love The Barrows House so much that they come back here often and play house.
Rooms: $150-$180, including breakfast and dinner.

Marble West Inn

West Rd. (off Rte. 30)
(802) 867-4155
Open year-round.
Cash or personal check only.

This intimate country inn is owned by charming, sincere partners who are committed to creating a welcoming ambience and sense of comfort. Owners Ed Ferenc and Hugh Miller have turned a beautiful Federal-style house into a delightful inn, aptly named for the West family, who built their home from the profits of their marble trade. The marble columns, stepping stones and random slabs on the grounds are the Wests' legacy. They also left behind an incredible hooked stairway runner that's populated with a Noah's ark of wildlife. Opera singer Amanda West, who lived here with sister Lizzie, must have been a diva of the little people—the stairway bannister and doorknobs are scaled more for a toddler than an adult. (Those who believe in the paranormal side of life say the girls are still around.)

Hugh and Ed have a deft decorating touch, as evidenced by the sixteen lovely rooms; the moss-colored suite downstairs is particularly engaging, with a fireplace, fine sense of space, and coveted privacy. The other rooms, though smaller, are just as pleasant. The Wicker Room has a bathroom larger than most people's bedrooms. Breakfast is served by Ed's mother every morning in the cheery dining room. The view across the street of the farm field (held in perpetual trust by the West family, ensuring no intrusions from condos or latter-day Federal-style architects) perpetuates the inn's state of suspended bucolic animation.

Rooms: $85-$120, including breakfast.

SHOPS

American Sporting Antiques

Rte. 30
(802) 867-2271
Open by appt. or chance.

Harold Smith has an extensive collection of New England fishing lures, antique reels and rods, rifles, decoys, fish and fowl prints, creels, carved birds and even a small stuffed brown bear, which keeps curious kids busy. The affable Pendleton-clad owner is helpful and passionate about his brand of collectors' items; don't be surprised if you catch his spirit and leave with a rare hand-carved frog or a New England catfish lure.

The Wood Duck

Rte. 30
(802) 363-2413, 867-5925
*June-Dec.: open daily 9
a.m.-5:30 p.m.; Jan.-May:
open by appt. or chance.*

You don't have to be a serious collector or compete in duck-carving competitions to appreciate the finesse of Marilynn Morrissey's talent for carving wildfowl. Her little shop is filled with beautiful carved ducks, birds, swans and butterflies. Some pieces are antiques; others are fresh off the carving block. Morrissey's pair of award-winning ducks is alone worth a visit. She spent more than 1,200 hours carving and painting these glorious creatures, and she'll sell them to you if you have $7,000.

EAST POULTNEY

QUICK BITES

**Whispering Pines
Restaurant**
Rte. 30
(802) 287-9715
*Open daily 6:30 a.m.-
9 p.m.*
No cards.

The weather-beaten green exterior of Whispering Pines may prompt you to pass it by. Resist your first impulse and instead stop at this unpretentious family restaurant to sample one of the home-baked pies: the lemon meringue and the many cream varieties–banana, chocolate, orange, date, peanut, pineapple and coconut–are pure heaven. You can also get a decent sandwich, oyster stew, cube steak, fried chicken, scallops, clams or pork chops, served at the orange counter or at one of the tables surrounded by knotty pine walls. There is an enormous room hidden in the back that is filled to capacity on bingo nights. And the stately pines shading the restaurant and picnic tables really do whisper.

INNS

Eagle Tavern
Rte. 140
(802) 287-9498
*Closed March 15-April
& Nov.-Dec.*
Cash or personal check only.

When you see the Eagle Tavern at the crossroads in East Poultney, you'll probably want to stop out of sheer curiosity. The handsome 1785 yellow building, with its impressive white columns, is worth taking a look at—it's even better inside. Gertrude and Bill Horridge have filled the historical home with their own collection of American antiques. In fact, visiting the inn is like staying in a museum; the original Hitchcock chairs in the dining room, the beautiful card tables and side tables in the living room and the furnishings in the guest rooms are of the highest quality. It's not surprising that Gertrude used to run an antiques business in New Jersey before she and Bill became innkeepers.

The six sleeping rooms are just as memorable as the rest of the inn, especially the Ballroom bedroom. Occupying half of the former ballroom (the other half is another bedroom), this 26-foot-long room with a barrel ceiling is scaled for those who need a lot of space around them; the tall-post bed with a country-print canopy looks dwarfed in the sea of space. The room also has a table-and-chair seating area if you want to have a meeting, and Bill's childhood trucks and cars are on hand to entertain children. The other half of the ballroom, scaled on a more manageable level, is a pretty, romantic wash of pink and has a lace-canopy bed. There are also a snug single, the Horace Greeley room, with a tiger-maple bed, and three other country-perfect rooms; these four share a spacious bathroom.

Gertrude is a great cook who spoils guests with her substantial European-style breakfasts. Muffins, Irish soda bread, cheesecake, yogurt, tea breads, Vermont cheeses and breakfast meats revive even the slowest starters.

The Eagle Tavern was the meeting place of Ethan Allen and his boys, as well as home to Horace Greeley. The Tap Room in the cellar will give you a taste of what life was like during the days of the Green Mountain Boys. The rest of the inn will make you a fan of the Early American look, perhaps even inspiring you to start your own collection.

Rooms: $35-$60, including breakfast.

FAIR HAVEN

RESTAURANTS

Vermont Marble Inn
W. Park Pl. (on the town green)
(802) 265-8383
AMERICAN
Open Sun.-Mon. & Wed.-Thurs. 5:30 p.m.-9 p.m., Fri.-Sat. 5:30 p.m.-10 p.m.
Cards: AE, MC, V.

The owners of this fine inn have had the good sense to keep chef Don Goodman happy. As a result, he produces creative dinners that change every month. He has a deft touch with soups: delicately seasoned asparagus soup with curry, nicely balanced duck soup with mushrooms and wild rice, innovative eggplant minestrone and wonderfully refreshing orange-mango soup. The other starters are just as good: delicious tortellini with sweet squash, pesto and cream; terrific almond shrimp stir-fried with fresh ginger and orange; pasta and prosciutto tossed with a red-pepper purée; shrimp and onion flan; and a sauté of wild mushrooms with tomatoes and basil on a bed of pasta. And Goodman's skills don't flag after the starters, with such entrées as a perfectly cooked filet of salmon baked with lemon butter and chives and served with crème fraîche; pork tenderloin roasted with grainy mustard and served with apple-pear chutney; breast of chicken roasted with tarragon pesto; gulf shrimp stuffed with sweet sausage and shallots; and veal scallops served with ginger-spiced apples.

Innkeeper Bea Taube is in charge of desserts, which provide a lush ending to an excellent meal. The chocolate-mousse tart with a pecan crust, chocolate torte, sour cream cheesecake, white- and dark-chocolate pâté, dacquoise, berries-and-cream tart and chocolate satin pie are all sensational. About $55 for dinner for two, with wine.

INNS

Vermont Marble Inn
On the town green
(802) 265-8383
Open year-round.
Cards: AE, MC, V.

Luckily for Bea and Richie Taube and their partner, Shirley Stein, in 1867 there was a falling-out between the original owner, Ira Allen, and his partner. The result was that Allen built this extraordinary monument in marble in a fit of one-upmanship intended to drive his partner crazy. You can see his partner's model on the other side of the green, and there is no doubt that Vermont Marble Inn is the better of the two.

By the standards of the traditional-inn business, the delightful trio that owns and runs this beautiful place could be viewed as slightly eccentric. Fear not—they're fabulous. Considering that they've never run an inn before and never cooked professionally, it is a tribute to their sheer gutsiness and tenacity that they have been so successful.

The fourteen-room inn is filled with Victoriana. Pinks, roses and mauves are pervasive, as is a healthy dose of lace, along with impressive beds and decorative detailing. And it all suits this beautiful Victorian house perfectly. The architecture alone gave the trio a head start in creating a striking interior. The rooms are named after Bea and Shirley's most admired English authors. Oscar Wilde is especially lovely, with tall-post twin beds and a Victorian marble fireplace, as is Elizabeth Browning, with a lace-canopy queen-size bed, blue-and-peach coloring and its own Victorian marble hearth. Lord Byron has a majestic brass bed; Alfred Lord Tennyson, an enormous bath; and the charming third-floor rooms, gabled walls and step-up windows. There is also an art deco wing, added by a former owner, which has been decorated accordingly. All the rooms have private baths, and ceiling fans keep guests comfortable all summer.

The two high-octane hostesses make a terrific breakfast. Bea does all the baking, and Shirley prepares the breakfasts. You can expect the likes of succulent homemade muffins, Grand Marnier french toast, waffles studded with nuts, pancakes laden with fresh fruit, cheese omelets as light as soufflés, all served with sautéed fruit, ham or bacon. No indulgence is spared, which will seduce you into coming here as often as possible for the mouth-watering breakfasts, impressive dinners and romantic, ultra-private guest rooms.

Rooms: $65-$95, including breakfast.

> *Some establishments change their closing times without warning. It is always wise to call ahead.*

FAIRLEE

QUICK BITES

Fairlee Diner
Rte. 5
(802) 333-9798
Open Mon.-Sat. 6 a.m.-
8 p.m. (until 7 p.m. in
winter), Sun. 8 a.m.-
3 p.m.
No cards.

It's more than worth your while to get off Interstate 91 and travel pokey parallel Route 5 at breakfast or lunchtime, for that's where you'll find the Roberts family's restaurants—this place in Fairlee and Country Cookin' in East Thetford. Everything—french toast with real maple syrup, red flannel hash, and apricot, butterscotch and custard pies—is homemade, the clientele is local, and the atmosphere is small-town casual. It'd be hard for two to spend more than $12 for lunch.

GOSHEN

INNS

Blueberry Hill Inn
Off Rte. 73
(802) 247-6735
Closed April, Nov. & 1st
2 weeks of Dec.
Cards: MC, V.

After you've splurged on the latest boron fly rod at Orvis, stocked up on Hornberg flies and have your fish forceps in hand for easy hook release, the logical place to show them off is this upper-crust sportsman's lodge, which has a Western dude-ranch feel to it. It is simple in an expensive sort of way—only the confidently rich feel comfortable in such a no-frills setting. They tend to go to bed early anyway, and they're certainly not here to admire a frivolous decor—there are too many other things to do. If fly-fishing isn't your chosen avocation, you can bicycle (mountain bikes are provided), cross-country ski, hike and do all kinds of water sports at nearby Lake Dunmore. To keep your energy level up for all that activity, Blueberry Hill keeps chocolate chip cookies in plentiful supply. And the rooms, while hardly opulent, have an abundance of comfort and country warmth.

Despite all this rusticity, the inn caters to well-traveled palates with its quality regional cuisine. Blueberries dominate the menu during the summer (soups, pancakes, marinades, tarts and cheesecakes), along with herbs grown in the garden and locally grown produce. Dinners are adventurous and quite fine: scallops with a tomato-Cognac cream sauce, grilled beef with an Irish whisky mushroom sauce, grilled pork marinated in honey and soy, rack of baby Vermont lamb with basil butter, and swordfish steaks with a black-olive purée and spicy red hollandaise sauce. Breakfast is just as satisfying: apple puff pancakes, vegetable frittata, eggs baked with Brie, light herb omelets or homemade granola. Local bacon and sausage keep protein levels up.

Devotees of the Eddie Bauer life, New England style, will find Blueberry Hill a great place to spend a lot of money to be pampered and taken care of in a most wholesome way. Rooms: $152-$192, including breakfast and dinner.

HEALDVILLE

SIGHTS

Crowley Cheese Factory
(802) 259-2340
Open Mon.-Fri. 7 a.m.-4 p.m.

Vermont's cheese is famous the world over, and the state's oldest producer, the Crowley Cheese Factory, still makes the Colby variety by hand, just as Vermonters did a century ago. The factory, on a National Historic Site, is a living, working museum. The best time to visit is between 10:30 a.m. and 12:30 p.m., when the curd is weighed, put into forms and pressed.

Admission free.

JEFFERSONVILLE

QUICK BITES

Jana's Cupboard
Rtes. 15 & 108
(802) 644-5454
Open Mon.-Thurs. 6 a.m.-8:30 p.m., Fri. 6 a.m.-9 p.m., Sat. 7 a.m.-9 p.m., Sun. 7 a.m.-8:30 p.m. No cards.

No matter that there are big-ticket ski areas nearby (Stowe, Smugglers' Notch) drawing tourists aplenty—this place is the real thing. Take a seat at the counter or at one of seven tables and lean into a breakfast of three blueberry flapjacks the size of baby Frisbees. Pour on the real maple syrup, and plan to return again for the house burger topped with Canadian bacon, Swiss cheese, grilled peppers and onions. The walls are hung with old wooden sleds, skis and a toboggan. Breakfast for two, with juice and coffee, will run about $8.

Some establishments change their closing times without warning. It is always wise to call ahead.

KILLINGTON

RESTAURANTS

Hemingway's
Rte. 4
(802) 422-3886
AMERICAN/INTERNATIONAL
Open Wed.-Sun. 5 p.m.-
9 p.m.; closed 6 weeks in
April & May.
All major cards.

This is a destination restaurant, a place that will reward you for making the special trip. It conveys the taste and attention to detail of owners Linda and Ted Foundas, who oversee things with a friendly, calm grace. The ever-changing menu draws primarily from regional cuisine, so, for example, an appetizer of crispy soft-shell crab is accompanied by a delectable fresh corn- and-chive sauce. Fish chowder is a refined rendition of the classic, including as it does julienne vegetables and clams and mussels in their shells. And the entrées have also pleased us mightily: blackfish with a sorrel-tomato butter, and a subtle, tender roast pheasant in a pear-and-morel sauce. The kitchen is even confident enough to make potato crisps, which taste like the potato crisps that are surely made in heaven: weightless, greaseless, marvelous. If the hazelnut praline ice cream with chocolate espresso sauce happens to be on the menu, don't pass it up. These creations are all beautifully prepared and served in the three dining rooms, which include a garden room and a wine cellar. Service is proficient and the wine list excellent; you can sample more of the cellar's treasures by ordering the nightly changing tasting menu, which is accompanied by four wines. Dinner for two, with wine, will run about $100.

INNS

See Chittenden, East Poultney, Fair Haven, Ludlow, Quechee,
South Woodstock, Woodstock.

SIGHTS

Along with skiing, enjoying summertime in the mountains and playing tennis (see listings below), Killington is home to some fine cultural activities each summer, including the Green Mountain Guild's series of Broadway-style musicals at the Killington Playhouse, from early July to early September; the annual Killington Music Festival of chamber works, performed by the Vermont Festival Players (see "Music Festivals" chapter); and the Killington Showcase Series of concerts and other entertainment events. For more information on all three series, call (802) 422-3333.

Killington School for Tennis

(800) 343-3101
Clinics offered late May-early Sept.

Although skiing is Vermont's top sport, it's by no means the only game in town. The Killington School for Tennis is ranked among the nation's top ten tennis schools, boasting more than 18,000 alumni of its trademarked Accelerated Tennis Method. Five-day midweek schools and two-day weekend clinics are held each summer; prices, including accommodations, range from $325 to $800 per person.

Mount Killington

Killington Rd. & Rte. 4
(802) 422-3333, 773-1500
Mid-July-mid-Oct.: open daily 10 a.m.-4 p.m.; chair lifts.

Home to the steepest mogul slope in the Northeast, Mount Killington (comprising six mountains) takes good care of its customers—primarily New Yorkers getting away from it all—with seventeen lifts, 100 trails, a full ski resort (rentals, ski school), condominium rentals (call 802-773-1330 for information), snowmaking, shops, restaurants, cafeterias, even a healthy nightlife. The snow can be on the icy side, but that's made up for with especially pretty ski trails. For snow information, call (802) 422-3261.

Ski season winds down in March or April, but the same lifts that carry skiers high into the mountains make excellent vehicles for summer sight-seeing. At Killington, two lifts—an open double chair lift and an enclosed gondola—run daily from mid-July to early September, and mid-September to mid-October for fall foliage viewing. From the end of Killington Road, the chair lift embarks on a 2.5-mile round trip to the summit of Mount Killington Peak, 4,200 feet above sea level, which offers 360-degree views into five states and Canada. The gondola, which leaves from U.S. Route 4, also reaches the peak—on a 25-minute ride that covers a seven-mile round trip (making it the longest ski lift in North America).

Adults $8-$12, children $5-$8; winter hours and lift prices vary.

LUDLOW

INNS

Governor's Inn

86 Main St. (Rte. 103)
(802) 228-8830
Open year-round (dining room closed in April).
Cards: AE, MC, V.

Governor's Inn may look all too familiar as you enter its 1890 front door—owner Deedy Marble has been so industrious in getting promotional coverage that countless magazines and newspapers have featured the inn and her good cuisine. (For those interested, these articles are proudly on display upstairs.) The coverage is warranted, because Deedy and her husband, Charlie, are serious about food. Students of the great chef Roger Vergé (their diplomas are also on display), they're always experimenting with their latest culinary discoveries—and unlike some experimenters, they know what they're doing (as attested by the many culinary awards they've won). Five-course dinners include seasonal chilled fruit or curried squash soups, salads, the prehistoric entremet, such entrées as salmon with Champagne sauce or game hens laced with Grand Marnier and for dessert, chocolate-walnut pie or poached pears in Kir. Deedy, who has published her recipes for guests, will happily pack a gourmet picnic for afternoon outings (for an extra charge). After indulging your way through a full dinner, you can head to one of eight snug bedrooms to sleep it all off. Family antiques, English armoires, lovely linens, lacy crocheted spreads and Victorian touches surround you in modest style. Morning brings Charlie's breakfast, which is a bit more restrained than dinner: strawberry-rhubarb or maple-walnut coffee cake, stone-ground hot cereal, rum-raisin french toast or the inn's popular puffs. For an additional charge, guests can start the day off with mimosas, delivered bedside.

Rooms: $160-$170, including breakfast and dinner.

SIGHTS

Calvin Coolidge Home
Rte. 100A, Plymouth Notch
(802) 828-3226
Late May-mid-Oct.: open daily 9:30 a.m.-5:30 p.m.

For insight into Calvin Coolidge's origins, visit the home off Route 100A in nearby Plymouth Notch where silent Cal was born, spent his boyhood and was sworn into the Presidency by his own father, a local justice of the peace, after Warren Harding died in the middle of the night in 1923. Admission $2.

MANCHESTER VILLAGE

INNS

1811 House
Rte. 7A
(802) 362-1811
Closed Dec. 25-26.
Cards: AE, MC, V.

What do you do when your own home is so saturated with English and American antiques that you can barely move around? You open a country inn and go public with your collection. At least that's what Mary Hirst decided to do, and now perfect strangers are spoiled with her extraordinary family furniture displayed in an impeccable Federal home. Carrying on British tradition, English-born Mary and her family/partners, Pat and Jeremy David, offer guests a cozy pub (certainly better looking than the too-often-ratty real thing) and an authentic English breakfast in the morning.

The eleven bedrooms are as stunning as the rest of the house. Elegant and tastefully furnished, all have private baths and distinct personalities, and each is named after a local legend. The Mary Lincoln Isham room, at the top of the stairs, is indisputably the most exquisite, with fireplace, large canopy bed, demure pink-and-blue wallpaper and Victorian-era bath. But the bathroom is better in the Robinson Room, as long as you prefer tall pencil-post single beds. A hidden room, tucked away in the back of the house, is named after the well-known Franklin Orvis, and the Jeremiah French Suite downstairs is a spacious hideout. All the rooms are full of Mary's beautiful furniture.

If you like to eat your bacon, eggs, fried bread, sautéed mushrooms and tomatoes, and sliced apples while seated on Chippendale chairs and surrounded by chandeliers, an impressive porcelain collection and barnyard oils, the 1811 House will never disappoint.

Rooms: $100-$150, including breakfast.

The Equinox Hotel, Resort & Spa
Rte. 7A
(800) 362-4747,
(802) 362-4700
Open year-round.
Cards: AE, MC, V.

For those travelers who need to be pampered, wrapped, massaged and scrubbed, The Equinox is a welcome alternative to Vermont's heartier winter-sports hideaways. And for those who want to mix some exercise in with their personal restoration, the inn also offers golf and tennis. There may be some competition, however, for the spa facilities: With 140 rooms, The Equinox is usually pretty crowded with guests who certainly aren't there for attractive accommodations. Checking into the inn is somewhat like checking into the Plaza; business-meeting participants dot the heavy-handed Victorianish lobby, the receptionist tries to keep up with the demands, guests mill about, and the uniformed doormen and staff are busy looking efficient. The Equinox is an institution—its impressive colonnaded facade tells you as much. But the rooms are dreary, the place looks faded, the pace is too hectic for a so-called relaxing country inn, and there's little sense of privacy.

Rooms: $99-$150.

Wilburton
River Rd.
(802) 362-2500
Open year-round.
Cards: AE, MC, V.

When A. M. Gilbert wanted to get a message to his good friend Robert Todd Lincoln, all he had to do was yell down the hill from Wilburton to Hildene. This handsome brick Victorian 24-room mansion has been converted to a spacious, historically accurate inn. You can almost imagine what it might have been like to live here at the turn of the century. Oversized fireplaces, handsome wall coverings, well-crafted woodwork and a lovely seventeen-acre site make Wilburton a unique inn, and the large rooms are a welcome change from those intimate, sometimes-too-cozy back-roads inns. But though the scale borders on the monumental, the feeling inside is warm and gracious.

You could do far worse than to dine in the paneled former billiards room, with its horse prints, large fireplace and soft green tones, enjoying well-prepared, sophisticated cuisine. Breakfast is served in the second dining room, with cabbage-rose wallpaper, and on the porch, furnished with garden furniture.

The bedrooms are as handsome as the upper-class dining rooms. Large and airy, the back rooms have fabulous views of the valley; in the summer, you can even hear strains of Hildene's concerts floating through your bedroom window. All of the ten bedrooms have private baths, some of which have large claw-footed Victorian tubs with pink toenails. There are also four full-scale houses on the property, each with bedrooms that are more modest but perfect for traveling families. The two tennis courts inspire activity, and the surrounding property inspires lovely evening strolls.

Innkeepers Albert and Georgette Levis up and bought Wilburton after celebrating Albert's 50th birthday there, a seemingly rash move that you'll find easy to understand after visiting the place.

Rooms: $60-$145, including breakfast.

SIGHTS

The American Museum of Fly Fishing
Seminary Ave. & Rte. 7A
(802) 362-3300
May-Oct.: open daily 10 a.m.-4 p.m.; Nov.-April: hours vary.

To some people, to paraphrase author Norman Maclean, there is no clear line between religion and fly-fishing. For those people, walking through this door is like walking through the pearly gates.

$2 donation requested.

Hildene
Rte. 7A South
(802) 362-1788
May-Oct.: tours daily 9:30 a.m.-4 p.m.

Silent Cal wasn't Vermont's only resident of the White House. Robert Todd Lincoln, the only one of Abraham Lincoln's four sons to survive into adulthood, made his home at Hildene in Manchester Village. The 24-room Georgian Revival house has been restored by a nonprofit organization, and most of the furnishings actually belonged to the Lincoln family.

Adults $5, children 5-14 $2, children under 5 free.

SHOPS

Equinox Antiques
Rte. 7A
(802) 362-3540
Open Tues.-Sat. 10 a.m.-5 p.m., Sun. 11 a.m.-4 p.m.

You may be among the fortunate ones, as we were, to wander into this small shop while co-owner Mark Reinfurt plays Mozart on his $30,000 antique harpsichord. It is so enthralling that you'll want to snap up a stunning English Regency bull's-eye mirror with carved, gilded deer trim, or an inlaid bird's-eye maple Hepplewhite four-drawer bureau, or a Queen Anne cherrywood bonnet-top bureau, or a Chippendale ox-bow mahogany chest, or a tiger-maple and flame-birch worktable, or a pair of Staffordshire dalmatians. Mark and his partner, Charles Dewey, drive a hard bargain, so if you're dying for one of these big-ticket items, you'd better be big-ticket rich.

Orvis
Rte. 7A
(802) 362-3622
Open daily 8 a.m.-6 p.m.

You would expect to see a cross section of preppy matrons, robust-looking young people, Blazer-driving sportsmen, affluent-looking retirees, executive duck hunters, professional dog breeders and serious fishermen at the Orvis headquarters. And you will. They come here for the cashmere sweaters, Adams flies, doggy nests, practical oilcloth jackets, graphite rods, Arietta shotguns, waders, tweed blazers, camouflage vests, bird feeders and durable private-line luggage. The sales are good, and the Rod Shop down the hill is open for tours each morning at 10:30, when you can see master craftsmen constructing Orvis's famous bamboo rods. Orvis also hosts a fishing camp, held April through August. Be advised: You'll have to book well in advance, for people from all over the country come here for the two-and-a-half-day course, which includes fly-tying and outings to the Batten Kill river to practice what they preach. For information, call (802) 362-3900.

MARLBORO

INNS

Longwood Inn
Rte. 9
(802) 257-1545
Open year-round.
Cards: MC, V.

To improve yourself, or to enjoy the summer Marlboro Music weekend concerts, book a room at Tom and Janet Durkin's inn for all seasons. It's an ideal place to visit during the chamber-music season, or for one of the Durkins' special weekends when guest lecturers are in residence. Guests have become overnight experts in arts, crafts, small businesses—even dream interpretation (one can only assume that the dreams here are most pleasant). The 1790 house has eleven bedrooms, most with private baths and all with a simple, Colonial decor; many rooms have working fireplaces.

The inn serves some appetizing food. The specialties are salmon en papillote with lemon butter or dill sauce, fresh pastas, its own smoked turkey and sausage, and tangerine-glazed roast duckling. There is a grazing menu for light eaters, and some less-than-light but luscious desserts. Breakfast is properly robust and country style: fresh pastries, Vermont cheese omelets, french toast, pancakes and home-made breads.

Longwood is a true surprise. You may look up from your own dinner conversation to spot Rudolf Serkin and his party, or an intellectual gathering with John Galbraith and Katherine Graham, all enjoying their meals and the inn's honest ambience.

Rooms: $85-$135, including breakfast; $110-$175, including breakfast and dinner.

MIDDLEBURY

RESTAURANTS

Otter Creek Café
Frog Hollow Mill, Mill St.
(802) 388-7342
AMERICAN/INTERNATIONAL
*Open Mon.-Sat. 11:30 a.m.-2:30 p.m. & 5 p.m.-10 p.m.
Cards: MC, V.*

Unlikely as it may seem, Middlebury is a small gastro-nomic center. The Otter Creek Café, the newest of several good restaurants, achieves high marks. Tucked into the river level of an old stone mill, the restaurant puts you in the mood immediately with the retail bakery at the entrance featuring an enticing spread of desserts. The dining room is small and pink, with white tablecloths, and looks onto a wooden deck filled on summer nights with happy diners. The carefully selected menu favors fish and game birds in silky sauces, with a nod to fresh pastas. The appetizer ragoût of wild mushrooms and vegetables in white wine and cream sauce has just the right blend of earthy taste and sophisti-cated smoothness. You'll find duck on many Vermont menus, but none will have a better honey and wine sauce; and if you've had a hankering for roast partridge in a rich plum sauce, save time searching and hie yourself here. Excellent breads and pastries round out a special meal. For dinner with wine, two will spend about $65.

Swift House
25 Stewart Ln. (off Rte. 7)
(802) 388-2766
AMERICAN
*Open May-Oct. Thurs.-Mon. 6 p.m.-9 p.m.
All major cards.*

As if she didn't have enough to do, Andy Nelson (who runs Swift House Inn with her husband, John) has under-taken the ambitious task of cooking dinner every night for the inn's handsome dining room. The historical room is lush with lavender and grape-garland wallpaper that dates back to 1905, when Jessica Swift lived in this beautiful home. Seating is Queen Anne and Chippendale, and the feeling is calming, with views of the rolling lawns outside. It is a gathering place for both inn guests and locals, all of whom appreciate the joys of gourmet home cooking.

Andy's culinary touch is sincere and sure. She changes the menu nightly, taking advantage of the freshest local ingredients. For example, springtime is a celebration of fiddlehead ferns, those Early American delicacies that are an acquired taste. Starters range from fettuccine with smoked scallops and asparagus and a perfect tomato soup with bacon and fennel to delicate seafood ravioli, black-bean soup with cob-smoked ham and Madeira, and crabcakes with capers and a sweet red-pepper mayonnaise. Entrées are well prepared, well garnished and delicious. Grilled swordfish is presented with lemon butter and a nostalgic potato-cheese pie. Calves' liver is tender and properly cooked, served with cob-smoked bacon and caramelized onions. Cheese tortellini is tossed with fresh vegetables and pesto. Andy's version of jambalaya is spicy, with Cajun-flavored shrimp, chicken and smoked sausage mixed with the traditional peppers, onions, tomatoes and rice. And lamb chops are tender and pink, infused with garlic and rosemary. Desserts are richly comforting, the perfect finale to this simple, honest cooking. Bananas Foster, fudge toffee-pecan torte, cheesecake with raspberry Chambord, an old-fashioned banana split of the kind you probably haven't dreamt of in the last decade at least, Black Forest cake—all are equally dense and divine. The wine list has quite a few California boutique labels and the comme-il-faut French varietals. About $75 for two, with wine.

Woody's

3 Bakery Ln.
(802) 388-4182
INTERNATIONAL
*Open Mon.-Sat. 11:30 a.m.-
3 p.m. & 5 p.m.- 10 p.m.,
Sun. 10:30 a.m.-3 p.m. &
5 p.m.-9:30 p.m.
All major cards.*

12/20

Woody's sits on a bank of Otter Creek (a swift-running river despite its name), looking like a clapboard box from the outside and a classy art deco ocean liner within. We may have been born too late for the *Normandie*, but we were on time for a meal on one of the three deck levels of this peach-and-gray architectural flight of fancy. The look isn't overdone, but the effect is slick '30s nautical. Owner/chef Woody Danforth holds a steady standard for fresh ingredients from fish to pasta. A luncheon salad plate of coho salmon gravlax arranged on fettuccine combines the two nicely. Sturdy, spicy Portuguese soup is thick with white beans, cabbage and ham. The semi-open kitchen also passes out a good steak au poivre for carnivores. Try homemade ice cream or a tall three-layer chocolate-mousse cake with whipped cream for dessert. There is a real outside deck for summer dining, and a snug little bar just inside the door. For dinner for two, with wine, figure on about $55, less if you order from the list of eclectic light entrées.

INNS

Swift House Inn
25 Stewart Ln. (off Rte. 7)
(802) 388-2766
Open year-round.
All major cards.

Swift House Inn is a superb place to visit; Andy and John Nelson's vibrant hospitality makes a trip to Middlebury well worth the effort. In the original home of Samuel Swift (governor of Vermont in the early 1800s), the Nelsons have done an excellent job of creating a lush, intimate inn. The decor is lovely: beautiful wallpaper prints, large bathrooms with a Victorian feel, oversized beds, pretty linens, handsome antiques and inviting sitting areas. Each of the seven bedrooms is charming and all have phones. The Jessica Swift Room is particularly luxurious, with its own balcony off the large bathroom, as is the Governor's Room, which has a whirlpool bath and king-size brass bed; the five other bedrooms, although smaller, are just as pleasant. And the Nelsons have rehabilitated the gatehouse at the bottom of the hill, which holds five more rooms, all decorated in a Victorian theme consistent with the house's 1901 construction.

In the beautiful sitting rooms in the main house, soft colors, comfortable chairs, blazing fires and attractive, well-dressed guests will have you sighing with gratitude for the good life you've hit upon. The small bar is staffed by interesting young people, and the dining room, with its original hand-blocked wallpaper intact, is run by a team of efficient (and also young) men and women. Andy does the cooking at night, and does it well (see "Restaurants" above). Breakfast runs to such things as pastries, popovers, eggs Benedict, french toast, blueberry pancakes and scrambled eggs.

Rooms: $55-$99, including breakfast.

SIGHTS

Robert Frost National Recreation Trail
Off Rte. 125, Ripton
(802) 388-4362

Admirers of Frost's work may follow his footsteps in the woods of nearby Ripton. The Robert Frost National Recreation Trail offers a leisurely one-mile walk through woods and meadows; quotations from Frost and insights into his art are mounted on plaques along the route. A wayside picnic area adjoins Frost's cabin, which is not open to the public.

Morgan Horse Farm
Off Rte. 23, Weybridge
(802) 388-2011
May-Oct.: open daily 9 a.m.-4 p.m.

Just outside Middlebury in Weybridge, the University of Vermont pays tribute to one of the state's best-loved symbols: the Morgan horse. The Morgan, considered "America's first horse," is a genetic mutant descended from a single stallion that lived in the area in the late 1700s. It's considered a particularly versatile breed, good in any role from family pet to work horse to show animal. The tours and slide shows at the Morgan Horse Farm provide a fine introduction to this noble (and historic) animal.

Adults $2.50, teenagers $1, children under 12 free. Reservations required.

Sheldon Museum
1 Park St.
(802) 388-2117
*June-Oct.: open Mon.-Sat.
10 a.m.-4:30 p.m.; Nov.-
May: open Wed. & Fri.
1 p.m.-4 p.m.*

Not to be confused with the Shelburne Museum near Burlington, Middlebury's Sheldon Museum is a nineteenth-century house with period furnishings, a Victorian garden and its own research library. Guided tours are given during the museum's open hours. Middlebury College (802-388-3711) also has two museums—the Christian A. Johnson Memorial Gallery (open daily noon to 5 p.m.; admission free) and the Egbert Starr Library, featuring first editions and Robert Frost memorabilia (open Monday to Friday; admission free).

SHOPS

**Vermont State
Craft Center at
Frog Hollow**
Frog Hollow
(802) 388-3177
*Open Mon.-Sat. 9:30 a.m.-
5 p.m., Sun. 11 a.m.-
5 p.m.*

This is more than a craft store—it is the heart of the state's considerable craft movement. The first such facility in the country, it displays the work of more than 200 craftspeople in both the shop and in major exhibits that center on a theme or the work of an individual. In addition to regular classes, three resident craftworkers have studios in the building, and visitors are invited to observe art in the making.

MONTPELIER

RESTAURANTS

**The Elm Street
Cafe**
38 Elm St.
(802) 223-3188
AMERICAN
*Open Mon.-Fri. 7 a.m.-
10 a.m., 11:30 a.m.-1:30
p.m. & 5:30 p.m.-9 p.m.,
Sat. 8 a.m.-10 a.m., 11:30
a.m.-1:30 p.m. & 5:30
p.m.-9 p.m.
Cards: MC, V.*

12/20

The Elm Street Cafe, like Tubbs Restaurant (see below), is a training ground for students at the New England Culinary Institute. The school's course of studies is geared more to short-order and American cooking than to classicism, which in its way makes for a rewarding playfulness on the menus. There has recently been an attempt here by chefs David Miles and Max Hansen to experiment with modernizing New England cookery by using Vermont and New England products to their best advantage. The farms in the area supply the kitchen with excellent provender throughout the year, from fresh goat cheese to fiddlehead ferns.

The premises are wood-paneled, wallpapered and casual, and prices are remarkably low. The service has gotten better, but it is still understandably amateurish and too often apologetic. At lunch you can get anything from a first-rate, juicy hamburger to a bowl of delicious spiced lentil soup; dinner can range from a spicy osso buco to a New England boiled dinner punched up with horseradish cream. The salad may contain that Vermont goat cheese, the winter squash soup will be enriched with a little Vermont maple syrup, and the ham will be corn cob–smoked at a local smokehouse. Desserts are wholesome and quite American— perhaps an apple popover with maple walnut ice cream. All the baked goods—including breakfast rolls and croissants from La Brioche bakery—are made by the students as well. The only caveat we have about The Elm Street Cafe is that this is still student cooking, and your enjoyment depends on just how far along that particular student is in his classes. A dinner here for two, with wine, should run about $50.

Horn
of the Moon Café
8 Langdon St.
(802) 223-2895
AMERICAN
Open Mon. 7 a.m.-3 p.m.,
Tues.-Sat. 7 a.m.-9 p.m.,
Sun. 10 a.m.-2 p.m.
No cards.

10/20

Step across the threshold of the Horn of the Moon Café and you'll think you've somehow gotten stuck in a time warp back to the late 1960s, when Victorian oak furniture, hanging spider ferns and "natural foods" were all chic and part of the movement toward more "healthful" eating. Times have changed, and health-food stores now stock more pills than organically grown rice cakes, but the charming Horn of the Moon Café (actually opened only eleven years ago) represents a moment suspended in time. Owner Jinny Callan continues to turn out some delectable vegetable soups and sandwiches made of Vermont Cheddar, bean sprouts and whole-wheat bread (accompanied by nothing stronger than cider or tea) that will make you think of the days when you dressed in leather vests, Bangladeshi print shirts and Frye boots, and took courses with names like "Macrobiotic Marxism." The other good reason to come here are the wholesome—dare we say scrumptious?—baked goods: wonderful earth mother–style cookies, muffins and pies made with honey. It would be difficult for two to spend more than $30.

Tubbs Restaurant
24 Elm St.
(802) 229-9202
FRENCH/AMERICAN
Open Mon.-Sat. 11:30 a.m.-
1:30 p.m. & 6 p.m.-
9:30 p.m.
All major cards.

12/20

The spacious, high-ceilinged Tubbs is the main dining room for student chefs at the New England Culinary Institute, a small school with a dedicated staff and students who come here to learn cooking the right way, by hands-on preparation from the day they arrive. Cooking at Tubbs is part of the senior curriculum, and the food preparation here is classic but not without a sure degree of imagination on the part of the instructors, Michel Leborgne and Michel Dederan.

Since Tubbs is subsidized by the school, prices are bargain-basement, and the wine list, though not very substantial, is also decently tariffed. We've found that the service, which tries to be quite formal, ranges from the completely inept to the studiously professional. You must never forget that these are students, but you may be amazed at the quality of the food that issues forth from the kitchen: a soup of scallops and coriander, roasted lotte with salsify, a good duck confit, lamb with couscous. Seasoning—either too much or too little—may compromise a dish now and then, but the desserts are almost always of a decidedly high order.

In this neck of Vermont's woods, Tubbs is a worthwhile respite from the dreary clichés at all the proximate ski-resort restaurants that serve veal piccata and stuffed mushroom caps ad nauseam. If you hit a particularly good class in the kitchen one evening, you will dine splendidly. If not, you'll still dine better than at most places in the area. Dinner for two, with wine, should be about $60 to $70.

INNS

See Stowe, Waterbury.

SHOPS

Artisan's Hand
7 Langdon St.
(802) 229-9492
Open Mon.-Sat. 10 a.m.-5:30 p.m.

This small co-op has an urbane sensibility that can be seen in its large ceramic dishes and baskets, which could double as sculpture. The open, airy space makes it a pleasure to browse among such items as silk-screened pillows, stained-glass hangings with chandelier drops, and hand-painted silk scarves.

MOUNT SNOW

INNS

See Arlington, Newfane, Marlboro, West Dover, Wilmington.

SIGHTS

Mount Snow
235L Mountain Rd.
(off Rte 100)
(802) 464-3333

Now run by the same people who own Killington, Mount Snow is one of New England's best—and sometimes most crowded—ski resorts. It's also one of the largest: eight double chairs, five triples, a gondola, snowmaking and 75 miles of cross-country trails. The intermediate skiing is particularly good. Nearby inns can be found in the towns mentioned in "Inns" above; call (802) 464-8501 for more lodging options.

NEWFANE

RESTAURANTS

Four Columns Inn
West St. (off Rte. 30)
(802) 365-7713
INTERNATIONAL
Open Wed.-Mon. 6 p.m.-
9 p.m.
Cards: AE, MC, V.

Flanking the exquisite green-shuttered buildings of New-fane's town green sit two inn/restaurants—Four Columns and Old Newfane (see "Inns")—whose reputations were made in years past largely by the same chef, René Chardain. And since Chardain was more strongly identified with Four Columns, it is still the better known of the two. The question, then, is how well chef Greg Parks has maintained the tradition over the last few years since Chardain's departure. After our first visit to the place in some time, we'd say Parks is doing just fine.

The menus run to a wide variety of ingredients; seafood, veal, chicken, rabbit and game main courses are generally included. Our meal began with a rich and robust veal and chicken pâté that set the tone for the occasion. The following bit of sherbet added not only a touch of class but also a welcome moment of lightness, though that was all too quickly erased by the strong house dressing on the salad. Our main course was assorted seafood poached in fish stock, a sort of super-bouillabaisse, which, as it happens, can also best be described as rich and robust; that description also applies to the house wine, Côtes du Ventoux. A concluding blueberry tart was notable merely for the pleasure of chomping down on the fat berries.

On the whole, each dish was plenty good, but in the long run we found the intensity a bit wearing: Like a novel or a symphony, a meal needs proper buildup, suspense, peaks and valleys of feeling. For all of its virtues, we'd say the kitchen needs to learn the art of modulation. About $110 for two, with wine.

INNS

Four Columns Inn
West St. (off Rte. 30)
(802) 365-7713
Closed April & Nov. 1-
Thanksgiving.
Cards: AE, MC, V.

Jacques Allembert (aided by his wife, Sandy) runs this celebrated plantation-style inn like a potentate in a private fiefdom. His indefatigable presence is everywhere: in the seventeen tastefully appointed guest rooms, around the manicured lawns, swimming pool and pond, and in the luxuriant gardens, which each year take over more of the wilderness on the mountain behind the inn. But his fanatic attention to detail is most evident in the dining room, where a young chef named Greg Parks works wonders with sweetbreads, poussin (baby chicken) and Vermont-bred veal (see "Restaurants" above). Never have the words "country elegance" been more appropriate: Rough-hewn ceiling timbers and walls hung with antique copperware make a romantic setting for leisurely dining. And after dinner you can take in the night air, strolling the most-often-photographed village green in Vermont. Like the dining room, the bedrooms have a rustic elegance. They range from smallish to spacious, but all have private baths and are spotlessly clean and attractively decorated with antiques. (Allembert has a fine collection of antique sleds.)

In the morning, a buffet breakfast puts forth fruits, cheeses and pastries. A more robust breakfast is offered for an additional charge: prosciutto-and-basil omelets, fresh fruit with crème fraîche and sorbet, chicken salad and smoked salmon.

Rooms: $75-$115, including breakfast (winter, spring and summer); $150-$190, including breakfast and dinner (mid-September to October 31).

The Old Newfane Inn
Court St.
(802) 365-4427
Closed Mon., April-mid-May & Nov.-mid-Dec.
Cash or personal check only.

This venerable inn has sheltered weary wayfarers since 1787. The gently sloping floors and absence of perfect right angles in the building attest to its age, as does a dining room with a manorial hearth and Paul Bunyonesque ceiling beams. The furnishings in the ten guest rooms (eight with private bath) run to old-fashioned wallpaper and country antiques. You wouldn't call the inn luxurious, but it doesn't lack for comfort. No surprises lurk in the dining room: The kitchen turns out serviceable Continental cuisine. Veal is the house specialty. The Old Newfane Inn overlooks one of the prettiest village greens in New England.

Rooms: $65-$80, including breakfast.

SHOPS

Newfane Country Store
Rte. 30
(802) 365-7916
Open Mon.-Sat. 9 a.m.-6 p.m., Sun. 10 a.m.-6 p.m.

Country crafts and knickknacks are the staples here: quilts, hand-knit sweaters and caps, wooden children's toys, candles, soaps, honey and the ubiquitous Vermont maple syrup. Most people can't leave without buying a little bit of Vermont to take home.

The prices listed in this guide reflect what restaurants and hotels have informed us they plan to charge at press time. Please don't blame us if they don't coincide exactly with reality.

PITTSFIELD

SIGHTS

**New England
Maple Museum**
Rte. 7
(802) 483-9414
*Memorial Day-late Oct.:
open daily 8:30 a.m.-5:30
p.m.; late Oct.-Dec.: open
daily 10 a.m.-4 p.m.*

The secrets of maple sugaring and syrup making are un-
locked in this humble little museum, which tells the sappy
story via a slide show, demonstrations and displays of antique and contemporary sugaring equipment. A small gift
shop sells plenty of the resulting syrup and candy.
Adults $1.25, children 50 cents, children under 6 free.

PUTNEY

QUICK BITES

**Curtis All American
Barbecue**
Rte. 5 off Rte. 91
(no phone)
*April-Oct.: open Thurs.-
Sun. 10 a.m.-8 p.m.
No cards.*

Curtis operates out the side of an old blue school bus
parked next to Rod's service station in Putney, just off
Route 91. He bills himself as the Ninth Wonder of the
World; we don't know about that, but he sure does make
fine barbecue. You'll find all you need—you got your ribs,
your chicken and your combo. You got baked potato (extra
toppings 25 cents each). You got baked beans, coleslaw,
potato salad, corn on the cob. There are also plenty of picnic
tables, swings, a volleyball net for those so inclined and
ample parking. The chicken is surpassingly tender and moist,
the sauce more on the subtle than the robust side and not
particularly smoky. Baked beans are rich and fine. We've
had better barbecue, but it sure wasn't in Putney or anywhere else en route from someplace to someplace else in
these parts. We figure Curtis is there to make the interstate
a better place. A whopping meal for two will run ten bucks.

SHOPS

**The Putney
Woodshed**
S. Main St. (Rte. 5)
(802) 387-4481
*Open Mon. & Wed.-Sat.
10 a.m.-5 p.m., Sun. noon-
5 p.m.; off-season hours
vary.*

This is the Vermont that hasn't quite made its way out of
the '60s. Housed in the woodshed of an old farmhouse, this
shop has the feel of being stocked by former granolaheads
who are still making batik T-shirts and colorful celebration
banners. The pottery, the woodenware, the musical instruments all feel very natural and organic. They even have
wooden telephones you can use to call Jerry Rubin for
advice on investments.

QUECHEE

INNS

Parker House
16 Main St.
(802) 285-6077
Closed April 1-15.
Cards: AE, MC, V.

Parker House gives new meaning to the concept of country-inn room service. Dinner—salmon mousse, butternut squash soup, ballotine of squab and clafouti of fresh plums and apples—can be served in your romantic room by a tuxedoed waiter. The four guest rooms, some named after members of the Parker family, are spacious and pretty, with brass beds, private dressing rooms, art nouveau furniture suites, large bathrooms, sitting rooms and views of the Ottauquechee River. Owner Roger Nicolas has made every effort to create a setting of luxury and to offer first-class service. If you choose to dine more publicly, dinner is also served in three beautiful dining rooms or outdoors on the summer porch. Breakfast, in the French Continental manner, is just as formal as dinner, with crystal, silver and lovely table linens.

Quechee is a pretty little place. The balloonists come to town every June; the hydraulic display of power and energy at the gorge is worth seeing. The handsome 1857 Victorian Parker House will draw you back at any time of year, to celebrate a special event or milestone birthday.

Rooms: $75-$120, including breakfast.

RUTLAND

QUICK BITES

Seward Family Restaurant
N. Main St. (Rte. 7)
(802) 773-2738
Open daily 7 a.m.-10 p.m.
No cards.

The vintage '40s exterior, with glass-block detailing and curved lines, is still intact, but indoors, the Sewards have caught up with the times, remodeling what was once a wonderfully nostalgic interior complete with a superb soda-fountain counter. Today, unfortunately, the interior is more in line with that of a fast-food chain restaurant, but the food is still just as old-fashioned: sandwiches, burgers and all that forgettable American diner chow that is so irresistible when you're on the road. The best thing about this place is its homemade ice cream, the centerpiece of sundaes, banana splits, frappés, milkshakes, ice cream sodas and ice cream rolls, as well as the topping for brownies, Belgian waffles and strawberry shortcakes. It's even served au naturel in cones.

INNS

See Chittenden, East Poultney, Fair Haven, South Woodstock, Woodstock.

SIGHTS

The second-biggest city in Vermont, Rutland is the commercial hub of this inn-rich part of the state. Come here for the things you won't find in the quaint little villages: movie theaters, supermarkets, an airport and even discount outlets (try Tennybrook Square on Route 7). Rutland is also home to the annual Vermont State Fair, which runs for a week starting Labor Day weekend. For information, call the chamber of commerce at (802) 773-2747.

SHELBURNE

INNS

See Burlington, Waterbury.

SIGHTS

Shelburne Farms
Bay Rd. & Harbor Rd.
(802) 985-8686
Open June 1-mid-Oct.; hours vary.

Not to be confused with the Shelburne Museum (see below) is Shelburne Farms, two miles away on the lake shore. This 1,000-acre agricultural estate, dating from the 1880s, was planned with the help of noted landscape designer Frederick Law Olmsted. The property includes a Queen Anne Revival mansion, now a 24-room inn; a coach barn; a farm barn; and formal gardens. It's also a haven for bird-watchers; more than 60 species are known to nest there, and dozens of others have been sighted. Naturalists should also venture to the seven-acre Vermont Wildflower Farm, located five miles south on Route 7 in Charlotte. It's open daily from May to October 10 a.m. to 5 p.m.; admission—$2 for adults, $1 for senior citizens—is charged only in July and August.

Walking trails $1; guided tours $2.50-$5.

Shelburne Museum & Heritage Park

Rte. 7
(802) 985-3344
Mid-May-mid-Oct.: open daily 9 a.m.-5 p.m.; off-season hours vary.

A prime repository of Americana, the Shelburne Museum, with 45 acres and 35 buildings, is a microcosm of New England. It began with the personal collections of Electra Havemeyer Webb, a Vanderbilt relative who accumulated everything from paintings and dolls to entire houses that she moved to her estate long before historic preservation became fashionable. The rolling grounds include three fine-art galleries, a barn filled with carriages and sleighs, six historic houses, a covered bridge and even a 220-foot steam paddle wheeler, the S.S. *Ticonderoga*, which once plied the waters of Lake Champlain.

Adults $10, children $4, children under 6 free.

SHOPS

Vermont's Own Products

Tennybrook Square, Rte. 7
(802) 985-2505
Open Mon.-Thurs. & Sat. 9 a.m.-6 p.m., Fri. 9 a.m.-8 p.m., Sun. noon-5 p.m.

If you have time for just one Vermont shopping stop, come here. The owners have assembled in one room a fine collection of the finest-quality Vermont-made items, including such Upcountry gourmet foodstuffs as an array of salad dressings, dessert toppings, Thai marinades, peanut sauces and all sorts of maple goods—from dehydrated sprinkles and maple butter to the expected syrup.

Visitors Center and Farm Store at Shelburne Farms

Bay Rd. & Harbor Rd.-
(802) 985-8442
Open daily 9 a.m.-5 p.m.

The former gatekeeper's cottage at a unique 1,000-acre Gilded Age estate on Lake Champlain is now home to a shop that sells an excellent selection of high-quality Vermont food products: farmhouse cheese, smoked meats, lamb pâté, crème fraîche, fromage blanc, honey, mustards and jams, in addition to New England goat cheeses. The Shelburne Farms Farmhouse Cheddar made from the resident Brown Swiss herd and the dense sourdough bread baked on the estate pair up for a nice picnic; we suggest Vermont's own Catamount beer, which is also sold here, as their accompaniment.

Unless otherwise noted, the prices given for restaurants are for a complete dinner for two, including an appetizer, main course and dessert. The prices also include tax, fifteen-percent tip and one of the least expensive bottles of wine on the wine list. Please don't hold it against us if you end up spending a bit more!

SOUTH WOODSTOCK

RESTAURANTS

Kedron Valley Inn
Rte. 106
(802) 457-1473
AMERICAN
Open nightly 6 p.m.-
9:30 p.m.
Cards: AE, MC, V.

One of the most pleasant surprises when staying at a country inn is finding a talented chef in the kitchen; there are so many innkeepers serving their grandmothers' home cooking that it can break the spirit of any sophisticated traveler after too long. But chef Tom Hopewell does an admirable job of putting interesting food in front of visitors to Kedron Valley Inn's pretty dining room. The menu changes seasonally; Hopewell's starters run to the likes of grilled garden vegetables with Vermont goat cheese, fresh oysters with shallots and raspberry vinegar, scallops sautéed with a citrus-saffron butter, hearty country pâté, chilled cucumber soup with minced smoked salmon, wild mushroom and scallop bisque, and good old escargots in puff pastry with roasted fennel and garlic butter.

Entrées are well prepared, properly seasoned and not out of Hopewell's reach. Grilled butterflied game hen is pleasantly marinated with fresh herbs, duck confit has a surprising fruity glaze over its crispy skin, grilled Vermont rack of lamb is tender and scented with rosemary, a veal chop is topped with sweet red- and yellow-pepper sauces, and pepper steak is flavored with five different peppercorns. The pastry chef's creations include pumpkin cheesecake, flourless chocolate cake, fruit-topped marzipan tart and chocolate-bourbon flan, all of which are appropriate endings to a satisfying country dinner. About $75 for two, with wine.

INNS

Kedron Valley Inn
Rte. 106
(802) 457-1473
Closed 3 weeks in April.
Cards: AE, MC, V.

Merrily and Max Comins escaped the brutal pace of Wall Street and the world of investing to run this pleasant country inn. But they didn't leave their business prowess behind—it's evident in the smooth operation, the creative marketing approach, the sideline T-shirt and sweatshirt business and the excellent restaurant. The large 30-room inn has a relaxed feel to it, reflected in the simple decor, mix-and-match furnishings, soft color schemes and collection of family quilts. Some of the rooms are quite large and equipped with fireplaces, and others are charming and snug; some have beamed ceilings, and others have stenciled walls. The main house has fifteen rooms, the Tavern (the 1822 brick building next door) has seven, and the log lodge provides six more. The lodge rooms, although quite simple and rustic, are particularly sweet, with log walls, Merrily's stencil work and simple furnishings. All the rooms have private baths, some have televisions, and all are charming.

Breakfast—cheese omelets, eggs any style or buttermilk or blueberry pancakes—is served in the peach-toned dining room. There are plenty of things to do in and around the inn: The swimming hole has a sandy beach and a lifeguard, horseback riding is available, all sorts of sports activities are nearby (including Killington), and Woodstock is up the road a piece. But relaxing in the casual sitting room or on the front porch is just as acceptable. So is prowling through the many quilts and antique clothes on display at the inn. Merrily's family history reveals itself in the many hand-printed plaques, which show the intricacies of the quilt patterns and piecework.

Rooms: $95-$176, including breakfast and dinner.

SPRINGFIELD

QUICK BITES

Shanghai Garden
129 Clinton St.
(802) 885-5555
*Open daily 11:30 a.m.-
10 p.m.*
No cards.

This is one of those roadside surprises that keeps road-weary travelers optimistic. The unexpectedly authentic Chinese food served at breakneck speed by a Chinese family in a tiny old pink diner includes fiery kung pao beef and other hot items that are hard to come by up here. Bypass the Americanized selections on the large menu, be warned that the drafty diner is cold in winter, and enjoy a good meal for two, including egg rolls, hot-and-sour soup, entrées and Tsingtao beer, for about $24.

> *Unless otherwise noted, the prices given for restaurants are for a complete dinner for two, including an appetizer, main course and dessert. The prices also include tax, fifteen-percent tip and one of the least expensive bottles of wine on the wine list. Please don't hold it against us if you end up spending a bit more!*

STOWE

RESTAURANTS

Austrian Tea Room
Luce Hill Rd.
(Trapp Family Lodge)
(802) 253-8511
AUSTRIAN/AMERICAN
Open daily 10:30 a.m.-
5:30 p.m. (July-Oct. until
8 p.m.); closed parts of
April-May & Nov.-Dec.
All major cards.

10/20

When the Trapp family fled Austria and settled on a wooded hilltop overlooking Stowe, they stumbled upon a very marketable view—and as we know from those alive hills in *The Sound of Music*, the Trapps knew a good view when they saw one. The Tea Room is perched over a sweeping valley that enthralls in every season except possibly spring, which is a frequent no-show in Vermont. Sit on the deck in summer and enjoy the flowers; sit inside for the fall foliage show or the Christmas-card winter scene. This informal place is a fine stop for lunch (hearty Cheddar-cheese soup, knockwurst with potato salad) or an afternoon dessert (large wedges of Linzertorte, Sachertorte and the ubiquitous Black Forest cake) served by waitresses in traditional dirndls. Children love this place. Happily, the Tea Room is fully licensed and serves a warming Glühwein in the cold months. Lunch for two, with beer, is about $25.

Ten Acres Lodge
Barrows Rd.
(802) 253-7638
AMERICAN/INTERNATIONAL
Open daily 6 p.m.-
9:30 p.m. (closed parts of
May-April & Nov.-Dec.).
All major cards.

One of the nice things about dining at Ten Acres is its isolation, a mile down a country road from the hustle of Stowe's resort life—it will give you the illusion of a farmhouse inn, with its bucolic view of Mount Mansfield. The menu, however, is anything but down-home, and the ambience is cozily elegant, with white linens, candles, fresh flowers and unobtrusive service. The food is equally elegant. Starters include a circle of littleneck clams on the half shell with a splash of sushi flavors, and a lovely platter of smoked bluefish and salmon with slices of avocado and a grapefruit mayonnaise. Grilled butterflied leg of lamb with rosemary and roasted garlic is both particularly rare and good, served with lightly cooked fiddleheads with the crunch of early spring in them. The handsome mound of black pasta in a subtle cream sauce crisscrossed with roasted peppers, asparagus, black olives and Vermont goat cheese makes for a successful combination of strong flavors. And the slim, warm chewy French bread is excellent. Country-inn desserts demand a bit of excess, and the mud pie, involving ice cream and hot fudge, does its job admirably. No smoking is permitted. After dinner, you can repair to one of the serenely comfortable, antiques-filled rooms for a sound night's sleep. (We especially like the quiet rooms in the Hill House out back, which have private baths and decks, fireplaces and cable TV; they go for $120 to $130.) Dinner for two, with wine, will run at least $90.

QUICK BITES

Hapelton's
Rte. 100
(802) 253-4653
Open daily 11 a.m.-2 a.m.
Cards: MC, V.

This quite dark café is wonderfully cozy in winter. There's a sunken dining area in front of a blazing fire, the last glimmers of sunlight filter through stained-glass windows, and the atmosphere is friendly and enthusiastic. Fill out your own sandwich order from the mix-and-match options, selecting your own bread, toppings, extras and preparation requests. There is also a selection of snack foods and soups available from lunchtime on. Dinners are of the prime-rib-and-game-hen genre; brunch offers eggs Benedict, red flannel hash, huevos rancheros and a Vermont specialty, apple-cinnamon pancakes with Vermont Cheddar. About $15 for a sandwich and a beer for two.

INNS

Aside from the Trapp Family Lodge (see below), you can try Ten Acres Lodge (see "Restaurants") or the area's large resort hotel, Top Notch at Stowe (Mountain Road, 802-253-8585), a costly place with ice skating, indoor tennis, cross-country skiing, sleigh rides, endless views and pretty good food. Rooms are $220-$250, including breakfast and dinner. Skiers seeking further lodging options should call the Stowe Area Association, (800) 253-7321.

Trapp Family Lodge
Luce Hill Rd.
(800) 826-7000,
(802) 253-8511
Open year-round.
All major cards.

We'll have to be honest and say there's really no place particularly unusual or elegant to stay in Stowe, a tiny mountain town that caters to winter-sports aficionados who expect only warmth and a good bed. The place with the most visitor interest is undoubtedly the Trapp Family Lodge up the hill. A cross between a motel and an Austrian lodge (the European influence is hard to find, but they promise it's there), this 95-room complex, with its time-share condos, at least offers a room with a view. The rooms also have balconies and a utilitarian decor. Run by the *Sound of Music* Trapps, it is an efficient operation that would make any Austrian proud.

There are a scenic pond, a fitness center with indoor pool and workout equipment, cheerful solarium sitting areas, a library with large leather chairs and a pine-filled bar and restaurant. The Trapps also run a gift shop and clothing boutique, in case you didn't pack the right things.

Rooms: $120-$370, including breakfast and dinner.

SIGHTS

Stowe Ski Area
Mountain Rd. (Rte. 108)
(802) 253-7311

Although not as alpine as places like the Trapp Family Lodge would lead you to expect, Stowe is still (by New England standards) a first-rate ski resort with all the amenities—a ski school, rentals, shops, restaurants, cross-country trails and a good range of downhill slopes for all levels.

We like Stowe just as much in the green summertime, when you can ride the gondola to the mountaintop for a dazzling view and a refreshing shot of mountain air.

SHOPS

Samara
Mountain Rd. (Rte. 108)
(802) 253-8318
Summer & winter: open daily 10 a.m.-5 p.m.; fall & spring: hours vary.

Samara sells the quaint New England–style crafts—clay pots, honey dippers and wooden items with Swiss motifs—that people expect to cart home after a ski vacation. But there is also a nice assortment of traditional-design quilts, and prices are reasonable given the location.

Stowe Pottery and Craft Gallery
Rte. 108 & Rte. 100
(802) 253-4693
Open Mon.-Sat. 10 a.m.-5 p.m., Sun. 11 a.m.-5 p.m.

Step into this wooden-beamed former blacksmith shop and you're in the quintessential New England craft store. Though the place specializes in small glass items, woodenware and ceramic utensils, its diversity is amazing. Tree spirits carved from branches peer from one wall; in another corner is a cabinet of handmade knives; in still another, wooden duck decoys.

STRATTON

INNS

See Arlington, Dorset, Ludlow, Manchester, Newfane, West Dover.

SIGHTS

Stratton Mountain
Rte. 30
(802) 297-2200

Its southwestern location (near the New York border and lots of charming small towns), its complete range of facilities (ski school, restaurants, rentals), its snowmaking, its cross-country trails and its sleigh rides make Stratton a favorite of skiing New Yorkers. Mount Snow and Killington (see "Mount Snow" and "Killington") are in this same general neck of the woods, as are several towns with good country inns (see "Inns" above). For more lodging information, including details on the resort's Stratton Mountain Inn, call the number above.

SUGARBUSH VILLAGE

SIGHTS

Sugarbush
Rte. 100
(802) 583-2381

Smaller and a bit more peaceful than the state's major ski resorts—Killington, Mount Snow and Stratton—Sugarbush is actually three ski mountains: Sugarbush, Sugarbush North and Mad River Glen. There are twelve chairlifts in all, good cross-country trails and all the necessary services. Call the number above for lodging information.

WATERBURY

INNS

Inn at Thatcher Brook Falls
Rte. 100
(802) 244-5911
Open year-round.
Cards: AE, MC, V.

Old-fashioned rusticity in a country inn certainly has its merits, but sometimes we appreciate the modern comforts—floors that don't squeak, spotless contemporary bathrooms, not too much turn-of-the-century-style clutter. The Inn at Thatcher Brook Falls, recently taken over by Kelly Fenton and Peter Varty, combines the best of both worlds: the charm of a handsome white Victorian farmhouse and the scrubbed-fresh appeal of a top-to-bottom renovation, including a well-designed new wing and a pleasant dining room. The furnishings may not be priceless antiques, but they're handsome, well made and appropriate to the inn's all-American look. Each of the twelve quiet, attractive bedrooms has a private bath; most are pretty good-size, and some have canopy beds. The location is excellent for indulging in a tour of Ben & Jerry's Ice Cream Factory in nearby Waterbury Center (see below), also the home of the superb Villa Tragara restaurant; for exploring the antiques shops and Vermont-style country stores along Route 100; and for skiing the local slopes, including Stowe. Both the gourmand and the hearty skier will be pleased with the delicious breakfast: pancakes, fresh berries, homemade muffins and breads and the like.

Rooms: $75-$130, including breakfast.

WATERBURY CENTER

RESTAURANTS

Villa Tragara
Rte. 100
(802) 244-5288
ITALIAN
*Open Mon.-Sat. 5:30 p.m.-
9:30 p.m.*
All major cards.

12/20

Route 100 makes for a lovely drive, whether or not you're a skier. Book a room at the Inn at Thatcher Brook Falls (see "Waterbury"), then head north, stopping to visit Ben & Jerry's Ice Cream Factory (see "Sights" below), browsing through some of the antiques stores and pausing at one of the roadside farm shops to pick up some Cabot Cheddar, Harrington's ham and fresh apple cider. Then have dinner at Villa Tragara, set atop a hill by the side of the road in a converted 1820 farmhouse overlooking the Green Mountains. Actually, the renovation was done only marginally along antique lines—a little flowered wallpaper here, some wall sconces there—and the dining rooms are rather drearily lighted at night. But owners Antonino and Patricia Di Ruocco run a fine kitchen, beginning with the olive oil–scented bread (baked twice each night) that might dissuade you from bothering with the antipasti. But if you can keep your hands off the bread, try the fried calamari or the mozzarella in carrozza (battered and fried mozzarella-and-bread). Then move on to a "pasta mista"—a mix of three pastas that shows off Di Ruocco's favorites that evening, perhaps gnocchi al pesto, cannelloni with veal and ricotta, and fettuccine sauced with sautéed fresh vegetables. Then order lightly, perhaps snowy filets of sole cooked with wilted lettuce and pine nuts. You may accompany all of this with a selection from a short but well-chosen wine list, weighted with some of the better Italian bottlings available in this country. Then have a well-made espresso (ask the chef to make it for you the way he takes it), then drive back in the moonlight to your little inn and sleep like a good bambino. A several-course dinner for two, with wine, should cost about $90.

SIGHTS

**Ben & Jerry's Ice
Cream Factory**
Rte. 100
(802) 244-5641
*Tours Mon.-Sat. 9 a.m.-
4 p.m.; retail shop open daily
9 a.m.- 4 p.m.*

New Englanders (especially Bostonians) claim the country's highest per-capita rate of ice cream consumption. If you're set on increasing that rate, get in your licks at Ben & Jerry's Ice Cream Factory, on Route 100 just off Interstate 89. As they tell their story in an aw-shucks multimedia slide show, Ben and Jerry were just two regular guys who, in 1978, started a little ice cream shop in an old gas station with a five-gallon freezer. Since then, they've purveyed their rich, incredibly creamy product (bolstered by one of the highest butterfat contents on the market) into what *Time* magazine has declared "the best ice cream in the world." A visit includes a tour of the modern factory and free samples cold off the assembly line. If a taste just whets your appetite, visit the old-fashioned ice cream parlor and gift shop, stocked with a staggering variety of ice-cream paraphernalia.

Adults $1, children under 12 free.

WEST DOVER

INNS

**The Inn
at Sawmill Farms**
Rte. 100
(802) 464-8131
*Closed the Sun. after
Thanksgiving-mid-Dec.
Cards: AE.*

The setting may be rural, but there's nothing rustic about The Inn at Sawmill Farms. How many "country" inns serve high tea from a silver samovar and stock a 15,000-bottle wine cellar? Each of the 21 guest rooms has a king-size bed and color-coordinated spread and curtains; there are ten spacious cottages with flagstone fireplaces and views of the well-stocked trout pond. But clearly it is dining that's the main activity around here: The restaurant serves Continental classics in a setting of candlelight and nineteenth-century paintings. And the lounge, with its copper bar and eighteenth-century floorboards, is as popular as the dining room—even the tomato juice in the Bloody Marys is homemade. Amenities include a swimming pool and tennis, and skiers will find themselves close to Mount Snow's slopes. The manicured grounds afford a fine view of the white steeple of the West Dover Congregational Church. All is pure serenity, which is further ensured by the innkeepers' ban on children under 10.

Rooms: $160-$230, including breakfast and dinner.

WILMINGTON

INNS

The Hermitage
Coldbrook Rd.
(802) 464-3511
*Open year-round.
All major cards.*

"The best way to experience my inn," says Jim McGovern, "is to be stranded here during a snowstorm." And should that fate befall you, you can rest assured of one thing: You won't go hungry. McGovern's 24-acre domain has a sugar house, a trout pond, a game-bird breeding facility and a 30,000-bottle wine cellar. Add to this a sauna, eleven bedrooms with fireplaces, and 55 miles of cross-country ski trails, and you'll want for neither activity nor comfort. Built in 1870, The Hermitage belonged for many years to Bertha Eastman Barry, editor of the redoubtable *Social Register Blue Book*. Many of the rooms are furnished with Federal-era antiques; all have private baths. A solid Continental bill of fare is served in four rustic, candlelit dining rooms; the house specialty, as you may guess from the breeding quarters, is game. After dinner you can sit by a roaring fire in the lounge and listen to McGovern hold forth about his latest project. During the fall foliage season, you may have to dodge tour buses filled with the senior citizens who flock to McGovern's compound to buy maple syrup and homemade jams.

Rooms: $160-$180, including breakfast and dinner.

SHOPS

Craft Haus
Top of the Hill Rd.
(802) 464-2164
Mid-May-mid-Jan.: open Mon.-Tues. & Thurs.-Sun. 10 a.m.-5 p.m.

This out-of-the-way shop (take Route 100 to Stowe Hill Road, then go up the hill two miles and turn right) is in the basement of Ursula and Ed Tancrel's home. In addition to Ursula's cloisonné jewelry, which she sells at wholesale prices, the Tancrels carry a good selection of pottery, porcelain, glass and lithographs. Regardless of its remote setting, the place is usually crowded with people who have been here before and liked what they found.

Quaigh Design Centre
W. Main St.
(802) 464-2780
Open daily 10 a.m.-6 p.m.

Step into the shop, laddies and lassies, and you'll find yourself in a wee bit of Scotland. If you're not as thrifty as a good Scotsman should be, you can stock up on mohair blankets, Shetland sweaters, kilts, pottery and jewelry from Scotland, in addition to an assortment of more traditionally American ceramics and jewelry.

WINDSOR

SHOPS

Vermont State Crafts Center at Windsor House
Main St.
(802) 674-6729
June-Jan.: Mon.-Sat. 9 a.m.-5 p.m., Sun. noon-5 p.m.; Feb.-May: Mon.-Sat. 9 a.m.-5 p.m.

Located in a stately Greek Revival building in the center of town, this store is one of two such centers in the state. As such, it has assembled an impressive array of work in virtually all media. Always outstanding are the quilt selection and the furniture, which is handmade along very traditional lines.

WOODSTOCK

INNS

Jackson House
Rte. 4
(802) 457-2065
Closed Nov.-mid-Dec. &
April-mid-May.
Cards: AE, MC, V.

It is to Laurence Rockefeller's credit that he had the good taste to bury Woodstock's power lines, helping to create a perfect New England town with little noticeable urban-development intrusion. Woodstock is a Norman Rockwell kind of a town. Galleries, antiques stores, shops, restaurants, historic buildings, the town green—it's a small-town dream that smacks of the good life, country style. For an extended taste of it, check into Jackson House, a large yellow Victorian inn surrounded by three acres of landscaped grounds, complete with brook and trout-stocked pond. Owners Jack Foster and Bruce McIlveen have created a refined place that befits the original home of Wales Johnson, a sawmill baron in the late 1800s. The house is a tribute to his business, and the curly maple and cherry floorboards make it clear that you're not in an ordinary home. The ten bedrooms are civilized, comfortable and stylish. Ceiling fans help deal with summer heat, Chinese rugs as soft as cashmere warm the place in winter, and decorative touches enliven every room. Ask for the inn's brochure before booking a specific room—it gives a preview of each room, ensuring that you get what you want.

Breakfast is served in the elegant Queen Anne–style dining room. Foster is a formidable cook who will keep you happily full with his Santa Fe french toast, eggs Grisanti, cheese blintzes, sourdough pancakes, poached eggs Creole served on eggplant, and zucchini omelets with mushrooms and peppers. Foster and McIlveen also offer guests wine and Champagne in the evening, along with an hors d'oeuvres buffet of pâtés, cheeses, caviar and lobster or shrimp quiche.
Rooms: $110, including breakfast.

The Woodstock Inn
14 The Green
(802) 457-1100
Open year-round.
All major cards.

To call this Rockresort a country inn is like calling Manhattan a secluded island. A "country inn" with 120 rooms isn't exactly what we would call intimate. And even if the lobby does have braided rugs and a ten-foot fireplace, the decor of the guests rooms is about as "country" as that of an airport motel. And don't look to the dining room for consolation. The menu features Yankee-style Continental cuisine, but we have found the food as tired as a farmer's mule after harvest. So why is it so difficult to book a room here? First, because it's a popular meeting place for the corporate crowd. Second, because it's located in one of the most picture-pretty towns in Vermont. Third, because of its on-grounds amenities, which include a state-of-the-art sports center and an adjacent eighteen-hole golf course. Another plus: Tucked away on the wine list are some excellent Vermont fruit wines.

Rooms: $99-$315, including breakfast.

SIGHTS

**Billings Farm
and Museum**
River Rd.
(802) 457-2355
*May-Oct.: open daily
10 a.m.-5 p.m.*

In telling the story of Vermont dairying, the Billings Farm and Museum mixes the old with the new. The museum's permanent exhibits focus on rural life in the 1890s, with daily demonstrations of such crafts as rug braiding, butter churning and chair caning. And the farm is a modern dairy farm, home to a herd of Jerseys (milked daily at 3:30 p.m.), as well as sheep and horses.

Adults $4, children $2, children under 6 free.

SHOPS

**F. H. Gillingham
& Sons**
16 Elm St.
(802) 457-2100
*Open Mon.-Sat. 8:30 a.m.-
5:30 p.m.*

This updated country store comes by its wood floors honestly. For a century it has been the town market; today its shelves are crammed with all manner of kitchen accoutrements and an up-to-date mix of Vermont-made gourmet products in attractive jars with handsome labels. These home-based firms of mustard and marinade makers have proliferated, tapping into the national taste for natural ingredients in interesting new forms. The expected honey and maple syrup can be found here, along with some more unusual things: berry applesauce, dark, chunky ketchup, and jellies made from cucumber and red pepper.

Log Cabin Quilts
9 Central St.
(802) 457-2725
*Open Tues.-Sat. 10 a.m.-
5 p.m., Sun. 11 a.m.-5 p.m.*

In the midst of what may be the ultimate New England town sits this repository of wonderful quilts. All are made in the region, and the traditional designs are beautifully executed. The store also has supplies for do-it-yourselfers.

NEW HAMPSHIRE

BARTLETT

SIGHTS

See Mount Washington Valley.

CENTER BARNSTEAD

RESTAURANTS

The Crystal Quail
Call for directions
(603) 269-4151
CONTINENTAL/AMERICAN
Open Tues.-Sun. 5 p.m.-
9 p.m.
No cards.

We like a restaurant in which guests walk through the kitchen on their way to the dining room—particularly when the kitchen sparkles with copper cookware and the dining room has massive ceiling beams, a working fireplace and seats for a mere dozen guests. Both kitchen and dining room are housed in a charmingly restored eighteenth-century farmhouse. This restaurant lovingly operated by the Huckaby family: Howard runs the kitchen, his wife tends the vegetable garden, and his daughter bakes the bread and waits on the handful of guests. The recited menu changes daily; a recent visit fetched us airy calves'-liver quenelles, a salad of wild greens, a brace of quail and home-grown rhubarb meringue tart. Guests must bring their own wine (a plus to our thinking), which will be poured into etched-crystal goblets. Locating The Crystal Quail requires the detective skills of Sam Spade. But persevere—it's worth it. About $80 for two.

CENTER SANDWICH

INNS

Corner House Inn
Rte. 113 & Rte. 109
(603) 284-6219
Closed April & Nov.
Cards: AE, MC, V.

Center Sandwich is well known as a craft center. It is also home to Corner House, which has a craftsy look of its own. Husband-and-wife innkeepers Don Brown and Jane Kroeger renovated this sweet 1849 house located at the crossroads in town. Its four charming bedrooms are stocked with antiques and have been decorated with a light touch, creating quiet, calming havens.

Corner House has a good restaurant with four separate barnyard-craftsy dining rooms, serving such traditionalist fare as roast duckling with orange-raspberry sauce, filet mignon Dijon and homemade soups. A hearty breakfast is also served: yogurt and fruit, omelets or pancakes, served with Virginia ham, sausage or bacon.

Rooms: $60-$70, including breakfast.

CHESTERFIELD

INNS

Chesterfield Inn
Rte. 9, West Chesterfield
(603) 256-3211
Open year-round.
All major cards.

It makes a difference when innkeepers are young, lean and ambitious. Consider Phil and Judy Hueber of the luxurious Chesterfield Inn. They bought the inn in July 1987. Within twelve months, they'd installed a much-lauded restaurant, a truckload of antiques and, in most of the spacious rooms, quilts personally stitched by Judy. The inn occupies a farmhouse and barn built in the late eighteenth century, though you'd never guess it from looking at the inside of the nine guest rooms, with their dramatic architecture, deep carpets, towering plants, telephones and minibars. Four of the rooms have working fireplaces, two have Jacuzzis, and two have balconies overlooking the foothills of the Green Mountains. The king-size beds are so comfortable that it's easy to snooze through dinner. Don't, or you'll miss the estimable cooking of chef Carl Warner. He's the tall, dark, handsome guy at the stove, and you can peek over his shoulder on your way through the kitchen to one of three cozy dining rooms. His food makes a virtue of simplicity: corn and shrimp chowder, maple-glazed game hen, berries with zabaglione. Dinner will run about $90 for two, with wine.

Rooms: $95-$145, including breakfast.

CHOCORUA

INNS

Staffords
in the Field
Off Rte. 113W
(603) 323-7766
Open year-round.
Cards: AE, MC, V.

Ramona and Fred Stafford have been innkeepers for so long that their longevity is surpassed only by those New Hampshire families that have passed their innkeeping businesses down for generations. Twenty-five years ago, the Staffords left their ranch in San Diego and headed for New England to run this comfortable inn. Three children later, their fourteen-room inn is still flourishing, and son Fritz is following in his parents' footsteps.

The decor is family simple: The homey rooms are furnished with second-hand pieces the Stafford boys rescued from local auction houses; the rooms in the back of the house are slightly more updated. Some of the fourteen share bathrooms, and all are unpretentious and relaxing.

Ramona is an accomplished chef (the inn sells a cookbook filled with her recipes), and her dinners have a country flavor: pork with apples and walnuts, duckling, blackened fish, pork Dijon and black-raspberry chicken, along with a few Cal-Mexican specialties. Desserts range from frozen apricot mousse and Southern pecan pie to dark-chocolate cake with raspberry ganache and chocolate mousse. The ambience in the handsome dining room is restful: Lush blue-and-gold print walls, a collection of antique butter molds, an antique stove and an impressive old grandfather clock give the place spirit. Breakfast, which is also served in this room, runs to Cheddar or sour-cream-and-green-chile omelets, blueberry pancakes, warm applesauce, homemade fruit preserves and freshly baked breads. The Staffords also make their own maple syrup.

The inn is perched on top of a hill and flanked by a large barn. Extras include a tennis court, a swimming hole, about 30 acres in which you can get lost, marked cross-country ski trails, and plenty of books if you prefer a less-active pace.

Rooms: $120-$180, including breakfast and dinner.

CONCORD

INNS

See Henniker.

SIGHTS

Audubon House
3 Silk Farm Rd.
(603) 224-9909
Open Mon.-Sat. 9 a.m.-4 p.m.

More than just politicians and history buffs flock to Concord, the state capital—so do bird lovers (and more than a few birds, we would hope). Headquarters of the Audubon Society of New Hampshire, Audubon House contains its own library and exhibits, and self-guiding nature trails wind through the grounds. Look here for information on the society's other major facilities in New Hampshire, including the Depierrefeu–Willard Pond wildlife sanctuary in Antrim, a habitat of bobcat, beaver, otter and loons, and Ponemah Bog in Amherst, a 100-acre botanical preserve.

Coach and Eagle Trail

244 N. Main St.
(chamber of commerce)
(603) 224-2508

The State House (see below) is just one of seventeen historic sites on the Coach and Eagle Trail, a walking tour of downtown Concord. The trail, which begins at Eagle Square, includes the New Hampshire State Library and Historical Society, three historic churches, the League of New Hampshire Craftsmen and the Pierce Manse, which was once occupied by President Franklin Pierce. The free, self-guided tour takes one and a half to two hours; before you begin, stop in at the Greater Concord Chamber of Commerce for a map.

Self-guided tour; admission free.

State House

107 Main St.
(603) 271-1110
Open Mon.-Fri. 8:30 a.m.-4:30 p.m.

From its locale on the Merrimack River, Concord serves as New Hampshire's capital, and its double-porticoed State House is considered a small jewel of its genre. The visitors' center sponsors guided tours of the legislative chambers and the Hall of Flags.

CONWAY

INNS

Darby Field Inn

Bald Hill Rd. (off Rte. 16)
(603) 447-2181
Open year-round.
Cards: AE, MC, V.

We arrived at Darby Field in the dead of night with the feeling that we were driving through an enchanted forest, far from the Yellow Brick Road. The winding dirt road, the encroaching pine and birch forest, the sound of the wind whistling through the fields—we knew we were somewhere far north of Oz. But in the light of day, we were grateful that this pretty place is so far off the beaten path. We were enraptured by the mountain vistas, rolling hills, gushing brook, hiking trails, peaceful surroundings and wonderful swimming pool surrounded by fieldstones.

The common room has an enormous stone fireplace, the cozy bar has an uninterrupted view of the mountains, and the dining room serves excellent food. Dinners are acclaimed: roast duckling with Grand Marnier, chicken marquis (sautéed with tomatoes and mushrooms), veal piccata and fresh fish. Breakfast the morning after is a hearty feast of buttermilk or oatmeal pancakes with sour cream; whole-wheat pancakes with apples, strawberries, peaches or bananas and honey; or Swiss cheese and basil omelets. While waiting for that first cup of coffee to kick in, consult the flip side of the menu to survey the distant mountain range—each peak is outlined on a map, to help you keep track of the view.

Rooms: $120-$150, including breakfast and dinner.

CORNISH FLAT

INNS

Chase House
Rte. 12A
(603) 675-5391
Open year-round.
Cards: MC, V.

Peter Burling opened Chase House as one in a series of his special projects. Another Burling endeavor can be seen down the road in Cornish: He bought and rehabilitated the old Trinity Church and gave it back to the town, with the stipulation that it remain nondenominational. He also sold the town a cherry-picker fire truck for one dollar. An attorney by training, Burling is community oriented, as evidenced by his restoration of this lovely inn. Chase House was originally the home of Salmon Portland Chase, another community-minded man, who served in Lincoln's cabinet and lived out his life as a Supreme Court Justice (he also founded the Republican Party—surely an irony for liberal Burling—and is namesake of the Chase Manhattan Bank).

The house today is a charming six-room inn. Decorated by professional interior designer Gilberte, the house has a real 1770s look: wide-plank floorboards painted in Colonial colors, tall-post beds, lace canopies, beautiful Oriental bird-print wallpaper in the hallway and antique furniture. Marilyn and Hal Wallace, the resident innkeepers, will make your stay pleasant. After indulging in one of Marilyn's breakfasts—fresh-fruit compote with grenadine, eggs any way you like them, blueberry pancakes, french toast, cereal—you can cross-country ski nearby, put your own canoe in the Connecticut River across the street, hike throughout the property or visit Trinity Church to see Burling's other restoration.

Rooms: $65-$85, including breakfast.

SIGHTS

Augustus Saint-Gaudens House
Rte. 12A
(603) 675-2175
Mid-May-Oct.: open daily
8:30 a.m.-4:30 p.m.
(grounds open until dark).

Like so many other sophisticated artists, the American master sculptor Augustus Saint-Gaudens sought a simpler life in New England. His Classical Revival summer home and studio in Cornish Flat are now open to the public; in them you'll find, among other things, replicas of some of his best-known works, including the Adams Memorial in Washington and the Robert Gould Shaw Memorial bas-relief on Boston Common. This National Historic Site is just two miles from America's longest-surviving covered bridge, which in 460 feet spans the Connecticut River from Cornish to Windsor, Vermont.

Adults $1, children under 12 free.

ETNA

INNS

Moose Mountain Lodge
Moose Mountain Hwy.
(603) 643-3529
Closed April-May & Nov.-Dec. 26.
Cards: MC, V.

Maria von Trapp would be in heaven here: glorious mountain views, fresh, clean air, a pet goat named Kirby, impressive hand-hewn four-poster beds, trails for hiking and skiing, copious amounts of delicious, robust food and the attractive, accommodating Peter and Kay Shumway as hosts. The lodge is an outdoors-enthusiast's Technicolor dream. The inn's ski shop can outfit a family of cross-country skiers; Kay leads day-long hikes through the surrounding countryside; the serene vistas of Killington Peak and Sugarbush are akin to an all-American Valhalla; and in rough weather, the hike up the road to the inn is an invigorating initiation rite (four-wheel-drive owners will have no problems, and the Shumways will retrieve anyone who needs a lift). Inside is a rustic, reassuring decor: oversized stone fireplaces, handmade log furniture and rooms done in soft pastels, all protected by the watchful resident moosehead trophy. Bathrooms are shared; there are two additional Scandinavian baths on the lower level. Guests eat family style at an enormous dining room table, and the musically inclined can duel it out on the two baby grand pianos in the handsome living room. Moose Mountain is spectacular in any season, and it's the perfect place for well-behaved children over five years old—they can bring the surrounding hills alive with their own sounds of music.

Rooms: $120-$150, including breakfast and dinner.

EXETER

SHOPS

Exeter Craft Center
61 Water St.
(603) 778-8282
Open Mon.-Sat. 9:30 a.m.-5 p.m.

Because this center is within easy reach of both the coast and Boston, the crafts displayed here are a touch more sophisticated, more sculptural than you'll find in parts north. Like all the shops affiliated with the League of New Hampshire Craftsmen, this one juries work monthly, and the selection includes work from around the state, as well as from local artists (who must live within a few miles of the store). Look for Shaker-influenced wooden-chip boxes, magnificent stained glass and furniture, as well as more standard ceramic, wood and jewelry items.

FRANCONIA

SIGHTS

Cannon Mountain
Rte. 3
(603) 823-5563

State-owned and -operated Cannon Mountain is the state's largest ski area, boasting particularly good expert runs, miles of incredibly beautiful cross-country trails, complete ski-resort services and a view-crazy gondola. The gondola remains open in summer, when it carts visitors atop 4,200-foot-high Cannon Mountain for a panoramic view of not just the Franconia area but, on a clear day, all the way to New York State's Adirondacks. Also on Cannon Mountain is the most appropriate museum possible for this part of the country: the New England Ski Museum on Cannon Mountain (603-823-7177). It's open from late May to mid-October, daily 10 a.m. to 5 p.m.; and from late December to early April, daily 10 a.m. to 4 p.m. Admission is $1 for adults and free for kids under 11.

Franconia Notch State Park
Franconia Notch Pkwy.
(off Rte. 93)
(603) 823-5563

In Pennsylvania they're called "gaps," in the West "passes," and here they're "notches." New Hampshire has any number of these deep valleys between mountain ranges—Dixville, Crawford and Pinkham notches, to name just a few. But the granddaddy of the notches is Franconia, between the Franconia and Kinsman ranges of the White Mountains. If you have any doubt about it, just look up—1,200 feet, to be precise—to the Old Man of the Mountain, a 40-foot-tall natural rock formation that looks like the profile of a man.

The Great Stone Face is just one example of the natural wonders in Franconia Notch State Park. There's also the Flume, which is not an amusement-park ride but an 800-foot-long gorge with granite walls 70 to 90 feet high and only 12 feet wide in some places—instant claustrophobia. The 6,440-acre park comprises a variety of lakes, campgrounds and scenic drives. To plan your sight-seeing, stop in at the Flume visitors' center, approached from the Franconia Notch Parkway. The visitors' center is open from late May to late October, daily 9 a.m. to 4:30 p.m.; admission to the Flume is $4. The park itself is open year-round, except for maintenance periods in the spring and fall.

Some establishments change their closing times without warning. It is always wise to call ahead.

GLEN

RESTAURANTS

Bernerhof Inn
Rte. 302
(603) 383-4414
SWISS/AUSTRIAN/GERMAN
*July 1-Oct. 30: open daily
11:30 a.m.-2:30 p.m. &
5:30 p.m.-9:30 p.m.; off-
season hours vary.
Cards: AE, MC, V.*

At the risk of sounding like sticks-in-the-mud, we always order the same dishes when we dine at the "Hof": Glühwein (hot mulled wine), délices de Gruyère (Swiss-cheese fritters), the house salad, dressed with cider vinegar and cream, Wiener Schnitzel à la Holstein (fork-tender veal topped with fried eggs and anchovies), homemade Spätzle (small noodle or dumpling) and the heart-stoppingly rich chocolate silk pie for dessert. That may not be fair to chef Mark Prince, who also does a fine job with seafood dishes and attractively garnished daily specials. It's simply that while fine fish and modern French fare can be found at any number of Mount Washington Valley restaurants, no one can even remotely approach the traditional Swiss and Austrian fare that has made the Bernerhof famous. The dining rooms have the rustic elegance of pine paneling, antique mirrors and brass lamps, and the alpine mood of the menu is echoed in the dirndls worn by the waitresses. But to come here for dinner alone would be to overlook the enormous effort and expense the owners, Ted and Sharon Wroblewski, have put into transforming the Bernerhof from a humble bed-and-breakfast to a luxurious inn. A massive renovation completed in July 1988 endowed all the rooms with private bathrooms and many with wood stoves and Jacuzzis. Located midway between Attitash and Black Mountain, the inn is popular with skiers. Cooking enthusiasts take note: The Bernerhof is the home of the Taste of the Mountains Cooking School. About $70 to $80 for dinner for two, with wine.

SIGHTS

See Mount Washington Valley.

HAMPTON BEACH

INNS

See Portsmouth.

SIGHTS

New Hampshire doesn't have much of a seacoast—only about twenty miles' worth—but what there is, as Spencer Tracy might say, is *cherce*. Hampton Beach, the primary coastal resort, offers a full summer of beach-centered activities, including band concerts, flea markets, children's programs and just plain sun. The visitors' center at 180 Ocean Boulevard (603-926-8717) is open mid-April to mid-October, daily 9 a.m. to 10 p.m. For basic transportation or sight-seeing, two companies, the Hampton Trolley Co. and Olde Port Trolley Co., run trackless trolleys along the major routes. Both run daily from noon to 10 p.m. during the season (late June to early September); each ride costs $1. On the entertainment scene, the Hampton Beach Casino (603-926-4541) will keep the younger set happy; it features big-name entertainers, especially in pop music, as well as an arcade and rides. It's open from late May to mid-September, daily 7 a.m. to 1 a.m.

HANCOCK

INNS

John Hancock Inn
Main St.
(Rte. 123 & Rte. 136)
(603) 525-3318
Open year-round.
Cards: MC, V.

Owners Pat and Glynn Wells have done an admirable job maintaining the Colonial look and feel of the Hancock Inn. A gray exterior and bright-red front door invite you inside to explore the ten rooms. Each has a private bath and is charming, with Colonial colors, original planked floorboards and a simple decor. The best room is Sixteen, which boasts original paintings by Rufus Porter. The inn was once full of his artwork, along with Moses Eaton stencils. Sadly, little remains today.

Local residents come here frequently to dine on old-fashioned New England fare, such as cranberry shrub, clam chowder, roast duckling, rib roast, Boston scrod and seafood casserole. The pub is cozy and convivial, the pace relaxed and informal. But the best part of the inn is its location in beautiful Hancock, a sleepy Federal-era village in which each of the striking Main Street homes has a different fan light. In fact, every impossibly charming small-New-England-town ingredient is here, from the meeting house and scenic pond to the history-laden cemetery and pristine Congregational Church.

Rooms: $56-$63.

HANOVER

RESTAURANTS

The Ivy Grill
(Hanover Inn)
Town Common
(603) 643-1410
INTERNATIONAL
Open Mon.-Sat.
11:30 a.m.-10 p.m., Sun.
5:30 p.m.-10 p.m.
All major cards.

12/20

The Ivy Grill reminds us of those TV commercials in which determined young stockbrokers stride among computers while waving profitable pieces of paper. No doubt they go to places like The Ivy Grill for their power lunches. The Ivy is a postmodern intrusion into the plush heart of old-school Hanover Inn. The lights are low, the colors are shades of gray and salmon, the music is minimalist/pop, and everything is chilly but chic—it's an atmosphere to make deals in. The same holds true for the food, which is consistently good but hardly distracting. You might call the menu pretentiously unpretentious: cheeseburgers and pizza rub shoulders with thyme-roasted rack of lamb and grilled rainbow trout with shrimp and scallions; the wine list starts with low-priced natives and escalates to pricey imports. On our visit, after some brusque and peppery chowder, we tucked into the rainbow trout, finding it done perfectly; the accompanying grilled shrimp and vegetables made a fine effect. (The fries on the side were the unpretentious part.) This solid meal was capped by a crème brûlée (though there is also a startlingly rich chocolate mousse). We propose the theory that if you love The Ivy Grill's atmosphere, you'll love the food; and if you find the decor soulless, at least you'll have a pretty good meal.

During New England's brief interregnum of civilized weather, The Ivy also serves meals outside on a shady, spacious terrace, easily the nicest spot in town for eating and schmoozing. There the mix of items on the menu really comes into its own: You can pass long hours on a hot day sipping frozen drinks and having snacks while deciding whether to have a plain or fancy entrée— a pleasant prospect, in any case. Dinner will run about $70 for two, with wine.

QUICK BITES

Peter Christian's Tavern
39 S. Main St.
(603) 643-2345
Open daily 11:30 a.m.-
12:30 a.m., Sun. 11:30
a.m.-11:30 p.m.
Cards: AE, MC, V.

Yes, this is an informal cellar restaurant in a college town, but don't mistake it for a burger burrow. Descend into the cramped, convivial quarters, settle into a wooden booth and select from an eclectic menu. Big sandwiches made of things like boursin cheese, spinach and roast beef are favorites, but we've also had a thick, tangy tortilla soup and creamy turkey lasagne. Desserts are rich and worth it. Other branches in

Keene and New London, New Hampshire. Dinner for two, with beer, runs about $25.

INNS

See Etna, Lyme; in Vermont, Quechee, Woodstock.

SIGHTS

Hanover is a college town and proud of it: The manicured look of the Dartmouth campus spills into the neat streets of the town. Not surprisingly, the college is a cultural leader in western New Hampshire. The ten galleries of its Hood Museum (603-646-2900), widely recognized as one of New England's best, houses collections of artworks that span the ages, including Paul Revere silver and Native American art. It's open Tuesday to Friday 11 a.m. to 5 p.m., Saturday 11 a.m. to 8 p.m., Sunday 11 a.m. to 5 p.m., except during semester breaks (college is in session year-round). Also of interest on campus is the Hopkins Center for Creative and Performing Arts (603-646-2422), which presents programs of dance, music, film and theater. Except during semester breaks, it's open daily 7:30 a.m. to 11 p.m.

SHOPS

Kaleidoscope
3 Lebanon St.
(603) 643-4327
Open Mon.-Sat. 10 a.m.-6 p.m.

This store has its work cut out for it, competing as it does with the League of New Hampshire Craftsmen outlet down the street (see below). But it succeeds admirably, with the cluttered feel of a good antiques store—except that the wares are the antiques of the year 2086. The furniture is particularly notable (representing the work of more than 100 furniture designers who work in both contemporary and traditional styles), and Kaleidescope helps pay the bills by also stocking an impressive selection of fine cabinet, plumbing and door hardware.

League of New Hampshire Craftsmen
13 Lebanon St.
(603) 643-5050
Open Mon.-Sat. 9:30 a.m.-5 p.m.

As with most of the league's stores throughout the state, this one has nice stuff nicely displayed. Furniture is upstairs, and the variety is excellent. Definitely a cut above most college-town stores.

HENNIKER

INNS

Colby Hill Inn
The Oaks
(off Western Ave.)
(603) 428-3281
Open year-round.
Cards: AE, MC, V.

Don Glover is a man with a lot of time on his hands. He's been amassing a clock collection for years, and a personal tour (when he happens to be at the inn) of his many timepieces makes for an entertaining history lesson in clock design and workmanship. But don't worry, you won't be rudely awakened—thank God, only a few of the chimes have been set.

Colby Hill, run by Don's son, Don Jr., is classic New England. Beautiful antiques fill the twelve-bedroom inn, some of the wallpaper is authentically hand blocked, many of the beds have canopies, a few of the rooms have fireplaces, and all have private baths. If you visit during the summer, you'll appreciate the Glovers' swimming pool, with its uninterrupted view of the countryside. A full breakfast is served, and the restaurant dishes up acceptable home cooking for lunch and dinner.

Rates: $75-$85, including breakfast.

INTERVALE

INNS

Riverside Country Inn
Rte. 16A
(603) 356-9060
Open year-round.
All major cards.

The former summer home of the Cotter family has been retrofitted and is now a pleasant country inn full of family history—from Uncle Charlie's hand-painted winter scene in the pantry to the names of the seven bedrooms, tributes to the Cotter family and their governess and chauffeur. It was built in 1906, when life was slow and easy (especially for affluent types who built houses like this). Life's just as easy today, especially when enjoying the sensational cooking of Anne Cotter, wife of innkeeper Geoff.

The bedrooms upstairs are simple and spacious, with a decor leaning to the summer side, as befits the original role of this summer cottage. The sitting room is more formal, the wicker-laden front porch is a calming place to rock away an afternoon, and Auntie's Bar on the side porch is a great place to relax before dinner in the lovely dining room. Anne's cuisine wonderfully blends regional New England with her own inventiveness, with Maine represented by smoked trout, sausage, pork, ham, Sauerkraut and cheese;

New Hampshire by the ingredients for Anne's beet relish; and Vermont by maple syrup. Entrées are both creative (veal Regina, sautéed with apples, walnuts and maple syrup) and simple (fresh Maine fish and scallops). Desserts change daily; Anne makes her own ice cream and a delicious Key lime pie and mango Grand Marnier puff served with lemon curd.

An equally ample breakfast—baked custard, roast beef hash, eggs Benedict (with ham or salmon), chicken shortcake, Welsh rarebit, pork pie, fruit pancakes and salmon scrambled eggs—will convince you of the need to exercise all day to prepare for dinner (touring the discount stores in nearby Conway and North Conway ought to be enough of a workout).

Rooms: $55-$95, including breakfast.

SIGHTS

See Mount Washington Valley.

JACKSON

RESTAURANTS

Wildcat Inn & Tavern
Rte. 16A
(603) 383-4245
CONTINENTAL/AMERICAN
Open daily 11:30 a.m.-10 p.m. Cards: AE, MC, V.

Owner/chef Marty Sweeney is as high-spirited and amply proportioned as the generous meals he prepares. There are always specials on the dinner menu; you might start with a tasty exotic vegetable soup, a baked artichoke heart wrapped with bacon and Stilton or a crispy salad. Entrées provide just the sort of substantial fare you'll crave after a day on the local slopes or after eighteen holes of golf: delicious chicken Creole; pork seasoned with Dijon mustard and herbs and baked in puff pastry; simple shrimp and scallop scampi; satisfying chicken with sweet Italian sausage, apricots and mushrooms laced with apricot brandy; and lobster fettuccine. Desserts are equally oversized: chocolate silk pie, peppermint-stick ice cream pie, strawberry shortcake and a bevy of old-time pies, from pumpkin-almond and pecan to peanut butter and Boston cream. From $50 to $65 for dinner for two, with wine.

QUICK BITES

Yesterdays
Rte. 16A
(603) 383-4457
Open daily 6:30 a.m.-3 p.m. No cards.

The Zeliffs, owners of Christmas Farm Inn (see "Inns" below), also own this lively local restaurant, which they call "the home of the all-day breakfast." And it's so good that you won't mind having breakfast for breakfast *and* lunch. The decor is simple—beamed ceilings and yellow country curtains—and there's a friendly counter that you'll share with fiercely loyal locals who look like models from the L. L. Bean catalog. Though it takes an eternity to eat because of its chewiness, the homemade granola remains one of the best we've had. The pancakes, waffles and loaded-up omelets are equally delicious. But just because the Zeliffs serve breakfast all day doesn't mean that that's all you can eat: Lunch includes generous and tasty sandwiches, hot dogs, homemade soups, chili and fattening desserts (homemade brownies, sundaes, Indian pudding). Breakfast for two shouldn't be more than $8.

INNS

Christmas Farm Inn
Rte. 16B
(603) 383-4313
Open year-round.
Cards: AE, MC, V.

Bill and Synda Zeliff have made Christmas Farm Inn memorable since they became its proprietors in l982. The main inn (dating to the 1780s), the Salt Box building (circa 1777) and eight other structures (the barn, five cottages, a log cabin and a sugar house) make up the resort complex. It's a virtual village, complete with swimming pool, golf course and putting green, winter sleigh rides, children's playground, hiking trails, cross-country trails and a restaurant that serves sophisticated cuisine. The location is beautiful, and conveniently situated near three of New Hampshire's ski mountains (Attitash, Mount Cranmore and Wildcat; see "Mount Washington Valley").

The 37 rooms (with private baths) are peaceful and pristinely simple, with a virtually invisible decor—a cross between country inn and efficient motel (although the honeymoon cottage is more romantic, as befits the occasion). The practical setting suits perfectly those visiting Jackson for a healthy dose of outdoor exercise.

The cheery dining room serves some interesting food. Given the inn's understatedness, you'll be surprised by such dishes as crab ravioli with saffron and chives, sautéed scallops with asparagus and tomato, grilled salmon, veal scallops with Japanese eggplant and fried parsley, medallions of pork with endive, and grilled steak with red-wine sauce. And the fourteen blessedly peaceful acres make an after-dinner digestive stroll a delight.

Rooms: $124-$144, including breakfast and dinner.

The Inn at Thorn Hill

Thorn Hill Rd.
(603) 383-4242
Open year-round.
All major cards.

This is the house that Stanford White built, and a stately house it is. The Victorian architect, known for the Copley Church and Cambridge City Hall, endowed it with a distinctive gambrel roof and a peerless view of Mount Washington. The past lives on in the Victoriana-filled parlor and in the dining room, with its crackling fireplace and flickering hurricane lamps. The rooms—sixteen in all—combine antique furnishings and modern comfort: inviting beds and private baths. There's a VCR in the game room, and the spacious cottages behind the inn are equipped with working fireplaces.

One could never accuse chef Hoke Wilson of being old-fashioned: His specialties include smoked-chicken ravioli and fried-quail salad, each as prettily decked out as a debutante on her way to the prom. After dinner you can retire to the cozy, fire-warmed pub appropriately named "The Snug." But not before you've raided the kitchen for more of that irresistible chocolate bread, sure to ward off an attack of the midnight munchies. Dinner will run from $60 to $80 for two, with wine.

Rooms: $120-$140 per person, breakfast and dinner included.

Nestlenook Inn

Dinsmore Rd.
(off Rte. 16A)
(603) 383-9443
Open year-round.
Cards: MC, V.

Just as we were going to press, we discovered that the Nestlenook Inn had changed hands and closed for extensive renovations, which will be completed by the time you read these lines. We cannot provide a personal report (or a ranking), given the closing, but we can say that new owner Robert Crye is turning the once-rustic inn into a small but fairly lavish year-round resort. Crye hopes to make Nestlenook one of New Hampshire's leading Nordic ski centers, thanks to a complete ski shop, rental equipment, lessons and miles of cross-country trails in and around the property. Other wintertime amenities will include ice skating and sleigh rides—there will even be an honest-to-goodness one-horse open sleigh! And, of course, there's plenty of downhill skiing nearby (see "Mount Washington Valley"). Other seasons will see guests trout fishing, swimming in the pool, hiking, enjoying hay rides, touring nearby Ellis River and just plain relaxing.

The inn, formerly a family-farmhouse sort of place, is being redone from top to bottom in a Victorian style, complete with period antiques. Rooms are being enlarged and equipped with upscale amenities, and a full-service restaurant is under construction. All in all, Nestlenook has considerable promise.

Rooms: $135-$200, including breakfast.

Wildcat Inn
& Tavern
Rte. 16A
(603) 383-4245
Open year-round.
Cards: AE, MC, V.

The Wildcat Inn is an absolutely simple place designed to withstand the rigors of skiers, children and hearty mountain men. The sixteen rooms are unpretentious and rustic; some have bunk beds and private baths, and all have furnishings that look vaguely familiar. If you're a baby-boomer, it'll remind you of sleeping over at a friend's house in the '50s. You get what you see, for the Wildcat doesn't pretend to be anything else.

Extras include a pretty backyard garden, a lively, popular tavern and a very good dining room (see "Restaurants" above). A large box of antique trucks and cars will entertain young children waiting for dinnertime. The Wildcat is a manly sort of place, booming during ski season (see "Mount Washington Valley") and relaxing when everyone else is home watching the NBA playoffs.

Rooms: $60-$68, including breakfast.

SIGHTS

See Mount Washington Valley.

JAFFREY

INNS

Benjamin Prescott
Inn
Rte. 124 East
(603) 532-6637
Open year-round.
Cards: MC, V.

Richard Rettig is one of those rare individuals who seem to master anything they tackle. Business manager at Franklin Pierce College by day, a superb innkeeper by night, he has made the Benjamin Prescott Inn a fabulous place to visit— for the decor, the ambience, the food and the host. He is a perfectionist, his breakfast as flawless as his selection of the bed linens that coordinate with each room's individual decor.

Eleven rooms are scattered about the meandering 1820 house, which is full to the brim with toy bears (regular guests send him their own to add to the collection), antique postcards, decorative details and a willowware ceramic collection. One of the best rooms in the house is the John Adams Suite in the attic, with a sitting room overlooking the back forty, a lush bedroom and sleeping lofts tucked away behind curtains, making the place perfect for families of eight traveling together. The other rooms are a bit more modest but no less charming. The first-floor suite practically constitutes its own house, with a sitting room, two bedrooms, two bathrooms and a complete kitchen. All the rooms have private baths, are impeccably decorated and are tributes to Rettig's good taste.

Breakfast, served by candlelight in the dining/sitting room, is delicious—due, no doubt, to Rettig's training as a professional cook. And the egg casseroles, lemon loafs, blueberry tea cakes, pumpkin bread, crumb coffee cake and french toast are served on his charming blue-and-white china.

Rooms: $45-$110, including breakfast.

KEENE

QUICK BITES

176 Main
176 Main St.
(603) 357-3100
*Open Mon.-Sat. 11:30
a.m.-11 p.m., Sun. 5 p.m.-
11 p.m.*
Cards: AE, MC, V.

See Peter Christian's Tavern in Hanover; the name isn't the same, but the operation is.

LINCOLN

SIGHTS

Loon Mountain
Kincamagus Hwy
(603) 745-8111

Several miles south of Franconia Notch is this pleasant ski resort, particularly good for the intermediate skier. Along with seven chairlifts, there's a gondola that also whisks sightseers to the top of the mountain for summertime views. Ski-resort features include cross-country trails, snowmaking on almost the entire mountain, a complete ski school, rental and dining facilities and a lodge on the mountain.

> *We are always happy to hear about your discoveries and to receive your comments about ours. We want to give your letters the attention they deserve, so when you write to us, remember to state clearly exactly what you liked or disliked. Be concise, but convincing. Do take the time to argue your point.*

LITTLETON

INNS

Beal House Inn
247 W. Main St.
(Rte. 18 & Rte. 302)
(603) 444-2661
Open year-round.
All major cards.

If you spend Christmas with Brenda and Doug Clickenger at Beal House Inn, you'll wallow in romantic nostalgia, complete with Colonial costumes, antique cuisine, garland-strewn rooms, and stockings hung by the chimney with care. The Clickengers got into innkeeping for the fun of it, and they'll make sure you have fun, too. Their handsome 1833 farmhouse has fourteen bedrooms throughout its many levels and wings. Brenda's decorating instincts are sentimental: antique furnishings, canopy beds, fresh flowers in spring and restful color schemes. The Annex over the carriage house has smaller rooms and its own book-filled sitting room. The Garden Room has a massive high-post bed, the Blue Room has a climb-up-into-it high bed, and the Family Room has three beds, one of which has a canopy.

Guests eat breakfast in the comfortable, fireplace-warmed dining/sitting room with its twig chairs and antique kitchen paraphernalia. Doug prepares the creamy scrambled eggs served in milk-glass covered hens, french toast and oversized popovers, all of which Brenda serves dressed in 1800s clothes.

The Clickengers' antiques store is next door, much of the furniture in the inn is for sale, and nearby are some of the White Mountains' ski slopes. All of this, along with comfort and old-fashioned appeal, makes Beal House a charming alternative to the motel-style inns in the area.

Rooms: $40-$120, including breakfast.

Unless otherwise noted, the prices given for restaurants are for a complete dinner for two, including an appetizer, main course and dessert. The prices also include tax, fifteen-percent tip and one of the least expensive bottles of wine on the wine list. Please don't hold it against us if you end up spending a bit more!

LYME

RESTAURANTS

D'Artagnan
13 Dartmouth College
Hwy. (Rte. 10)
(603) 795-2137
FRENCH
Open Wed.-Sat. 6 p.m.-
9:15 p.m., Sun. noon-
1:15 p.m. & 6 p.m.-
9:15 p.m.
Cards: AE, MC, V.

In the restaurant-reviewing racket you learn to live with disappointment: places not measuring up to their reputations, entrées not living up to appetizers, pleasant meals sullied by grudging service. But on our last memorable afternoon at D'Artagnan, everything lived up to everything. We'd heard about the place for some time: The husband-and-wife team of chef/owners Rebecca Cunningham and Peter Gaylor are well known in the East. Peter's twin passions are fencing (thus the swashbuckling name) and cooking; he and Rebecca were prize students of Yannick Cam at Le Pavillon in D.C. Their place is in the basement of an old inn—wood beams, stencils, a primitive mural, glass doors looking out onto a shady garden and stream.

Our meal started out quite well with the rolls—firm-crusted, nonflaky, major rolls. A galantine of shrimp mousseline and some Scottish smoked salmon were fine, the latter especially silky and firm; but really, those rolls. . . . When the main courses arrived, we finally forgot about the rolls. Delicate filets of trout enclosed a salmon mousse, with mushroom duxelles and a beurre blanc sauce. After the first bite of this dish, one of our party shed a tear and began talking of old lovers and Mozart and other peak experiences. It was the kind of dish in which every bite is like a phrase of a song, each with its own full shape, and it played trills on the palate. But let's not forget the sautéed salmon on a bed of julienne vegetables—awfully good, with a rich sauce that needed only a touch to make its point. These entrées lived up beautifully to the ideals (but not the excesses) of nouvelle cuisine, each ingredient making its contribution in the grand counterpoint. Waiting for dessert, we sat buttering the last of our excellent rolls and staring dreamily into the garden. Then came a galette citron and a fruity charlotte: satisfactory, not oversweet codas, the kind of desserts that look so pretty you hate to tear into them. It was as near-perfect a meal as you're going to find for anything approaching these prices—which, at the Sunday afternoon meal, came to an amazing $48 for two, with tip and without wine. For that once-a-week lunch (which has a full menu), there are two prix-fixe meals for less than $20, and the prix-fixe dinner is $30. Menus change daily, to keep abreast of fresh ingredients. The wine list is as good as one would expect, and most of the selections are less than $30. Hey you, Chez Panisse: En garde!

INNS

Lyme Inn
Dartmouth College Hwy.
(Rte. 10)
(603) 795-2222
Closed 2 weeks in April &
3 weeks in Dec.
Cards: AE, MC, V.

The large yellow Lyme Inn (circa 1809) commands a powerful vantage point of the town green. The lovely three-story building is a welcome home-away-from-home for Dartmouth students' parents, leaf peepers, tourists from the West Coast, and East Coasters who want a good dinner and pretty room to escape from the ravages of business, children and community relations. (Some bring their children with them, as long as they are 8 years or older. There's a room perfect for them: Nine has a suite of hand-painted furniture and is connected to another charming room for the kids.) Each of the fourteen rooms is different, two share baths, and a few have working fireplaces. Owner Judy Siemons has done an admirable job creating the beautiful decor, making skillful use of canopy beds, soothing colors and even (in one room) black wicker. The third-floor rooms are smaller but still quite attractive.

Judy's husband, Fred, makes breakfast, which is served in dining rooms bedecked with beamed ceilings, antique baskets and samplers. Fred's french toast, homemade muffins and egg dishes are quite good. Dinner is pretty tasty, too; prime rib, roast leg of lamb and German Hasenpfeffer are popular with the regulars.

Amusements include Judy's craft boutique on the second floor, which features good-looking clothes and home items, all made locally. You can also explore the town of Lyme, walk along the Connecticut River and ride bikes, or simply use the inn as a restful stopping-off point en route to the White Mountains.

Rooms: $50-$95, including breakfast.

MANCHESTER

SIGHTS

Currier Gallery
of Art
192 Orange St.
(603) 669-6144
Open Tues.-Wed. & Fri.-
Sat. 10 a.m.-4 p.m., Thurs.
10 a.m.-10 p.m., Sun.
2 p.m.-5 p.m.

The Currier Gallery of Art is considered one of America's best small museums; its permanent collections of American and European art include works by Henri Matisse, John Singer Sargent, Frederic Remington and Alexander Calder. A special attraction is the small gallery displaying works on paper. Special exhibits rotate about every two months.

Admission free.

SHOPS

**Shop
at the Institute**
148 Concord St.
(603) 623-0313
*Open Mon.-Fri. 9:30 a.m.-
5 p.m.*

This small shop stocks an assortment of fairly standard craft items, many made by teachers at the Manchester Institute of Arts and Sciences. It's hard to get terribly excited about the inventory, but there's not much competition in Manchester.

MARLBOROUGH

INNS

**Thatcher Hill Inn
Bed & Breakfast**
Thatcher Hill Rd.
(off Rte. 124)
(603) 876-3361
Open year-round.
Cards: MC, V.

Cal Gage was lucky enough to inherit his ancestors' home, the extraordinarily handsome Thatcher Hill farmhouse, built in 1794 and complete with barn and 60 surrounding acres. He and his wife, Marge, abandoned the fast-paced advertising world to become innkeepers, with the goal of offering guests the kind of accommodations they appreciated during their own business and leisure trips. That's why you'll find towel-warming racks, toiletries, European showers in the Victorian bathtubs, lovely bed linens and a beautiful country-inn decor. We felt fortunate that the Gages have such high standards and good taste, since they created the inn as a place *they* would want to visit.

The seven rooms are beautifully decorated with individual color schemes, matching hand-woven rag rugs, handsome quilts and impressive beds. One of the most winsome rooms is Three, in the front of the house, with strawberry-print wallpaper, terrific twig furniture, a massive green iron bed and a sunny view. The Honeymoon Suite has a more urban look, with green colors, a four-poster bed, fireplace and a sitting area. Seven is patriotic in red, white and blue; a graphic quilt doubles as a wall hanging. All the rooms, in fact, are stunning. What makes the decor so special is its simplicity, restraint and coordination of color and furnishings. The parlor downstairs is elegant in rose and mauve, and the more relaxed sitting room has a fireplace, comfortable chairs and a cozy feeling. In the country dining room, you'll select from a breakfast buffet of fresh fruit with yogurt, homemade fruit breads and muffins and a variety of hot dishes with breakfast meats.

Thatcher Hill is a lovely getaway. The barn cupola has a great view, and Cal's collection of antique music boxes fills the house with delicate sounds. And the Gages are pleasant hosts who will make you a loyal overnight regular.

Rooms: $55-$75, including breakfast.

MEREDITH

SHOPS

Leighton/Tracy Gallery
Mill Falls Marketplace
(603) 279-4553
Open Mon.-Thurs. 10 a.m.-5:30 p.m., Fri.-Sat. 10 a.m.-9 p.m., Sun. 11 a.m.-5:30 p.m.

Tucked away halfway up the state is this second-story wonder. Unlike the ten League of New Hampshire Craftsmen shops, Leighton/Tracy brings in craftwork from all over the country, and the shop demonstrates exquisite taste. In addition to such unusual items as the Winnipesaukee Table, whose top is ornately carved with the flora and fauna of the lake, the gallery displays elegant ceramic sculpture, tables with basket forms as a base, and glass that is both functional and decorative. It also has a terrific selection of geometric woven rugs.

MILFORD

SIGHTS

American Stage Festival
Rte. 13
(603) 673-7515
Late June-late Sept.: hours vary.

Every summer the American Stage Festival mounts professional productions ranging from new works to stalwarts of the Broadway stage, and they're always worth checking out. The 500-seat theater is located ten miles west of Nashua, just over the Massachusetts border.

SHOPS

The Golden Toad Gallery
65 Elm St.
(603) 673-4307
Open Mon.-Sat. 10 a.m.-5:30 p.m., Sun. 1 p.m.-5 p.m.

A renovated home supplies the perfect setting for this collection of homey country crafts, which spill from every square inch of space. This is classic New Hampshire stuff—lacy pillows mounded on a bench, soft-sculpture animals nestled together and ceramic pots and kitchenware in abundance. Here and there, however, is a more contemporary note, such as small postmodern wooden clocks and colorful glass jewelry.

Some establishments change their closing times without warning. It is always wise to call ahead.

MOUNT WASHINGTON VALLEY

INNS

See Chocorua, Conway, Intervale, Jackson, Snowville, Tamworth.

SIGHTS

See also North Conway.

Mount Washington
Mount Washington
Chamber of Commerce
(603) 356-3171

You see the bumper stickers all over New England (and even on the streets of New York City): "This car climbed Mount Washington." It's no mean feat. The highest peak in the eastern United States (6,288 feet), Mount Washington has always fascinated explorers and tourists alike. Even in summer, the rugged peak is usually covered with snow, and the winds at the National Weather Service Observatory can be notoriously brutal. (The greatest wind speed ever recorded, 231 miles per hour, was clocked at its summit.) In winter, New Englanders frequently seek out hints on their own weather by asking, "What's it doing on top of Mount Washington?"

The road to the top is steep and hard on the gears, not to mention drivers' nerves. If you and your car are game, the auto route to the top begins at Glen House on Route 16 in Pinkham Notch. The privately owned road is open mid-May to mid-October, daily 7:30 a.m. to 6 p.m.; the toll is a costly $10 per car, plus $4 per adult and $3 per child (free under age 5). If you'd rather sit back and relax, hop on the Mount Washington Cog Railway, a three-hour steam-powered trip to the summit. It runs daily 9 a.m. to 5 p.m. and costs even more than the road: $27 per person (free for children under 6 who ride on an adult's lap). Once atop the mountain, you can enjoy the 52-acre state park and visit the Mount Washington Observatory Museum.

Mount Washington Valley
(603) 356-3171

Down in the valley, the small towns in the region—among them Albany, Bartlett, Conway, North Conway, Glen, Intervale, Jackson, Madison and Snowville—make excellent bases for exploring and particularly for partaking in the variety of winter sports popular in the area (see "Skiing" below). The Appalachian Mountain Club in Pinkham Notch

(603-466-2727) can acquaint you with the mountains and the valley through its year-round programs (guided hikes, workshops and seminars), all of which are open to both members and nonmembers. And for more information on any area attraction, call the Mount Washington Valley Chamber of Commerce at the number above.

Skiing

Mount Washington Valley is a skiers' paradise; from any of its small towns—Jackson, Conway, Intervale and others—you can reach several fine downhill-skiing mountains and the cross-country skier's dream come true: Jackson Ski Touring Center (603- 383-9355), which provides access to 100 miles of lovely trails. The best of the downhill mountains are Attitash (Route 302, Bartlett, 603-374-2369), a moderate-size, not-too-crowded resort popular with families; Mount Cranmore (North Conway, 603-356-5544), another midsize full-service resort that draws families; and Wildcat Mountain (Pinkham Notch, Jackson, 603-466-3326), which features challenging runs, great views, a gondola (which also runs in summer) and a lively crowd of young skiers, including lots of college students.

NASHUA

SHOPS

Options Gallery
115 Main St.
(603) 889-7676
*Open Mon.-Wed. & Fri.
9:30 a.m.-5:30 p.m.,
Thurs. 9:30 a.m.-9 p.m.,
Sat. 9:30 a.m.-5 p.m.*

This classy space carries an eclectic inventory: everything from African baskets to ceramic furniture to traditional prints. Surprisingly contemporary in its outlook, the store features exhibits between September and May.

NORTH CONWAY

INNS

See Conway, Intervale; in Maine, Center Lovell, Fryeburg.

QUICK BITES

Elvio's Pizza
Main St.
(603) 356-3307
*Open Sun.-Thurs. 11 a.m.-
10 p.m., Fri.-Sat. 11 a.m.-
11 p.m.
No cards.*

Some seven years ago, a rotund baker from New York City named Elvio moved to New Hampshire's White Mountains and opened a pizzeria. We're not about to dispute his claim that his is "the best pizza north of the Bronx." Elvio's specialty is a thin-crust pizza so crisp that it crunches when you bite into it. It's available with both red sauce and white—the latter a pungent mixture of garlic, mozzarella and ricotta cheese. But New York–style pizzas are only part of the story, for amid the clouds of flour and steam, the kitchen also turns out hearty deep-dish Sicilian pizzas and crusty calzones. Elvio recently renovated his storefront dining room. Another plus: His fabulous pizzas are available by the slice. About $13 for pizza and beer for two.

SIGHTS

See also Mount Washington Valley.

Conway Scenic Railroad
Rte. 16 & Rte. 302
(603) 356-5251
*May & Sept.-Oct.: hours
vary; June-Aug.: open
daily 10 a.m.-5:15 p.m.*

Though dominated by motels, fast-food restaurants and shops, North Conway, at the edge of the White Mountain National Forest and within sight of Mount Washington, remains a pleasant place for getting away from it all. Among its most popular attractions is the Conway Scenic Railroad near the junction of routes 16 and 302. Steam engines pull antique coaches on one-hour, eleven-mile trips through the lovely countryside.

Adults $5, children $3, children under 4 free.

SHOPS

League of New Hampshire Craftsmen
Main St.
(603) 356-2441
Open daily 9 a.m.-5 p.m.

The beauty of ski country is reflected in the representational work displayed here, which often takes nature as its theme. You may find a 3-D stained-glass pheasant, warmly quilted vests, tapestry jackets or bird carvings. Functional ceramics, rag rugs and a large children's section remind you that North Conway is a rural-shopper's paradise.

Richard Plusch
Rte. 16
(603) 356-3333,
383-9222
*June-Oct.: open daily
10 a.m.-5 p.m.; Nov.-May:
open by appt. or by chance.*

If you were to travel to this little shop every six months or so, you might get the impression that Richard Plusch loves his collection so much that he is unwilling to part with any of it. The same fabulous country-Chippendale chest, the same stunning marine oil and the same set of tempting George Jones majolica plates are right where you saw them during your last visit. But don't take a chance if you're hesitating over a purchase—many of his quite reasonably priced gems do move quickly. We've counted among our finds such pieces as a four-drawer Chippendale bureau, an 1820 shelf clock, a fabulous naïf drawing, Leedsware and a pair of children's beds. The shop is outcharmed only by its owner, who helps customers find pieces major or minor to stuff into the back of their Range Rovers or to lash on top of their Cherokee Chiefs for the long drive home.

ORFORD

INNS

White Goose Inn
Rte. 10
(603) 353-4812
Closed 2 weeks in March.
Cards: MC, V.

Karin and Manfred Wolf have created a stunning fifteen-room inn in an 1833 brick house, its wraparound porch containing the trunk of a large elm tree. The quiet exterior conceals a lovely, lush inn filled with Karin's brand of country crafts: Stencils, wreaths, pierced lampshades, quilts, pillows and hand-carved geese fill the pretty place. The rooms are decorated with a creative eye, and each has a charm of its own, thanks to rich pastel colors, beautiful beds, towel-filled baskets, handcrafted mirrors, lacy curtains and barnyard motifs. And you'll be reminded of whatever impending holiday you almost forgot via Karin's inventive displays (Easter eggs, valentines, Christmas trees) saluting the seasons.

Come breakfast, you'll sit in a ladderback chair at a pine table in the cozy dining room, which is dominated by a majestic fireplace mantle; the fare runs to raisin-bran muffins, pancake soufflés, sour-cream cake, cranberry bread and french toast. Afternoon tea offers scones, cookies and madeleines.

Rates: $65-$115, including breakfast.

PETERBOROUGH

SIGHTS

Monadnock Music

Monadnock Music, based in Peterborough, runs a well-known concert series each July and August. Concerts are given at various locations throughout the Monadnock region. See listing in "Music Festivals" chapter.

SHOPS

The Cobbs
83 Grove St.
(603) 924-6361
*Open Mon.-Sat. 9:30 a.m.-
5 p.m.*

This friendly shop is home to the occasional country-Chippendale tall bureau, Hepplewhite serving table and corner-shape sideboard, to Queen Anne chairs, country baskets and wooden trenchers, and perhaps even to a rare set of intricately carved shield-back chairs, with provenance (for a mere $19,000). Owner Charlie Cobb is pleasant and helpful, and the attic in his pretty yellow frame house looks much like your great-grandmother's, full of similarly nostalgic but, of course, costlier memories.

**North Gallery
at Tewksbery's**
Rte. 101E
(603) 924-3224
*Jan.-June: open Wed.-Sat.
10 a.m.-5 p.m., Sun.
1 p.m.-5 p.m.; July-Dec.:
open Mon. & Wed.-Sat.
10 a.m.-5 p.m., Sun.
1 p.m.-5 p.m.*

This converted 1812 barn in the town that inspired Thornton Wilder's *Our Town* houses both traditional and contemporary work by about 60 craftspeople. The barn's loft showcases paintings and graphics.

PINKHAM NOTCH

SIGHTS

See Mount Washington Valley.

PORTSMOUTH

RESTAURANTS

Blue Strawbery
29 Ceres St.
(603) 431-6420
AMERICAN
*Seatings Mon.-Sat. 6 p.m.
& 9 p.m., Sun. 3 p.m. &
6 p.m.
No cards (checks accepted).*

Every evening at 5:45, a well-dressed crowd gathers in front of an ancient brick building on a steep street next to Portsmouth's waterfront. The only sign of their destination is a brass plaque the size of a business card bearing the words *Blue Strawbery*. (No, this is not a spelling mistake—the first white settlers called the area Strawbery Banke.) At 6 p.m. the door opens, and the crowd enters an old ship's chandlery, its interior lined these days with antique paintings, massive ceiling beams and time-worn exposed-brick walls. Blue Strawbery was the brainchild of enfant terrible James Haller, and not the least of his accomplishments is the fact that his vision has survived even though he and his partners have parted ways. The $36 fixed-price menu still changes daily; it is still recited out loud; and the entrées—a mere three in number—are still served from mismatched platters, family style. The flavor combinations are as zany as ever: snails with black olives and feta cheese, swordfish with sea beans and lemon grass, New Hampshire veal sautéed with Dijon mustard and cèpes. As on numerous visits in the past, we had no trouble cleaning our plates. The wines change daily, too. Our waitress won our hearts by offering free tastes of two vintages that sorely tempted us. The dessert, thankfully, has not changed in the eighteen years Blue Strawbery has been open: an irresistible combination of fresh strawberries, sour cream and sugar. About $100 for two, with wine.

QUICK BITES

Gilly's PM Lunch
175 Fleet St.
(603) 431-6343
*Open Mon.-Sat. 11 a.m.-
3 a.m., Sun. 6 p.m.-3 a.m.
No cards.*

After making many a sentimental journey, this Worcester Dining Car Co. trolley car–cum–diner named after long-time employee Ralph Gilly has been stationed at Fleet Street for fourteen years. Every day for more than 55 years, Gilly religiously took the wagon to the town square, where he served sandwiches, burgers, Boston baked beans and franks from the tiny kitchen. Today, diners sit at soda-fountain stools in the black-and-yellow car, watching the tiny TV over the stove. It's an institution that demands a visit when you're in Portsmouth; the food is good, the price is right, and nostalgia runs rampant. A mere $5 will fill up two people.

INNS

See also Cape Neddick, Kennebunkport (both in Maine).

Sise Inn
40 Court St.
(800) 232-INNS
(603) 433-1200
*Open year-round.
All major cards.*

Sise Inn, an elegant place to stay in touristy Portsmouth, is a large inn that has been restored and decorated with a nice blend of reproduction furnishings, antiques and lovely wall-papers. The original 1881 Victorian home sets the theme, and the new wing gracefully added onto the back retains the appropriate feeling. Each of the 32 rooms has a private bath, a TV and VCR discreetly hidden behind a closed armoire or cabinet, a telephone, a ceiling fan and, in summer, air conditioning. Rooms vary from snug ones with Victorian beds to large ones with lofts, meeting tables and sitting areas; the overall colors run to dusty pale tones. The Honey-moon Suite is a duplex, while the carriage house has two suites with whirlpool baths and saunas. The point of view throughout is first-class, from the lush carpets to the tranquil atmosphere; you'll feel like you're staying in a miniature luxury hotel. A generous breakfast buffet is served downstairs: fresh fruit, yogurt, croissants, cereals, English muffins, and bagels with cream cheese.

Rooms: $78-$120, including breakfast.

SIGHTS

Along with the history-rich sights in the listings below, Portsmouth has a few other noteworthy places and/or events to see. Families should check out the Children's Museum in the South Meeting House (280 Marcy Street; 603-436-3853), which presents hands-on exhibits that include a Yellow Submarine, a computer center and a lobstering exhibit. If you visit Portsmouth in summer, we suggest you pay a visit to Prescott Park on Marcy Street, the site of a running arts festival with craft displays and performances. In fact, visit the park in spring and fall, too, when its gardens peak. And to remind you of Portsmouth's seafaring history, one of New Hampshire's oldest cruise lines, the Isle of Shoals Steamship Co., operates the *Thomas Laighton*, a 90-foot diesel-powered steamboat replica, to the offshore Isle of Shoals twice daily from mid-June to early September. Tickets cost $10; the boat leaves from Market Street. The cruise line also offers whale-watches and dinner cruises. For more information, call (603) 431-5500.

Portsmouth Trail
(603) 436-1118
June-mid-Oct.: hours vary.

Even outside acclaimed Strawbery Banke (see below), Portsmouth has its share of historic houses. The Portsmouth Trail covers six of them, including the 1759 John Paul Jones House, Middle and State streets; the Georgian-style Wentworth Gardner Mansion on Mechanic Street, once the official governor's residence, showing changes in architecture from the 1690s to the 1750s; the Warner House, 150 Daniel Street, which has stood relatively unchanged since it was built in 1715; and the Gov. John Langdon Mansion, 143 Pleasant Street, where George Washington was a guest. Call the chamber of commerce at the number above to find out which houses are open when, or stop in at the chamber's office, 500 Market Street, to pick up a ticket book covering admission to all six houses for $6—roughly half the price of the regular admission.

Admission $2-$2.50 per house, $6 for all 6.

Strawbery Banke
Marcy St.
(603) 433-1107
*May-Oct.: open daily
10 a.m.-5 p.m.*

No contest—the biggest and best show in this city built where the Piscataqua River meets the Atlantic Ocean is Strawbery Banke, a ten-acre complex that's part museum and part boutique. The Marcy Street site includes 35 homes dating from the seventeenth to the nineteenth century, 30 of them on their original sites. Exhibits focus on early construction techniques, gardening and New England archaeology.

Adults $6, seniors $5, children $3, family rate $15.

SANDWICH

SHOPS

Sandwich Home Industries
Main St.
(603) 284-6831
*Mid-May-Oct.: open daily
10 a.m.-5 p.m.; hours may
vary.*

This tiny village was instrumental in founding a movement to promote the state's crafts, and the small white building on the town common sells small-scale work that has the distinct feel of being produced just around the corner, along with crafts from around the state. Look for hooked and braided rugs, leather, woven items and prints.

SHARON

SHOPS

Sharon Arts Center
Rte. 123
(603) 924-7256
*Open Mon.-Sat. 10 a.m.-
5 p.m., Sun. 1 p.m.-5 p.m.*

This teaching center sponsors seven to eight yearly exhibits of fine arts and crafts. The adjacent store sells the work of some 350 New Hampshire craftspeople, who occasionally give demonstrations of their techniques.

> *The prices listed in this guide reflect what restaurants and hotels have informed us they plan to charge at press time. Please don't blame us if they don't coincide exactly with reality.*

SHELBURNE

INNS

Philbrook Farm Inn
North Rd. (off Rte. 2)
(603) 466-3831
*Closed April & Oct.
31-Dec. 26. Cash or
personal check only.*

The Philbrooks have managed to hold onto this extraordinary inn for 127 years, keeping the 1861 farmhouse in the family for five generations. Visiting their lovely inn is like going back in time. The rooms are farmhouse simple, with beautiful tiger-maple and bird's-eye furnishings, understated fabrics and country coverlets. The nineteen-room house is surrounded by five summer cottages.

Philbrook is sort of like upscale camp. There's a game room in the basement for kids, a Victorian parlor filled with memorabilia and scrapbooks of the farm's history, beautiful gardens in summer and 1,000 acres surrounding the house, which hold enough activities to tire out even the most stubborn 3-year-old. Dinner is unimaginative and totally safe, perfect for camp: Sunday roast chicken, baked beans and ham with brown bread, pot roast, and New England fishballs with cornbread.

Days can be spent exploring the swimming holes, cross-country trails, hiking paths and the most amazing forest of silvery birch trees. First-time visitors often start their own traditions here; in fact, many guests have been returning throughout several of their own families' generations. Some of the rooms are even named after these loyal families, which must make the inn more like coming home than coming home.

Rooms: $110-$176, including breakfast and dinner.

SNOWVILLE

INNS

Snowvillage Inn
Off Brownfield Rd.
(off Rte. 153)
(603) 447-2818
*Closed April & first 2
weeks of Nov.
All major cards.*

From the porch of the Snowvillage Inn, the snow-covered peak of Mount Washington looms almost close enough to touch. But the breathtaking view of the Presidential Range is only part of what makes this secluded inn such a tonic for the tired traveler. Located on the side of Foss Mountain, Snowvillage offers tennis on clay courts and hiking and cross-country skiing on 150 acres of woodlands, not to mention the tranquility of book-lined parlors, a blazing hearth and award-winning English gardens. The Snowvillage Inn was built in 1916 as a summer home for historian Frank Simonds; the current owners are Frank Peter and Trudy Cutrone, the latter a fine cook with a charming Austrian accent. The inn's fourteen rooms have been renovated, and as we went to press, the owners were in the process of building six new rooms, each with fireplace and private bath. The dining room bathes you in the romance of oil lamps and red-checked tablecloths. Loaves of bread are baked fresh each day.

Rooms: $130, including breakfast and dinner; special packages available.

SIGHTS

See Mount Washington Valley.

SUNAPEE

INNS

Seven Hearths Inn
Old Rte. 11
(603) 763-5657
Closed April & 2 weeks in Nov.
Cards: MC, V.

Miguel Ramirez does things with panache. For wife Marianne's 40th birthday, he invited her closest friends to Seven Hearths for a festive black-tie celebration. The Ramirezes became so enamored with the place that they bought it a week later. Today, they run the handsome ten-room inn with style and attention to upscale detail, making it a welcome escape in an area otherwise dominated by run-of-the-mill inns and restaurants. And the kitchen at Seven Hearths is one of the better ones in New Hampshire.

Marianne has decorated the bedrooms with sophistication. Devoid of typical country-inn clutter and cuteness, Seven Hearths is refined and elegant. Count Rumford fireplaces blaze away during the winter; the rooms have beamed ceilings and pastel dhurrie rugs and are filled with fresh flowers and flowering plants year-round. Outside is an impressive deep-black granite pool that reminds us of a black lagoon, and there are five acres for walking in complete privacy. Back inside, the tranquil living room has contemporary seating, a grand piano and a fieldstone fireplace. Hors d'oeuvres are served here to get diners in the mood for an excellent dinner, which runs to such sophisticated fare as vichyssoise, grilled fresh tuna with red-wine sauce, sautéed scallops with lemon-chive butter, asparagus with tomato hollandaise, grilled swordfish with shrimp butter, roast leg of lamb en croûte and filet mignon with a blue cheese–horseradish cap. And the desserts—perhaps the irresistible chocolate custard with toasted almonds and Chantilly cream—will finish you off indulgently. Then, after a sound sleep, it's time to eat again! Breakfast is served in the same country dining rooms: home-baked pastries, breads, apple pancakes and french toast.

Rooms: $73-$138, including breakfast.

TAMWORTH

INNS

Gilman Tavern
Main St.
(603) 323-8940
Closed April-May.
Cash or personal check only.

If you can't make it to Vermont's Shelburne Farms Museum to tour its overwhelming collection of American antiques, folk art and crafts, come instead to Gilman Tavern, an enchanting inn run by the talented Sue McCarthy and her husband, Bill. The four-room inn is a virtual tribute to folk and country art. The house is overflowing with yellowware, antique clothes, painted hat boxes, clipper-ship models, stoneware, Shaker boxes and baskets, stencils, quilts, Pennsylvania Dutch–country pieces, wall murals, needlework and a collection of handsome beds and antique coverlets. The living room is dense with these naïf treasures, as are the lovely bedrooms. The Village Room has a canopy bed, stenciled pickled-wood floors, a doll house filled with bears, and a view of the village. The Swift River Room echoes this front room; the Herb Garden Room has children's toys and clothes, circa 1860; and the Mountain View Room has high solid-maple twin beds. Bathrooms combine a country look with (thankfully) modern fixtures.

Breakfast is served in the dining room on antique plates with crystal. Sue makes breads, muffins, french toast and a variety of egg dishes, served with country sausage, bacon and fresh fruit.

Rooms: $60-$85, including breakfast.

DON'T FORGET: Gault Millau introduces you to the Best of New York, the Best of Washington D.C., the Best of Los Angeles, the Best of San Francisco, the Best of Chicago, the Best of France, the Best of Paris, the Best of Italy, the Best of London.

TEMPLE

RESTAURANTS

The Birchwood Inn
Rte. 45
(603) 878-3285
INTERNATIONAL
Open Tues.-Sat. 6 p.m.-8:30 p.m.
No cards.

12/20

Sitting beside the exquisite little town green in lovely little Temple, New Hampshire, the cozy Birchwood Inn is decked out with the usual Yankee-inn trappings, down to the antique toys and the parlor cat. Patrons of the restaurant are a mix of inn guests, locals doing the town and not a few outlanders willing to take a long drive for the food. The small dining rooms (one with a classic New England primitive mural) are stages for some excellent cookery by the innkeepers. There are three entrées each night—meat, fish and veal—and on Saturday night the owner presents his specialty, a duck à l'orange that is one of the better in our memory. Like the entire place, the food is lovingly done: One tends to leave with the feeling, however temporary, that all's right with the world. Bring your own wine, and expect to pay about $40 for two.

WATERVILLE VALLEY

SIGHTS

Waterville Valley
Rte. 49
(603) 236-8371

Nestled within the White Mountain National Forest and certainly New Hampshire's most complete and elegant ski resort, Waterville Valley is a privately owned, completely self-contained haven for the athlete. Wintertime finds visitors skiing the two mountains (Mount Tecumseh and Snow's Mountain), exploring the miles of cross-country trails, snowshoeing and ice skating. Come summer, they make use of the eighteen-hole golf course, the abundance of clay tennis courts, the rental bicycles, the hiking trails, the swimming pools and the nearby fishing. For information on condo rentals and other lodging, call the number above.

Remember to phone ahead to reserve your table or your room and please, if you cannot honor your reservation, be courteous and let the restaurant or the hotel know.

344

WEIRS BEACH

SIGHTS

Weirs Beach may be a small town, but it's one of the gateways to the biggest of New Hampshire's many mountain lakes, the majestic Winnipesaukee. The lake, whose name translates from the Indian as "beautiful water in a high place," covers 72 square miles and is bordered by sandy beaches, forests and vacation homes. Weirs Beach itself seems to be dominated by arcades, palm readers and water slides, but it redeems itself as the home port of the *Mount Washington*, a 230-foot steamer that carries up to 1,250 passengers on a three-hour, 50-mile cruise around the mountain-ringed lake and its more than 200 islands. The boat leaves Weirs Beach at 9 a.m. and 12:15 p.m., making a stop at Wolfeboro across the lake. The *Mount Washington* (603-366-5531) runs from late May to mid-October; adults are $11, kids are $5, and kids under 5 are free. For those who prefer to travel under sail, the *Queen of Winnipesaukee*, a 46-foot sloop, also runs excursions from Weirs Beach from late May to early October. For cruise schedules and reservations, call (603) 524-1911.

WEST OSSIPEE

QUICK BITES

The Yankee Smokehouse
Rte. 16 & Rte. 25 West
(603) 539-7427
Summer: open daily 11:30 a.m.-9 p.m.; fall & spring: open Thurs.-Sun. 11:30 a.m.-9 p.m.; hours may vary.
No cards.

"We will sell no swine before its time," reads the slogan on the staff's T-shirts. Welcome to one of the best rib joints north of the Mason-Dixon line. Yankee Smokehouse owners Lloyd and Mary Ann Kerr, who learned their pitsmanship in Florida, smoke all their meats over maplewood fires in a towering cinder-block smokehouse. The hearty rib and chicken dinner for two (about $24) is the restaurant's bestseller, but we would also like to put in a good word for the luscious baked beans. The furnishings run to picnic tables and inexpensive paneling. The long lines of contented customers attest to the quality of the food.

WESTMORELAND

INNS

Partridge Brook Inn
Hatt Rd. (off Rte. 63)
(603) 399-4994
Open year-round.
Cards: MC, V.

Renee and Don Strong have turned a 1790 farmhouse that once served as a safe house during slavery times into an elegant, comfortable country inn. The original owner, Abiathar Shaw, must have been affluent, for the house retains traces of style and luxury. The downstairs parlor room is superb—the beautiful circular floor stencils, intricate woodwork and Indian shutters date from the original house. A king-size bed and private bath make this a unique and luxurious sleeping room. The Shaws' master bedroom upstairs, another showpiece, boasts similar woodwork detailing, another lovely fireplace and sought-after spaciousness. The other four bedrooms are equally wonderful, albeit slightly smaller in scale. All the beds are large—the king-size canopies look something like lace-topped circus tents. The Brass Room has a royal-size brass bed and a brass single bed. All the bedrooms have fireplaces, lovely fabrics and modern baths. In the common rooms, barn-siding meets city sophistication with great success. Renee has used elegant wallpaper in the front room, but wicker furnishings in the back room create a more relaxed, summer look. The living room is ruled by the original cooking hearth, and the original barn-siding is still in the dining room.

Renee serves a civilized breakfast of apple pie, french toast with cream cheese, walnuts and fruit sauce, whole-wheat pancakes and homemade muffins. After breakfast, you can fish for trout in Partridge Brook, hike or help Don with his 500 blueberry bushes.

Rooms: $65-$80, including breakfast.

MAINE

AUGUSTA

SIGHTS

Augusta, Maine's capital, also serves as the state's hub, the link between the coastal cities and the sparsely populated north. The towering Capitol building, built of granite quarried just a few miles away, is open to visitors Monday to Friday 8 a.m. to 5 p.m. (207-289-1110). Also worth a visit in the Capitol complex on State Street is the Maine State Museum. Once primarily a museum of natural history, it has expanded greatly in recent years to show a broader picture. Those in doubt would do well to walk through the "Made in Maine" exhibit, which takes in the state's industries, from nineteenth-century mills to present-day production. The museum (207-289-2301) is open Monday to Friday 9 a.m. to 5 p.m., Saturday 10 a.m. to 4 p.m., Sunday 1 p.m. to 4 p.m.; admission is free.

Augusta's location on the banks of the Kennebec River makes it a perfect site for the Great Kennebec River Whatever Race, a parade of anything that will float. The eight-mile race from Augusta to Gardiner is the highlight of Whatever Week, an annual ten-day festival held in late June. For more information, call the Kennebec Valley Chamber of Commerce at (207) 623-4559.

BAR HARBOR & MOUNT DESERT ISLAND

RESTAURANTS

The Brick Oven Restaurant
21 Cottage St., Bar Harbor
(207) 288-3708
AMERICAN
May-Oct.: open nightly
5 p.m.-9 p.m.
Cards: AE, MC, V.

If at first you don't see the new Brick Oven Restaurant, persevere—this delightful place is well worth seeking out. Owner Fred Pooler and his wife, Susan Jackson (of the same Jackson family that feeds and shelters Bar Harbor guests so well), have created a magical restaurant that will thrill antique-toy collectors. An entrepreneurial craftsman, Fred is in love with old toy trucks, cars, trains, mechanical dioramas—seemingly everything amusing from generations past. Above the bar is an old country-store scene, complete with gas pump and nostalgic signs; a marionette show lurks above the door. Cases and shelves of toys provide the perfect entertainment for children who are bored with their parents' conversations. Setting the stage for Pooler's collection is a bright-white interior with Victorian tin paneling, arched church windows and the occasional church-pew bench.

The hearty, generous, casual food suits the decor perfectly. The satisfying starters include clam chowder, onion soup, baked mushrooms and fresh, crunchy salads with ten vegetables. Pastas are filled with perfectly cooked seafood or dressed with good old spaghetti sauce with meatballs. Entrées run to grilled steaks; some more complex, mannered dishes like sole Florentine and chicken Cordon Bleu; fresh Maine seafood, fried and served with traditional tartar sauce; and lobster served four different ways (we like it boiled with drawn butter). And the broiled shellfish and North Atlantic fish are always fresh and perfectly cooked. Desserts, as dense as the entrées, include chocolate mousse, chocolate-mousse cake, lemon-mousse pie and chocolate layer cake. True, some of the dishes could use a lighter touch with sauces, but there is something wonderfully nostalgic about indulging in this type of old-fashioned, satisfying American fare. About $40 for two, with wine or beer.

INNS

Cleftstone Manor
92 Eden St. (Rte. 3),
Bar Harbor
(207) 288-4951
Closed mid-Oct.-mid-May.
Cards: AE, MC, V.

Phyllis Jackson would abhor living in a vacuum. Her lush inn is filled to the brim with Victorian and European furniture and objects. She collects lace, dolls, silver, crystal candelabra—a host of decorative details that may make the claustrophobic feel slightly faint. And the collection grows steadily: She and her husband, Donald, escape to Europe every winter to stock up on more Schloss-size furniture for Cleftstone. But we don't find the place annoyingly cluttered; instead, the dense decor has a calming effect, possibly due to the rich carpeting and sound-absorbing tapestries hanging around the house.

The sixteen bedrooms are as dramatic and lavish as the common rooms, and each is named after someone Phyllis admires (Tennyson, Churchill, Keats, Wilde, Gainsborough, Sherlock Holmes, Romeo and Juliet), usually someone from the England she adores. The suite named after the young lovers is something to reckon with. Part of the original ballroom, it is enormous, with a monumental fireplace, oversized bed and romantic decor. But all the rooms are impressive and ornately furnished.

The overflowing decor is matched by the Jacksons' gracious service. Phyllis, never lacking in energy and the desire to please, serves a generous buffet breakfast on the wicker-furnished porch: fresh fruit, yogurt, English teas, home-baked breads, muffins and coffee cakes. Afternoon high tea is poured, and a midnight snack is served by candlelight, in the impressive dining room. You can also order a picnic lunch to take with you for a Sunday in the country.

Rooms: $80-$175, including breakfast.

Grey Rock Inn

Rte. 198, Northeast Harbor
(207) 276-9360 (summer),
(207) 276-5526 (winter)
Closed Nov.-May.
Cash or personal check only.

If you had had the foresight to invest in one of the summer cottages of the once-rich-and-famous when you were raising six children, perhaps you, too, would have converted your jewelbox of a home into an inn, room by room, as your progeny left home. That's what Janet Millet did, and she's now the proud owner of one of the loveliest inns in New England. You'll think you've died and gone to country-inn heaven if you stay in the downstairs suite, which has a canopy bed, lovely Japanese screen, impressive carved furniture, handsome fireplace and luxurious space. But the upstairs rooms are just as stunning, albeit with a more feminine touch, as befits the feminine, British-born Janet. Most of them have sensational views of the harbor, and all have private baths.

Breakfast is served in the sunny living room, converted overnight into a separate-tables breakfast nook. On the menu are fresh fruit and the cheese and blueberry danishes, honey buns, blueberry turnovers, pecan buns and croissants that are all baked in the Millet kitchen. Victorian lace and a decidedly soft touch abound, but even the most manly man will enjoy a stay here, pampered and seduced by such lovely surroundings.

Rooms: $90-$150, including breakfast.

The Inn at Canoe Point

Rte. 3, Hulls Cove
(207) 288-9511
Open year-round.
Cash or personal check only.

Sometimes even the most dedicated fan of the sweet country inn gets fed up with Laura Ashley wallpapers and bed linens, Victorian bureaus and beds, dense clutter, canopies and lace curtains. That's what makes The Inn at Canoe Point so refreshing. Owner Don Johnson (no, not that one) has done an admirable job of decorating his exquisite little inn in a contemporary, clean-lined, stylish way. The six bedrooms are lovely. The Garden Room is one of the most charming: Large windows overlook the garden, with a view of Frenchman Bay just beyond, and pale beige colors, a private entrance and a sitting area with a fireplace create a warm haven. The Master Suite is also attractive, with a fireplace, a deck, handsome furnishings and a peaceful view. Johnson has done a marvelous job of keeping things simple, from the striped sheets and colorful plaid comforters to the clean colors and uncluttered decor.

Breakfast is served in the sunny sitting room overlooking the water (or on the deck during the summer): blueberry pancakes, french toast, Cheddar quiche, fresh fruit and homemade breads. The oversized granite fireplace is welcome in winter, as is its fieldstone partner in the more formal foyer seating area. One visit to this enchanting inn will turn you into a regular, ready to brave the Maine winter for a shot of civilized living.

Rooms: $50-$190, including breakfast.

The Tides
119 West St., Bar Harbor
(207) 288-4968
Open year-round.
Cards: MC, V.

This large Victorian home is well situated on a rolling lawn, with a peaceful view of Frenchman Bay and its own rocky beach. You may feel compelled to take off your shoes as you enter, faced with a sea of ivory wall-to-wall carpeting that contributes to The Tides' sense of serenity. Owned by Susan and Barry Jackson (a son of the Jackson innkeeping dynasty), the inn is a tribute to gracious, luxurious living. The oversized living and dining rooms are simply beautiful, with creamy walls and mauve and pale- blue detailing. Upstairs is a sitting room that's larger than most city-dwellers' apartments. And each of the (only) three bedrooms is palatial in size and elegantly furnished with Victorian and Empire pieces that preserve the original tone of the house. The Master Suite has a separate dressing room, as well as a balcony, canopy bed and fireplace; the more modest Center Room is a period-perfect tribute to Victoriana and has its own view of the bay; and the lovely apricot-and-blue East Room boasts its own balcony. All the beds are queen-size, the bathrooms are as beautiful as the bedrooms, and a sense of refinement pervades the house.

Breakfast is served in the formal dining room, a stage set for Susan's fabulous meals: delightful shirred eggs with bacon rings, sausage soufflé, crêpes, pancakes and baked french toast, along with homemade muffins and breads. The entire Tides experience is a treat. A visit here will bring forth the good taste you've always known you had—somewhere.

Rooms: $150-$175, including breakfast.

SIGHTS

The largest of Maine's islands and the third largest on the East Coast, Mount Desert comprises 22 square miles of such varied environments as the unspoiled beauty of Acadia National Park, of which the island forms only a part, and the rich resort of Bar Harbor. The island's primitive landscape of spectacular mountains, lakes and ponds, cut by glaciers in ice ages past, entices travelers to take the scenic route, Ocean Drive on the eastern side. We suggest then driving to the summit of Cadillac Mountain for panoramic views of the island and Maine's coast.

It's no wonder that Bar Harbor, as well as such neighboring villages as Hulls Cove and Northeast Harbor, attracts so many well-to-do vacationers and cruise ships, given its location on Mount Desert and its up-to-the-minute shops and galleries. A summertime center for the arts, it boasts among other attractions the annual Bar Harbor Festival, which has nurtured hundreds of young musicians for almost a quarter of a century. The series, which runs from mid-July to mid-August, includes jazz and chamber-music performances, pops concerts and even musical teas, all centered at the Bar Harbor Congregational Church. For schedules and ticket information, call (207) 288-5744. For information on other Bar Harbor activities and on accommodations, call (207) 288-5103; for information on the entire island, call (207) 288-3411.

If you'd like to blend in with the natives while in Bar Harbor and environs, remember to pronounce the name of the island *Mount Dessert*, as if it were a sweet treat after the main course rather than a hot, sandy expanse. The pronunciation originated with Samuel de Champlain, the French explorer who discovered the area in 1604. He dubbed it *L'Isle des Monts Déserts* or "island of deserted mountains" for its bare-rocked summits, punctuated only by the occasional scrub pine tree. More than 200 years have elapsed since the island's first permanent English settlement in 1763, but the steadfast Mainers stick with their own Down East version of the French pronunciation.

Mount Desert Island is approached via a small bridge from Trenton, southeast of Ellsworth. The *Blue Nose–to–Nova Scotia* car ferry also leaves from Bar Harbor, and if you're extending your trip into Canada's Maritime Provinces, it's a pleasant way to shave off hundreds of driving miles. For schedules and reservations, call (207) 288-3395.

SHOPS

Caleb's Sunrise
115 Main St., Bar Harbor
(207) 288-3102
*Memorial Day-Labor Day:
open daily 9 a.m.-11 p.m.;
off-season hours vary.*

The clean, open design of this store serves as backdrop for a variety of woodenware, leather bags, ceramics and graphics. The quality ranges from exquisite inlaid knives and letter openers to the standard tourist trinkets.

Island Artisans
99 Main St., Bar Harbor
(207) 288-4214
*May-Oct.: open daily
10 a.m.-10 p.m.*

Visitors sated with stuffed red-plush lobsters can step into this co-op and find a good selection of porcelain and stoneware, weaving, silkscreen prints and stained glass. The eleven artists represented all live on Mount Desert Island, and its rugged beauty permeates their work.

BATH

SIGHTS

One of America's shipbuilding capitals, Bath was once America's fifth-largest seaport, and until the turn of the century it supported more than 200 shipbuilding firms. Although the industry has sharply declined in the decades since, the Bath Iron Works still produces vessels for the U.S. Navy and Merchant Marine. Visitors to the city may get an overview of the shipyards from the Route 1 bridge just outside town. For a historical perspective, visit the Maine Maritime Museum's Sewall House, 963 Washington Street (207-443-1316), and its restored ten-acre shipyard on the Kennebec River, where traditional shipbuilding crafts are demonstrated. The museum is open mid-May to mid-October, daily 10 a.m. to 5 p.m.; admission is $4.50 for adults and $2 for children under 16. Bath also boasts a historic district of restored mansions of sea captains and shipbuilders, making the town eminently suitable for strolling.

BELFAST

RESTAURANTS

Penobscot Meadow Inn
Rte. 1
(207) 338-5320
AMERICAN
*Open nightly 5:30 p.m.-
9 p.m. Cards: Discover,
MC, V.*

The excellent cooking is the first reason to visit this comfortable, attractive inn on the edge of the charming town of Belfast, but the owners' warm, genuine hospitality runs a close second. At our last visit, our party elected to stay on the open deck intended for cocktails to watch an incoming storm boil across the countryside, rather than be sensible and move to the pleasant glassed-in porch. We were brought cushions for greater comfort and a candle to fight the flies (didn't work), and our meal was served with as much serenity and courtesy as if we were sane. And the meal was as good as the dinner show. The mushroom caps, firm, moist and filled with herbs, bubbled cheerfully in a cheese sauce; the swordfish steak had an orange hollandaise napping; and the chicken in brandy sauce with red grapes, like the other entrées, was surrounded by fresh, bright flowers. Desserts always feature two or three flavors of homemade ice cream, and on this memorable occasion, lemon mousse in a chocolate shell circled with raspberry sauce was consumed seconds before the downpour. A lot of very good food and drama for about $65 for two, with wine.

SHOPS

Goose River Craft Collection
48 Main St.
(207) 338-1168
Open Mon.-Sat. 9 a.m.-5 p.m.

Traditional New England crafts go with the coast of Maine as lobster goes with sweet corn, and these are about as archetypal as they come. Wooden and woven things predominate, and a stop here provides an excellent break on the drive up to Bar Harbor.

BOOTHBAY HARBOR

RESTAURANTS

Fisherman's Wharf Inn
40 Commercial St. (Pier 6)
(207) 633-5090
AMERICAN
Summer: open daily 11:30 a.m.-2:30 p.m. & 5 p.m.-9 p.m.; off-season hours vary. All major cards.

10/20

Fisherman's Wharf, which sits on a pier that dates back more than 100 years, first opened its doors in 1946. But you'll be pleased to hear that it has added such modern amenities as air conditioning and has put in enough glass to afford the best possible view of Boothbay's frenetic little harbor; if you're lucky, you'll see one of the great windjammer schooners glide into home port. The menu treats the local produce (lobsters, clams, scallops, mussels, halibut) with the respect for tradition that you'd expect from such a venerable restaurant. You can get your scallops deep-fried or broiled and your lobster boiled plain or tucked into a stew or Newburg; the other dishes are no more exotic. Pork chops are served with applesauce, chicken with cranberries, and steak with mushrooms, and the most daring side dish (in capital letters on the menu) is SPECIAL ONION RINGS. Exciting this place isn't, but all of the above are freshly prepared with skill and an eye to visual appeal. Somewhat unexpectedly, the place takes wine pretty seriously, suggesting something appropriate in italics after each entrée. The broiled chopped sirloin, for example, rates a Beaujolais Villages or Chianti Classico; a Muscadet or Pinot Blanc is paired with the fried fresh Maine clams. Personally, we prefer a beer with our hamburger or fried clams, but those with more refined tastes will appreciate the restaurant's concern. And you'll appreciate the prices: Even if you go for wine, two people shouldn't spend more than $35 for dinner—unless, of course, you opt for a lobster blowout.

Gilchrist's East

Commercial St.
(Waterfront)
(207) 633-5692
AMERICAN
*Summer: open daily
11:30 a.m.-2:15 p.m. &
5:30 p.m.-11 p.m.; off-
season hours vary.
All major cards.*

11/20

Gilchrist's provides a quiet retreat from the bustle of downtown Boothbay Harbor, yet it still gives you a panoramic view of the bay. The menu harbors no surprises, but the restaurant has come up with an innovation that will appeal to those who can never make up their minds: a fixed-price menu that includes *everything*. Well, not quite everything, but the "Candlelight Dinner" does present (in order of appearance): a lettuce and vegetable salad, a glass of white wine, broiled haddock, fresh broccoli, a glass of red wine, tenderloin strips with béarnaise sauce, a demitasse and a mint—all for $14.95. The trick is that the portions are tiny, served on little bitty plates in the aforementioned candlelight. It's fun for a change, and children love it (parents can drink their wine). But if you're not in a multicourse mood, you can choose from among twenty other entrées. Or if you're just a tad indecisive, try the seafood sampler, which has a nice variety and lets you choose your own beverage. Whatever you select, don't pass up the rum chocolate mousse for dessert. As you've undoubtedly deduced from the Candlelight Dinner tab, this is not a pricey place: $30 should do two of you just fine, with wine.

INNS

See Wiscasset.

SIGHTS

If your idea of something to do on vacation is actually doing something, Boothbay Harbor is the place to go in Maine. Next to Portland, it has more in the way of activities than most Mainers can deal with. The harbor town is located on one of those prototypical ragged peninsulas that offer the traveler blessed relief from Route 1. Route 27, just north of Wiscasset, takes you down to the harbor (shaped, by some natural whimsy, like a lobster claw), where there are a bed for every breakfast and no shortage of cabins, cottages, campgrounds, motels and inns (for lodging information, contact the chamber of commerce at 203-633-2353).

Once settled in, you can leave your car where it is and either walk or take the summer trolley to the many clothing, gift and antiques shops that crowd the main street. For high-quality, rigorously conservative clothing, try the House of Logan on Townsend Avenue; for gentle, beautifully made ceramic sculptures of seagulls, seals and other local fauna, visit the Anderson Studio in East Boothbay.

Most of the goings-on, naturally, center on the surrounding sea. July offers Windjammer Days, the area's biggest draw, when the tall ships parade through the harbor under full sail for a three-day celebration that also includes lobster-boat races, live music, fireworks and an antique-boat parade. The smaller but classically lovely Friendship sloops also get together in Boothbay for two days of racing. August brings bluefish- and tuna-fishing tournaments; come fall, there's the annual Fall Foliage Country Fair. For details on these events, call the chamber of commerce at the number provided above.

Between events you can amuse yourself at the Marine Aquarium at McKown Point (203-633-5572); visit Railway Village (203-633-4727), a re-created early Maine village complete with a steam narrow-gauge train and antique autos and trucks; get a gull's-eye view of the area from Downeast Flying Service (203-882-6752); take in a play at either the Boothbay Dinner Theatre (203-633-6186) or the Carousel Music Theatre (203-633-5297) (parts of the movie *Carousel* were filmed in Boothbay, and the town has never forgotten it). Or take advantage of one of the many opportunities to get out on the water—excursions, charters and day trips abound. You can haul a few lobster traps, watch seals, whales or puffins, fish for anything that's out there, go to a lobster bake or simply cruise around, under sail or motor, the little coves and islands that dot the area. Try the Argo & Linekin II cruises at Pier 6 (203-633-4925) or Cap'n Fish's at Pier 1 (203-633-3244).

If all this activity gets to be too much, take a day trip to ruggedly beautiful and relatively unspoiled Monhegan Island, a longtime artists' community. You'll be able to escape Boothbay's tourist crowds and revel in the island's peace, quiet, flora and fauna—especially if you hike a bit off the beaten path. Cruises aboard the *Balmy Days* depart daily for Monhegan from Pier 8; call (203) 633-2284.

BRUNSWICK

RESTAURANTS

22 Lincoln
22 Lincoln St.
(207) 725-5893
AMERICAN
Open Tues.-Sat. 6 p.m.-
9:30 p.m.
Cards: MC, V.

22 Lincoln—named for its address, which is lucky because it's a little hard to find—takes dead aim at originality and excellence and almost always hits right on. A restaurant review that simply lists the menu is usually a bore, but in this case it's the essence of the place—as well as wonderful reading. Consider, for example, such appetizers as a warm salad of soft Maine goat cheese and smoked mussels with pine nuts and oregano or a black-currant sorbet with Champagne and cassis; and such main dishes as lobster with summer truffles and sweet corn essence, turbot with Chardonnay and chervil, or breast of Barbary duckling with ginger, citrus and dates. A clam shack this ain't. In case the decision-making process is too much for you to handle, the kitchen is kind enough to put together some complete fixed-price dinners that do an excellent job of combining the unusual flavors and textures into a coherent meal. Oh, occasionally the dishes get a little precious or some of the combinations don't quite work, but it's never because the ingredients aren't the freshest and best available, or the chef is cutting corners. 22 Lincoln generally puts forth a wonderful dinner; it's definitely a night out, and by local standards, it costs an arm and a leg: about $100 a couple, with wine.

CAMDEN

QUICK BITES

Ma Ma & Leenie's
Cafe and Bakery
27 Elm St.
(207) 236-6300
Winter: open Mon.-Sat.
8 a.m.-7 p.m.; summer:
open Mon.-Sat. 8 a.m.-
9 p.m.

There's an earth-mama feeling to this pink, hearts-and-flowers place. Everything is homemade: The cookies are fabulous (particularly the orange-sugar ones), the lunches are generous (chunky egg salad, meatloaf, crab plate, macaroni and cheese and hearty homemade soups), and the bakery treats are delicious (scones, beer bread, shortbread, muffins, Maine blueberry pie and chocolate fudge cake). It's a pleasant place to rest a spell and watch the street traffic, refueling for more Camden sight-seeing or a hike into Camden Hills State Park. Better yet, have them pack you a movable feast to take on a day-long windjammer cruise from the wharf. About $10 for lunch for two.

INNS

Edgecombe-Coles House
64 High St.
(207) 236-2336
Open year-round.
All major cards.

Edgecombe-Coles may be the most attractive inn in inn-filled Camden. Hidden behind a tall private hedge, this nineteenth-century house offers serene views, wonderfully decorated rooms and the charm of owners Terry and Louise Price. It's hard to imagine anything more civilized than relaxing in bed with a view of Penobscot Bay sparkling in the distance, a privilege that can be yours if you reserve one of the two front rooms upstairs. The other four rooms are equally tempting, filled as they are with the Prices' collections of primitive art, Early American furniture, Oriental rugs, prints, antique toys, country pieces, lace and crocheted accessories, beautiful beds and flattering colors. It'll make you want to chuck it all and move in here for good.

Terry serves a hearty breakfast: seafood omelets, roast beef hash with eggs and hollandaise sauce (sounds odd, tastes good), Dutch babies (popover-like pancakes), strawberry waffles, scrambled eggs with bacon and cheese, amaretto french toast and fresh fruit. This nourishing feast will motivate you to conquer nearby Mount Battie, where you will be captivated by the extraordinary views of Camden Harbor and the wooded coastline.

Rooms: $65-$120, including breakfast.

Norumbega
61 High St.
(207) 236-4646
Open year-round.
Cards: AE, MC, V.

You can expect a somewhat austere and impersonal welcome at this otherwise impressive Victorian summer palace. The architecture alone is worth a visit, as is the spectacular view of Penobscot Bay and beyond. The original woodwork, ornate fireplaces and architectural detailing conjure up turn-of-the-century Newport; in fact, Norumbega looks slightly out of place in rustic Camden. Nonetheless, the eight rooms are pleasantly accommodating, each with a king-size bed and private bath. The two turrets house rooms with fine vantage points, and fireplaces in four of the second-floor rooms offer winter warmth (the furnishings, however, are hardly memorable).

The downstairs sitting rooms, embellished with marvelous carpentry detailing, are period masterpieces, and the sitting area on the impressive stairway landing is a seductive spot for private conversation. In the grand dining room a full breakfast–breads, fruits, cakes, waffles, pancakes, french toast, egg and meat dishes—is served at 8:30 a.m.; late sleepers are served a Continental breakfast in bed.

Come to Norumbega if you don't mind paying a lot of money for show. And in any case, you can always keep your eyes riveted on the view, which will make it easier to forget that this place could be stunning if it were only furnished in the style to which it was accustomed in 1886.

Rooms: $130-$180, including breakfast.

SIGHTS

Camden Hills State Park
Rte. 1
(207) 236-3109
Mid-May-mid-Oct.: open daily 9 a.m.-sunset.

Camden's harbor isn't the town's only attraction, thanks to Camden Hills State Park, two miles north of town along coastal Route 1. The park's 5,000 acres include a campground and a paved road that climbs 900-foot-high Mount Battie. A hike to Battie's summit will reward you with panoramic views of Penobscot Bay.

Admission $1.

Windjammer Cruises
(800) 624-6380

Approaching from the sea, you can't miss Camden, set on the coast against a backdrop of hills, some reaching 1,400 feet skyward. A favorite among yachtsmen, Camden's harbor is a frequent port of call for windjammer cruises, which run from late May to late October. For information and reservations, contact the Maine Windjammer Association in nearby Rockport at the number listed above.

SHOPS

Ducktrap Bay Trading Co.
28 Bayview St.
(207) 236-9568
Summer: open daily 10 a.m.-5:30 p.m.; off-season hours vary.

In this aviary of handsomely carved birds—mostly, but not exclusively, ducks—antique decoys nest next to the work of some of New England's best carvers, who can put a finish on a bird that will make you expect to see it hop off the shelf and fly south for the winter. Even if you're not a birder, it's worth a peek to see how closely wood can resemble feathers.

Good Hands
Harbor Square
(207) 236-8700
Summer: open Mon.-Sat. 10 a.m.-5 p.m. & 7 p.m.-9 p.m., Sun. noon-5 p.m.; off-season hours vary.

Get away from the hassle of touristy downtown Camden and step into this serene gallery. In addition to the gold jewelry made by owner Thomas O'Donovan in his studio at the back of the store, Good Hands beautifully displays furniture, ceramics, prints and paintings. You'll have to look for the stairs to the second level, but don't miss it.

Scheuler Antiques
10 High St. (Rte. 1)
(207) 236-2770
Mid-June-mid-Oct.: open Tues.-Sat. 10 a.m.-5 p.m.

The price tags on these handsome antiques may be on the high side, but the quality is excellent, the service more than just helpful, and the collection an honest representation of New England's finest.

CAPE NEDDICK

INNS

Wooden Goose Inn
Rte. 1
(207) 363-5673
Closed Jan.
Cash or personal check only.

Passing through tourist-infested York Beach in the middle of summer may make you consider abandoning the human race, but you'll reconsider the moment you arrive at Wooden Goose, a refined bastion of civilization. If you arrive at teatime and are greeted by what appears to be a hanging garden of blazing crystal candlesticks, don't be daunted— it's just a flair for the dramatic on the part of partners Jerry Rippetoe and Tony Sienicki. The decor here is lovely but dense, making the Wooden Goose no place for a happy, tail-wagging golden retriever.

If you have a penchant for le grand style yourself, check into the Honeymoon Suite, which has a canopy bed and large bathroom with a freestanding claw-footed tub. Or try the upstairs room, snug and intimate with Chinese detailing and a customized bed. The two suites in the back have Early American furnishings, and all six rooms have air conditioning and wall-to-wall carpeting, creating welcome tranquility and quiet.

A stay at the Wooden Goose also means a temporary abandonment of any hopes for being thin again. Afternoon tea—pâté, mocha-pecan torte, cheesecake, raspberry tart, profiteroles—is de rigueur. Breakfast is even less restrained: There are eighteen different menus, allowing you to stay here on a long-term basis before meals start repeating themselves. Poached pears with Grand Marnier custard sauce, julienne potato nests filled with steamed broccoli and poached eggs with hollandaise, eggs Oscar (the tourists love it), sausage-mushroom strudel, French bread topped with poached eggs and a mushroom-béchamel sauce. . . those are just the beginning. After such indulgences, you'll have to crawl back to your pretty room to sleep it off in time for tea.

Rooms: $85-$95, including breakfast.

We are always happy to hear about your discoveries and to receive your comments about ours. We want to give your letters the attention they deserve, so when you write to us, remember to state clearly exactly what you liked or disliked. Be concise, but convincing. Do take the time to argue your point.

CENTER LOVELL

INNS

**Westways
Country Inn**
Rte. 5
(207) 928-2663
*Closed Nov. & April.
Cards: AE, MC, V.*

What does it take to keep employees interested and enter-
tained? To William Fairburn, original owner of the Diamond Match Company in the 1920s, it took the creation of
this executives' playground on the shores of Lake Kezar.
Fairburn regularly imported his management team to this
summer camp to hold board meetings. But who had time to
work? The 120-acre compound is equipped with a softball
field, tennis courts, stables, a fives court (to play the Brits'
version of handball) with impressive cathedralesque architecture, a recreation hall with billiards and Ping-Pong tables,
an astonishing inlaid bowling alley (you have to spot your
own pins) and a boathouse. And today, thanks to Fairburn,
you can enjoy this place without having to attend any
tedious meetings. The Lodge (his former private home) has
that odd hodgepodge decor beloved by the rich: Renais-
sance-style furniture (created by Italian craftsmen who Fairburn brought over), a heavy European decor, beautiful late-
eighteenth-century Japanese woodcuts and an unusual
combination of reproduction prints. The bedrooms have
kept their looks over the years; the Master Suite is particularly lovely, with a nonstop view of the lake and a bathroom
not unlike those in Newport's summer palaces. The Blue
Room, also spacious and attractive, boasts custom-made
carpet and antique furnishings. Even the servants' quarters
make cheery little guest rooms, with a more country-style
look. Excellent food, including a creative breakfast, is served
in the peaceful dining room overlooking the lake.

Rooms: $120-$180, including breakfast and dinner.

DEER ISLE

INNS

Pilgrim's Inn
Main St.
(207) 348-6615
*Closed 3rd week of Oct.-
3rd week of May.
Cash or personal check only.*

Those who prefer their country-inn experience plain and
simple will love Dud and Jean Hendrick's Pilgrim's Inn. a
pristine 1793 Colonial house perfectly situated between
Northeast Harbor in front and a picturesque millpond in
back. The decor is spare, which gives the place a certain
countrified elegance. The thirteen bedrooms have lovely
antiques, wood-burning stoves, Laura Ashley linens, rag

rugs, beamed ceilings and authentic Colonial colors. Because the inn doubles as a gallery for local artists, you can bring home the print or photograph that hung over your bed. The library upstairs is full of books that will interest any taste in literature; comfortable chairs and good reading lights make it a popular spot.

Downstairs, the sitting room is the heart and soul of the inn. Elegant couples, bike-tour groups, best friends and summer regulars toast each other with selections from Dud's extensive collection of imported beers, comparing notes on another perfect Maine day, while Jean offers delicious hors d'oeuvres before serving her ambitious dinners. The handsome, barn-sided dining room, with a country-casual raffia rug, fresh flowers and hand-thrown ceramics (a reminder that Haystack Mountain School of Crafts is nearby), is always full of activity. Dinner is a hearty affair, a tribute to the inn's physically fit, outdoorsy guests. Jean's range is broad: pork stuffed with apples and prunes, paella, pasta with roasted red peppers and scallops, halibut grilled over applewood. There is always a selection of home-baked breads, fabulous soups and a baker's dream of desserts: Linzertorte, sour-cream apple tart, raspberry pie and other down-home sweets. All ingredients are fresh, and the vegetables come from Jean's own garden on Cape Rosier. She's a veritable Alice Waters, State o' Maine style.

After you recover from dinner, clear-headed from a refreshing Deer Isle night of sleep, Jean will do an encore at breakfast. Apple- and apricot-stuffed french toast, scones, eggs, sour-cream coffee cake, blueberry pancakes and the inn's staple, homemade granola with fruited yogurt, are the breakfast norm. This sort of early-morning retanking will make you jump up, borrow one of the Hendricks' bikes and race around the island.

Rooms: $125-$145, including breakfast and dinner.

SIGHTS

Haystack Mountain School of Crafts
Rte. 15
(207) 348-2306
June-early Sept.: open Thurs.-Sun. 10 a.m.-4 p.m.

One might think the spectacular scenery—coves and inlets, tiny granite out-islands, cottages dating back a century or two—would be reason enough to visit Deer Isle. But there's more. Among its other beauties, Deer Isle (which is connected to the mainland and requires no ferrying) is the home of this craft school, a series of connected studios where artists from all over the world gather to produce works in metal, textiles, wood, glass, pottery and paper. Refreshingly, none of the work is for sale at the school.

FREEPORT

INNS

Isaac Randall House
Independence Dr.
(off Rte. 1)
(207) 865-9295
Open year-round.
Cash or personal check only.

When you're planning your next assault on L. L. Bean's bunker-style headquarters to stock up on the latest camping gear and outerwear, book a room at the Isaac Randall House. This innocent-looking inn makes a nice contrast to Freeport's burgeoning commercialism and end-to-end factory outlets. The eight bedrooms in the 1823 farmhouse are on the sweet side, decorated with canopy beds, floral wreaths, lace, ribbons and a palette of pastels. You'll always have a room with a view, since each overlooks the six peaceful acres surrounding the inn.

Jim Friedlander's breakfasts are served in the farmhouse kitchen. His traditional country menu features french toast, blueberry pancakes, fruit breads and homemade granola. It's the sensible way to fuel up for another day of discount shopping at Laura Ashley, Ralph Lauren, Anne Klein and Benetton.

Rooms: $50-$85, including breakfast.

SHOPS

Time was when L. L. Bean was a 24-hour-a-day beehive of activity tucked away in this otherwise sleepy little New England town. Even in the wee hours of the morning, the rustic, wood-frame shop on Main Street (207-865-4761) would be filled with bleary-eyed Bowdoin College students taking a study break to replenish their supplies of Bean boots, chamois shirts and down vests, and hunters and fishermen stocking up on camouflage binoculars and neoprene waders.

Soon other smart merchants and manufacturers realized that they, too, could make a nickel or two plying their trades to the passing hordes of tourists, and soon commercialism sprawled along Main Street like a creeping Maine fog. Factory outlets offering everything from Frye boots and Cole-Haan shoes to Ralph Lauren crew-neck sweaters and Laura Ashley frocks transformed tiny Freeport into a bargain-hunter's dream come true.

Praxis
136 Main St.
(207) 865-6201
Open daily 10 a.m.-6 p.m.

Sick of looking at factory outlet stores in which the merchandise doesn't seem to be much less expensive than it is back home? Drop into this co-op run by a dozen Maine craftworkers whose specialties range from weaving, leaded glass and tableware to leather and jewelry. Though the selections are somewhat limited, at least they're not seconds.

FRYEBURG

INNS

Oxford House Inn
105 Main St. (Rte. 302)
(207) 935-3442
Open year-round.
All major cards.

What every compulsive shopper needs as restorative tonic before another foray into North Conway's factory outlets is a decent meal, some peace and quiet and a pleasant room in which to sleep off the high of buying at discount. If this sounds like a reasonable alternative to the endless stream of impersonal sleeping factories along Route 16, head for Oxford House, just a few miles away in Fryeburg. The 1913 Victorian house has an unusually good restaurant run by owner John Morris. His wife, Phyllis, who runs the front of the house, will cheerfully install you in a Victorian-style bedroom, where you can freshen up for dinner. John is an excellent self-taught cook. His specialties are poached salmon with Pommery mustard sauce, fresh scallops in puff pastry and a heartier grilled pork tenderloin with black-currant sauce. While waiting for your dinner, you can decompress by soaking in the peaceful view across the back forty.

The five upstairs bedrooms are modest but pleasant, and you can be assured a quiet sleep. The master suite is the most attractive, with Victorian antiques, a welcome spaciousness and an extra bed, helpful for traveling families. Whether you spend the evening on the sleeping porch or in the quaint sewing room, you'll awaken to the comforting fragrance of John's excellent breakfast. Scones, fresh fruit, blueberry buttermilk pancakes, and french toast stuffed with cream cheese and homemade marmalade are just a few of his morning temptations.

Rooms: $60-$75, including breakfast.

SIGHTS

Most visitors to Maine come up the coast from Boston, but the state's western gateways should not be neglected. Fryeburg, which traces its roots back to an old Indian settlement, sits almost atop the Maine–New Hampshire border. From late May to late October, the Maine Publicity Bureau operates a visitors' center on U.S. Route 302, where those approaching from the west will find help in planning their Maine travels. Route 113 from Fryeburg also leads into the Maine side of the White Mountain National Forest. Located in the plain of the Saco River Valley, the town is also a canoeing center; day rentals are available if you haven't brought your own. If your fall foliage tour includes Maine, plan to stop at the Fryeburg Fair, a traditional country fair that's been going strong for nearly 140 years. It's held the first week of October at the Fryeburg Fair Grounds on Route 5.

GARDINER

QUICK BITES

A-One Diner
3 Bridge St.
(207) 582-4804
Open Mon. 5 a.m.-2 p.m.,
Tues.-Sat. 5 a.m.-9 p.m.,
Sun. 7 a.m.-noon &
5 p.m.-9 p.m.
No cards.

In 1946, the Worcester Diner Car Company delivered this stylish diner to Eddie Heald, and it's been sitting here ever since. The curved deco-looking interior—prerequisite black-and-white tile floors, wooden cabinetry, polished granite countertop and "Time to Eat" blue neon clock—is in mint condition. And, fortunately, the food is just as authentic: fried tripe, meatloaf platters, fried haddock, macaroni and cheese and countless sandwiches. The homemade coconut-cream, coconut-custard and chocolate-cream pies are as delicious as the hot cinnamon-apple bread pudding, strawberry shortcake and cheesecake.

SHOPS

Kenneth and Paulette Tuttle
Rte. 4
(207) 582-4496
Open Mon.-Fri. 9 a.m.-
4 p.m., or by appt.

It's easy to spot the Tuttles' enclave in Gardiner's outback. The sparkling white picket fence, the cluster of white Federal-era buildings and the former Congregational church with its "Antiques" sign are traffic stoppers. They sure stopped us in our tracks, and we were convinced that these buildings would house an extensive collection of eighteenth- and nineteenth-century collectors' gems, the kinds of things displayed in their colorful magazine ads. Alas, the one small showroom wasn't exactly bursting at its seams, the secretary on duty wasn't particularly knowledgeable about the semiprecious items on display, and we found the withholding of prices and histories of each piece to be supremely arrogant. You have to ask for everything and must rely on the limited information you get. Naturally, if you have already established a relationship with Ken, he'll greet you at the door and help you decide whether the Hepplewhite sideboard ($28,000), 1790 lolling chair ($7,500), ultra-expensive tall-case clocks, Chippendale high-boys or highly polished secretaries are right for your home.

GREENVILLE

SIGHTS

S.S. Katahdin
East Cove
(207) 695-2716
Late May-Sept.: cruises daily 10 a.m.-2 p.m.

Situated at the foot of Moosehead Lake, Greenville is the gateway to rugged northwest Maine. The lake itself, 40 miles long and 10 miles wide, is a recreational center with spectacular scenery. A popular way to view it is on board the S.S.*Katahdin*, a 1914 steamboat that serves as the floating Moosehead Marine Museum of logging and steamboat lore. The sole survivor among a lake fleet of more than 30 vessels, the*Katahdin*, known locally as "Katie," runs two-and-a-half-hour cruises from Greenville's East Cove.
Admission $12.

KENNEBUNKPORT

RESTAURANTS

Windows on the Water
Chase Hill Rd.
(207) 967-3313
AMERICAN
Open Mon.-Sat. 11:45 a.m.-2:30 p.m. & 5:30 p.m.- 9 p.m., Sun. 11:30 a.m.-3 p.m.
Cards: AE, MC, V.

11/20

Kennebunkport is what our mother calls a "spendy" little place, crammed with gift shops, craft centers and art galleries perched on wharves around its lovely harbor. Once you've made your purchases, and admired the truly remarkable architecture of many of the town's old-money summer homes, drive to Windows on the Water to relax over a decent meal. After all the crowds and charming clutter of the port, it's a real pleasure to sit in the spacious, high-ceilinged dining room, with its huge arched windows overlooking, as promised, the water—or what you can see of it between all the sailboats. Half the menu, naturally, is devoted to seafood (a Madeira-laced lobster bisque, filet of sole stuffed with crab and dill Havarti cheese), but there is also a refreshing emphasis on red meat (remember red meat?): prime rib, tenderloin, filet mignon, rib-eye sirloin or that dinner-party favorite of yesteryear, beef Wellington, all tender, trimmed and cooked the way you ask. We finished up our last meal here with a Key lime pie, which was tinted a little too brightly green—but overall we enjoyed a satisfactory, if not distinguished, meal in an exceptional location. The two of us were out the door for $63, including wine by the glass from a better-than-usual selection.

INNS

Captain Jefferds Inn
Pearl St. & Pleasant St.
(207) 967-2311
Closed Nov.
Cash or personal check only.

It's hard to imagine anyone owning more quality majolica than Warren Fitzsimmons. The vintage ceramics are loaded four-deep in cupboards and on every available shelf in this extraordinary inn. The collection is matched only by Fitzsimmons's assured taste in American furnishings and decorative arts. In a former life, he was an antiques dealer in Southampton, Long Island, and his collector's eye and first-class taste are amply evident in this handsome inn. The solarium is a symphony of deco wicker; the lively living room is brightened with flower-splashed upholstery; the tranquil dining room is a display of every American collector's dream; and the twelve bedrooms are models of good taste. Cottage-painted bedroom suites, Early American weather vanes, doll houses, hobo art mirrors, root furniture, folk art and quilts run rampant. And for those traveling en masse, the carriage house has three apartments filled with even more American treasures.

Breakfast is a feast: eggs Benedict, blueberry crêpes, New England flannel (hash and poached eggs), french toast with Grand Marnier, fresh fruit and frittatas. The Captain Jefferds makes it possible to forgive Kennebunkport its commercial mentality. It's also conveniently located for those who can't resist seeking out a glimpse of George Bush's well-protected, preppy compound.

Rooms: $75-$95, including breakfast.

Captain Lord Mansion
Pleasant St. & Green St.
(207) 967-3141
Open year-round. Cards:
Discover, MC, V.

This handsome old sea captain's home painted a notice-me yellow is an impressive place to spend a weekend. Owners Beverly Davis and Rick Litchfield believe that a visit to the mansion should be memorable, and it is. You'll feel like royalty on holiday, despite the somewhat impersonal service from an otherwise-efficient staff. Most of the sixteen large rooms have working fireplaces, private baths, amazing beds and oversized furnishings that complement the 1812 architecture. Summer guests relax on the wicker lawn furniture in the yard, refreshed from an endless supply of iced tea and pleased with their good sense in reserving their rooms early. And the view-struck widow's walk is a great place to get away from it all while you're getting away from it all.

With Oriental chimes, Rick summons guests to breakfast in the kitchen, where they sit extended-family style and try to master the delicate art of eating soft-boiled eggs in their shells in eggcups. If you are successful, you can purchase your own egg cutters and accessories in the inn's little shop, so that you can relive the experience back home.

Rooms: $59-$195, including breakfast.

SIGHTS

As any reader of *Town & Country* knows, Kennebunkport and its surrounding towns are almost synonymous with "summer," especially for the set comfortable enough to afford to pass the entire season here. George Bush has spent just about every summer of his life on Walker's Point in Kennebunkport, and his family's vacation home has been a magnet for both admirers and detractors, who have sometimes protested in the neighborhood. Politics aside, the area is a haven for nature lovers, pleasure-boaters and especially fishermen. The waters off Kennebunkport are rich in striped bass, cod, mackerel and even tuna; both professionals and weekend fishermen regularly bring in good catches. Among the companies running deep-water boats are Cape Arundel Cruises (207-967-5595) and Deep Water Fishing Charters (207-967-4938). Although Kennebunkport's main season is summer, social activities continue in the off-season—Santa Claus arrives by lobster boat for the Christmas Prelude the first weekend in December. For more information on the Prelude or any other aspect of life in Kennebunkport, call the chamber of commerce at (207) 985-3608.

LIMINGTON

SHOPS

Robert O. Stuart
Jo Joy Ln. (off Rte. 117)
(207) 793-4533
Open daily 8 a.m.-5 p.m.

Rob Stuart himself may greet you at the door of his recently refurbished barn to take you on a tour of his fabulous collection of museum-quality American antiques. Or perhaps you'll be met by his vivacious wife, Lorna, who is just as knowledgeable and enthusiastic about the treasures they have collected. This high-powered couple has settled in a Maine version of Shangri-la, combining their families of seven children and tending store for a select clientele. The setting alone is enough to make you weep. Cattle grazing on rolling, rocky hills, friendly Labradors announcing your arrival, bucolic views, a picturesque pond—all of it will mellow even the most nervous customer into considering at least one major purchase. And the view inside isn't bad, either—a collection of stunning American jewels that are hard to resist, though the prices will give you pause. Prices like $22,500 for a Hepplewhite secretary, $55,000 for an exquisite miniature tall-case clock, $3,600 for a child's Windsor chair, $5,500 for a rare Chippendale armchair and $14,000 for a Pennsylvania sofa make it clear that this is a shop intended for serious collectors. The selection is deep, most pieces have provenances and histories, and there is plenty of information available about every piece.

Stuart left his position as professor of ethics at Princeton to live out his dream of being a collector and inventor. This Renaissance man also started another company, which creates reproduction pieces from the originals in his collection. Well made, with design integrity, these pieces are affordable and boast a rare attention to detail. And the sophisticated Stuarts realize that not everyone is crazy enough to drive down their backwoods lane in the middle of January, so they cleverly sell their pieces by videotape. If you're interested in chairs, take a look at the chair tape, or secretaries, the secretary tape; each is narrated by Rob, who shows the undersides and innermost workings of each piece.

OGUNQUIT AREA

INNS

See Cape Neddick, Kennebunkport.

SIGHTS

Kittery, York, Ogunquit, Wells... as one crosses the border from New Hampshire and travels north along the coast, southeast Maine seems to be nothing but one glorious beach after another. And if, on a summer day, one beach is too crowded for your liking, just hop in the car and move on to the next. The name *Ogunquit* comes from an Indian word for "beautiful place by the sea," which is exactly how vacationers have always found it. (These vacationers have been multiplying in recent years, which has unfortunately made the area more touristy in spirit.) In addition to beaches, Ogunquit is the home of a thriving summer artists' colony and the Ogunquit Playhouse on Route 1 (207-646-2402). The playhouse, a fixture since its establishment in a converted garage by a Hollywood director in 1933, mounts a ten-week season each summer, usually producing three musicals and four dramatic plays featuring major stars in national tours. And Kittery is abloom with factory outlets, rivaling Freeport for bargain-basement appeal.

See also "Wells" below.

POLAND SPRING

SIGHTS

Shaker Museum at Sabbathday Lake
Rte. 26
(206) 926-4391
Late May-mid-Oct.: open Mon.-Sat. 10 a.m.-4:30 p.m.

If you recognize the name of this village near Lewiston as a brand of bubbly water but nothing else, think again. Poland Spring also plays host to the Shaker Museum at Sabbathday Lake. If you missed Hancock Shaker Village in Massachusetts, this museum, founded in 1931, will give you a picture of Shaker life with its guided or self-guided tours of exhibits that showcase folk art, textiles and especially the prized Shaker furniture.

Adults $4.50, children $2.25.

PORTLAND

RESTAURANTS

Alberta's Café
21 Pleasant St.
(207) 774-1336
AMERICAN
Open Mon.-Fri. 11:30 a.m.-2:30 p.m. & 5 p.m.-10:30 p.m., Sat. 5 p.m.-11 p.m.
Cards: AE, MC, V.

Alberta's is a happening place, thanks to its excellent cuisine and relaxed, no-problem atmosphere. The nondescript decor belies cooking that is serious but not without a sense of humor; the menu changes weekly, as does its clever artwork. You'd think you were in a college hangout, except that the quality of the cooking begs a sophisticated palate and a slightly more endowed wallet than those found in the traditional university soup kitchen.

It would be tempting to say that the chef here has an even touch, because you can expect every meal to be good. But the consistency is all the more commendable when you realize that there are actually four or five chefs taking turns at the ovens. Even more improbable: All of them are consistent in producing good, innovative food. Starters can include such things as an excellent smoked-ham-and-vegetable bisque, calamari and wild mushrooms in a vol-au-vent with lobster tamale cream sauce (somewhat of a mixed metaphor), and delicate sautéed scallops with leeks, bacon and roasted almonds vinaigrette. Entrées run from solid sirloin chili and barbecued chicken and ribs to the more fragile salmon with Choron sauce, lotte sautéed with capers, lemon and thyme, sautéed calamari with julienne vegetables in a black-bean sauce and an Oriental sauté of shark with ginger sauce. And things can get a little wilder: bluefish with pear salsa, pork loin pané with a pecan-Marsala brown sauce. The thick-crust sourdough pizza is heavenly and generous, and the pan-blackened chicken filets wrapped with flour tortillas and sauced with a spicy Cajun rémoulade are inventive.

Desserts are worth saving space for: praline ice cream truffle with raspberry purée, apple spice cake, fresh fruit laced with a vanilla custard sauce, ginger pound cake with orange sauce. The wine list is modest (no bottle is more than $17), there is a good selection of lagers and ales, and service is affable and helpful. Alberta's Two, located at 27 Forest Avenue, is more elegant and refined in decor; the menu offers similar fare. Dinner for two, with wine, will run $65 or $70.

Brattle Street

19 Brattle St.
(207) 772-4658
CONTINENTAL
Open Tues.-Sat. 6 p.m.-
9:30 p.m.
Cards: AE, MC, V.

If a restaurant can be compared to music, Brattle Street would be a piece by Chopin or Mozart: cool, classical and, in both senses of the word, *composed*. The food is perfection, from the little appetizers set at your place before you order through the between-courses grapefruit sorbet to the imaginative desserts, which have the sweet richness you dream of without trying to win the "Most Calories in a Single Dessert" contest that seems to be sweeping today's restaurants. Entrées tend toward the classic—lobster in puff pastry, melting tenderloin of beef, pheasant—each prepared with respect and affection, and each given the nuances of flavor and presentation it deserves. The setting is a small Greek Revival brick building, tastefully restored and obviously uncomfortable with the huge Federal buildings across the street. But at last parking is available, and inside Brattle Street is a world of its own. It is *not* the place in which to hang out with a group of friends, doing a lot of catching up and laughing. But if you want to feel elegant, civilized and deserving of the best in life, you won't find a better place. There's no such thing as an average dinner here, but the average price for two, with wine, will run about $80.

Cafe Always
47 Middle St.
(207) 774-9399
INTERNATIONAL/AMERICAN
*Open Tues.-Sun. 5 p.m.-
10 p.m.*
Cards: AE, MC, V.

The only things that say "Maine" about Cafe Always are the relatively reasonable prices for such high-quality food and the unfailingly cheerful, helpful waitresses. No driftwood and pine decor for these folks—the look is jazzy and bright, with chrome-yellow oilcloth, mermaid-topped swizzle sticks and some of the freshest art in the state on the well-lit walls. The food is kinda California, but it also circles the globe; Thai, Tex-Mex, a Japanese touch here and there, some nouvelleties—you name it, it'll show up sooner or later on the often-changing menu. Regardless of where the ideas come from, the dinners are always prepared with quality, charm and the freshest of ingredients. An example? The appetizer we had recently: ravioli filled with shiitake mushrooms and cottage cheese and lightly covered with a saffron cream sauce. Our latest dinner, including an exceptional Australian wine, came to $73 for two.

Madd Apple Cafe
23 Forest Ave.
(207) 774-9698
AMERICAN/SOUTHERN
*Open Tues.-Sat. 11:30
a.m.-2:45 p.m. & 5:30
p.m.-9 p.m.*
Cards: AE, MC, V.

12/20

You might hesitate to bring someone with a hearty appetite to a place called the Madd Apple Cafe. But we're not talking watercress sandwiches here. The lunch menu lists beef brisket po' boys, Carolina chopped-pork barbecue, Creole sausage with red beans, and a "grilled Ivan," which consists of roast beef, Swiss cheese, Bermuda onions and Russian dressing grilled on pumpernickel. That should hold you until supper. Lighter eaters, however, could graze on a niçoise salad or a vegetable pocket. The barbecue here is the best in town (or the state, to our knowledge), with a zingy, lime-scented sauce and the meat thoughtfully deboned, so that you don't wind up wondering what to do with all those sticky fingers when you're dressed up for a night out. Nobody has given much thought to the decor or the table settings— there's no real commitment to ambience—but maybe that's because they're too busy back in the kitchen, turning out that good Southern cooking for us Mainers. Country prices, too: $40 did us for dinner, with beer.

INNS

The Inn
at Park Spring
135 Spring St.
(207) 774-1059
Open year-round.
Cards: AE, MC, V.

This urban bed-and-breakfast inn is a welcome change from the impersonal lodging at the nearby large hotel chains. Perfectly located within walking distance of the resurrected historic waterfront, the Portland Museum of Art, the Performing Arts Center and some wonderful restaurants, the seven-bedroom inn was built as a townhouse in 1885. Each room has attractive furnishings, its own color scheme and pleasant art; you'll be impressed by the ingenuity used in creating modern bathrooms out of no space at all. The Murphy Room has a pull-down bed that is something out of the Arabian Nights—a billowy paisley print creates a sophisticated Bedouin tent-alcove. Park, downstairs, is a spacious room with a tall-post bed and Victorian marble fireplace. Museum, upstairs, is cheerful in apricot and green, Spring is serene in dusty blue, and the two rooms on the third floor are cozy and perfect for a traveling family (as long as the kids are over 12).

Breakfast is served in the vibrant kitchen, Walton-family style, with fresh fruit, home-baked breads, pastries, cereals and plenty of tea and coffee to keep the conversation alert. The inn is overseen by extremely capable, professional managers who are helpful and gracious. They will point you in the right direction for dinner, suggest walking tours and answer all of your questions with patience and good spirit. Rooms: $60-$85, including breakfast.

SIGHTS

As Maine's commercial capital (and an important shipping port), Portland has always been important to the state—but never so much as in the last several years. As in so many American cities, the once-forbidding waterfront area has a new lease on life—old warehouse buildings have been restored and transformed into shopping complexes, among them the Old Port Exchange. Gentrification? Perhaps, but in the best possible sense.

The city is proud of its cultural attractions, especially the Portland Museum of Art, 7 Congress Square (207-773-2787). Among its drawing cards, so to speak, are works by artists with Maine connections, including Winslow Homer and the Wyeth family. It's open Tuesday to Saturday 10 a.m. to 5 p.m., Thursday to 9 p.m. and Sunday noon to 5 p.m.; admission is $2.50 for adults, $2 for students and senior citizens, $1 for children and free on Thursday from 5 p.m. to 9 p.m. The Portland Symphony (207-773-8191), a professional orchestra, performs regularly, and the Cumberland County Civic Center draws major concerts and entertainment events to the Maine coast. Portland is also a city of festivals, ranging from the Old Port Festival each June to New Year's/Portland, a ten-hour arts festival (similar to Boston's First Night) that rings in the New Year.

The city is the gateway to Casco Bay, whose 136 islands are popular summer colonies (some quadruple in population during the season), drawing scores of day-tripping visitors for sunning and sight-seeing. Various cruise lines run excursions from the Portland piers to the islands in season, among them Casco Bay Lines, which has been operating a ferry service to the islands since 1845. Boats leave from Custom House Wharf on Commercial Street; for information on seasonal schedules, call (207) 774-7871.

SHOPS

Abacus
44 Exchange St.
(207) 772-4880
Open Mon.-Sat. 10 a.m.-6 p.m. (later in summer), Sun. noon-6 p.m.

This is the Bloomingdale's of craft stores: big, well-stocked and diverse, with something for every taste. The gold and silver jewelry is rather conservative; other items tend toward the postmodern, and many of the artists will be familiar to craft-store devotees.

Maine Potters Market
376 Fore St.
(207) 774-1633
April-Dec.: open daily 10 a.m.-6 p.m. (later in summer); Jan.-March: open Tues.-Sun. 10 a.m.-6 p.m.

The work of fifteen Maine potters is displayed here, and because it is a co-op, you'll meet at least one of the potters whose work you're looking at. The extensive offerings are largely functional, with lots of blue-and-white and floral motifs.

Nancy Margolis Gallery
367 Fore St.
(207) 775-3822
Open Mon.-Sat. 10 a.m.-6 p.m., Sun. noon-5 p.m.

A sign of Portland's transformation, this chic craft gallery is located in what used to be a rundown waterfront area but is now the trendy Old Port Exchange. Formerly the Maple Hill Gallery in Ogunquit, the store is a serious collector's dream. You'll see little production-line stuff here, and even the functional items display a high level of design awareness. The back room usually contains an exhibit, often of ceramics or glass, the store's specialties. If you're looking for the antiques of the future, bring a charge card with an extremely high credit limit.

Unless otherwise noted, the prices given for restaurants are for a complete dinner for two, including an appetizer, main course and dessert. The prices also include tax, fifteen-percent tip and one of the least expensive bottles of wine on the wine list. Please don't hold it against us if you end up spending a bit more!

SOUTH HARPSWELL

RESTAURANTS

**Estes Lobster
House**
Rte. 123
(207) 833-6340
AMERICAN
*Open daily 11:30 a.m.-
9 p.m.*
*No cards; cash or
personal check only.*

11/20

If you're a visitor to Maine, this is probably what you came for—and if you're a native, it's one good reason to put up with February and March. This quintessential lobster house sits on a narrow strip of land connecting the hybrid town of Brunswick, with its mixture of French Canadians and Naval air base and Bowdoin College residents, with this tiny community where summer people and lobstermen coexist in relative harmony. On a summer's day you can take your food to an oceanside table that's cooled by the salt breeze and enjoy fish chowder, steamed clams, Maine shrimp, a one-pound lobster, coleslaw and strawberry shortcake, parting only with a $20 bill and the ability to move for the rest of the afternoon. Or you can stay in the barn of a restaurant, haphazardly decorated with marine artifacts, and let the most pleasant of summer waitresses serve your meal. If you're not up for the full treatment, you can simply dig into a lobster, sensibly served in a broth-catching tray with melted butter, potato chips and enough wet-wipes and napkins for a first-timer. We can't honestly recommend the prepared dishes, such as the lobster pie, but for pure Maine seafood, pulled that morning from the waters by the man at the next table, you've come to the right place. Prices vary considerably: If you're just getting the kids hamburgers, you'll escape for $10, but hearty lobster feasts—with the available wine or beer—can run to $50 for two.

STONINGTON

SHOPS

**Eastern Bay
Cooperative Gallery**
Main St.
(207) 367-5006
Hours vary.

Difficult to reach it may be, but the harbor view from this gallery perched in a small seaside fishing village is worth the effort involved. And the work on display is of surprisingly high quality. The place is close to the Haystack Mountain School of Crafts in Deer Isle, a top-notch craft school that also has a superb gallery, though the work there is not for sale.

VAN BUREN

SIGHTS

Acadian Village
Rte. 1
(207) 868-2691
Mid-June-mid-Sept.:
open daily noon-5 p.m.

This is the forest primeval. Longfellow's Evangeline and her fellow Acadians fled south from Nova Scotia to Louisiana, but in 1785 some of the group settled in what is now Maine's Aroostook County, just over the border from Canada. The Acadian Village in Van Buren is a living memorial to Acadians of the past built by their present-day descendants. The complex includes sixteen homes, a country store, a blacksmith shop and exhibits on the Acadians' wilderness way of life.
Adults $2, children $1.

WELLS

SIGHTS

Wells doesn't look much different from any other seaside town—T-shirt shops, ice cream stands, plates of fried clams everywhere. In most places these signs of a summer colony might be expected to do the natural environment far more harm than good, but Wells has two major organizations dedicated to preserving it. The 1,600-acre Wells National Estuarine Research Reserve (207-646-4521) is one of only fifteen of its kind in the United States. Visitors may tour the reserve's various habitats—fields, woods, tidal rivers, sand dunes—to see many varieties of shore and forest birds. The reserve is open for guided tours from late June to early September on Tuesdays, Thursdays and Saturdays; in spring and fall, it's open only on Saturday mornings. Visitors are asked to call in advance; admission is $1 per person or $3 per family. Upon completion, the nearby Rachel Carson National Wildlife Refuge on Route 9 (207-646-9226) is projected to cover 4,000 acres of salt marsh between Portland and Kittery. Visitors to the Wells section are invited to stroll a one-mile trail through the pines and onto the marsh. The refuge is open daily year-round from sunrise to sunset; admission is free.

SHOPS

R. Jorgensen Antiques
Rte. 1
(207) 646-9444
Open Thurs.-Tues. 10 a.m.-5 p.m.

If you plan to visit the Jorgensens' family of shops, you may have to check into a local inn so that you'll have time to see them all. All sorts of antiques, from the formal to the casual, are here, and many of the pieces are advantageously priced for the more modest collector. American highboys, card tables, sets of Chippendale chairs, secretaries—it's a virtual one-stop shopping experience. Spongeware, stickware, Minnesota fish decoys, fire fenders, baby cradles, Chinese exportware porcelain... it's all deliciously tempting. The barn in the back is full of English imports, along with tall-case clocks, tables and other examples of the Jorgensens' collection. The whole family is involved in the business; each member has his or her own specialty. You can trust any of them and expect them to be friendly, helpful—and pros at closing the sale.

Ida & Ken Manko
Seabreeze Dr.
(207) 646-2595
Open daily 9 a.m.-5 p.m.

Ken Manko told us that no one knows more about antique weather vanes than he does, and we believe him. So do the experts. They come to him for help and information, as you should if you are as in love with this all-American art form as the gregarious Manko. His intimate barn-cum-studio houses wonderful treasures at affordable (and sometimes not so affordable) prices. It's well-nigh impossible to walk away without buying a weather-beaten fish, pelican or horse weather vane, an antique basket, a charming whirligig, a naïf drawing, country furnishings or a piece of ancient scrimshaw.

WISCASSET

RESTAURANTS

Le Garage
Water St.
(207) 882-5409
AMERICAN
*Open Mon.-Sat. 11:30 a.m.-4 p.m. & 5 p.m.-10 p.m., Sun. noon-10 p.m.
Cards: DC, MC, V.*

Wiscasset claims to be the prettiest village in Maine, and while there are several other contenders, we admit that it has a good shot at the title. After a few hours of examining its credentials—the extraordinary brick homes, the winding roads with a view of the water around each corner, and the high-quality craft and antiques shops—we repair to Le Garage, a cool, cavernous restaurant that offers good food in a relaxed atmosphere. It's worth waiting for a table on the glassed-in porch overlooking the two derelict schooner hulks from the early 1900s. If they were cars they'd be junkers, but being boats, they're history—and they do provide a picturesque foreground to the vistas of the Sheepscot River flowing right by your table. Le Garage keeps the cooking traditional, fresh and tasty and does not omit the touches that make a meal an occasion. After our plate of sweet and abundant steamed clams, for example, we were given a large lemon-scented finger bowl rather than those sticky little wet-paper things. Our charbroiled garlic lamb kebab was accompanied by a separate skewer of broiled vegetables, so that each was done to perfection; the rice pilaf was improved with almonds and raisins. Our dessert was a bird's-nest meringue with homemade vanilla ice cream, whipped cream and hot fudge: a simple but triumphant mixture of textures, temperatures and tastes. The whole, entirely satisfactory dinner came to $43 for two, with wine by the glass.

INNS

Squire Tarbox Inn
Rte. 144
(207) 882-7693
Closed Nov.-mid-May.
Cards: AE, MC, V.

If you fancy yourself a latter-day Marie Antoinette, Karen and Bill Mitman's miniature Colonial Trianon and their family of affectionate goats may keep you returning for years. We've seen otherwise staid matrons in evening dresses get down on their knees to help Karen out with the evening milking chores. And when you're not visiting your adorable new floppy-eared friends, you can relax in the Mitmans' 1825 inn or 1763 barn, which has been converted to rustic sleeping rooms. If you're so inclined (as we were), the pigsty may be your room of choice. The other eleven rooms are equally charming in a modest sort of way. The Colonial-style dining room has its original cooking hearth intact; its adjacent deck affords a peaceful view of the surrounding countryside, making it a particularly lovely spot at cocktail hour. The dinner fare is ample and quite good, especially if you go for fresh goat cheese. Karen is partnered with her goats in a successful sideline business; she produces wonderful cheese, which is wrapped in personally created gift packages and sold to friends and family.
Rooms: $100-$160, including breakfast and dinner.

SHOPS

Viewpoints
Water St.
(207) 882-6328
Open Mon.-Sat. 10 a.m.-
5:30 p.m.

Only if you're told (so we'll tell you) would you guess that this bright, airy store used to be the Wiscasset Ford dealership. Upstairs is a large open space for exhibits and displays of larger items, such as furniture and quilts; downstairs, look for a menagerie of stuffed animals, enough toys to fill a terrific playpen, functional ceramics and woven blankets.

WOOLWICH

RESTAURANTS

A Taste of Maine
Rte. 1
(207) 443-4554
SEAFOOD
March-mid-Dec.: open
Sun.-Thurs. 11:30 a.m.-
8 p.m., Fri.-Sat. 11:30
a.m.-9:30 p.m. (nightly to
9:30 p.m. in summer).
Cards: AE, MC, V.

10/20

On scenic Route 1 north of Portland lurks this huge decade-old seafood house. A lounge/bar area downstairs has plenty of room for those waiting for a table in the window-rimmed upstairs dining room, which overlooks the pine-scattered slopes of the bay. The unpresumptuous clientele ranges from local prom dates and birthday celebrants to eager-eyed tourists in pairs and families; the room, service and presentation are open and informal, reminiscent of a summer-camp eating hall. But the food's a lot better than summer-camp chow: succulent lobsters only hours out of Maine waters, platters of native shrimp and, of course, other heavier, traditional New England entrées. Stick to the fresh, simply prepared dishes and you'll enjoy a good, honest meal. About $65 for a lobster feast for two, with wine; less for other seafood dinners.

YARMOUTH

SHOPS

W. M. Schwind
17 E. Main St. (Rte. 88)
(207) 846-9458
Open Mon.-Sat. 10 a.m.-
5 p.m., or by appt.

The Schwinds' beautiful four-story house is filled with a selection of antiques that will please most tastes. For the country-minded, there are ceramics, tiger-maple work tables and the random hobbyhorse. For the more formal, there are wing chairs, beautiful English glassware and decanters, card tables, silver tea sets and creamware. The inventory is always changing, and the Schwinds are in love with antiques, so you're assured an enjoyable conversation about any piece in question. They want to help you become a regular collector.

TOQUE TALLY

17/20

Chillingsworth, Brewster, MA
Robert Henry's,
   New Haven, CT
Jasper's, Boston
Le Marquis de Lafayette, Boston

Maxime's, Granite Springs,
   NY (see CT)
La Panetière, Rye, NY (see CT)
Restaurant Jean-Louis,
   Greenwich, CT

16/20

Aujourd'hui, Boston
D'Artagnan, Lyme, NH
L'Espalier, Boston
Fine Bouche, Centerbrook, CT

Julien, Boston
Michela's, Boston
Restaurant du Village, Chester, CT
Seasons, Boston

15/20

Alberta's Café, Portland, ME
Allegro, Waltham,
   MA (see Boston)
Bee and Thistle Inn,
   Old Lyme, CT
Bertrand, Greenwich, CT
Blue Strawbery, Portsmouth, NH
Brattle Street, Portland, ME
The Colony, Boston
Le Coq Hardi, Ridgefield, CT
Golden Lamb Buttery,
   Brooklyn, CT
Hamersley's Bistro, Boston

L'Hostellerie Bressane, Hillsdale,
   NY (see Cent. & West. MA)
Locke-Ober Café, Boston
Lucky's, Providence, RI
Old Lyme Inn, Old Lyme, CT
Panache, Boston
Rarities, Boston
Ritz-Carlton Hotel/
   The Dining Room, Boston
Il Toscano, Boston
Upstairs at the Pudding, Boston
Wheatleigh, Lenox, MA

14/20

Al Forno, Providence, RI
L'Américain, Hartford, CT
Azteca's, New Haven, CT
Beardsley's, Northampton, MA
Cafe Always, Portland, ME
Clarke Cooke House,
    Newport, RI
East Coast Grill, Boston
La Grange at The Homestead,
    Greenwich, CT
Green Street Grill, Boston
Grill 23 & Bar, Boston
Griswold Inn, Essex, CT
The Harvest, Boston
Hemingway's, Killington, VT
Hopkins Inn, New Preston, CT
Icarus, Boston
Kedron Valley Inn,
    South Woodstock, VT
Pasta Nostra, South Norwalk, CT
Pauline's, Burlington, VT
Penobscot Meadow Inn,
    Belfast, ME
St. Cloud, Boston
Second Story, Nantucket, MA
Suntory, Boston
Toscano's Restaurant,
    Providence, RI
22 Lincoln, Brunswick, ME
Vermont Marble Inn,
    Fair Haven, VT

13/20

Another Season, Boston
Barnard Inn, Barnard, VT
Bay Tower Room, Boston
Beach Plum Inn,
    Martha's Vineyard, MA
Bernerhof Inn, Glen, NH
The Bluepoint Oyster Bar and
    Restaurant, Providence, RI
The Brick Oven Restaurant,
    Bar Harbor, ME
Bruxelles Brasserie and Bar,
    New Haven, CT
Cafe Budapest, Boston
Café du Bec Fin,
    Old Greenwich, CT
Church Street Cafe, Lenox, MA
Condé's, Old Greenwich, CT
Copper Beech Inn, Ivoryton, CT
Cornucopia, Boston
The Crystal Quail,
    Center Barnstead, NH
L'Etoile at the Charlotte Inn,
    Martha's Vineyard, MA
Four Columns Inn,
    Newfane, VT
Le Garage, Wiscasset, ME
Kebab 'N' Kurry, Boston
Legal Sea Foods, Boston
Maison Robert, Boston
Mr. Leung, Boston
Miyako, Boston
Otter Creek Café,
    Middlebury, VT
Rocco's, Boston
Savoir Fare, Martha's
    Vineyard, MA
Straight Wharf Restaurant,
    Nantucket, MA

The Student Prince,
  Springfield, MA
Swift House, Middlebury, VT
Ten Acres Lodge, Stowe, VT

21 Federal Street,
  Nantucket, MA
Wildcat Inn & Tavern,
  Jackson, NH

12/20

Adesso, Providence, RI
The Birchwood Inn,
  Temple, NH
Block Island Broiler,
Block Island, RI
Blue Diner, Boston
Bnu, Boston
Cafe Brazil, Boston
Cafe China, Boston
Cajun Yankee, Boston
Daily Catch, Boston
The Daily Planet, Burlington, VT
Dartmouth Street, Boston
Déjà Vu Café, Burlington, VT
Delmonaco's, New Haven, CT
The Elm Street Cafe,
  Montpelier, VT
Feasts, Martha's Vineyard, MA
Five Seasons, Boston
Hampshire House, Boston
Ho Yuen Ting, Boston

Hot Tomatos, New Haven, CT
The Ice House, Burlington, VT
The Ivy Grill, Hanover, NH
Mad Hatter, Nantucket, MA
Madd Apple Cafe, Portland, ME
Marty's Riverside Restaurant &
  Bakery, Shelburne Falls, MA
Mary's, Bristol, VT
Morton's of Chicago, Boston
The Orchards, Williamstown, MA
John B. Parmelee House
  (The Inn at Chester),
  Chester, CT
Sakura, Burlington, VT
Siam Cuisine, Boston
Tubbs Restaurant,
  Montpelier, VT
Twin Oaks, Cranston, RI
Villa Tragara, Waterbury
  Center, VT
Woody's, Middlebury, VT

11/20

Anthony's Pier 4, Boston
Carmelina's at the Commons,
  Hadley, MA
Chef Chandler's, Boston
Chef Chang's House, Boston
The Elm City Diner,
  New Haven, CT
Estes Beach Lobster House,
  South Harpswell, ME

Gilchrist's East, Boothbay
  Harbor, ME
Golden Palace, Boston
Leo's, Providence, RI
The Mooring, Newport, RI
Tap Room at Jared Coffin House,
  Nantucket, MA
Windows on the Water,
  Kennebunkport, ME

10/20

Austrian Tea Room, Stowe, VT
Ciro & Sal's, Provincetown, MA
Ciro's Flagship Restaurant,
  Provincetown, MA
The Common Ground
  Community Restaurant,
  Brattleboro, VT
Durgin-Park, Boston
Fisherman's Wharf Inn,
  Boothbay Harbor, ME
Hillside, Hartsville, MA
Horn of the Moon Café,
  Montpelier, VT
A Taste of Maine, Woolwich, ME

NO RANKING

Sally Ling, Boston

MAPS

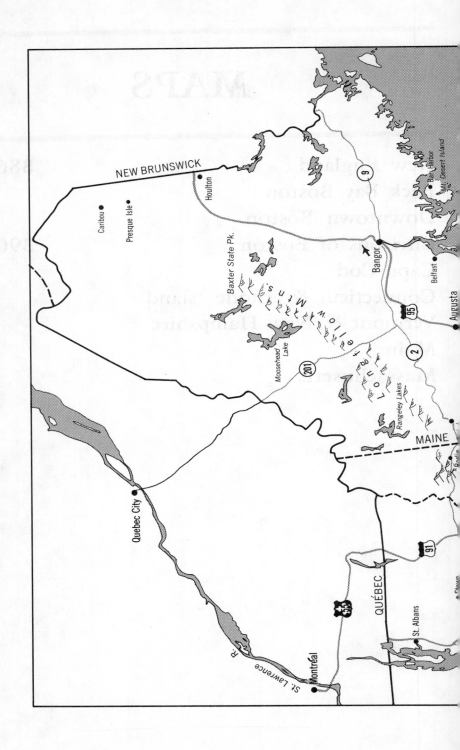

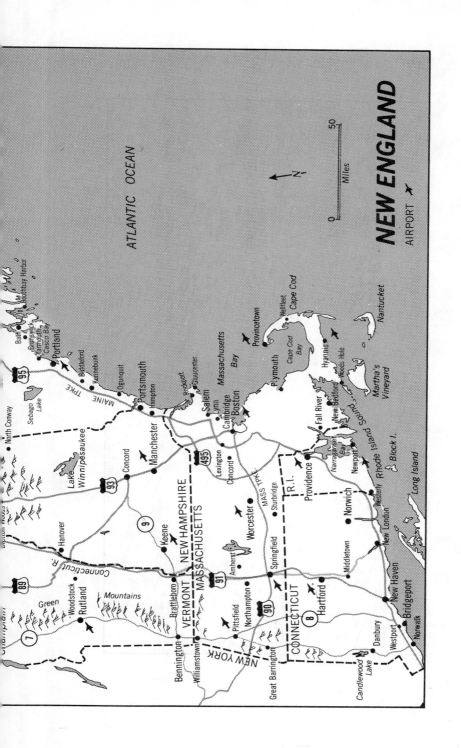

ATLANTIC OCEAN

NEW ENGLAND
AIRPORT ✈

50

Miles

0

N

MAINE

MAINE TPKE.
Sebago Lake
North Conway
95
Portland
Biddleford
Kennebunk
Ogunquit
Bath
Brunswick
Yarmouth
Casco Bay
Boothbay Harbor

NEW HAMPSHIRE
Hanover
Concord
93
Manchester
9
Keene
Lake Winnipesaukee

Portsmouth
Hampton
Rockport
Gloucester
Salem
Lynn
Cambridge
Boston
Massachusetts Bay

Provincetown
Cape Cod Bay
Cape Cod
Wellfleet
Plymouth
Hyannis
Woods Hole
Nantucket
Martha's Vineyard

VERMONT
Green Mountains
7
Woodstock
Rutland
Connecticut R.
89
Lake Champlain
Brattleboro
Bennington
Williamstown

MASSACHUSETTS
495
Lexington
Concord
MASS TPKE.
Worcester
Sturbridge
Amherst
Springfield
91
Northampton
Pittsfield
90
Great Barrington

NEW YORK

Fall River
New Bedford
Providence
R.I.
Narragansett Bay
Newport
Westerly
Rhode Island Sound
Block I.
Norwich
New London
Long Island

CONNECTICUT
8
Hartford
Middletown
Danbury
New Haven
Bridgeport
Westport
Norwalk
Candlewood Lake

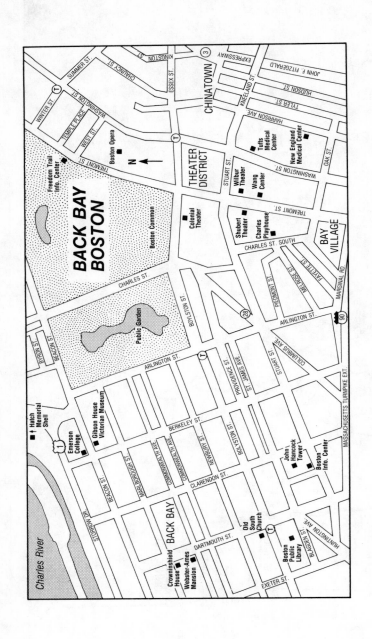

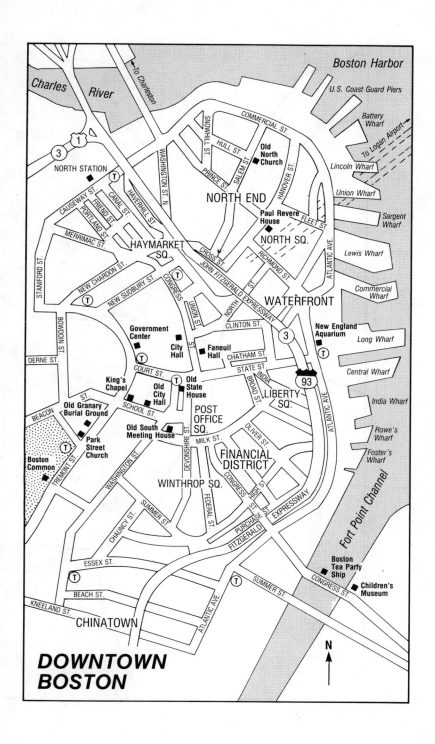

DOWNTOWN BOSTON

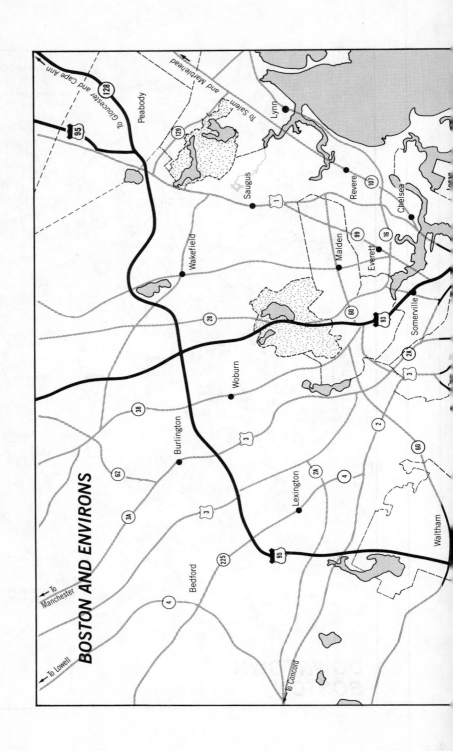

BOSTON AND ENVIRONS

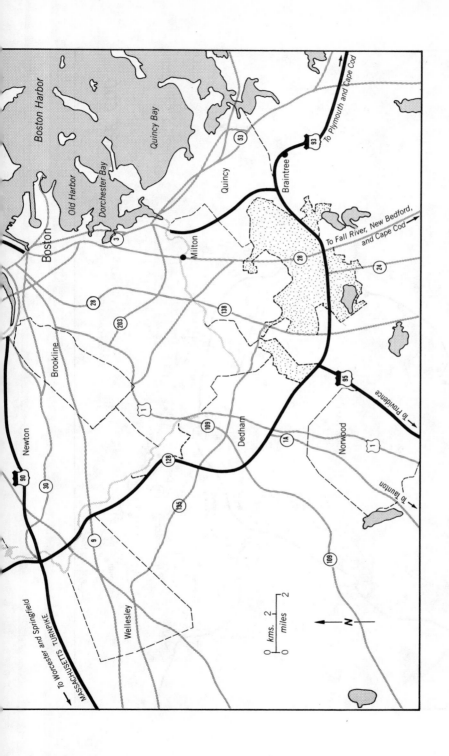

Boston Harbor

Quincy Bay

Old Harbor

Dorchester Bay

Boston

Milton

Quincy

Braintree

53

93

To Plymouth and Cape Cod

To Fall River, New Bedford, and Cape Cod

3

28

24

28

203

138

Brookline

1

95

To Providence

Dedham

109

1A

Norwood

1

To Taunton

Newton

128

90

30

135

9

Wellesley

MASSACHUSETTS TURNPIKE

To Worcester and Springfield

0 kms. 2
0 miles 2

N

109

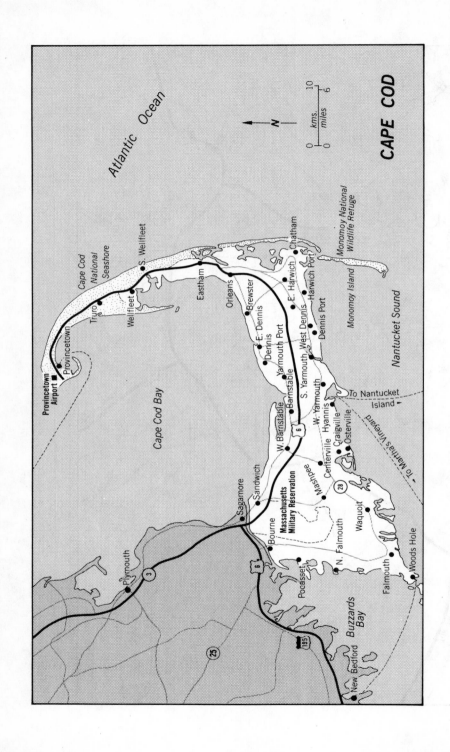

CAPE COD

Atlantic Ocean

Cape Cod National Seashore

Provincetown Airport
Provincetown
Truro
Wellfleet
S. Wellfleet

Cape Cod Bay

Eastham
Orleans
Brewster
E. Dennis
Dennis
Yarmouth Port
Barnstable
W. Barnstable
S. Yarmouth
W. Yarmouth
Hyannis
Centerville
Craigville
Osterville

E. Harwich
Harwich
Harwich Port
West Dennis
Dennis Port

Chatham

Monomoy National Wildlife Refuge

Monomoy Island

Nantucket Sound

To Nantucket Island

To Martha's Vineyard

Sagamore
Sandwich
Mashpee
Waquoit

Massachusetts Military Reservation

Bourne
N. Falmouth
Pocasset
Falmouth
Woods Hole

Buzzards Bay

Plymouth
New Bedford

kms.   10
miles   6

N

0

0

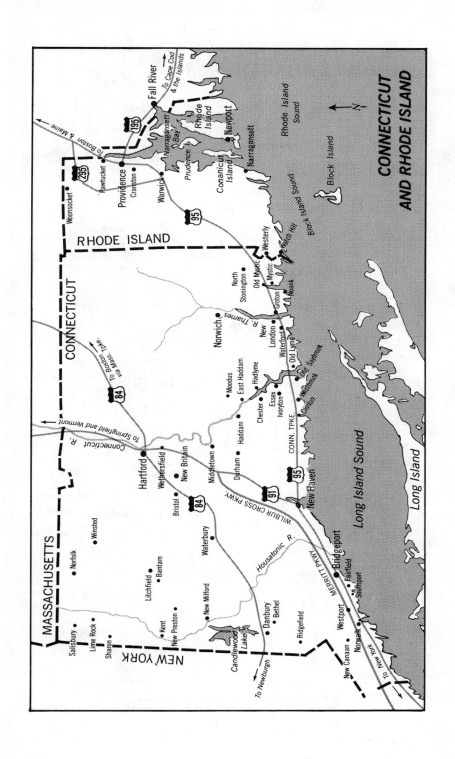

CONNECTICUT
AND RHODE ISLAND

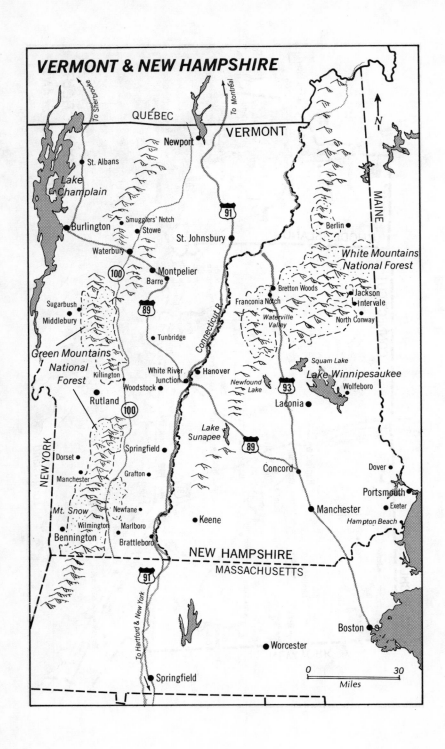

VERMONT & NEW HAMPSHIRE

QUÉBEC

VERMONT

To Sherbrooke

To Montréal

N

Newport

St. Albans

Lake Champlain

Burlington

Smugglers' Notch

Stowe

Waterbury

MAINE

Berlin

91

St. Johnsbury

White Mountains National Forest

100

Montpelier

Barre

89

Bretton Woods

Jackson

Intervale

Sugarbush

Middlebury

Franconia Notch

Waterville Valley

North Conway

Green Mountains National Forest

Tunbridge

Connecticut R.

Squam Lake

Killington

White River Junction

Hanover

Lake Winnipesaukee

Wolfeboro

Woodstock

Newfound Lake

93

Rutland

Laconia

100

Lake Sunapee

NEW YORK

Springfield

89

Dorset

Grafton

Concord

Dover

Manchester

Portsmouth

Mt. Snow

Newfane

Wilmington

Marlboro

Bennington

Brattleboro

Keene

Manchester

Exeter

Hampton Beach

NEW HAMPSHIRE

MASSACHUSETTS

91

To Hartford & New York

Boston

Worcester

0   30

Miles

Springfield

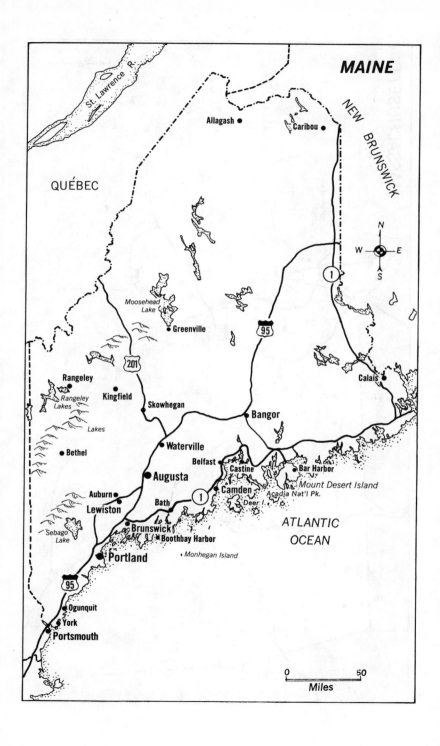

MAINE

NEW BRUNSWICK

QUÉBEC

St. Lawrence R.

Allagash •

• Caribou

N
W · E
S

① 1

Moosehead Lake

⑨5 95

• Greenville

② 201

Rangeley •
Rangeley Lakes

• Kingfield

Lakes

Skowhegan

Calais

• Bethel

Waterville

Bangor

Belfast

Castine

Bar Harbor

Augusta

Camden

Mount Desert Island

Acadia Nat'l Pk.

Auburn •

Bath

① 1

Deer I.

ATLANTIC
OCEAN

Lewiston

Sebago Lake

Brunswick

Boothbay Harbor

• Portland

• Monhegan Island

⑨5 95

• Ogunquit

• York

Portsmouth

0   50
Miles

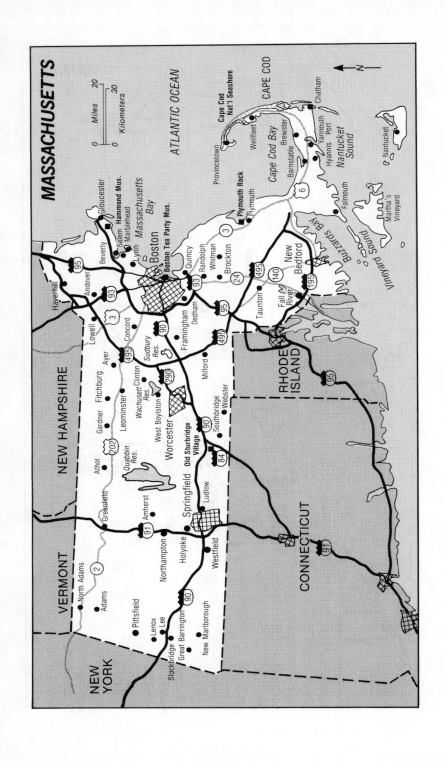

INDEX

BO/E: *Boston/Environs*
BO/H: *Boston/Hotels*
BO/N: *Boston/Nightlife*
BO/Q: *Boston/Quick Bites*

BO/R: *Boston/Restaurants*
BO/S: *Boston/Shops*
BO/SI: *Boston/Sights*
BO: *Boston*

T

U

The Gault Millau series of guidebooks reflects our readers' demand for insightful, incisive reporting on the best (and worst) that the world's most exciting destinations have to offer. To help us tailor our books even better to your needs, please take a moment to fill out this anonymous (if you wish) questionnaire, returning it to:

Gault Millau, Inc., P.O. Box 361144, Los Angeles, CA 90036.

1.   How did you hear about the Gault Millau guides: newspaper, magazine, radio, friends, other (please specify)?

....

....

2.   Please list in order of preference the cities (or countries) on which you would like to have a Gault Millau guide, aside from the already existing destinations.

....

....

3.   Do you refer to the Gault Millau guides in your travels or for your own city?

A. (Travels) .... B. (Own city) .... C. (Both) ....

4.   Do you use any other guides than Gault Millau?

If yes ....

5.   Please list, starting with the most preferred, the three features that you like most about the Gault Millau guides.

A. ....

B. ....

C. ....

6. What are the features, if any, you dislike about the Gault Millau guides?

.   ...
....

7. Please list any features you would like to see added to the Gault Millau guides.

.   ...
....

8. Please list the features you like most about your favorite guidebook series if it is not Gault Millau?

   A. ....
   B. ....
   C. ....

9. How many trips do you make per year for business and for pleasure?

   Business: International: .... Domestic: ....
   Pleasure: International: .... Domestic: ....

10. Is your annual household income over (check appropriate choice)?

   $ 20,000 .... $ 40,000 .... $ 60,000 ....
   $ 80,000 .... $ 100,000 ....   Other (please specify) ....

11. If you have any comments on the Gault Millau guides in general, please enclose them on a separate sheet of paper.

We thank you for your interest in the Gault Millau guides and we welcome your remarks and your recommendations about restaurants, hotels, shops, services.

NE

MORE GAULT MILLAU "BEST" GUIDES

Now the series known throughout Europe for its wit and savvy reveals the best of major U.S. and European areas—New York, Washington, D.C., Los Angeles, San Francisco, Chicago, New England, France and Italy. Following the guidelines established by the world-class French food critics Henri Gault and Christian Millau, local teams of writers directed by André Gayot, partner of Gault Millau, have gathered inside information about where to stay, what to do, where to shop, and where to dine or catch a quick bite in these key locales. Each volume sparkles with the wit, wisdom, and panache that readers have come to expect from Gault Millau, whose distinctive style makes them favorites among travelers bored with the neutral, impersonal style of other guides. There are full details on the best of everything that makes these cities special places to visit, including restaurants, diversions, nightlife, hotels, shops, the arts—all the unique sights and sounds of each city. These guides also offer practical information on getting around and coping with each city. Filled with provocative, entertaining, and frank reviews, they are helpful as well as fun to read. Perfect for visitors and residents alike.

Please send me the books checked below

☐	The Best of Chicago	$15.95
☐	The Best of London	$16.95
☐	The Best of Los Angeles	$14.95
☐	The Best of New England	$15.95
☐	The Best of New York	$14.95
☐	The Best of Paris	$16.95
☐	The Best of San Francisco	$14.95
☐	The Best of Washington, D.C.	$14.95
☐	The Best of France	$16.95
☐	The Best of Italy	$16.95

PRENTICE HALL TRADE DIVISION
Order Department—Travel Books
200 Old Tappan Road
Old Tappan, New Jersey 07675

In U.S. include $2 shipping UPS for 1st book, $1 each additional book. Outside U.S., $3 and $1 respectively.

Enclosed is my check or money order for $ —————————————————

NAME ——————————————————————————————

ADDRESS ——————————————————————————————

CITY ————————————— STATE ————— ZIP —————